AMERICAN LIFE, AMERICAN PEOPLE

VOLUME II

Timothy J. Crimmins
Georgia State University

Neil Larry Shumsky
Virginia Polytechnic Institute and State University

HARCOURT BRACE JOVANOVICH, PUBLISHERS
San Diego New York Chicago Austin Washington, D.C.
London Sydney Tokyo Toronto

Preface

AMERICAN LIFE, AMERICAN PEOPLE began at a chance meeting in Chicago in the spring of 1979. We took advantage of this meeting to assess the state of history teaching, to explore recent advances in American culture by seeing the latest movies, and to visit Water Tower Place, a shopping mall at the epicenter of modern culture. Our discussions led to the preparation of these readers. We wanted to introduce an element of comparability in the selections of articles that accompany textbooks in American history and to emphasize aspects of everyday life in our nation's past. Therefore we began to search for selections that focused on how earlier generations of Americans and their institutions have changed.

The result of our efforts is a two-volume reader that illustrates the nature of life in the United States during the past 350 years. The focus is not on wars and politics or reform movements and economic trends. Rather, the selections illustrate activities that we all share, the everyday events that occupy us from the time we wake until the time we go to sleep.

Cultural anthropologists divide human activity into six categories: religion, family, education, politics, society, and economy. In terms of daily life, these six areas are concerned with how people worship, how they structure their families, how they are educated, how they are governed, how they fit into society, and how they make a living. Each selection in these books deals with some aspect of one of these major categories, with the single exception of politics.

The selections are organized into four chronological time periods that we call Preindustrial and Industrializing (Volume I), and Industrial and Modern (Volume II)—a terminology chosen because, in our opinion, nothing in human history has changed daily life as quickly or as radically as the process of industrialization. Within each of these four periods are eleven selections on the topics of establishing a family, of raising children, of being old, of working, of praying, of housing, of communicating, of shopping, of socializing, of managing the environment, and of having heroes. Since these topics exemplify major human activities or stages of life, the repetition of them in each section allows readers to see what has changed and what has remained constant.

The selections do not simply elucidate the lives of individuals; they also illustrate relationships among people as well as relationships between people and institutions. For example, some selections show how people organized themselves into families and how those families functioned in the external world. Several articles reveal how people were organized into social institutions beyond the family and how they related to those institutions. Finally, a few of the articles say something about the importance of religion and about how

Americans have conceived their relationship with God. Each of the four sections of the two volumes has an introduction that briefly explores these social issues and shows how larger social changes have occurred over time.

We are indebted to Drake Bush, our editor at Harcourt Brace Jovanovich, who saw merit in our idea and offered us help and counsel in carrying it out. We also owe gratitude to Virginia Polytechnic Institute and Georgia State University for the travel assistance that brought us together in Chicago and permitted us to attend conferences in San Francisco, Chicago, and Minneapolis, where we continued our collaboration. We also appreciate the help of a number of our colleagues who offered us leads to just the right article. Finally, we want to thank our wives, Marcia and Carolyn, and our children, Eric and Michael, Tim and Meghan, whose good humor and encouragement have helped to bring this project to fruition.

Neil Larry Shumsky
Timothy J.Crimmins

Contents

v

Topical
Table of Contents

The listings that follow incorporate selections found in both Volume I and Volume II.

THE FAMILY

RAISING CHILDREN

OLD AGE

WORK

RELIGION

PART THREE

LIFE IN INDUSTRIAL AMERICA

From 1870 to 1920, the forces of industrialization continued to transform the daily lives of Americans. By 1920, the United States was an urban nation bound together not just by rivers and canals but also by train, telegraph, and telephone. Immigrants and native Americans alike flocked to newly available factory jobs that helped increase the production of the goods of the Industrial Revolution. And, sparked by such sales innovations as the Sears Roebuck catalogue and Macy's Department Store, there was a corresponding rise in the demand from consumers in all parts of the country.

The price that people paid for the wonders of the industrial age was a dramatic increase in the pace of life. "Retreat from the City" describes how the rush of business and the relentless movement of the factory contributed to a sharpening of the boundaries between community and family. Middle-class Americans came to see the family as a refuge in which they might find shelter from the unrestrained competition of the workplace. Within the family, husbands and wives had to work out new relationships. Women were given the impossible task of creating and maintaining a utopian home environment for the family through ceaseless housework and concern with domestic detail. Men, on the other hand, had to venture into the world of work, from which they had to be careful not to bring any contamination into the home. "Privacy," a watchword for late nineteenth-century home life, represented the effort of the middleclass family to shield its members from an intruding world. Unfortunately, the family could not function that way: both men and women were frustrated in their attempts to make the home a private Eden.

"Frank Lloyd Wright, the Family and the Prairie House" details how the homes designed by the famous architect represented the growing demand for privacy, another indication of the detachment of individual families from their communities. The exterior arrangements of Wright's houses emphasized distance and enclosure: yards were carefully screened and doors were often not visible from the street; overhanging roofs and high windows prevented those outside from looking in; living areas were frequently raised to permit residents to look down on the street without being seen. The internal configuration of the home, however, emphasized family intimacy. An open floor plan fostered a feeling of togetherness since everyone in the household knew where the others were and what they were doing.

If middle-class Americans could afford to seek a private refuge in homes on the outskirts of towns and cities, the working class could not. In the class-segregated world in which they lived, the poor found little privacy. Crowded, unsanitary tenements and noisy, sometimes unsafe workplaces were far removed from the suburban homes and bustling offices of middle-class life. "The Poor Man's Club" shows how working-class men found their own refuge from a hostile environment. The saloon provided a place for comradery and amusement, away from work and family. For many, this was the only place they could relax socially with neighbors or fellow workers. Because of its attraction, the saloon became a place where ward and precinct leaders garnered votes, where information about job openings was passed around by word of mouth, and where developing labor unions could meet safely. Even though saloons were public establishments, they often functioned as private places where working-class men of similar background escaped from the pressures of urban life.

Although many activities of daily life were divided by class, there were places where the classes mingled. "The Department Store" focuses on such a location, in which women of varied economic backgrounds joined together. If men could escape to clubs and saloons for companionship, women could spend their leisure time shopping in an entertaining environment. By bringing together a vast array of goods under one roof, department stores catered to a mass audience in industrial society. Although it was primarily the growing middle class who frequented these emporiums, all customers were made to feel important and valued. Department stores displayed their wares in creative ways, introduced seasonal changes in fashions, provided guaranties and credit, and offered such facilities as rest rooms, reading rooms, and nurseries. Shopping was no longer merely the purchasing of daily necessities; it was a leisure activity for women on many social levels.

The technological advances that made possible the mass-produced goods sold in department stores also brought new methods of communication to Americans. When Alexander Graham Bell invented the telephone in 1876, the telegraph was the principal means of communicating business information and news over distances. "The Telephone" describes how Bell labored to establish his invention not just in the world of work but also in the domestic sphere. By making it easier for people to communicate over distances, the telephone transformed the way Americans interacted with the world. Not only could businessmen talk to their colleagues across town or across country; their wives in suburban homes could phone orders to their grocer, butcher, or baker. In addition, public telephones in most parts of the city and in post offices and stores in small towns made available to all levels of society what was first thought to be only an electrical toy.

"New" was the watchword as technological breakthroughs brought rapid change. For the elderly, however, the "new" world was one that favored youth. At the time they were benefiting from technological advances that extended their lives, older Americans were also being pushed aside in favor of younger people. Medical researchers who studied the elderly began to define a life stage that was characterized by decline and disorder. Business leaders responded to those discoveries by introducing mandatory retirement as a means of eliminating the old from the workforce and making room for the young.

Changes in the industrial workplace also affected young Americans. With the introduction of child labor laws and compulsory school attendance and the expansion of the high school curriculum, the time of growing up was extended. "Coping with Adolescence" describes how Americans developed programs to deal with this new phase in life, when children were moving away from the control of the family but were not yet ready for the discipline of the workplace. The Boy Scouts and the YMCA sponsored activities after school and on weekends that were designed to build character, provide adult supervision, and instill old-fashioned values. While preteenagers responded enthusiastically to these programs, the adolescents for whom they were intended found their own peer groups more attractive. Despite the best efforts of organizations such as scouting and the Y to discourage it, by the early twentieth century a youth culture was already in the making.

As the size of work groups increased in factories and in white-collar occupations, efforts were made to rationalize, systematize, and closely monitor jobs at all levels. "Making Workers More Efficient" describes how new management controls developed in the factories were applied to the sales staffs of department stores. In efforts that were typical of the modern efficiency movement, managers sought to remake shopgirls into successful saleswomen through careful supervision and an elaborate set of guidelines. But while the regimentation of the workplace *did* influence dress, record keeping, and hours, coworkers were more likely than supervisors to help new saleswomen develop good sales technique. Efforts to link people to the routine of the factory were more successful than attempts to create human selling machines, though. In industrial society, few workers could escape the controls of scientific management.

For many Americans, the machines that powered factories were threatening. Proponents of picturesque urban parks such as New York City's Central Park sought to give relief from the machine age by creating an environment in cities that imitated nature, providing a refuge from the din of urban life. For many others, however, the machine was an object of fascination. "Designing Places for Mechanized Leisure" shows how the power of the Industrial Revolution was applied to leisure-time activities. Coney Island became the site of several amusement parks whose twirling machines and flashing lights dazzled millions. In amusement parks, machines helped people to escape from the cares of everyday life by whirling thrill-seekers in an environment that was as carefully planned as that of the urban park. Turn-of-the-century amusement parks had unified architectural themes, landscaped grounds, and rules of conduct that gave a sense of order to the excitement of the ever changing environment.

The spiritual world of Americans was reshaped by the materialism of the industrial age. "The Gospel of Success" describes how leading ministers sanctified the virtues of industry, frugality, and sobriety—attributes that they promised would lead to rewards in this life, as well as in the next. The austere God of Puritan society was replaced by a benevolent God who looked with pleasure at the material advancements of the American people. The wealthier classes welcomed the message from many pulpits that God rewarded hard work. They were confirmed in their belief that affluence was a gift from God and that the poverty of others was a punishment.

The machine age in America was characterized by a number of dramatic upheavals, from the demographic changes of European immigration and rural-to-urban migration, to the creation of the controlled environment of the modern factory. People were forced to search for beliefs that were appropriate for the new industrial society. "Log Cabins and Lone Prairies" focuses on heroes who made a place in the new age and whose feats reconciled the conflicts between the demands of an organized urban workforce and the earlier ideal of an independent pioneer. The heroes of the stories by Horatio Alger, who displayed the old-fashioned values of hard work, self-denial, and reliability in an urban setting, exemplified the gospel of success because their virtue was rewarded. For the millions of Americans who read Alger's stories, the heroes exemplified the potential of industrial society, in which virtue and fortuitous circumstance could lead to riches.

While the aspiring middle class emulated Alger's characters, the working class could look to the cowboy for inspiration. Like factory workers, cowboys were hired hands. Their valor in chasing outlaws or in fighting Indians was an essential element in bringing civilization to the West. Long after the West had been settled, cowboys remained popular in the American imagination. They provided an alternative to the rags-to-riches business leaders like Andrew Carnegie, whose success was tainted in the eyes of the working people by the control he exerted over the laborers in his industries.

Americans in the industrial age were adjusting to a new environment. Depending on their sex and economic circumstance, they sought refuge from the pressures of a regulated workplace in their homes, working-class taverns, department stores, or amusement parks. The old and the young alike had to find new roles. Many sought a meaningful God and relevant heroes. Like earlier generations, these Americans showed that they could adapt to new and complex conditions.

THE FAMILY

Retreat
from the
City

KIRK JEFFREY

Goose dinner, Christmas, Wesley, Rhode Island

FAMILIES PROVIDE A BACKDROP for child-raising and a legal setting for sexual relations. They also serve as buffers between the individual and society. The family maintains and perpetuates the social system, and it provides a focus for the acquisition, consumption, and distribution of wealth.

"The Compassionate Family," by James Reed, a selection in the first volume of this anthology, showed that the importance of family life increased during the early nineteenth century and that the boundaries between family and community sharpened. The selection that follows shows that later in the century Americans further distinguished between family and society and in fact perceived them as two independent worlds. The family became a separate sphere in which the individual was thought to be able to find the greatest satisfaction in life. Moreover, Americans thought of the home as a perfectable utopia—a heaven on earth—in which each individual could attain perfection.

Kirk Jeffrey shows that this new concept of the family resulted from Americans' response to the rapid urbanization and industrialization of the United States. Americans feared the new social and economic order. In particular, they considered their burgeoning cities to be amoral centers of unrestrained competition and homes to the uncontrolled pursuit of money.

The new definition of the family modified the roles of husband and wife. It also created serious tensions for each of them. Men had to learn how to function in the outside world. But if they had to venture outside the family, how could they avoid harming the family, or even destroying it, when they returned? The ideal solution of popular moralists was for men to spend their free time at home, practice sexual abstinence, and model themselves on their wives, who came to be seen as the source of piety and morality. Women had to learn to create and maintain the perfect home for their families, and make it a retreat from the harshness of the outside world. Ceaseless work—especially housework—and attention to domestic detail would theoretically allow women to create a refuge for their families. Jeffrey concludes that, tragically, neither women nor men could possibly satisfy the ideal, and the result was frustration and guilt for both sexes.

DURING THE YEARS from about 1800 to 1870, and particularly after 1825, the values and expectations about family life which many Americans share today became implanted in middle-class American culture for the first time. These included beliefs about the nature and proper behavior of women and children, attitudes about sex which were widely accepted well into the twentieth century, and a general sense of sharp disjunction between the private world of the family and the larger society. This last assumption pervaded the writings of the popular moralists and advisers of that age—the physicians, phrenologists, clergymen, "scribbling women," and others who instructed middle-class Americans about their "duties and conduct in life." In the sermons and novels, the magazines and hortatory literature of the mid-nineteenth century, they asserted over and over that home was a distinct sphere, an enclave emphatically set apart from the activities and priorities of "the world," as they usually called the non-domestic part of their society. Associated with this idea was a second one which could be stated in a good many ways but which amounted to an affirmation that, ultimately, the individual found meaning and satisfaction in his life at home and nowhere else.

Our ancestors thus were encouraged to nurse extravagant hopes for the domestic realm. Whether they regarded home as an utter and permanent retreat from life in a shocking and incomprehensible social order, or as a nursery and school for preparing regenerate individuals who would go forth to remake American society, they agreed that domestic life ought to be perfect and could be made so. Through careful design of the home as a physical entity, and equally painstaking attention to the human relationships which would develop within it, the family could actually become a heaven on earth. Many of the significant features and patterns of middle-class family life in the nineteenth century, as well as significant points of strain, tension, and guilt, arose directly from these extravagant expectations.

A risky but potentially illuminating way of coming to terms with dominant American ideas about the family both in that day and in our own may be to

RETREAT FROM THE CITY   By Kirk Jeffrey. Originally published under the title "The Family as Utopian Retreat from the City." From *Soundings*, LV (1972), pp. 21–39. Reprinted by permission.

analyze the middle-class family as a kind of utopian community, analagous in many respects to the more famous communities which some reformers attempted to plant and nurture during those same decades prior to the Civil War, when recognizably modern family patterns were developing in some parts of American society. Certainly three utopian themes—retreat, conscious design, and perfectionism—pervaded nineteenth-century writings about the family.

What strikes one immediately, as one reads into the ephemeral popular literature of that era, is the intense seriousness with which middle-class writers discussed the home and the family. Often their words seem comical as they strain for the sonorous phrase, the classical allusion, which may succeed in capturing that intensity, that seriousness. "Home!—sweet word and musical!" wrote Mrs. Lydia Sigourney, a noted household poet, "key-tone of the heart, at whose melody, as by the harp of Orpheus, all the trees in its garden are moved, holy word! refuge from sadness and despair, best type of that eternal rest, for which we look, when the journey of life is ended!" This gush was typical of many writers in a sentimental and declamatory age; beneath it, though, was a serious statement. Others could be equally effusive, equally serious: "Home! the very word calls up a thousand feelings of thrilling interest; what ear is there so dull as not to hear it with delight? what heart so cold as not to respond with pleasure to the welcome sound?" Still another writer asked, "Is there any brain so dull into which [the word 'home'] does not flash with a gush of suggestive congruous fascinations?"

In Mrs. Sigourney's statement the dominant theme is retreat. In this connection it is noteworthy that idealized homes of the nineteenth century were invariably described in the context of a generalized, usually sentimentalized rural setting, surrounded by gardens and orchards. An entirely typical description is the following, from Mrs. A. J. Graves's novel *Girlhood and Womanhood* (1844). Here one of the heroines gazes for the first time at the landscape around her family's new home:

> A beautiful prospect stretched away before her. A fine range of green, softly swelling hills, bounded the horizon, behind which the sun was setting, in all the splendor of a richly tinted canopy of clouds. At their base, a lovely valley lay in shadow, through which a stream was gliding, fringed here and there with clumps of trees and shrubs, and upon its grassy banks, her father's herds were quietly grazing. A fine grove of old oaks rose beneath the window, whose trunks were lighted up with the red rays of the declining sun, and the green sward from which they sprung, was beautifully varied by long lines of sunshine and lengthened shadows, as intervening trees or intermediate spaces admitted, or obscured the brilliant hues of sunset.

The language of this description, clotted with "softly swelling hills," "grassy banks," and "green sward," suggests that such scenes—which can be found quite frequently in popular fiction and illustrations—were debased pastorals: middle-class Americans, that is, regarded the most important feature of the ideal home as its location in ordered natural surroundings. But so great was the gulf between aspiration and the social realities of the nineteenth century, and so unequipped were most writers for the task of discovering adequate ways of relating the two, that they fell back upon stale literary conventions.

The hortatory writings of the same period also betrayed the same assumptions. In their massive and famous compendium of domestic advice entitled *The*

American Woman's Home, Catharine Beecher and her sister Harriet Beecher Stowe made the rural home their ideal model despite the fact that their audience was largely urban. Much of their instruction on matters domestic, the sisters explained, "is chiefly applicable to the wants and habits of those living either in the country or in such suburban vicinities as give space of ground for healthful outdoor occupation in family service. . . ." They offered advice on the cultivation of flowers, fruits, and vegetables, and the care of "horse, cow, and dairy." "Each and all of the family, some part of the day," they asserted, should "take exercise in the pure air, under the magnetic and healthful rays of the sun. Every head of a family should seek a soil and climate which will afford such opportunities. Railroads, enabling men toiling in cities to rear families in the country, are on this account a special blessing."

This was in 1869. As the illustration of "The Christian Home" and phrases such as the one about "magnetic and healthful rays" suggest, the Beecher sisters too fell back upon a prettified image of country life which was probably far removed from the mundane realities confronting the average farm family. Home, they were suggesting, belonged neither in the city nor too far away from it on the American frontier. Like Mrs. Graves, they believed that it ought ideally to be found in an ordered but natural setting—that is, a timeless one.

The development of this middle-class cult of the rural home must be understood as a response to the historical experience which members of this group were undergoing during the middle decades of the nineteenth century. What it betrayed was an intense fear, a shock of non-recognition, with which such Americans greeted their society. As Marvin Meyers has remarked of them, they "were not inwardly prepared for the grinding uncertainties, the shocking changes, the complexity and indirection" of the economic and social order which was beginning to confront them by the 1830's and 1840's. The trends toward rapid change, extreme diversity, and new psychic demands had developed most fully in the larger cities of the Republic by then, and we should recall that the forty years prior to 1860 witnessed a higher rate of urban growth in proportion to total population growth, for the Eastern part of the nation, than at any later time in the century. Hence it was appropriate that the city appear to popular moralists and their readers as a symbol of all that distressed them in society outside the home. The cities housed the slums and immigrants, the gambling-dens and saloons which the Protestant clergy so frequently attacked.

The shocking features of urban life were magnified for many middle-class Americans because they were themselves rural-bred migrants to the city. Their very notable propensity to idealize the villages and farms of their childhood years and to excoriate the cities of their adulthood ones is a good index to the "profound alteration in human experience" which they were undergoing. The present discussion can do no more than offer a few examples from the considerable literature of wailing and gnashing of teeth about the city which was appearing as early as the 1830's. One typical volume by the Reverend John Todd, entitled *The Moral Influence, Dangers and Duties, Connected with Great Cities*, offered readers a comprehensive analysis of urban life. Most striking, according to Todd, was the set of purposes that men pursued in the city: "Wealth and Fashion are the deities which preside over the great city. . . . [There] you see the young, the ardent, the keen, and the gifted, rushing into these great marts of nations, to court the smiles of Mammon;—all hoping for his gifts." The frenzy and cultural diversity of the city thus alarmed him most. "On all sides . . . are the songs and the invitations of pleasure, the snares and the pitfalls covered with flowers. . . . To these very many yield. . . . All hope by-and-by to be able to retire on a competency. A few can do it; but what an amazing proportion fall in the race! and the tide rolls on, and they and their hopes are forgotten!"

Here, then, was one central meaning of the city: the frantic and relentless pursuit of wealth, a quest at which few would succeed. It was "*the universal unconquerable desire for money*," according to Todd, which both gave the city its *raison d'etre* and rendered it utterly iniquitous. The pursuit of riches was intrinsically evil; but it had some side consequences which further compounded the dangers of urban life, even for those few who might withstand its central mania for riches. Of particular importance among these was the transiency of human ties: "Your acquaintances come and go,—are here to-day, and off to-morrow, and you have hardly time, or opportunity, to form deep attachments. The unceasing hurry, and perpetual pressure for time, prevent our forming those deep attachments which we do in country life."

Similar lessons were purveyed to Americans through the didactic fiction of the same era. In the Reverend Daniel Wise's *Young Man's Counsellor*, for instance, one finds the parable of Arthur—"Arthur in Babylon." . . . Arthur is a kind of failed Horatio Alger hero; everything he does turns out wrong. Aged nineteen, "educated, handsome, of fascinating manners, and manly spirit," Arthur arrives in "a certain city" determined to make his fortune. Here is the very archetype of the middle-class migrant. But the city, it transpires, contains perils that Arthur is wholly unprepared to withstand. The youth "unhappily fell into dissolute society, and began to run the giddy rounds of deep dissipation." Soon his money is gone and he must pay a bill. Arthur's next error brings down the catastrophe upon him: "he took the fatal step of selling an opera glass, which he had borrowed from a gay friend; and thus paid his bill." Next day Arthur learns to his dismay that friendship in the city is not to be counted upon: "his quondam friend had the heart of a Shylock, and hurried the astonished and mortified young man to the police court."

At this point Arthur collapses: "'Cut my throat! kill me! trample me to death!'" he howls to his astonished cell-mates. Delirious, he is pronounced by a physician to be "in imminent danger of dying." Bailed out by an anonymous philanthropist, Arthur collapses once again when told that his father has been summoned from the hinterland. "'I can't see him! I can't—I can't!'" groans the piteous Arthur, and dies just as his "venerable father" enters the room. . . .

> This brutal little yarn, so equally devoid of mercy and moderation, was printed as a true story; and was intended, and surely accepted by some, as an edifying and moral tale. Arthur's reckless hysteria, his pathological sense of guilt, his panic, and his egregious moral vanity, are blandly recounted by the author as something just and genteel. The story's excessive melodrama is in itself revealing. The fear and hatred of urban demoralization was so great that its condemnation was correspondingly enormous. The story serves well to polarize city and country, stigmatizing the one and, by implication, unreservedly approving the other. Arthur's downfall commences from the day he comes to the city; in the country he was happy, useful, and ornamental. The city is the villain and Arthur is its victim.

Indictments of the city such as Todd's and Wise's were based on a common nineteenth-century psychological theory: "We all know," wrote Todd, "that familiarity with any thing has a wonderful effect upon our feelings, and that it is a principle in human nature, that what is in itself revolting, will, by familiarity, cease to disgust." By implication, few if any city-dwellers could long hold out against the inevitable taint of experience; sophistication and virtue were incompatible. Indeed, such was precisely the lesson of "Arthur in Babylon."

Thus the necessary conclusion to such a despairing theory of the impact of urban experience was the recommendation that it be avoided entirely. And the only sure way to do so, naturally, was to remain in the country. But there was a second possibility—an outpost of the country, as it were, within city walls. This was, of course, the family; and for those who could not return to rural America, or who found the opportunities of city life too attractive to allow them to heed the warnings of the Todds and the Wises, the second-best choice was to establish a little sphere of peace and order to which they could retreat. Ideally the family ought to be rural; and a later generation, blessed with more efficient means of transportation, would discover that it was possible to commute to the city while still enjoying a home life far removed from its terrors, in houses surrounded by a few hundred square feet of well-trimmed grass. But more than a century ago the essential perception of the city had already been formulated, along with the response which has remained the most popular one for the American middle class: complete retreat.

> We go forth into the world, amidst the scenes of business and of pleasure; we mix with the gay and the thoughtless, we join the busy crowd, and the *heart* is sensible to a desolution of feeling: we behold every principle of justice and of honor, and even the dictates of common honesty disregarded, and the delicacy of our moral sense is wounded; we see the general good, sacrificed to the advancement of personal interest; and we turn from such scenes, with a painful sensation, almost believing that virtue has deserted the abodes of men; again, we look to the *sanctuary* of *home*; there sympathy, honor, virtue, are assembled; there the eye may kindle with intelligence, and receive an answering glance; there disinterested love, is ready to sacrifice every thing at the altar of affection.

For the most part, as such statements indicate, popular writers tended to define the ideal home as an Edenic retreat, a rural haven utterly distinct from the terrors of urban life and the loneliness which could assail men there. As one clergyman put it, home was "a sweet bower of peace and joy in this desert world, where hope brightens, and love gathers its linked, confiding circle;—a blissful retreat for jaded and weary hearts when the busy world drives on its votaries in the train of Mammon and pampered self;—a safe and alluring shelter for *yourselves* amid the vicissitudes of life, becoming more and more the abode of peace and love as the world grows dark without." This conception was nowhere more memorably stated than in Donald Grant Mitchell's best-seller of the 1850's, *Reveries of a Bachelor*:

> Sending your blood in passionate flow, is the ecstasy of the conviction that *there* at least you are beloved; that there are you understood; that there your errors will meet ever with gentlest forgiveness; that there your troubles will be smiled away; that there you may unburden your soul fearless of harsh, unsympathizing ears; and that there you may be entirely and joyfully—yourself.

Retreat, companionship, possibly even the surcease from moral striving—these were the elements of Americans' notion of the Edenic home. Sometimes, to be sure, popular writers—often the very same ones—also asserted that home and the surrounding society were vitally connected: that the regenerate family would train up moral children and gradually reform adult males, so that ultimately, through thousands of such trickles of perfected individuals, a mighty tide of social reform would sweep aside all the evil features of nineteenth-century society. Through "family discipline and instruction," rather than any public institutions or agencies, Americans could achieve some deeply-desired goals: "the preservation of manners, the maintenance of religion, and the perpetuity of national freedom." But this second conception of the relationship between family and society, like the first, posited no extended day-to-day contact between the two "spheres." Middle-class Americans, that is, took care to define the social role of the family in such a way that it did not demand many significant forays from home out into the larger society, or even much detailed knowledge of it. Thus both definitions of the ideal home—as perfect retreat or as school for a moral citizenry—were premised upon the assumption that a serious and practically unbridgeable gulf existed between the two spheres, family and society.

In a more extended discussion of the nineteenth-century middle-class family it would be possible to consider the underlying structural changes which certainly stimulated the intense preoccupation in domesticity and the sense of a sharp disjunction. It was not merely the transformation of the outer society but rapid alterations in family patterns themselves which sensitized middle-class Americans to the problem of the family. Notable among these changes, but difficult as yet for the historian to examine with precision, were a disruption of the internal unity of the family due to the separation of the husband's work from the home in nineteenth-century cities, and the attenuation of informal ties to relatives and neighbors which had characterized rural and village life. The latter development was particularly significant, for without a rich web of kinship and friendship, urban middle-class family members were seriously hindered from meeting other city-dwellers on intimate terms, gaining detailed knowledge about the processes of urban life, or becoming more involved in these processes. In fact, one might hazard the guess that the isolation wrought by the withering of kin ties probably contributed as much as the chaos of the urban environment itself to the notable middle-class alienation from the city by mid-century.

The middle-class sense of a gulf between family and society was by no means inevitable and natural, and it had not existed, as far as historians can tell, in colonial America. I have suggested that the growth of this perception can be understood as the *consequence* of social changes, some of them external to the family and others within the family and kinship system itself. Now I want to raise a different question: Did the nineteenth-century sense of a disjunction between the two realms in turn act as a *cause* of other changes in family and society, or at least reinforce changes already occurring?

Let us first consider the results for intimate family life of the cult of the idyllic home. It seems that life in the isolated, Edenic homes of the middle class, to the degree that the perfectionist definition of home was taken seriously, probably exacerbated the compulsive self-examination of many Protestant, middle-class husbands and wives and enormously increased the burdens of anxiety and guilt which they bore. Here was an unexpected and particularly ironic result of the cult, for it encouraged its votaries to expect near-perfect repose and emotional fulfillment in the domestic sphere.

The precise nature of the difficulties differed for husbands and wives. For husbands, there arose what we may call the "commuting problem." If a virtuous sophistication in the city was truly impossible, as writers like Todd and Wise affirmed, how then could men dare to leave home at all to pursue careers in American society? Or if they did leave, even for a few hours a day, what would happen to their wives and families when they returned? This quandry, arising from the literal way in which middle-class Americans took their own definitions of the pure home and the depraved world, was at the center of many novels and stories of the period. In no case were popular authors able to fuse domestic and worldly experience into a coherent whole.

One typically spectacular expression of the problem appeared in a story entitled "The Prodigal's Return," by Timothy Shay Arthur. Arthur, whose temperance novel *Ten Nights in a Bar-Room* rivalled even *Uncle Tom's Cabin* in sales, published over one hundred volumes of didactic fiction between 1840 and 1870. In "The Prodigal's Return" young William Enfield leaves home to go to college. His mother's anxious question as he sets out, "'You won't forget your mother, William?'" sets the theme for the tale. At college William falls under the influence of evil companions, becomes a card-sharper and a prankster, and is finally expelled. He spends years as a professional gambler—the road from college high-jinks to adult depravity was apparently a broad and easy one—but finally experiences an instantaneous conversion in the form of a dream about home and mother. Resolving to put aside his evil ways, William returns to his childhood home and is forgiven by his parents. There he remains, presumably, forever after. This version of the prodigal son parable failed adequately to solve the dilemma of home's relation to the world. What would William Enfield *do* now that he had returned home? Could he be the kind of vigorous, ambitious, independent man that Americans admired, without venturing outside again? Equally important, was it really so easy to put aside everything he had learned and become since leaving home? And was it really true that all experience was worthy only of being forgotten?

A second and even more interesting pattern in popular fiction also tried to deal with the problem posed for men by the notion of two spheres. In this case we find that worldly men, instead of being saved by home and women, destroy the domestic enclave itself. Lydia Maria Child's story "Home and Politics" provides an example. George Franklin and his wife are at first a happy married couple preoccupied with their domestic life together. But "in an evil hour a disturbing influence crossed their threshold. It came in the form of political *excitement*; that pestilence which is forever racing through our land, seeking whom it may devour; destroying happy homes." George's increasing interest in caucuses and campaigns, growing largely out of desire for office and power, draws him away from home night after night. On election night, 1840, while he is gone, his child falls sick and dies. Then in 1844 he loses all his money by betting on Henry Clay; this time his wife goes mad. "When he visits her, she looks at him with strange eyes, and still clinging to the fond ideal of her life, she repeats mournfully, 'I *want* my home. Why don't George come and take me home?'"

Essentially Mrs. Child was wrestling with the same difficulty: experience in the world inevitably changes a person, but the cult of home demanded that one return absolutely intact. Implicit in both stories, and made fully explicit in the numerous volumes of advice to young men during the mid-nineteenth century, was the exhortation for American men to love domestic life and to model themselves after their wives. This suspicion of men and their worldly doings followed necessarily from the Victorian "cult of true womanhood" which placed middle-class women on pedestals and proclaimed that they were naturally more cultured, affectionate, and pious than their husbands. Only by becoming women in significant respects could American men, it seemed, be considered fit for sustained presence in the home.

In concrete terms, this boiled down to a number of extreme demands which popular moralists quite literally expected men to meet. The first was that they stay home—indeed, this was their fundamental commandment to American men. "*Virtue, purity, spiritual excellence* are the great purposes of our being. And where can you acquire these qualities better than at home?" Such writers regarded ambition for fame or fortune as a base impulse, the moral equivalent of uncontrollable lust for sex or gambling. One clergyman lamented, for example, that in many young men

> you may see in the very outset of life a passion for Gain towering above every thing else; so that ease, even the necessary rest of night, time, talents, and not seldom reputation itself, are sacrificed on the altar of Mammon. He, who feels this burning desire to get rich, cares usually but little for the pleasures of home. He is never, indeed, so uneasy as when seated by his own fireside; for he feels, while conversing with his kindred, that he is making no money. And as for fireside reading, there is to him no interest in that; 'he reads no book but his ledger.'

Once at home, men must consult with their wives and defer to them. As purer beings, women were more trustworthy guides on matters of morals and often, too, with respect to more worldly decisions. "Nothing," wrote the health reformer William A. Alcott, "is better calculated to preserve a young man from the contaminations of low pleasures and pursuits, than frequent intercourse [of the Platonic variety, one judges] with the more refined and virtuous of the other sex."

But how could women be safeguarded from the sexual lust of men? Might not husbands prove so coarse and passionate that the purity of their wives, and hence of the home itself, would be endangered? This was an issue of explicit discussion during the generation before 1860. Whether the passions of men resulted from their innately bestial natures or were vastly heightened by worldly experience, men were always perceived in middle-class writing about the home as extreme threats to the peace and unity of the family. The natural conclusion was that husbands must exercise a continual self-restraint in sexual matters, in order to enable wives to remain pure enough to save them through their mild influence. Clearly there was something circular about this line of thought, for if men successfully practiced sexual continence, was that not a good indication that they already had their base propensities well under control? Which was to come first, the influence of the pure wife or masculine self-restraint? Unaware of this problem with their regimen, domestic advisers went right ahead in affirming that "there is no lust in true marriage, and two rightly mated never run to excess in anything in any of the indulgencies [*sic*] of their natures." In more explicit terms, physicians and others were not shy about spelling out precisely what this meant. Alcott, an extremely popular arbiter on matters of medicine and health, urged late marriage, told young married couples to live with their parents during the early months of marriage, and warned them to refrain from sexual relations during pregnancy and lactation. The rest of the time "one indulgence to each lunar month, is all that the best health of the parties can possibly require."

In the case of middle-class husbands, then, we might say that the demands upon them—that they stay home, practice a continual sexual continence, and model themselves upon their wives—were heavy and almost impossible to carry out to perfection. Yet popular moralists demanded perfection. Moreover, their advice disguised a significant contradiction, for the intimacy and affection which they promised American husbands and wives was probably difficult to achieve in the context of the rigid sexual formality and self-control which the same writers also urged.

For American wives the difficulties arising from the definition of home as a separate and perfect realm were, if anything, more poignant, for women had few alternatives to their domestic role. Curiously, though, the precise nature of these difficulties has been little noted and discussed by social historians.

While it is an overstatement to speak of the "oppression" or "subjection" of middle-class wives in the nineteenth century, there seems little doubt that they suffered a notable decline in autonomy and morale during the three-quarters of a century following the founding of the American republic. Essentially this decline occurred as an indirect result of underlying changes in family patterns, and particularly in expectations about family life, which we have been examining. Most women in this group failed to perceive the "correct" causes for the sense of desperation which many of them seem frequently to have felt. In particular, they failed to see the unfortunate side-effects of the "cult of true womanhood" which defined them as the pious, pure keepers of the hearthside and bearers of genteel culture.

Almost all middle-class American wives accepted these ideas quite seriously, as far as the historian can tell. They did not regard confinement to the home as an indication that they were oppressed. On the contrary, if home was more pure and joyful, as women were continually assured, then it was a definite privilege to be allowed to remain there, unsullied by the outside world. Over and over again, women writers commented on the exalted position of their sex and thanked men for treating them with the respect which was their due. Thus Mrs. Sarah J. Hale, editor of *Godey's Lady's Book* and probably the most influential spokeswoman for her millions of sisters in nineteenth-century America, dedicated her *Woman's Record* to American men, "who show, in their laws and customs, respecting women, ideas more just and feelings more noble than were ever evinced by men of any other nation."

In the home middle-class wives had an arena in which they exercised much genuine responsibility and power. Their husbands were absent often; yet even when present, men were urged by popular moralists to model themselves after women and treat their wives with affection and deference. But it appears that the very set of ideas which endowed them with significant responsibility and power in the domestic sphere also weighted women with a heavy burden of anxiety and guilt. It was their duty to make home perfect, for only in a perfect home could husbands and children be redeemed and the outside society thereby reformed and saved. Or, to put it another way, only a perfect home could be a genuine alternative, a genuinely Edenic retreat from the horrors of the larger society.

Whether perfection was defined in terms of retreat and affection or training and order, it followed that every mundane household duty of women could be invested with the gravest implications. No matter how apparently routine and trivial, *every last chore* could be made to seem enormously significant. "Who knows but the Mexican war may be traced to an ill-cooked, ill-assorted, contradictory and irritating cabinet dinner?" asked "A Lady of New York" in *The American System of Cookery*. This was an unusually bold claim, or at least an unusually specific one. But many others spoke in the same vein. "It is within your power," Daniel Wise told young American wives, "to create a domestic heaven in the lowliest cottage." Catharine Beecher was especially prominent in the campaign to endow homemakers with a sense of the grave significance of their every action. Her advice books covered dozens of minute topics, abounded with technical illustrations, and always conveyed the message that if such seemingly unimportant matters were not attended to by American wives, the family and society would suffer grievously.

Ideas of this sort obviously led directly to a belief in the pressing need for conscious, sustained domestic training for women. Housekeeping, in fact, was a science "of broad extent, and minute detail. It cannot be grasped without due preparation, any more than a course of history could be achieved without laborious reading." This notion could take ludicrous forms when combined with the ruthless perfectionism of popular moralists. "For my own part," wrote William A. Alcott in *Letters to a Sister; or Woman's Mission*, "I see not how a Christian woman of but common intelligence, should dare . . . to make a loaf of bread without a thorough knowledge of Chemistry." In the same book he summarized the message to American wives: "There is not an act of your lives so small but you should labor with all your might, and resolve, and if necessary re-resolve concerning it."

The task of perfecting the home through ceaseless work and attention to detail was ultimately an impossible one; indeed, the constant effort and bustle of trying to perfect it probably would have ensured that family life would never succeed in being perfectly restful and joyous. But American domestic advisers encouraged women to believe that perfection was really theirs to attain, and that if they failed at it the responsibility was their own and the consequences vast. Inevitably, in a culture which entertained perfectionist dreams and looked to the home for their attainment, women would bear much of the sense of failure and guilt when perfection failed of being achieved.

Perhaps, then, historians should seek indications that middle-class women felt a sense of futility and guilt arising from the inevitable gap between expectations and reality. Presumptive signs of such feelings abound, but as yet little systematic study of this problem has been done. It appears, for one thing, that women devised a number of ways to "drop out" of the domestic role without explicitly rejecting it. One way, of course, was to develop a non-domestic avocation or career in which one continued to pay lip-service to domesticity without personally trying to live up to it. This path was the one taken by many "scribbling women," most of whom apparently felt somewhat uneasy about their effective rejection of domesticity in favor of a literary career, but few of whom were able to face the fact that they had indeed rejected it. A second path was to develop interests in charity work, Sunday School societies, tract societies, sewing circles, or other similar activities which the historian William L. O'Neill has called "social feminism." These pursuits, like journalism and literature, were premised upon two of the fundamental tenets of the "cult of true womanhood": that women were too pure to associate safely with anybody except other women, and that nurture, religion, letters, and the like were peculiarly feminine activities. Still a third avenue was to become involved in movements for political reform, including feminism. Even this alternative to domesticity did not necessarily result in a rejection of prevailing expectations and ideals about women and the home, as O'Neill and others have shown. Another path is less clearly understood from the distance of a century or more, but some women—how many is anybody's guess—dropped out, temporarily or permanently, through sickliness and the use of drugs. By developing vague physical or psychological maladies a woman could reduce to more manageable proportions the expectations focused upon her in her roles as wife, mother, and housekeeper. By turning to patent medicines, many of which were laced with alcohol or narcotic drugs, she could find more immediate and temporary respite.

Let us attempt to summarize the foregoing discussion, and in the process we can perhaps note some consequences for the society at large of the middle-class tendency to perceive a virtually unbridgeable gulf between the domestic and worldly realms.

It seems clear, first, that these nineteenth-century Americans entertained utopian aspirations about the family. At least, they told themselves that the domestic sphere could truly and literally become an isle of bliss in which their hopes for leisure, harmony, and joy could be fulfilled. Even when they affirmed that the family ought to concern itself with moral training of its members, they still emphasized that this would occur through gentle, loving techniques. Thus the ends of family life were emphatically individualistic, libertarian, even anarchic. In the perfected American home that perennial American aspiration, individual freedom, could at last be attained—and without a corresponding increase in social disorder.

In practice, as we have seen, these aspirations were more difficult to realize, even in such a small theater as the family, than most Americans had anticipated. Indeed, it even appears that the aspirations were so high as to breed greater frustration with family life than they might otherwise have been forced to endure. Internally, the perfectionist expectations placed heavy burdens of guilt upon adults of both sexes.

In terms of the relationship between family and community, the middle-class yearning for a small corner of peace in the form of a happy family may actually have furthered the social trends which Americans deplored and which encouraged them to turn inward in the first place: the misgovernment of the city, the frantic race for status through conspicuous consumption, the degradation of politics in the Jacksonian era, and the rest. It is notable in this connection that nineteenth-century writings on the city and on other problems of American society usually betrayed a deep ignorance even as they lamented the national decline and called for reform and renewal. Popular writers and their audience strike one as unable to perceive their society in any complexity; they tended to view it, and particularly the city, in stereotyped images, as a hellish place dotted with brothels, saloons, gambling-dens, race-tracks, and Catholic churches. What brought about this ignorance? The retreat to domesticity was hastened by fear of the city, but also by structural changes such as the withering of ties to kin and neighbors. These probably resulted from the migration of many middle-class families from small towns to cities, and were further exacerbated by the high rates of geographical mobility which apparently prevailed in nineteenth-century cities.

Whatever the cause of the fear of the city and the ignorance about its workings, the point is that middle-class Americans increasingly opted for retreat rather than for active engagement in the life of their society. They thereby ensured that the abuses they perceived would be perpetuated and that their reasons for despairing about their society would grow ever stronger.

The foregoing indictment also raises the question of the "privacy" of the family. Middle-class Americans valued privacy in the nineteenth century as never before. In a sense their isolated families enjoyed a significant amount of it. Certainly this was one of the things implied in the distinction they customarily drew between home and the world. But their privacy was far from complete, and in some ways it has declined further since that time. The family was being penetrated by society at large at the very moment that its members discerned a gulf between family and society. It was being penetrated, most significantly, by the popular novels, magazines, and advice-books of the day. Unthinking, traditional ways of proceeding—in sexual behavior, child nurture, task allocation—were being replaced by impersonal instruction provided by outsiders. Custom was being replaced by fashion.

Thus the vaunted privacy of the middle-class family, its emphatic otherness from the evil world beyond, did not run so deep as many believed. Uprooted, half-educated, self-scrutinizing, middle-class Americans turned eagerly to the new mechanisms which seemed ready to assume responsibility for telling them what to believe and how to behave. The "Jacksonian era," then, may have witnessed not a breakdown of institutions, as some historians contend, but rather the beginnings of a switch in the sources from which Americans would take their cues.

And yet, if total privacy did not really exist, this was due to society's penetration of the family, not to any intense participation of family members in the life of the society. The emerging ideology of the happy family was an outgrowth of the pervasive American ideology called "privatism" by Sam B. Warner, Jr.:

> Already [Warner writes] by the time of the Revolution privatism had become the American tradition. Its essence lay in its concentration upon the individual and the individual's search for wealth. Psychologically, privatism meant that the individual should seek happiness in personal independence and in the search for wealth; socially, privatism meant that the individual should see his first loyalty as his immediate family, and that a community should be a union of such money-making, accumulating families; politically, privatism meant that the community

should keep the peace among individual money-makers, and, if possible, help to create an open and thriving setting where each citizen would have some substantial opportunity to prosper.

One might conclude, then, that middle-class Americans in the mid-nineteenth-century city were able to isolate themselves with sufficient thoroughness to retreat from responsibility for dealing with urban governance and urban reform; but they were unable to isolate themselves to the degree needed for a genuinely different set of values, priorities, and configurations of personal interaction to take hold. Indeed, as one studies the supposedly Edenic family of the urban middle classes, one discovers that the very qualities by which Eden was defined—the possibility for isolation and individual fulfillment—and the implacable perfectionism with which such hopes were pursued, were quintessentially American. To these Americans of the nineteenth century there was no necessary conflict between the demands of domestic life and the desire for personal freedom. . . . [D]omesticity itself came to seem a pleasurable and emancipating escape-hatch from the cares and anxieties of life in nineteenth-century society. . . .

Coping
with
Adolescence

DAVID I. MACLEOD

Early Boy Scouts learn survival skills.

AS THE CENTURY PROGRESSED, the advent of compulsory school attendance laws and the expansion of high school programs meant that more children were attending school for longer time periods. Despite this development, many parents were concerned about the spare time that children—especially teenagers—still had after school, on the weekends, and during the summer. Prolonging the period of growing up led to the definition of a new phase of childhood: adolescence. For those parents who did not want to leave their children on their own during this phase, a variety of character-building organizations, such as the Boy Scouts and the Young Men's Christian Association, and the Girl Scouts and the Young Women's Christian Association, offered leisure activities that stressed old-fashioned values under adult supervision. In these organizations, children could be sheltered from the attractions of the city and be prepared for the rigors of adulthood. In the following article, David Macleod shows how the Boy Scouts and the YMCA developed programs in response to the particular problems of adolescents in an industrial society.

Both the Scouts and the Y sought to augment the influence of the church and school, but since participation was voluntary, they had to sponsor activities that would hold boys' interests. While scouting was particularly successful in attracting preteenagers and those just experiencing pubescence, it was not able to retain many members beyond the age of fourteen. The schedule of troop activities, even if it included a healthy mix of camping and hiking, did not attract older boys, who wanted to spend more time with others their own age and less time with "little kids." For those who spent their teenage years in school, the peer group of the classroom seemed preferable to the mixture of ages in the troop. Macleod concludes that in resisting the efforts to organize their spare time, middle-class teenagers in the early decades of the twentieth century were already shaping their own subculture as they waited to join the work world.

. . . The search for order and social control is a pervasive theme in recent writing on the Progressive era. Although bureaucratic and professional structures reshaped middle-class life, historians tend to assume that the most blatant social control was directed against the lower class. But another imperfectly assimilated group was of equal concern to upper and middle-class adults: the rising generation of their own class. While some such adults sallied forth to impose social control upon the lower orders, others stayed inside the ramparts of the middle class and worked to keep the garrison loyal. The accepted first lines of control—family, church, and school—had enough gaps, it seemed, to need supplementing; and prominent among schemes to this end were character-building agencies. For boys, the main ones were the Boy Scouts of America and the junior department of the YMCA. Although these organizations have been neglected by historians, few Progressive-era innovations won more approbation from reformers and conservatives alike. Few won more participants either; for by 1921 the BSA had 16,910 Scoutmasters and 391,382 Scouts; YMCAs had 243,050 juniors.

Loss of control was not the only adult concern; for the conditions of middle-class urban boyhood—sedentary pursuits, pervasive feminine influences, and prolonged dependency—also raised widespread fears that the boys were growing weak in physique and will power. Adding to these fears was a broad complex of middle-class anxieties about the corrupting and debilitating effects of urbanization and social change. In response to this battery of concerns, character builders proposed simultaneously to strengthen and control boys, making them manly yet keeping them dependent. . . .

Boys' workers tried to manage boys by manipulating their peer groups; but peer pressure cut two ways, causing boys to drop out as well as join. Thus Boy Scout and YMCA enrollments by age offer revealing evidence on a subject which often eludes historians of schools and other youth agencies: the reactions of young people in the mass. If large numbers participated at a given age, they must have been willing to accept continued supervision, eager to develop strength and skills, or at least satisfied with the recreation they got. But if—as happened—many dropped out by their middle teens, then clearly what adults offered them must have disappointed their expectations or affronted their sense

COPING WITH ADOLESCENCE   By David I. Macleod. Originally published under the title "Act Your Age: Boyhood, Adolescence, and the Rise of the Boy Scouts of America," *Journal of Social History*, 16 (1982), 3–20. Reprinted by permission of the journal and the author.

of what self-respecting boys that age might do or submit to. Thus Scouting won preadolescent boys with its uniforms, achievement awards, and outdoor adventures. But it could not hold them long.

Boy Scouting was not the first major boys' work agency. The oldest, the Young Men's Christian Association, began in the 1850s, offering religious and social life to urban white-collar workers. Local Associations originally admitted boys of twelve or fourteen to full membership; but as young men tired of the small fry, YMCAs began in the 1870s and 1880s to form separate junior departments. Volunteers or part-time workers were in charge until about 1900, when rapid expansion led to the hiring of full-time boys' secretaries (the YMCA term for salaried staff), who ran sports, hobby clubs, and religious programs.

Boy Scouting was founded in 1908 by Robert Baden-Powell, a British general and Boer War hero who set out to enliven church cadet corps with elements of army scouting and ended up by producing a complete program. Scouting freed Edwardian boys from stuffy surroundings and soothed fears that the Empire's future workers and soldiers were turning politically radical, morally degenerate, and physically soft. Echoes of Scouting's popularity soon crossed the ocean, and YMCA men supervised formation of the Boy Scouts of America in 1910. Though independent, the BSA carried over personnel and ideas from the Y. Under Chief Scout Executive James West, a lawyer whose child welfare work had won praise from Theodore Roosevelt, the BSA Americanized its rules and set age limits at twelve through eighteen. Paid executives ran a centralized bureaucracy; but the troops of boys were led by volunteer Scoutmasters, mostly young ministers, teachers, other professionals, businessmen, and clerks. Troops also had institutional sponsors, mainly churches and a few schools.

"Boys' work" was a comprehensive term, encompassing not only Boy Scout and YMCA activities but also those of boys' clubs and many lesser organizations. What set YMCA and Boy Scout leaders apart from their counterparts in boys' clubs was their distinct favoritism towards older boys from good homes. Sons of business and professional men were most likely to become Scouts or YMCA juniors; those of lower-white-collar workers and skilled blue-collar workers joined less often; and sons of semiskilled or unskilled workers tended to stay away. Like all boys' workers, YMCA and Scout leaders hoped to get boys off the streets and keep them busy. But they expected to do more: they saw themselves as character builders, believing that superior raw material—adolescent boys from good homes—would enable them to inculcate ideals and build the social reliability and all-around strength called for in the American Boy Scout oath: "1. To do my duty to God and my country, and to obey the scout law; 2. To help other people at all times; 3. To keep myself physically strong, mentally awake, and morally straight." Theodore Roosevelt, the BSA's Chief Scout Citizen, epitomized the character builders' ideal of moralistic energy and forceful conventionality.

As every textbook writer knows, America underwent huge changes in the half century after the Civil War, changes which alarmed people whose moral and social frame of reference was the farm or small town and which ultimately spurred character builders to try to rebuild old strengths and virtues. As cities mushroomed, contemporaries lamented the steady drain of young people off the farms. In the evening light of nostalgia, rural communities appeared innocent, homogeneous places to grow up, whereas cities glared in the darkness of popular imagining as hellish centers of luxury and misery, where feverish debauch followed hectic work. To panicky observers, cities and their immigrant slums were like metastasizing cancers.

Meanwhile, the nature of work—traditionally central to masculine identity and the building of character—was changing. Farming declined and urban work, with its shorter days and faster pace, did not offer the same safe, steady preoccupation for men and boys; instead, moralists feared, it fostered nervousness and drove men to vice. Though white-collar jobs proliferated, large corporations and other bureaucratic structures compelled a growing segment of the middle class to accept lifelong paid employment instead of manly independence.

These social changes troubled character builders, boding enfeeblement and loss of social control. Ernest Thompson Seton, the famed nature writer who was the BSA's Chief Scout from 1910 to 1915, wrote that farmboys had once been "strong, self-reliant," yet "respectful to . . . superiors [and] obedient to . . . parents." But the rise of industry and growth of spectator sports had turned boys into "flat-chested cigarette smokers with shaky nerves and doubtful vitality. . . ." Luther Gulick, a specialist in physical education who revitalized YMCA boys' work in the 1890s and later helped found the Boy Scouts of America and the Camp Fire Girls, portrayed the urban middle class as unable to outbreed newcomers to the city and "pained to find that their children have less power and less vitality" than they themselves. Without toughening, their sons would be outnumbered and undercut by immigrants.

Underlying Gulick's alarm was widespread fear of race suicide; the best people, in their own imagining, faced submergence by inferior but hardier and more prolific immigrant stock. More generally, middle-class men feared loss of masculinity in an age of salaried dependence, soft living, and changing sex roles. To have women colleagues threatened the pride of male clerks and teachers; and women's rights undercut the simple equation of manliness with power.

A popular anodyne was to fantasize escape into an energetic, all-male world, through western novels, sports, or camping out. Scouting's outdoor program led some clerks, teachers, and clergymen to become Scoutmasters to prove their masculinity. But Scouting's tamed adventure appealed more directly to youngish boys; and for them it was sponsored fantasy to hold them in place.

In dealing with boys, after all, control remained basic. Freed of farm labor, urban boys were becoming an unsupervised leisure class. The BSA's James West spoke for most boys' workers when he complained that schools turned boys loose in midafternoon and that parental surveillance was weak. In small cities and towns, where Boy Scouting recruited best, the problem still looked manageable; but boys loitered about the streets and stables, and the growth of big cities in size and cultural hegemony made urban vices seem near enough. Parents needed little incitement to scent contagion and welcomed supervised recreation. Ideally, Scout leaders tried to root boys in a cohesive middle-class community. Locally, they set up supervisory councils of prominent men and tied boys to churches and schools through sponsored troops. Nationally, the BSA worked for conformity through citizenship training and insistent Americanism.

It remains to explain why character builders focussed their response to social change exclusively on boys twelve through eighteen. Obviously, the socioeconomic situation of teenagers had changed. In the mid-1800s, farming and commerce gave many teenage boys employment, including promising white-collar jobs. Working long hours and living with parents, these boys remained under sustained adult surveillance. But as farming ceased to expand and industrial and commercial technology changed, full-time jobs for the early and middle teens dried up and those that remained led nowhere. High school enrollments rose from 110,000 in 1880 to 2,200,000 in 1920, as demand for educational credentials compelled ambitious teenagers to stay in school. Middle-class adults realized they must hold boys in check well past fourteen, the usual minimum age for entering high school but also for quitting school. Middle-class boys generally stayed on but were often bored and restless. Since high school extracurricular activities were still limited in the 1910s and grammar schools had next to none, character builders saw a need for programs to keep schoolboys safely occupied.

Yet character builders worried that prolonged dependency exposed boys to effeminizing influences. They agreed that boys should stay under female control until age twelve, but then must begin to break free. As teenage boys ceased to work alongside men, however, women succeeded by default to the task of continuing supervision. Even in high schools, a majority of teachers were women, and character builders complained that schools geared their routine to the sedentary inclinations of girls. Sunday schools were worse, they charged. And when boys came home after school, father was away pursuing his career. Troubled by the conflict between dependency and vigor and by the guilty knowledge that men often ignored boys, character builders regarded home and mother with traces of misogyny. Edgar M. Robinson, a leader in YMCA boys' work, railed against "the boy who has been . . . so carefully wrapped up in the 'pink cotton wool' of an overindulgent home [that] he is more effeminate than his sister. . . ." More constructively, character builders devised supervised, strenuous, sex-segregated recreation to keep boys dependent but energetic.

This dual concern was pronounced among Protestant churchmen, whose churches were embarrassingly short of males. Mid-nineteenth-century remedies had centered on winning young men; but as Sunday schools became the churches' main recruiting grounds, concern shifted towards a younger group. Young people's societies sprang up in the 1880s to accommodate church members too young for adult prayer meetings, but boys shunned the societies' dull gatherings. By 1900, membership was two thirds female and two thirds over age eighteen; and boys' workers attacked the societies as effeminate. Meanwhile, experience accumulated that Sunday schools lost three quarters or more of their boys between twelve and eighteen. So concern gravitated towards the early teens, where the exodus began. To clergymen worried that the "boy problem" reflected their own or the church's lack of virility, muscular Christianity was a godsend; an enthusiast advised colleagues each to master "one athletic game so as to beat all the boys in the parish at it." Ministers adopted Boy Scouting with alacrity, comprising 29 percent of all Scoutmasters in 1912. More than half of all early troops were church-sponsored.

Physical changes drew further attention to the early and middle teens; for at fifteen the average American boy of 1920 was more than two inches taller and fifteen pounds heavier than his counterpart of 1880. (Younger and older boys grew less.) In addition, the median age of pubescence declined—to about fourteen in the 1910s. Had character builders simply wanted stronger boys, they should have rejoiced, but fears for control made them apprehensive of boys who seemed outsized and oversexed. The BSA's James West said the "most difficult" ages were fourteen and fifteen.

Dismay at physical and social changes among teenagers converged in hatred of precocity, an antipathy common among educated Americans. Threatening loss of control and moral and physical degeneracy, precocity subsumed whatever moralists decried in urban youth: debility, nervousness, independence, and above all sexuality.

It is well known that respectable Victorian opinion condemned sexual indulgence; the Christian gentleman was "continuously testing his manliness in the fire of self-denial." So, too, was the Christian boy, for the belief was well established that masturbation entailed penalties ranging from debility to madness. Though less alarmist, the Boy Scout *Handbook* warned boys against loss of "the sex fluid . . . that makes a boy manly, strong, and noble." Purity, in this view, was power—and thus essential if big business and mass immigration were eroding opportunity. *Scouting* magazine warned that a Scout must grow up "free from every blemish and stain—then and only then will he be fully equipped to . . . fight the battles of business life." Yet YMCA secretaries judged masturbation nearly universal among middle-class boys. And character builders regarded coeducational high schools as hotbeds of precocity. H.W. Gibson, a leading YMCA boys' worker who wrote frequently for Boy Scout publications, blamed "unnatural, hot-house forcing," especially overpressure in the schools, "for the highly nervous and sexually passionate adolescents. . . ." According to Norman Richardson, an educator and Scout commissioner who taught a course in Scouting at Boston University, certain high schools rivalled "Sodom or Babylon" because sedentary schoolwork had replaced physical labor.

The word adolescent—seldom used before the 1890s—gave character builders' worries a name. They got it from the famed psychologist G. Stanley Hall, who posited that growing children recapitulate human history, progressing upward as instincts implanted in past culture epochs emerge in sequence. In Hall's view, the boy from eight to twelve was an individualistic replica of an early pigmy. Then, after a massive infusion of new instincts, the adolescent emerged—similar to men of medieval times, imaginative, emotional, capable of idealism and altruism, but not fully mature. Echoing both antebellum expectations of teenage conversion and Victorian alarm at youthful sexuality, Hall depicted adolescence as promising yet dangerous. "The dawn of puberty . . . is soon followed by a stormy period," he warned, "when the very worst and best impulses in the human soul struggle against each other. . . ." His ideas rationalized hatred of precocity: since failure to assimilate new instincts meant "retrogression, degeneracy, or fall," adolescents must patiently live out their instincts and sublimate sexual drives into altruism and religious faith.

Hall's hyperbolic portrait of adolescent *bouleversement* made it logical to concentrate character building then, when all was in flux and susceptibility to moral and religious idealism was at its peak. Yet many character builders thought the threat of adolescence outweighed the promise. Hall's picture of storm and stress confirmed fears that teenage boys—even those from good homes—were hard to control and liable to enfeebling degeneracy. Since character builders had no wish to hurry boys into danger, many looked to boyhood, which was implicitly preadolescent, as a safer model for the teens.

Two traditions were involved. One was the cloistered life of the English public schoolboy, which underlay Baden-Powell's conception of Scouting. Although older schoolboys wielded great power within their little world, they were kept basically dependent until their late teens. Such prolonged segregation from adult affairs charmed American observers; and as prep schools multiplied towards 1900, Americans shaped their own version of the schoolboy life.

The home-grown tradition of American boyhood referred by the late 1800s to small-town lads aged six or eight to twelve or fourteen who foraged through the woods and frolicked at the swimming hole. Rural boyhood offered, it seemed, a moratorium during which boys could let off steam without threatening adults. Books on this sort of boyhood were popular, exploiting nostalgia for antebellum country life. The "real boy" in such tales played in an all-male world invaded only rarely by fussy mothers and timid girls; brimming with vigor, he was pure because he was energetic—and vice versa. Charles Dudley Warner claimed: "Every boy who is good for anything is a natural savage." In American stereotyping, Indians were violent but seldom lascivious; so too were preadolescent boys. Indeed, writers caught up in the turn-of-the-century celebration of energy lauded the boyish scrapes of famous men and professed to prefer boys with "life enough to get into mischief. . . ."

To vigor and basic decency, writers of the early 1900s added virtues for an urban age, emphasizing the group context of boyhood and its amenability to adult control. Researchers inspired by Hall reported that boys from ten or twelve to fourteen, fifteen, or sixteen had an instinct to form gangs or tribes. Referring synonymously to "Boyhood or the Gang period," boys' workers concluded that the secret of control was to form artificial gangs or take over existing ones and rule through boy leaders. Chief Scout Seton compared this technique, formalized in Scouting's patrol system, to Britain's imperial policy of governing tribes through their chiefs.

Interest in gangs reflected Progressive-era enthusiasm for cooperation and social concern. As service became a middle-class catchword and men went to work in large organizations, character builders looked to gang experience to teach boys rudimentary altruism and social conformity without compromising their masculinity. "Out among his peers God intends that he shall go," proclaimed William Byron Forbush, a student of Hall's and a leading writer on boys' work, "to give and take, to mitigate his own selfishness and to gain the masculine standpoint which his mother, his nurse, and his school-teacher cannot give. . . ."

Conveniently, the gang age overlapped the years which Hall assigned to early adolescence, forming a bridge from childish individualism to adolescent altruism. Yet character builders held to Hall's belief that dramatic adolescent changes began about age twelve. They expected middle-class boys to be under fairly close adult control until that age, but then to be potentially troublesome. Accordingly, acting under YMCA influence, the BSA's organizers barred boys under twelve, lest they limit Scouting's "effectiveness in dealing with adolescent problems." Even so, Scouting's answer to those problems was to encourage the boyish characteristics of gang-age boys and discourage the adolescent. In effect, the gang age carried aspects of small boyhood over into the early teens; by prolonging this sort of boyhood through the middle teens, Scout leaders hoped to give adolescent boys a refuge from female-infested, precocity-inducing situations.

YMCA boys' work and recapitulation-based theories of character building took root together. In the late 1890s, Luther Gulick, who had studied with Hall, enunciated a rationale for boys' work as the answer to adolescent problems. Under Edgar M. Robinson, who headed YMCA boys' work from 1900 to 1920, Hall's and Gulick's ideas became an ideology justifying rapid expansion of junior departments. Local YMCAs hired boys' work specialists who looked to knowledge of adolescence as their basis for professional status; the age range for juniors rose from ten to sixteen in the 1880s to twelve to eighteen after 1900; and membership grew rapidly.

To serve this new constituency, boys' secretaries tried to arrange a supervised adolescence in which crises were mild and age brought measured doses of recognition and authority. They sought "decisions for Christian living" from the boys and enrolled more than a third in Bible classes. But conversion was not to be convulsive; it was the first of many "forward steps": join the church; do committee work; give up some bad habit. Y men fought masturbation with purity talks and readings, but recognized the older boys' interest in girls and held occasional ladies' nights, urging respect for future wives and mothers. They also raised the problem of vocational choice, though their advice was undramatic: stay in school. Lest older boys chafe at dependency, secretaries portioned out authority to boys' cabinets and held older boys' conferences. By sponsoring an attenuated adolescence, in short, YMCA men tried to innoculate boys against adolescent turbulence, impurity, and independent-mindedness.

At the same time, Y workers sought to prolong boyish vigor and work off sexual or other forms of energy, but in ways that older boys would accept. Special interest clubs adapted to boys' changing hobbies and summer camps satisfied any lingering "savage" instincts. But sports and gymnastics were the key to pleasing older boys; for team sports were fashionable in high schools by the 1910s, and basketball, the leading YMCA sport, was distinctly a high school boy's game.

Whereas Y men tried to combine adolescent idealism with boyish activism, the BSA's answer to adolescent problems was simpler: extend boyhood and distract boys from adolescence. Baden-Powell had originally designed Scouting for boys as young as ten. In applying his program to boys twelve through eighteen, American Boy Scout leaders opted for delay and "preoccupation" as the remedy for adolescence. Chief Scout Executive James West said that Scouting "takes the boy . . . when he is beset with the new and bewildering experiences of adolescence and diverts his thoughts therefrom to wholesome and worthwhile activities." Fear of adolescent brooding led a camp committee to warn that during "the moody hours of twilight" Scouts were prone to "great thoughts" and must be kept busy. And Boy Scout officials shared the common belief that vigorous exercise would "short circuit" sexual impulses.

Boyish activism suffused Scouting. The better troops hiked often and camped in summer. Good Scoutmasters packed the weekly meetings with instruction, drills, and games. And the heart of the official program was a hierarchy of awards to tap the schoolboy's gold star mania, building strength and skills and filling leisure time. To reach first class rank, boys passed tests on woodcraft, reconnaissance, and civic service skills; then they could earn specialized merit badges and amass 21 to become Eagle Scouts. Since promotion became the main criterion of success, Boy Scouts faced pressure to keep busy.

Meanwhile, Boy Scout leaders skirted adolescent issues. A few merit badges explored vocations, but most were for hobbyists; and Scouting's woodcraft emphasis pointed away from careers. In order to please all faiths, the BSA left religious instruction to the churches; most Scoutmasters dodged the purity issue; and moral education came down to memorizing the Boy Scout Oath and Law, a chore which some Scouts skipped. Boy Scout leaders made a serious effort to teach altruism through individual and group good turns. But rather than risk the passionate enthusiasm and unsettling introspection predicted by Hall, they reduced adolescent idealism to a commitment to conventional morality.

Basically, Scouting systematized patterns typical of youngish boys. Although new team sports were displacing older pastimes toward 1900, small boys still roamed the woods. In Cleveland in the 1910s, for instance, 45 percent of elementary schoolboys said they went hiking. But tastes changed as boys grew older: fewer hiked and more played baseball, basketball, and football. An 1896 study of Massachusetts schoolboys found that interest in hide-and-seek held steady until age thirteen and then fell off, whereas interest in ball games kept rising. And small-town high school boys, surveyed in the 1920s, almost all named a team sport among their favorite recreations, while only a third mentioned swimming and a fifth said hiking or camping. By 1920, team sports played a major role in boys' lives, one that increased with age; the highly publicized example of high school, college, and professional athletics was more than woodcraft and camping could match. Scouting had its own games, but they resembled those like hide-and-seek that small boys played. Though Boy Scouts importuned for the new team sports, BSA headquarters discouraged Scoutmasters from giving in, lest they compromise Scouting's uniqueness. In effect, the BSA maintained a juvenile, somewhat old-fashioned form of boyhood.

To combat enfeeblement and bolster boyish pride, the BSA cultivated an air of determined masculinity, symbolized by awards for heroism, service alongside police at parades, and a uniform like the U.S. Army's. Women were barred even from supervisory committees. So it was no surprise that the BSA's Chief Scout Executive disliked the Girl Scouts and pressed them to change their name and program. West preferred the Camp Fire Girls, whose name suggested a stronger orientation toward hearth and home. As for the boys, some feared being called sissies if girls could also be Scouts. Young Boy Scouts wanted to avoid girls altogether; older ones would happily have met socially but sometimes balked at service projects on which they and Girl Scouts worked as equals. Still, Girl Scouting troubled Boy Scout leaders more than it did the boys. The leaders were trying to curb the boys' thoughts of independence while compensating them with a simulacrum of manliness. Scouting for girls unbalanced the trade-off.

How did boys react to Boy Scout and YMCA strategies? One need not accept the premise—fashionable in studying oppressed or neglected groups—that "youth makes its own history" to recognize that boys held a crude veto over character builders' plans, since they could always quit. . . .

We must also realize that masculinity was not the same issue for boys as for men. Boys saw manhood at least as much in terms of age as sex role; they wanted the status, amusements, and autonomy which they associated with growing older. When asked why boys left Sunday school, most boys replied that those of fifteen to twenty were "too old"; Sunday school was "kiddish." Far fewer said it was "only for girls." Even in relations with Girl Scouts, age was at issue, since girls could join at ten and that made Scouting seem juvenile, not just unmasculine.

For boys turning twelve, the Scout program of woodcraft backed by badges was enticing: just to attend evening meetings was a step towards independence, while summer camp promised the first week ever away from mother. So young boys flocked to join; two thirds of all new Boy Scouts in the 1920s were twelve or thirteen.

Yet runaway success with gang-age boys created problems, making it almost impossible to keep underage boys out and older ones in. Scoutmasters often admitted boys under twelve. Southerners claimed their boys matured faster; others simply found boys of ten or eleven eager to join and easy to lead. But older Boy Scouts felt demeaned, as extended graded schooling, by herding students the same age into the same classroom, had made them very sensitive to age differences. The YMCA's E.M. Robinson considered three years the maximum age span for a cohesive group of boys. Since few Boy Scout troops were divided by age, most suffered from the Gresham's Law of boys' work: younger boys drive out older ones. A dropout explained: "[We] got a bunch of little kids in the troop and they wanted to be with us all of the time and we wanted to be by ourselves. And I guess we wanted to do different things."

Baden-Powell's solution was to give older boys responsibility as patrol leaders; but the number of such offices was limited. Besides, Americans lacked the English faith in social hierarchy and would not give boys much authority. American Scoutmasters used simulated gangs as a thin disguise for direct control, reducing patrol leaders to monitors and seldom letting patrols hike or camp alone.

Underlying American losses of older Boy Scouts was enormous annual turnover in membership. From 1915 to 1925, 47 to 65 percent of each year's Boy Scouts did not reregister the next year. The problem was not unique to Boy Scouting, for YMCA persistence rates were equally low; but since the BSA recruited mainly boys of twelve or thirteen, rapid turnover made for a shortage of Boy Scouts past fourteen or fifteen. The median age of quitting was 14.5 in 1921, and 78 percent left before reaching sixteen. Current Scouts, of course, were younger still.

Boy Scouts quit for many reasons. Although some found badge work an exciting challenge—in 1921, one in 600 reached Eagle Scout and the proportion was rising—many showed little interest in promotion. At any given time, a majority were tenderfeet, the lowest rank. Boys who did not advance commonly dropped out; and BSA headquarters blamed Scoutmasters for not inspiring them to ambition. But some Boy Scouts found signaling and first aid dull, clamoring instead for sports and "fun." The outdoor program appealed best to youngish boys. In fact, age predicted length of membership just as well as rank:

the older a Boy Scout joined, the sooner he quit. Dropouts blamed accumulating dissatisfactions and distractions. In one survey, 25 percent mentioned the lure of sports, social life, or other duties; 14 percent each blamed poor leaders or the collapse of their troop; 12 percent said they got bored; 7 percent cited conflict with younger boys; and 28 percent gave other reasons. Not all these motives were age-related, but many gained in force as boys grew older.

Scouting's symbolism caused problems too. The very term *Boy* Scout gave offense. E.P. Hulse, a BSA publicist, warned: "Kids of 15 down South when called 'boy' used to retort, 'If I'm a boy where did Jackson and Lee get their men?'" The uniform, which looked manly to twelve-year-olds, struck older boys as childish; and in high schools with R.O.T.C., girls ostracized Boy Scouts as juvenile imitators. Yet adults delighted in the uniform's juvenility; Frank Gray, a New Jersey Boy Scout executive, condemned "the boy who wants to dress up like a man" and urged Scoutmasters to "see that the boy is living a boy's life. . . ."

The few older Boy Scouts from immigrant families faced added constraints. Just to walk their streets in uniform invited mockery or fights. And some Scout leaders—though not all—treated boys of immigrant stock as more juvenile than others the same age, making less effort to apply the patrol system and suspecting—in the words of a Scoutmaster at the Chicago Commons settlement house—that the full Scout program was "too hard and comprehensive for our Italian boys."

At best, efforts to recruit and retain older boys came up against increased restiveness about age fourteen or fifteen. Of 47 Boy Scouts whom *Scouting* magazine advertised as runaways from home in the late 1910s, 8 were fourteen-year-olds and fully 19 were fifteen-year-olds, whereas just 1 was twelve and 3 were thirteen. These were extreme cases, to be sure, but ordinary boys also grew impatient around fourteen or fifteen; and part-time jobs, high school life, and girls began to compete for their time. Boy Scouts who quit school usually left Scouting as well, seeking autonomy or simply lacking free time. High school boys came under pressure to concentrate on sports and study. They also met girls who looked on Boy Scouts as "little kids"—and by high school age, they cared. Yet Boy Scout leaders often regarded the "girl-struck boy" with distaste and discussed the "girl problem" in pathological terms, wondering how to cure boys "infected" with "girlitis."

Clearly, Y men catered more to older boys, since they provided lots of sports, prescribed no uniforms, divided boys by age, and sought out high school and white-collar working boys. By 1920, most YMCAs had a separate group for clerks and office boys; and Hi-Y clubs spread through the high schools. Because YMCA juniors were freer than Boy Scouts to choose their own activities— often paying fees separately for what they chose—older boys could pick what interested them. Most juniors signed up for gymnastics and sports (78 percent in 1920). They dodged vocational training, but otherwise showed an interest when Y men addressed adolescent problems. Although only one junior in fifteen professed conversion, large attendance at meetings for moral improvement, vocational choice, and religious decision-making suggested that boys wanted to assuage worries with some form of resolution. Some even found open condemnation of masturbation a relief.

Evidence that adolescents responded favorably when adults addressed their

problems and interests—as YMCA workers did—can be seen in the age differ-
ence between Boy Scouts and YMCA juniors. In the 1910s, a quarter of the
YMCA boys held jobs; and by 1921, two fifths were high school students;
whereas most Boy Scouts were still in grade school. In 1922, Trenton, New
Jersey had twice as many Boy Scouts as YMCA members among grammar
school and junior high pupils, but nearly four times as many Y boys as Boy
Scouts among senior high students. On average, Boy Scouts were younger than
YMCA boys. A survey of rural and suburban counties in the early 1920s found
a median age for Boy Scouts of 14.3, compared to 15.5 for YMCA juniors.
Nationwide, the Boy Scouts' median age in 1919 was 13.8 and fewer than ten
percent were sixteen or older. Fifteen years later, the median remained almost
unchanged at 13.9, although 16.5 percent were sixteen or above. By contrast,
the median age of YMCA juniors was about 15.0 and many were in their middle
or later teens.

In summary, the YMCA had fewer boys than Scouting, but a larger share of
those who did enroll were adolescents, that is, well into their middle or later
teens. The BSA enlisted many more boys of twelve and thirteen, but could not
attract or hold many boys more than a year or two past the average age of male
pubescence, then about fourteen. Even Sunday schools had more boys in their
late teens. So if Boy Scout leaders hoped to strengthen and control boys by
extending boyhood and distracting them from adolescence, such hopes often
went unfulfilled. To prolong the latency period by a controlled, somewhat
contrived promotion of masculine vigor and activism proved harder than Boy
Scouting's American organizers had foreseen.

Enrollments by age suggest limits, therefore, to adult success at voluntaristic
social control; for the tug of war across the generations ended near a draw. The
YMCA held older boys by adapting at least partially to their wishes, while the
BSA won its triumphs with boys twelve to fourteen, a bit older than the age at
which growing boys first clamored to join, but definitely younger than the BSA's
early leaders would have preferred. Scouting appealed vividly to the group
tastes—in a sense, the peer culture—of boys ten to thirteen or fourteen. But by
denying older boys the tokens of maturity and the fee-for-service autonomy of
the YMCA, Scouting branded itself too juvenile for boys in their middle teens;
and except for a few hardy souls devoted to the outdoors or Scout badge work,
it lost them.

The pattern of Boy Scout attrition may seem familiar today. So may adult
ambivalence towards adolescence and preference for the latency period, which
have survived not only the collapse of Hall's theoretical underpinnings but also
claims by scholars that adolescent upheaval is less dramatic or prevalent than
Hall believed. But in this regard the 1900s and 1910s *should* seem somewhat
familiar. For we cannot encompass the history of twentieth-century teenagers
simply by saying that they have grown more restive and sophisticated. That
may well be true; and adult anxiety may likewise have risen as adult authority
has weakened. But concern about adolescents was sharp and increasingly explicit in the decades around 1900; and many of our would-be agencies of
control date from that era. Furthermore, many of those institutions were—as
agencies of control—partial failures from the start. I have concentrated upon

middle-class boys' work, but one might make a similar argument regarding street boys' clubs, juvenile courts, perhaps even high schools.

As schooling engulfed teenagers, they looked to recreation for self-assertion and some limited autonomy. Teenage boys had definite tastes and a jealous regard for status marks of increasing maturity, however factitious these became. This does not mean there was a full-blown, self-conscious youth culture among middle-class teenage boys of the 1910s, though their removal from the mainstream of economic life met one precondition for the rise of modern youth cultures. By holding implicitly to certain roles for each age and sex they were forerunners of a sort, but not forerunners of a single youth culture. They were internally divided—as young people are to this day. Historians interested in masculine and feminine sex roles and in the changing context of adolescence must not forget that the young have not seen masculinity or youth whole; especially since the early 1900s, they have subdivided each condition by age as well as gender and social class and have acted in terms of those finer gradations. To control them, adults have had to accede in part to their desires.

Such an adaptation to the tastes of different age groups eventually reshaped boys' work. In the 1920s, YMCA secretaries relaxed their preoccupation with adolescence and set up groups of Friendly Indians for boys under twelve. More reluctantly, American Boy Scout officials began Cubbing (the early term for Cub Scouting) for boys nine through eleven in 1930 and lowered the minimum age for Boy Scouts to eleven in 1949. Only in the late 1940s, though, with Explorer Scouting, did the BSA provide separate groups for older boys and emphasize accepted needs of adolescence such as vocational guidance and a social life with girls. Boys could join at fourteen or remain regular Scouts.

The results suggest at first glance that the boys' downward pressure on age triumphed; for Cub Scouting mushroomed, while Explorer Scouting grew more slowly. Yet Scouting for older boys kept pace sufficiently that the ratio of Boy Scouts and Explorers fourteen and older to those aged twelve and thirteen changed little over the years. Furthermore, the proportion of American boys aged fourteen through seventeen enrolled in Scouting rose from 4 percent in 1919 to 9 percent in 1967. Since this increase reflected declining farm population, better organization by the BSA, creation of the Explorer program, and somewhat better recruitment among racial and ethnic minorities, it did not prove that traditional Scouting had grown more attractive to older boys. But neither did it show the movement losing ground. Age patterns established early in the century proved remarkably stable.

With programs differentiated by age, the BSA eventually enrolled crowds of preadolescents. An observer might see in this a downward extension of institutionalized adolescence; but the basic Boy Scout program, though originally promoted in America in response to concern about middle-class adolescence, was only marginally adolescent in design and practice. Boys under age twelve had *always* wanted to join, and most left by fifteen or so. In recreation they set their own timetable; and efforts to alter that timetable work about as well today as in the 1910s.

The
Obsolescence
of
Old Age

W. ANDREW ACHENBAUM

Brown Brothers

Hempstead Poor House, 1910–1915

IN COLONIAL AMERICA, THE SOCIAL IDEAL was to revere old people—although the ideal was not always practiced. But, by the late eighteenth century, Americans were showing less regard for the old and were beginning to idolize youth instead. Throughout the nineteenth century, American culture continued to devalue old age. In the following article, Andrew Achenbaum analyzes these attitudes after 1880.

Not only were older people not respected, but an increasing hostility and negativism were developing. Americans emphasized the disabilities of old age, rather than its advantages. They stressed the physical deterioration and bad health that often accompanied age, and they began to think of old people as morbid, ill-tempered, and bad-mannered.

Achenbaum explains this increased hostility toward the elderly by first of all pointing out the updated medical opinions. Medical researchers were uncovering and publicizing the pathological characteristics of age and discovering some of the actual reasons for physical decline. Ultimately, the medical world saw old age as a distinct stage of life with its own characteristics—and many of them were negative.

Achenbaum also notes that at the same time, business—especially big business—began to devalue age. Businessmen worried about inefficiency and the inability of old people to perform heavy physical labor as skillfully as they once had. Business leaders feared mental decline and wondered if older workers could concentrate or think as well as they did when they were younger. The result was the development of mandatory retirement systems, which forced the old out of the labor market and made a place for younger workers. Therefore, the growth of the "cult" of youth meant a corresponding decline in the attitude toward, and position of, the elderly in American society.

. . . ANALYZING THE OPINIONS OF POPULAR WRITERS, medical doctors, clergymen, intellectuals and businessmen constitutes a useful starting point for studying attitudes toward old age. Between 1865 and 1914, the number of articles and books this group wrote about aging sharply increased. Systematically surveying the pertinent literature reveals that definitions of old age changed significantly over time. In the earlier part of the period, old age was idealized: writers described the elderly as the true survivors of the fittest and emphasized the important societal roles they played. In the latter part of the period, writers challenged this idealistic image of old age: they stressed the physical, mental and behavioral deterioration accompanying old age and argued that the elderly contributed very little to the well-being of society. A preliminary profile of changing attitudes toward old age emerges from a consideration of four factors: the aging of the population; new scientific research into the physiological and psychological aspects of senescence; a deliberate effort by big business to retire workers arbitrarily at sixty-five; and the emergence of a cult of youth. Knowing the ways attitudes toward old age changed, even in a middle-class milieu, a historian can begin to set forth hypotheses to explain why they changed.

After the Civil War, Americans thought that "there (was) something highly impressive in the venerable appearance and corresponding sober manners of elderly men and women." Some said that old age accentuated a person's latent strength and endurance. Others thought that living a long life ripened a person's judgment because of the wisdom gained from many experiences. Most writers associated the qualities of benevolence, stability of character, self-control and piety with growing old. Before the 1880s, writers played down anything which might detract from "the very essence of the perfection of old age." They rarely mentioned problems such as illness and disability which accompanied senescence. And, although they acknowledged that youth and age differed in many ways, they were quick to point out that each stage of life had its distinctive merits, "Every period may be perfect in its kind. . . . Each has its advantage; each its peculiar experiences and enjoyments." This line of reasoning muted the liabilities of age and enabled writers to stress the special contributions old people could make to society.

Writers encouraged old people to keep active. Staying busy helped the elderly keep their mental and physical vigor, maintain their economic independence and advance their own and society's prosperity. As Ralph Waldo Emerson

THE OBSOLESCENCE OF OLD AGE   By W. Andrew Achenbaum. Originally published under the title "The Obsolescence of Old Age in America, 1865–1914." From *Journal of Social History*, 8 (1974), 48–60. Reprinted by permission.

noted, "We do not count a man's years until he has nothing else to count." In other words, old people mattered so long as they contributed to the well-being of others.

The elderly performed some of their most important duties in the home. Grandparents shared with parents responsibility for raising children properly: "The education of the young should properly commence with the grandmother, for it takes about two generations to eliminate plebian forms of character and constitution. Old people also improved the quality of adult life: "No one ever honors you with any kind of help, without being himself the better for what he does; for fellow-feeling with you ripens his soul for Him." Old age was a benefaction; service to it ennobled everyone.

References to the role of the aged in the family did more than reinforce the idea that the elderly had special roles to play. Associating the elderly with the home created an appealing and sentimental image of old age. Currier and Ives print, "Old Age" (1868), evoked the qualities of "perfect" old age as depicted in the first two decades after the Civil War. The old people in the print appear healthy, secure and contented sitting in a parlor filled with family portraits, books and other treasured possessions. The scene ably illustrated the mood conveyed by L. Maria Child's poem, "Old Folks at Home:"

> Near their hearth-stones, warm and cheery,
> > Where by night or day,
> They're free to rest when they are weary,
> > There the old folks love to stay.

Descriptions of old age were not based solely on notions derived from romanticism, however. Scientific interest in the causes of longevity and the attributes of people who lived long lives helped shape images of old age. Students of longevity postulated that heredity, a healthy environment, "sobriety of living," improved care of infants and the sick, fewer epidemics and increased understanding of basic rules of public health promoted long life. Analyzing such factors had practical as well as theoretical significance. Medical advisers to life insurance companies, for example, pointed out that those who were still healthy at sixty typically came from long-lived families and had met the problems of life successfully. On the basis of clients' medical histories, doctors recommended that "persons who have borne the battle of life well, and have passed the climateric unscathed, are good subjects for insurance." Other writers suggested that people's lives were becoming both longer and more fruitful. Authors cited the contributions of distinguished men over sixty to prove that an individual's public and private worth improved with age. A few even considered longevity a reliable measure of happiness. Believing that nature shortens a life of misery, one doctor proposed that "the survival of the happiest is also the survival of the fittest."

It is significant that writers thought in terms such as heredity, "survival of the fittest" and "surviving the battle of life" when they assessed longevity and the insurability of old age. While ideas about longevity and old age were not derived from Darwin's work alone, they were compatible with it. Darwinism suggested analogies and images which intrigued the imagination of speculative writers. As a result, conceptions of old age, which appeared shortly after the Civil War, seem to be a mixture of romanticist notions blended with newer scientific ideas

about evolution. Americans considered old people in good health the true survivors of the fittest. Those who had survived the battle of life deserved to rest,
to be honored and loved by their family and to enjoy the gift of good health.
Such beliefs underlined the positive attributes of old age.

Throughout the rest of the period we are considering, writers continued to
assert that one's heredity, health, medical history and personal habits directly
influenced life expectancy; everyone agreed that better sanitary conditions and
advancing medical knowledge constantly were improving public health and
increasing people's chances of living a long life. Furthermore, idealizing aspects
of old age persisted as one way of treating the subject. No dramatic event or
theory forced images of old age to change suddenly. After 1880, however,
predominant themes were challenged, and new ones emerged. Writers began to
distinguish between longevity and old age: "It's not old age, but length of life
which all men desire." Men wanted to live a long life, but they also wanted it
endowed with enough good health to make it enjoyable and permit them to
work. A longer life, plagued with increasing mental and physical debility, was
worth little. Implicit in this distinction between old age and length of life was a
new disesteem for old age.

Beginning in the 1880s, authors were less willing to proclaim old people the
survivors of the fittest. Although writers considered it axiomatic that man's
condition in general improved as society progressed, this did not mean that the
human life cycle necessarily followed the same pattern of evolution as society's.
Evolutionary progress portended disaster, in fact, for the elderly who no longer
found themselves adapted to the struggle for existence:

> The old man resents being pushed aside while at all capable . . . but there is such
> a rush for so-called progress, so bottomless a pit of appetite for that which is
> called new, that it creeps over the deepest marks the best of us can put in the
> sand.

Progress had a dualistic nature. Civilization, blessed with infinite possibilities
was evolving to its most perfect development. Human development, on the
other hand, was finite. A person reached his peak at a certain point in life and
then spent the rest of his years in decline.

By the turn of the century, most writers, believing that a longer life only
postponed the inescapable fact of decline, played down the blessings of old age
and spelled out the burdens of growing old. "We are marked by time's defacing
fingers with the ugliness of age." Old age meant wrinkled, parched skin; gray,
thin hair; sunken, listless eyes; drooped posture, unsteady balance and slow,
uncertain gait. Worse, old age meant poor health. Prolonged sickness and physical discomfort tormented elderly people. Mental as well as physical powers
declined with age. Authors pointed to old people's tendency to forget details
and events and their inability to express exactly what they meant. Many
doubted whether old age bestowed intrinsically better judgment.

Writers asserted that the aged's attitudes also differed from those of the rest
of society. Much of the pessimism and resignation associated with old age,
writers thought, stemmed from the elderly's loss of interest in the world and
unwillingness to keep abreast of recent developments:

> What is the old man's view? It is the view of one who has ceased to grow, whose
> ideas have crystalled, the sutures of whose mind, so to speak, have closed, who
> is no longer accessible to the teaching of new experience.

Longing for death was another depressing aspect of growing old: "One of the saddest conditions . . . is no longer to fear the shadow feared of men." Writers presented mortality statistics to corroborate the belief that old people welcomed death. Old men, they reported, committed suicide more frequently than young men; the aged poor were more likely to take their lives than those who were financially secure.

Although descriptions of old people's behavior did not focus only on its morbid features, they did contrast sharply with previous characterizations. Writers stressed that old people were not necessarily "paragons of all the virtues." Old people were often tactless, took little interest in their appearance, displayed poor manners and complained endlessly about their health and the way they were treated. New terms were coined to describe the way old people acted. A "geezer," for instance, was a derisive term first used in the 1880s to refer to the aged's behavior. A geezer said odd things and acted eccentrically.

By 1914, popular writers had overturned almost every sentimental notion about old age. Instead of depicting physical old age as hoary and stately, writers showed that it was ugly and sickly. Instead of emphasizing the experience and intrinsic judgment old people possessed, they pointed out that the elderly were forgetful and opinionated. Writers characterized the aged as alienated not fulfilled, anxious not tranquil, resentful not grateful, morose not helpful. The idea that moral goodness and decorum were synonymous with old age conflicted with evidence that the elderly were often suicidal, ill-mannered and unpleasant.

DEMOGRAPHIC FACTORS

How do we account for changes in definitions and descriptions of old age? An obvious explanation is that as the birth rate declined, people over sixty-five constituted an increasingly larger proportion of the total population. This age group's experiences, in turn, helped shape opinions of senescence. Realizing that the negative aspects of old age could not be ignored, writers began to temper their sentimental image of old age and paid more attention to the liabilities of growing old.

Changes in the age structure of the United States' population are part of the answer. Table 1 indicates that over time there was some increase in the proportion of Americans sixty-five and older.

Table 1   Percent of Americans Over Sixty-Five, 1870–1920

Census Year	% Total Pop. 65 Years & Older	% Males 65 Years & Older	% Females 65 Years & Older
1870	2.99	2.97	3.02
1880	3.43	3.40	3.47
1890	3.87	3.86	3.88
1900	4.06	4.02	4.11
1910	4.30	4.18	4.43
1920	4.67	4.61	4.73

And yet, note that the percent of the population over sixty-five increased gradually: the striking shift in attitudes toward old age was neither preceded nor accompanied by a dramatic upsurge in the percent of the aged. It is possible, of course, that writers perceived the increase which was occurring on the national level to be significant, or that there might have been a pronounced increase in the percent of older, middle-class males. Gross demographic changes seem too subtle, however, for increasing numbers of old people alone to be *the* crucial determinant shaping definitions of old age. We must go beyond a demographic explanation in order to understand why definitions of old age changed when and how they did.

FROM ROMANTICISM TO REALISM: MEDICAL VIEWS OF OLD AGE

Historians have suggested that during the latter half of the nineteenth century, a realistic perspective challenged and displaced countervailing elements of romanticism, which had influenced American culture since the 1840s. Distrusting crucial ingredients of romanticism, especially its emphasis on subjective experience and its idealistic world view, realists appealed to a more objective, dispassionate sensibility. In large part, the impact of the natural sciences—which called for scientific research and technological innovation and suggested a mechanistic, materialistic version of naturalized evolution—influenced the shift from romanticism to realism.

It is tempting to say that the broad shift from romanticism to realism taking place in high culture accounts for a comparable shift in emphasis in defining old age: earlier definitions idealized old age; later definitions its seamy side. The larger cultural shift from romanticism to realism is too general and its timing too vaguely defined, however, adequately to explain how, in the specific sphere of defining old age, new perceptions developed. In turning to high culture, therefore, we should consider how scientific and, in particular, medical opinions influenced definitions of old age. The articles medical doctors and scientists contributed to magazines like Harper's and *Popular Science Monthly* in addition to their own professional journals helped make popular attitudes toward old age less idealistic and more objective.

Ideas about longevity and old age in vogue among medical doctors in the 1860s and 1870s complemented popular ideas. Medical opinion supported the belief that heredity, climate and an individual's lifestyle affected longevity. Like popular writers, doctors usually couched references to old age in literary or philosophical terms. Although they offered advice on proper diet, exercise and personal habits, no American doctors were engaged in research directly related to the study of senescence.

Then, in 1881, Dr. Alfred L. Loomis, a lecturer at New York's College of Physicians and Surgeons, edited, expanded and published J. M. Charcot's research on old age. During the 1870s, Charcot, a professor of neurology and pathology, undertook a systematic study of the relationship between old age and disease among inmates at Salpetrière, a large public hospital for aged women in Paris. Charcot's key finding was that there were some diseases which were peculiar to old age, a second group of diseases that existed at other periods of life but presented special characteristics and dangers in old age and a third class of diseases from which old people seemed to be immune. Charcot and

Loomis' study proved conclusively that old age *per se* did not cause disease. Rather, specific organs deteriorating during the later stages of life caused specific diseases: "In old age, the organs seem, as it were, to become independent of one another; they suffer separately, and the various lesions to which they may become subject are scarcely echoed by the anatomy as a whole." By correlating localized structural lesions with certain symptoms and diseases, Charcot and Loomis laid the basis for a pathology of senility.

Although the medical profession hailed Charcot and Loomis' study as the definitive work on old age, most doctors remained more inclined to recommend ways to postpone the effects of old age than they were to devote years investigating its causes. Consequently, doctors' articles dealing with problems of old age in popular and scientific literature usually focussed on such practical matters as diet, exercise and medication. Nevertheless, during the 1880s and 1890s, a few doctors, following in Charcot and Loomis' path, did important research. Their discovery of schlerotic changes in blood vessels, degeneration of endocrine glands and dehydration of tissues contributed greatly to an understanding of the pathological characteristics of senescence.

Around 1900, some researchers went beyond studying only the pathological aspects of old age, and described senescence as a normal phase of the life cycle. I. L. Nascher was a chief spokesman of this emerging school of thought. Nascher believed that old age resulted from progressive changes in properties of cells and tissues as the human organism aged. New cells differed slightly in function and composition from older ones. Because cell modifications were cumulative throughout one's life, "the aged individual is in fact an entirely different individual from the one who was formed from the ancestors of the later cells." Old age, Nascher concluded, results from a natural physiological process.

One of Nascher's major contributions to the study of old age was his proposition that the medical profession had to view senescence from a broader perspective than it was accustomed. Nascher urged his colleagues not to limit themselves to diagnosing and treating the physical manifestations of old age. Doctors also had to consider the effect of an old person's mental outlook and attitudes about his physical condition.

> The psychic factor tends to exaggerate the objective and subjective manifestations of this condition . . . In many cases, the debility is apparently greater than the anatomical changes would warrant, while there is a profound mental depression without marked physical impairment.

The aged, Nascher contended, often suffer from "pseudo-debilities" brought on by their preoccupation with their ailments. To combat the mental factors aggravating the condition, Nascher recommended a change of scene, a new hobby, a new friend—anything which might stimulate the mind in other directions.

Nascher's other major contribution was to promote the study of old age as a legitimate medical specialty, complete with its own theories, area of study and professional standards. Nascher gave the discipline its name, geriatrics. He also served as first president of the New York Geriatrics Society, founded in 1915. During the early decades of the twentieth century, Nascher regularly contributed to medical journals both reports on his findings and appeals to others to enter the new field. Contemporaries considered Nascher's chief work, *Geri-*

atrics (1914), the most important study on old age since the work of Charcot and Loomis.

Between 1865 and 1914, the medical profession began to define old age in an objective, scientific manner. Scientists rejected the romantic image of aging, demonstrated the existence of a senile pathology and were diagnosing and researching ways to treat the physiological and psychological aspects of old age. The articles written by medical doctors and scientists provided theoretical and empirical support for the evolving popular notion that the coming of age brought more hardships than benefits. Medical research alone did not indicate, however, that the elderly were physically unable to continue working and thus should retire from their jobs; nor did it lead to the explicit deduction that old age was a period of obsolescence. Such convictions arose in the minds of observers and participants in big business.

BIG BUSINESS IDEAS AND PRACTICES MAKE OLD AGE OBSOLETE

Although romantic writers referred to the stage of life when people retired from their jobs as "the season of rest," we actually know little about retirement ideas and practices until the latter decades of the nineteenth century. Labor statistics for people over sixty-five are unreliable before 1870. Pensions provided by the federal and some state governments, fraternal benefit societies and corporations covered select groups of old people such as war veterans and their dependents, subscribers and those who had worked in specific occupations. Accompanying the postwar rise of the big business corporation, however, was an increased interest in rationalizing and instituting retirement policies. These emerging bureaucratic ideas and practices helped define old people's attributes and roles.

Writers argued that the presence of old people in the working force hampered a business' operation. As F. Spencer Baldwin, a professor of economics at Boston University, explained:

> In the first place there is the direct loss involved in the payment of full wages to workers who are no longer reasonably efficient, and in the second place, there is the direct loss entailed by the slow pace set for the working force by the presence of worn-out veterans, and the consequent demoralization of the service.

Corporations which placed a premium on cost-consciousness and productiveness considered the aged, who no longer retained their vitality, expendable. From management's viewpoint, therefore, retirement systems improved efficiency and morale by removing old people who could no longer keep up with the pace. Implicit in this rationale was a derogatory definition for retirement itself. From a larger perspective, pensions were part of an overall strategy to attract an ambitious, proficient work force: "The corporation that can assure its employees a reasonable permanency of employment, promotion in order of precedence and fitness, and a satisfactory program for old age, will inevitably attract the highest grade of men and obtain from them the most efficient work." The idea of pensioning the elderly gained wide acceptance: by 1910, major railroad companies and nearly every other large corporation, including branches of government, had instituted some old age pension policy.

It is reasonable to assert that big business' attitude toward old age was one of the reasons why employment statistics for people over sixty-five changed from 1870 to 1920.

Between 1870 and 1920, the percent of males over ten years of age gainfully employed in the United States steadily increased; at the same time, the percent of men over sixty-five in the labor force markedly declined. The evidence does not indicate what proportion of older men stopped working because of compulsory retirement. Other factors clearly were involved: some workers might have voluntarily withdrawn from the labor force; others may have been forced to quit because of disabilities, illness or obsolete skills. Nevertheless, comparing male and female labor statistics underlines the significance of old age in determining employment status for men.

Although the proportion of women over sixty-five was greater than that of men for each decade (see Table 1), older women constituted a far smaller sector of the labor force than older men. The fact that employment opportunities for women in general were improving probably explains why the percentage of older working women increased slightly between 1870 and 1920. Note, however, that the percent of older women working was always less than the figure for women workers over ten and that the former's employment rates began to decline by the end of the period. It appears that old age may have complicated, but was not the crucial factor influencing the nature of elderly women's employment. Thus Table 2 indicates why contemporaries may have referred to old age unemployment as a predominantly male phenomenon: finding a job after sixty-five was a more acute problem for men.

Other evidence supports these data. Magazine articles described how hard it was for men to get and stay on a job after a certain age. Recipes for men's hair

Table 2 Selected Labor Statistics, 1870–1920

Census Year	% of Male Pop. over 10 Gainfully Employed	% Males over 65 Gainfully Employed/ Males Over 65
1870	54.7	80.6
1880	57.8	76.7
1890	60.2	73.8
1900	61.2	68.4
1910	62.3	63.7
1920	62.7	60.2

Census Year	% of Female Pop. Over 10 Gainfully Employed	% Females over 65 Gainfully Employed/ Females Over 65
1870	7.5	5.8
1880	8.4	5.8
1890	11.3	7.7
1900	12.4	8.5
1910	14.9	8.6
1920	15.4	7.9

dyes appeared in health guides. A retired businessman published a best-selling exercise manual aimed at those trying to hide the "unfortunate fact that appearance of facial age is a deterrent and lessens (one's) values as an employee." Writers' concern to restore the superficial appearance of youth is suggestive: perhaps the declining status of elderly men in the labor market is reflected in the enhanced position bestowed upon youth. An essay entitled "The Superannuated Man" provides a clue to substantiate this proposition:

> Not all the sandwich men in our large cities or the sitters in our public parks are victims of intemperance or shiftlessness; they are, in many cases, the product of an industrial and economic system that thrives only on young blood.

It appears then, that around the turn of the century, contemporaries thought that America's economic system thrived on youth, not age.

YOUTH VS. AGE

The unprecedented emphasis Americans placed on youth represents an important shift in values. Before the 1890s, "youth" usually denoted an intermediate stage of life. By 1900, the word had taken on new meaning. Writers proclaimed youth as a vital social asset: "Youth is so vivid an element in life that unless it is cherished, all the rest is spoiled." Youth's increasing importance did not result from the age cohort's increasing numerical strength, for between 1860 and 1920, the percent of the population between the ages of fifteen and thirty remained remarkably stable.

"Youth" was extolled largely because of its ambiguous relationship to a society which itself simultaneously abhorred and craved the quest for power and order affecting every aspect of life. Rebelling against some societal restraints yet accommodating to others, youth were said to possess the vitality and creativity to advance society. In his monumental work, *Adolescence* (1905), G. Stanley Hall captured the promise of youth:

> Despite our lessening fecundity, our over-schooling, "city-fication," and spoiling, the affectations we instill and the repressions we practice, (youth) are still the light and the hope of the world.

Writers asserted that the young were the age group best able to engage in all facets of life. Some said that it was during youth that one faced nearly all the valuable experiences of living. By the turn of the century, people generally reached the same conclusion: "The whole world is charged with youth; old age, like death, is merely incidental." The rise of what might be called a youth cult weakened the position of the aged, who were thought to be incapable of contributing significantly to the world of the young.

This idea was most dramatically expressed by Dr. William Osler, a distinguished professor of medicine at Johns Hopkins and noted social critic. In 1905, at the age of fifty-nine, Osler set forth two thoughts about the contributions a man made to society after the age of forty. His first proposition was that men past forty were comparatively useless. "Take the sum of human achievement in action, in science, in art, in literature—subtract the work of men past forty, and while we should miss great treasures, even priceless treasures, we should be practically where we are today." Men accomplished their most significant work, Osler asserted, between the ages of twenty-five and forty. His second belief was that men past sixty were unequivocally useless. Accordingly, Osler urged mandatory retirement for men engaged in commercial, political and professional fields once they reached sixty.

Not everyone shared Osler's extreme position. Few were willing to say that the aged served no useful function whatsoever. Furthermore, writers disagreed about when a man's usefulness declined. Some said fifty, others sixty, a few said sixty-five. Nevertheless, Osler's position underscores an emerging cultural belief: the older a man was, the less people expected him to contribute in a society in which advances were "initiated by young or comparatively young men." Finally, although Osler did not refer to women, it is fair to suggest that their role was considered at least as negligible as that of men. Writers described their contemporaries treating older women as if they were baubles without purpose in life.

In short, popular writers created a new image of old age from the perspective of exalted youth:

> Slowly and with difficulty the septuagenarians climb the steep hill leading to the great temple of youth . . . They beat at the doors, and alas! these do not open. They crave only admittance, and a stool in a quiet corner, but the ruthless revellers turn a deaf ear.

The young refused the old admittance into their world. Youth no longer revered age; they excluded it. The stage of life romantics once characterized as the season of rest had become one of discontent.

CONCLUSION

We are now in a better position to understand some of the reasons why middle-class Americans gradually perceived the coming of age to be a burden not a blessing. While subtle demographic changes may have affected perceptions of the liabilities of age, there was no massive increase in the percent of old people in the population. Rather, new attitudes toward old age seem to have arisen from an interplay of cultural and structural phenomena. The medical profession's increasingly objective approach to old age exposed genuine biological fallibilities which had been masked by a blend of romanticism and optimistic evolutionism. In another area, new bureaucratic principles were applied in a deliberate effort to eliminate those who, from a "rational" point of view, appeared to be inefficient human machines.

Yet one must ask why the findings of medical men had such an impact and why businessmen shifted to an emphatically negative opinion of the worth of old people. Reverence for science and insistence on efficiency do not altogether explain the phenomenon. The vicissitudes of youth surely were as well documented as the infirmities of age. Any rational definition of efficiency must give weight to the experience and maturity of the elderly. Why did such considerations not prevail?

Part of the answer may lie in the cult of youth which swept late nineteenth-century American society in dramatic counterpoint to its depreciation of old age. Enthusiastic belief in the redeeming promise of youth might explain the ready acceptance and even exaggeration of the significance of medical research into the problems of growing old and the eager willingness to retire the elderly.

Ironically, this emerging youth cult is at once a product of a new realistic age and of the lingering romanticism of an earlier era, which once had encouraged writers to idealize the attributes of old age.

This framework suggests rather than exhausts plausible hypotheses concerning changing attitudes toward old age. Conceptions of aging, for example, should also be considered a topic in the history of the family. There might have been less need for the elderly in families as the birth rate declined and as other institutions assumed greater responsibility for education and welfare. Finally, we must keep a larger issue in mind: to what degree do middle-class writers' descriptions correspond to the actual policies and experiences of the aged at this time? Answering this question will help us to understand why a new attitude toward aging, which focussed on its liabilities and considered old age obsolescent, emerged and remains largely intact today.

Making Workers More Efficient

SUSAN PORTER BENSON

McCrorey's Five and Dime Store, ca. 1919

By 1900, MANAGERIAL PRACTICES that were developed in the factory were also being applied widely in other areas of the American workplace. As more people began working together and production processes became more complex, efforts were made by factory owners to rationalize, systematize, and control more closely all tasks in a given enterprise. In this article, Susan Porter Benson details the application of the standard management routines of the factory to the sales staffs of department stores. While efforts by the department store managers to increase the productivity of their workforce typified similar attempts elsewhere in the business sector, these efforts also demonstrate how class divisions and sex roles created particular variations common to retailing within the larger whole of American enterprise.

The shopgirl—the overworked and underpaid working-class operative in nineteenth-century department stores—was to be remade, Pygmalian-like, into a middle-class saleswoman knowledgeable about domestic concerns and able to guide her customers, largely female, in their search for ready-made products. Through careful supervision and elaborate rules of conduct, managers set out to create a new sales force. However, they soon discovered that empathy with the customer, the most important influence on sales, could not be regulated. Management then decided to try to improve the working conditions of the sales force and to teach good sales technique. But managers could not overcome the obstacles of class and sex that separated workers from their customers and their supervisors; the low pay for saleswomen would continue to distinguish them from their more affluent customers, while dress codes, separate entrances, and other demeaning workplace regulations set retail clerks apart from their male supervisors.

Like their counterparts in factories, department store workers were socialized into the complex dynamics of their roles in the workplace by their peers rather than by their superiors. In the end, they shaped their own selling style within the confines of the time limit, the dress code, and other management controls, and, in the process, showed how other workers might respond to the regimentation of the early twentieth-century workplace.

By the beginning of the twentieth century, the department store as Americans would know it until after World War II was a familiar feature of urban life. These giant emporiums, expanding rapidly after 1880, pursued policies distinctively different from their ancestors in wholesaling or small-scale specialized retailing. The dingy and cluttered store was eclipsed by a lavishly decorated palace of consumption, which not only presented goods in a well-organized and tempting way but also offered a variety of services and public accommodations. The simple newspaper announcement of goods for sale was replaced by aggressive and attractive display advertising. The one-price system put an end to the older custom of haggling between clerk and customer, and the free-entry policy replaced the habit of harassing customers until they bought something as the price of their escape. Finally, the male monopoly behind the counters yielded to a preponderance of females. By 1900, department store managers were beginning to realize that these changes in practices and personnel had not automatically produced an effective selling force; by 1910, the effort to develop a distinctive style of department store selling had taken first place on their agendas. This task was both difficult and complex, involving the peculiar demands of retailing in itself with vexing issues of class and sex affecting American society as a whole.

Because most business history concentrates on manufacturing enterprises, it is useful to begin by comparing the factory to the store. In the most general sense, managers of both types of business had begun by 1900 to face the twin problems of production and consumption with a new self-consciousness and determination. The impact of the new style of management on a given enterprise varied according to its size, location, competitive position, and the personal inclinations of its executives. Yet, despite this unevenness, trade associations in major production and distribution fields developed and codified a new managerial wisdom which framed the problems, possibilities, and goals

MAKING WORKERS MORE EFFICIENT   By Susan Porter Benson. Originally published under the title "The Cinderella of Occupations: The Work of Department Store Saleswomen, 1900–1940." From *Business History Review* (Spring 1981). Copyright © 1981 by the President and Fellows of Harvard College. Reprinted by permission.

for each industry, shaping both the consciousness and the actions of its executives. In industry after industry, the ultimate prescription was a thoroughgoing process of rationalization, systematization, and closer control of all aspects of the business. The concerns of the conscientious manager ran the gamut from the most minute aspect of production to shaping a new ethic of consumption in the society at large.

Although thoughtful executives in both stores and factories agreed on the ultimate goal of rationalization, the differences in social reality within their firms meant that they faced very different problems in implementing the new ideas. For the factory executive, efforts to rationalize production and consumption were neatly compartmentalized. Within the factory, the problem was to motivate workers to produce more goods in less time and at less cost; outside its walls, the task was to encourage people to buy these goods more freely and with less concern for necessity. While industrial managers could thus run their factories with a single-minded concern for productivity, and leave the fabrication of demand to advertising executives and copywriters, department store managers enjoyed no such luxury.

The heart of their operations—the selling floor—brought workers and customers face to face, creating the problem of simultaneously encouraging efficiency in the former and leisurely consumption in the latter. The store's basic accounting unit, the sales transaction, was used to measure both the salesperson's effectiveness in selling and the customer's willingness to buy. At best, the impossibility of separating the two made the store executive's task far more complicated than that of the factory manager; at worst, it enmeshed him in a web of contradictions that grew out of his curious betwixt-and-between position. Retailers sought on the one hand to control and supervise their workers and their firms as closely as any of their factory counterparts: they acted like managers pure and simple. Yet they also wished to make a complex social statement that involved issues of class and sex, psychology and aspiration, identifying consumption with a life of style, respectability, and urbanity: they acted, to use Stuart Ewen's phrase, like captains of consciousness.

From about 1900 to about 1940, the cornerstone of the retailer's effort to resolve this contradiction was what he called skilled or personal selling. Stripped to its essentials, skilled selling involved the use of trained salesclerks to increase both the size and number of sales transactions. It spoke to the problem of productivity by building more intensive sales efforts into the definition of skill, and to the problem of consumption by requiring the salesperson to appeal to customers' vanities of class and sex. Skilled selling, successfully implemented, would logically have resolved the department store manager's dilemma.

In reality, skilled selling did not solve the retailer's economic or social problems in any such neat way. In the broadest sense, department store managers were going against the grain of major twentieth-century trends in business management. They hoped to foster skill in an era when the central tendency of management policy was to expand unskilled and semiskilled labor. They undertook to monitor that skill with the supervisory and accounting methods developed elsewhere to deskill and regiment workers. Even more, they attempted to harness skill in social interaction, a most unmanageable quality and one even less susceptible to control than manual skill. In the factory, manual skill could ultimately though not easily be taken into the hands of management, mental and manual work could be divorced, and skill separated from the social relations of the workplace. In the store, however, the skill of selling was intimately and organically bound up with the social relations of the selling floor and the work group; only when left in the hands of the workers could it have the desired effect on sales. Ultimately, store managers had an apples-and-oranges problem: they were trying to combine elements that grew out of fundamentally different systems.

The reasons why they found themselves in this untenable position become clear only in the context of the historical development of large-scale urban retailing. For present purposes, we can divide the history of the industry at about 1900, bearing in mind that department stores developed unevenly and eccentrically and that changes did not occur simultaneously across the country. By about that time, department stores had seized center stage in the central business districts of American cities. The range of goods they offered, the luxury and excitement of their ambiance, and the appeal of their merchandising methods succeeded in attracting large crowds. In the estimation of the stores' controllers, however, these crowds spent their money too infrequently or too thriftily; the public spectacle of the department store was commercially viable only if financed by high sales levels.

Selling was the bellwether function of the store; as one industry writer phrased it in 1915, "The selling force is the best place to start at when a general speeding-up of the entire organization is necessary or desired. And in view of the position of the salesforce as a motive power, increase of salesforce efficiency will stimulate all the other parts of the machinery." No amount of cost-cutting efficiency behind the scenes could compensate for lackluster sales efforts, for only through skilled selling could the heavy burden of fixed costs for lavish public accommodations and "free" services such as delivery be materially lightened. Self-service was not an option in the minds of pre-World-War-II managers except in isolated instances; the culture of consumption rested on service and amenity, not on efficiency alone. Moreover, skilled selling was a response to the chronic problem that undermined attempts to rationalize retailing: the industry's built-in variability. The volume of customers and their willingness to buy varied according to the season of the year, the day of the week, and the hour of the day as well as with the weather and personal whim. Skilled salespeople would in theory maximize sales under all conditions and would respond resourcefully to changing opportunities and constraints.

During the first decade of the twentieth century, department store managers began to consider these questions with a new urgency. They shared with their factory colleagues the era's enthusiasm for efficiency, but the special demands of retailing sharpened their concern. Their tactics had solved one set of problems—the attraction of crowds—but had failed to touch another—the need to induce those crowds to buy more than they would from simple need or random impulse. Worried managers pinpointed the problem at the point of the sale and found a ready scapegoat in the "shopgirl," as the first generations of department store saleswomen were popularly dubbed with a mixture of scorn, condescension, and pity. Overworked and underpaid, they pleased neither their employers nor their customers.

An examination of industry and trade association periodicals, retail convention proceedings, and the store newspaper of the William Filene's Sons Company in Boston reveals that department store managers were deeply and persistently worried about the quality and behavior of their sales forces, and that they undertook extensive efforts to correct what they saw as salespeople's shortcomings. Although these sources do not trace the experience of any one firm with the thoroughness that a complete set of company records would, they do give a sense of the pervasiveness of managers' concern about their selling staffs. In stores large and small, in all parts of the country, retail executives redefined their expectations and treatment of their saleswomen. At national conventions, through personal contacts and local institutions such as Boards of Trade or the Research Bureau for Retail Training in Pittsburgh, and in the journals they discussed methods, traded experiences, testified to their successes and failures, and developed an industry-wide personnel stance. They did not of course speak with one voice, but what is striking about the sum of this literature is the notable agreement about basic goals and the shared conviction of the need to supplant the shopgirl with the skilled saleswoman.

The shopgirl was no accident; she was the direct result of management policies toward the salesforce. In the process of building, organizing, decorating, and systematizing the store, executives had given scant attention to the critical area of selling—the interaction across the counter. Believing on the one hand that selling as it had been practiced by men was an inborn knack, a talent, a fine art, and convinced on the other hand that attractive goods presented in a luxurious environment would practically sell themselves, managers in the great era of department store expansion between 1880 and 1900 had easily convinced themselves that they needed only to staff the counters with neatly dressed, polite women who would sell mechanically and inoffensively. A statement attributed to A. T. Stewart, a pioneer in large-scale retailing in New York, summarized well the personnel theory of department store managers in the last decades of the nineteenth century. Gazing at the army of workers in his Astor Place "palace dry goods store," Stewart is supposed to have commented, "Not one of them has his discretion. They are simply machines working in a system that determines all their actions." Convinced that all they needed were cogs on their wheels, department store managers wasted little time and energy on the development of their sales forces.

Stewart's view, and the inattention to the salesforce that it implied, came under sharp attack after the turn of the century. A perturbed industry observer summed up the difference between the old and new views on the subject: "As a rule, the salesforce grows up like Topsy. It is neither born nor made. No sensible attention is given to its creation nor to its training. The result speaks for itself more eloquently than any tongue can express. Every merchant should remember that his clerks are his personal representatives and that the public only know him, and pass their judgment upon him, from their CONTACT WITH HIS SALESFORCE." The idea that the salesperson was the merchant's emissary to the public was the foundation of the emerging retail personnel wisdom. There was an element of respect for the salesperson in the new view, but there was also an element of fear—and both were aspects of the retailer's uneasy recognition of the alarming power of a group that he had earlier considered, when he had considered it at all, as a mannerly adjunct to the store's elaborate accounting systems. Once he faced the issue, he could not turn back from the realization that all his efforts in other aspects of store operation would go for naught if a customer intent on purchasing were offended or inefficiently served, if her desire to consume were not nurtured.

When department store managers focused their attention on the salesforce with a view to managing it as closely as they did the other parts of the store, two central factors shaped their actions. The selling personnel of the typical department store around 1900 were overwhelmingly working-class and over-whelmingly female. Class and sex were the critical issues in the store manager's attempt to develop a skilled salesforce, but they interacted in extremely complex ways, sometimes complementary and sometimes contradictory. Executives be-gan by trying to change the class-based characteristics of their salespeople and by seeking to make use of their sex-based characteristics. In so doing, they unwittingly entered a maze of difficulties from which they never really extri-cated themselves.

The policies of late-nineteenth-century department store managers had built into their stores a class tension that troubled managers well into the middle of the twentieth. Their methods of attracting customers and their policies toward the salesforce conflicted sharply. Lavish stores and carriage-trade service enticed those who had the discretionary income to make the large purchases that were the stuff of department store profits. Although department stores ranged from the extremely exclusive to the popular-priced, it was the growing urban middle and upper classes whose trade managers most eagerly solicited, and whose cultural demands set the tone for the stores. The *Dry Goods Economist*, a major trade periodical, editorialized on the subject:

> [C]loser contact with Old World manners has created in our opulent citizens a relish for subserviency on the part of those who attend upon them; and this tendency on the part of the newly rich is spreading even to those who do not possess the golden talisman which crooks so many knees. . . .
>
> More consideration for the customer on the part of the clerk will be insisted on. The "take-it-or-leave-it" attitude will be less and less tolerated. Here will be a greater recognition of those assistants who make sales in a quiet, dignified, respectful manner and with a minimum of friction.

But department store selling was not attracting those who were of a mind to be "quiet, dignified, [and] respectful." The comparatively low pay, long hours, and difficult working conditions as well as the popular image of the tawdry shopgirl drove middle-class working women into other employment such as clerical work. Working-class saleswomen behaved in ways that were grounded in their own cultural background, but that offended their employers and cus-tomers alike. Contemporary portrayals of saleswomen frequently recall *Pyg-malion* on a grand scale. Some resented the ingratitude of those who dared to be different from themselves: "Who will dare tell you and me what a green, undisciplined, untrained stubborn girl is worth; and can any thinking person claim that the merchants of this country owe her a living wage?" Others con-demned specific offenses against proper demeanor, particularly those involving language and dress. Technically ungrammatical but widely used colloquial-isms and familiar forms of address appalled employers; one observer noted censoriously, "[T]he salespeople have become so forward as to call customers 'Dearie.' The use of such terms is a liberty which the woman of finer sensibilities quickly resents." Dress also conveyed a powerful class-laden message: customers were displeased when "they are approached by an employee who is overdressed and who bears on her person marks of opulence which apparently do not accord with her position." The social conflict that pervaded relations between saleswomen and customers was fundamentally of the store manager's own making: eager for the cheap labor of uneducated women, viewing selling as semi-automatic, setting his sights on an affluent clientele, he had created the problem for which he blamed his saleswomen.

While managers condemned clerks' class attributes out of hand, they found much to recommend in their gender characteristics, for sex was a unifying factor in the store. A journalist writing in 1910 captured the overwhelmingly female flavor of the department store:

> Buying and selling, serving and being served—women. On every floor, in every aisle, at every counter, women. . . . Down in the basement buying and selling bargains in marked-down summer frocks, women. Up under the roof, posting ledgers, auditing accounts, attending to all the complex bookkeeping of a great metropolitan store, women. Behind most of the counters on all the floors between, women. . . . Filling the aisles, passing and repassing, a constantly arriving and departing throng of shoppers, women. Simply a moving, seeking, hurrying mass of femininity, in the midst of which the occasional man shopper, man clerk, and man supervisor, looks lost and out of place.

Probably not more than one of eight department store customers was a man; and it was a rare department store after 1900 that did not have a clear majority of female salespeople.

Certain aspects of women's culture dovetailed with managers' developing conceptions of what a skilled sales effort involved. Qualities that had for a century been encouraged in women—adeptness at manipulating people, sympathetic ways of responding to the needs of others, and familiarity with things domestic—fit nicely into a new view of selling. Managers urged saleswomen to transfer skills from the domestic to the commercial sphere, to treat their customers as "guests" in a store so designed as to make it a "supplement to the home." Empathy and responsiveness constituted the irreducible core of selling skill; however definitions changed with fluctuations in the business cycle, twentieth-century selling always included the idea that the salesperson should be a lay psychoanalyst of the counter. A writer in 1911 urged, "Shop *with* the customer, not *at* her"; Macy's training director affirmed in 1940 that "interest in the customer's problems" was the major factor in selling success.

More than individual "womanly" characteristics was involved; the emphasis on interaction resonated as well with the collective aspects of women's culture. Recent research in women's history has called attention to the existence of affective and supportive female networks. From Italian and Jewish women in close-knit immigrant communities in Providence, to middle-class women dispersed around the country, solidaristic female networks have been a persistent feature of women's experience over the last century or more. They gave an important place to cooperative as opposed to competitive values, stressed the commonalities of female experience, and provided channels for the exchange of services and emotional support. As dimly as retail managers understood women's culture and its modes of functioning, in some unexamined way they defined selling skill in such a way as to reward women for being women, to give exchange value to their culture.

Department store managers' attempts to use women's culture were less explicit and self-conscious than their efforts to suppress working-class culture. The men who dominated the upper levels of department store management were understandably more at home in discussing the issue of class than that of sex. Class was an attribute that they shared with their customers; to manipulate class-based culture in the store meant to make their working-class saleswomen act in a way that was less disruptive to social relations within the store. Sex, on the other hand, was an issue that divided managers from customers and saleswomen alike. To manipulate sex-based culture was problematic from the point of view of managers, since it meant trying to exploit a sphere that by definition remained closed to them.

In elaborating their definition of skilled selling, department store managers rejected both the older ideal of the naturally. gifted salesman and the then-current model of the passive, unskilled, order-taking saleswoman. Managers undertook to shape a whole new breed of clerks; no longer would they be content to take salespeople as they were, for good or for ill. The new skill could be codified and taught; in the words of a Chicago department store manager in 1910:

> There is no mystery in the art of salesmanship. The qualities required are born in every one, and only a reasonable amount of training is needed to bring these qualities to the surface and make them serviceable. . . .
>
> As I say, good salespeople are made. They make themselves. . . . The expression, "He is a born salesman" may have meant something twenty years ago before modern experience had analyzed all the little secrets of the art, but to-day no one with common sense, industry and a real desire to learn need fear to tackle the task of soon becoming a leader in the ranks of truly good salespeople.

Most observers were more careful in asserting that the new skill would be under the control of managers; what was crucial was not that salespeople were self-made but rather that they be made by their superiors. As early as 1913, even a small-town retailer understood the importance of this point: "The success of salespeople is entirely the result of training, dependent entirely upon the opportunity for development and the result of the right working conditions. It lies within the power of every proprietor of every store, large or small, to re-create, re-construct, and re-organize the potential selling ability of his salespeople."

As if confident of the ease of their task, department store managers began their efforts to create a new sales force with more careful supervision and elaborate rules. Rules prescribing efficient performance of work, courteous behavior, and proper demeanor proliferated in department stores in the early years of the twentieth century. But managers soon learned that "simple rules and enforcement won't work." Similarly, early efforts at training salespersons focused almost exclusively on what was known as store system, or the proper use of forms and procedures for different types of sales. But the complex social dynamics of the selling floor demanded more than simple compliance with rules: it was at least as important how an item was sold as that it was sold at all.

The writer who asserted in 1913 that "The best salesperson . . . is *not necessarily* the one that *has the largest book*" ("book" was department store slang for a day's sales total) pointed to the difficulty of setting a clear quantitative standard for measuring sales performance. An item had to be sold with due attention to the cultural aspects of consumption and not simply foisted off on the customer. Otherwise, the store stood to suffer an immediate loss from the return of the goods, and a long term loss from the customer's reluctance to visit the store again; worst of all, she might come to regard shopping in general as a disagreeable experience. High production in a factory was an unmixed blessing so long as it did not destroy the machinery, but high sales totals were seriously undermined if customers were annoyed by overbearing sales tactics. Machinery had no consciousness and would bear no grudges, but a customer offended could be a customer lost.

The message was not an easy one to convey to department store saleswomen. The new skilled sellers were to be thinking but also obedient employees; they were to follow store procedures to the last rigorous detail and yet respond creatively to opportunities to sell as they arose; they were to develop independent judgment but yet display unquestioning loyalty to the store; they were to try very hard to sell but not *too* hard. Managers were clearly uncomfortable with these contradictions and periodically despaired of teaching controlled discretion to their saleswomen. During the grim years of the 1930s, for example, they succumbed to a vogue for drilling salespeople in "standard selling sentences" and in prescribed ways of dealing with various customer "types." By 1940, however, the dominant theme of the department store trade association's national convention was that these cut-and-dried answers had proved useless and that the best rule for successful selling was the old standby—empathy with the customer.

Since rules and procedures did not produce skilled selling, department store managers came to believe that nothing less than a thorough re-socialization of saleswomen would do. The customary agents of early socialization—the home and the school—had, in the view of these managers, failed to do their job. It was the fault, so they came to believe, of "unpropitious home surroundings and . . . defects in our education system" that so many salespeople "frequently speak and act in ways which do not commend them to people of refinement." Working-class and immigrant children were simply not being assimilated into the respectable middle-class mainstream fast enough to fill the places behind the counters of department stores. The schools, moreover, were falling short in their methods as well as in the ideology they taught: they did not encourage thinking, provided only "*admonition*", and not "EXPLANATION", failed to teach students to "ANALYZE, rather than *memorize*." These complaints are a measure of the degree to which department stores' labor requirements were different from those of manufacturers. Most of the latter would have been content had the schools inculcated the traditional virtues of hard work and obedience through admonition and memorization, while department store managers wanted initiative and independent judgment as well.

In order to work this transformation in those who became saleswomen, department stores undertook to "furnish the definitive, formative influences that the home and our educational facilities lack under present-day conditions." The school-and-family imagery was pervasive in the retail literature: a 1916 discussion of Marshall Field's personnel department described it both as "Dean of Women" and as "a conscientious mother." The theme was played out explicitly in the store as well. At Filene's, for example, the store manager and a counselor were known to the female employees as "Dad" and "Mother" respectively through the 'teens and 'twenties. Managers were confident that the sorry product of an unfortunate home and a misguided school would change through the benevolent influence of the store. Samuel Reyburn, President of Lord & Taylor and a key figure in department store management circles in the 'twenties and 'thirties, spoke glowingly of the impact of the store environment on such a girl:

> Constant contact with the woman who is in charge of her department will have an influence on her. Daily contact with other girls who have been subjected to influences in business will have an influence on her. Daily observations of customers in the building will influence her, and slowly she will change because of these influences. She will lower the tone of her voice, grow quiet in her manner, exhibit better taste in the selection of her clothes, become more considerate of others.

But, Reyburn continued, this "natural" process was too slow and haphazard, and in the enlightened store would be hurried along by training—the organized, deliberate effort to resocialize the department store saleswoman.

This process of resocialization can for present purposes be separated into two strands. The first, commonly known as welfare work, flourished during the first two decades of the century although its effects continued to be felt thereafter. The second, a variety of programs grouped under the heading of training, began in the second decade of the century but spread after 1920. The two phases were not in fact separate in aim and frequently overlapped in execution, but they focused on different aspects of the task of developing skilled selling: the first primarily concerned store facilities for workers, and the second involved activities explicitly designed to teach the new skill. Class and sex were central issues in both efforts.

Welfare work combined workers' facilities—rest rooms, lounges, dining rooms, gymnasiums, infirmaries, and libraries—with some rudimentary educational activities along the lines of personal hygiene, etiquette, and grammar classes. Welfare work, in the store as in the factory, had many meanings. Among these were the desire for good publicity, the hope of preventing union organization, and the belief that happier workers would be more efficient workers. In the store, however, welfare work assumed the added burden of dampening class conflict across the counter. One enthusiastic writer likened Jordan Marsh's employee facilities to a "high-class hotel," asking rhetorically: "If a girl, say, reared in humble surroundings, spends some part of her day amid pictures and cheerful furniture and tasteful rugs and books and sunlight, will she not insensibly acquire a clearer insight into the ideas and needs of the majority of the store's customers? Will she not, then, be better able to wait upon her trade deftly, sympathetically, and understandingly?"

Welfare work illustrates the double imperative under which retail managers were operating in fostering production and consumption simultaneously, and the retail literature reflects their delight that such measures served both ends. Medical programs, for example, could cut costs: in one store, described by the dean of department store doctors, a health program had so reduced absenteeism that the work force could be cut by fifty-four people. On the other hand, these programs could help to eliminate health problems related to class status and thus eliminate a jarring note in the palace of consumption: in the words of a journalist, "A customer is attracted to a person of wholesome appearance [and] will promptly and quite excusably shrink from a clerk whose hair shows the presence of vermin, or who is careless in controlling a cough." In the end, of course, welfare work promised to do even more than mollify the socially concerned customer and transform the working-class saleswoman—it sought to attract the elusive "better class" of salesperson to a store that was a more attractive and respectable place to work.

Welfare work helped to change the popular image of the shopgirl by improving the working conditions of the saleswomen and by beginning to attack the class-based characteristics that managers found so troublesome. Still, it gave no positive vision of what the new skilled salesperson would be like; clean towels, hot meals, and edifying literature could set the stage for skilled selling, but they could not write the script. This task fell to training programs. Tremendously varied in their specifics, these programs were in general an attempt to build upon the education aspects of welfare work, with a sharper focus on the specific demands of department store selling. Like welfare work, training programs had two components. One sought to increase immediate, quantifiable efficiency—for example, to train saleswomen to be punctiliously accurate in filling out sales checks. The other focused on developing the salesperson's ability to cope creatively with situations requiring discretionary behavior instead of cut-and-dried compliance with rules. It is the second that primarily concerns us here, for it was this aspect that defined and, in so far as possible, transmitted selling skill.

Discretionary selling training took many forms, but from its inception until at least 1940, it fell into two broad categories: merchandise training and salesmanship training. The first included instruction in the historical development of a given type of merchandise, its manufacturing process, its properties, and its uses. The content of merchandise training was a curious amalgam of high culture (in, for example, visits to museums), traditional womanly wisdom about homemaking and dress, newer "scientific" information about the care of merchandise, and the dictates of fashion. As a whole, however, the message was a simple one: to convey a respectable notion of "good taste" to the saleswoman. In the words of Helen Rich Norton, an important figure in retail training circles during this period, "the broadest and most important of the aims" of retail training was to convey to the students "[i]mproved standards of living, better habits of thought, higher interpretations, and ideals."

Some attempts to reach this goal verged on the absurd: the National Retail Dry Goods Association, the department store trade association, and the *Dry Goods Economist* both circulated films showing life in Palm Beach and Miami so that salespeople could develop the "mental 'atmosphere'" to properly advise resort-bound customers. Norton's textbook, *Retail Selling*, included a five-page list of essential French terms, with the cautionary note that they should be taught by a French teacher. Whether the goal was to apply a veneer of middle-class trappings or to remake the saleswoman's "inner consciousness," the target was the same: the saleswoman's class identity.

By contrast, salesmanship training attempted to build on the saleswoman's gender identity. Women had been trained to be consumers even before they were trained to be saleswomen: for example, they were encouraged to be conscious of dress, in terms of fashion as well as technical details. Such a consciousness became selling skill when saleswomen could guess a customer's size at a glance or estimate her budget by assessing the clothes she wore. Similarly, saleswomen had as women been socialized to deal with affect, to develop talents in sensing and meeting people's needs: once behind the counter, they had only to apply their interpersonal talents to dealing with their customers.

The specific techniques taught by training programs encouraged saleswomen to develop their skills at interacting with other women in order to create sales where there would have been none. Trainers counseled saleswomen to expand the individual sales transaction through what was known as suggestion selling, and to set the stage for future transactions by building up a clientele of customers. Suggestion selling was by far the most popular tactic urged upon salespeople; the literature abounds with inspirational pieces touting, quite correctly, its powers to expand profits and cut costs. Suggest a tie to go with a shirt—a second pair of hose—a handbag to match the shoes—a good buy on dishtowels—size up your customer's budget and preferences, and sell her the maximum amount of merchandise in a given visit to the store. Suggestion selling was as much a staple subject in the Filene's employee newspaper, *The Echo*, as it was in the trade press; a reading of *The Echo* shows that encouragement of suggestions went beyond mere exhortation, with prizes, bonuses, and write-ups as rewards to those who distinguished themselves at suggesting. Skilled suggestion selling tested the mettle of the saleswoman: if she were uninspired, too aggressive, or timid, her effort to suggest more merchandise could at best fail and at worst alienate the customer.

Developing a clientele required a long-term rapport with customers, an ability to anticipate their needs and whims, and the same delicate balance between increasing sales and avoiding offense. Saleswomen were urged to keep files of customers' addresses and buying habits, exhorted to remember their names, and encouraged to contact them about special merchandise. In order to deal successfully with her clientele, a saleswoman had to develop empathy with a varied group of comparative strangers, and to learn not only what sorts of merchandise they were interested in but also under what conditions and in what way she could approach them.

Both suggestive selling and developing a clientele were general techniques which saleswomen could only be urged and not forced to use; more than any other aspect of skilled selling, they demanded the discretion, resourcefulness, and independence of judgment that were at the heart of the new style of selling. There was in fact a contradiction in trying to teach these techniques at all. Properly speaking, all training programs could hope to do was to encourage saleswomen to channel their interactive skills into the best possible relations with customers through suggestion selling and developing a clientele. In fact, executives at all levels in department stores recognized that the implementation of these tactics was a delicate process that depended on the complex social situation on the selling floor. They would be successful only when grounded in the salesperson-customer interaction; used formulaically, they would fall flat.

Saleswomen became expert in knowing when and how to use these methods, and managers were eager to appropriate that knowledge so that they could recycle it in training programs. One of the most widely used textbooks on salesmanship, *How to Sell at Retail*, was mainly a compendium of the "practical methods" used by "three hundred expert salespeople." By and large, however, the evidence both from the trade press and from Filene's shows that managers waged a losing battle to wrest shop-floor secrets from their salespeople. They tried both the carrot—offering payments for suggestions about improving selling service and stories about feats of selling—and the stick—requiring employees to fill out "call slips" whenever a customer requested an item that was out of stock. Neither method persuaded salespeople that they should share their on-the-job wisdom with their superiors, and managers repeatedly argued the necessity and bemoaned the ineffectiveness of suggestion drives and call slips.

In the end, however, it was not just a classic workers' resistance to surrendering knowledge to managers, but rather the complex workings of class and sex, that undermined the attempt to turn shopgirls into skilled saleswomen. The women behind the nation's counters were alert to the fact that there was a disturbing two-sidedness to the vision of skilled selling that was presented to them by their bosses. Managers encouraged their saleswomen to forget the fact that department store selling was "looked upon by the public as the Cinderella of occupations" and to think of it as a highly trained vocation that conferred dignity on those who practiced it. John Wanamaker refused to have his employees called "shopgirls" or "help," and asserted that "We are men and women, living our lives, doing our share, doing it with dignity, doing it in the most respectable way." *The Echo* was somewhat more grandiose, likening the development of the art of selling to the work of ministers and lawyers; few made the exact comparison, but many referred to selling as a profession. Perhaps the fullest statement of the self-image that skilled selling was supposed to foster appeared in a discussion of the work of Lucinda Prince, the head of the National Retail Dry Goods Association's education department from its founding in 1915 until her death in 1935: "The change in the individual is a new conception of the dignity of work in general and of the chosen occupation in particular. There is a satisfaction that comes with mastery of certain of the forces of one's environment, and a pride inseparable from acquired skill and the achievements it makes possible."

In fact, managers' policies tended to foster dignity only rhetorically. For better or for worse, one criterion by which our society assesses an occupation's dignity is its compensation, and the pay of saleswomen remained low in comparison to alternatives available to women in office and factory. For a short period in 1920, the *Dry Goods Economist* urged that higher salaries would change both the image and practice of selling, but the argument convinced only an enlightened few among department store managers, such as those at Filene's. At about the same time, store executives began to use a variety of incentive-payment schemes such as commission and quotabonus, but they administered them so as to raise productivity and not earnings.

Perhaps even more important in the day-to-day conduct of the store, however, was the fact that saleswomen were not treated as dignified professionals;

if anything, they were treated more like servants. Generations of clerks chafed under John Wanamaker's pronouncement that the customer was always right. Although few stores enforced it literally—that would have been too costly— the maxim still prescribed servile and unquestioning demeanor for saleswomen: it was unacceptable to correct an error or parry an insult by a customer. A 1938 survey of both customers and salespeople about what they considered to be "successful" salesperson responses to customer objections to merchandise—a successful response being one to which customers reacted favorably—made clear the types of behavior that were necessary for fruitful interactions. The most successful responses involved *"encouraging," "deferential,"* and *"concili- atory"* remarks; the sales-squelching comebacks included those "indicating a *superior attitude," "indicative of personal opinion,"* or *"contradicting."* The same balance sheet would serve equally well if mistresses and servants had been questioned.

Department store life included more tangible signs of servitude for sales- women. Many, for example, objected to helping customers try on clothing since it involved the servile intimacy associated with being a maid. They loathed the systems that stores devised for special control or inspection of salespersons' personal packages; one manager testified that one of the most popular steps he ever took was to abolish his store's parcel-checking system. Saleswomen also resented rules that confined them to segregated store facilities, and made that resentment amply clear to management. They objected to separate employee entrances, particularly when they were tucked into dingy back streets and con- trasted too obviously with the customers' gracious doorways. Saleswomen at Filene's regularly violated rules restricting them to certain elevators and stair- ways and prohibiting them from using the customers' lounges and writing rooms. The two-class system of store facilities smacked of the upstairs-down- stairs division of the servant's experience and clashed with the rhetoric that termed selling a dignified profession. A writer for the *Dry Goods Economist*, who had once been a saleswoman, was distressed by the complaint of Minnie, a former comrade behind the counter: "Here I feel practically like a servant." The writer went on to say, "and there are hundreds of girls and women who feel more or less as Minnie did, but who are not so frank. Where on earth this 'servant' idea originated I was never able to figure out. I have known successful, mature saleswomen who would become defiant and belligerent at the mere mention of the word 'servant.' They loved their work and would have been miserable doing anything else, and yet they had that sensitive spot."

Dress rules intensified the impression of the servile status of saleswomen, and a detailed examination of the hotly argued issue of clerks' garb shows how a management policy could have unintended and contradictory effects. It is diffi- cult to date the appearance of dress regulations in department stores, but they were not yet universal by 1910. A *Dry Goods Economist* editorial made it clear that the question of dress had important implications for class relations within the store: "In certain departments of some stores the saleswomen are attired, hairdressed, and manicured to a point which seems to put them out of the class of business women, and thus tends to complicate their relations with the cus- tomer, or possible customer." Management attempted to eliminate this problem by requiring all saleswomen to dress in the same color, usually black or navy blue, in the hope that drab colors would minimize the "danger of display of poor taste and lack of background on the part of employees." In this case as in others, simple rules did not suffice to produce pleasingly dressed saleswomen, and a number of stores placed mannequins garbed in clothing deemed to be suitable in style and color near employees' locker or lunch rooms.

We can trace through the pages of *The Echo* the evolution of dress regulations at Filene's and glimpse the responses of saleswomen as well as the policies of managers. The net effect of these rules was clearly to undermine the saleswoman's sense of herself as a dignified worker and a handmaiden of consumption. No single issue aroused more interest in the selling force, and no single rule provoked more dislike. Filene's had mandated black for saleswomen as early as the turn of the century, but in 1902 the management considered uniforms; *The Echo*'s interviews showed that saleswomen were unanimously opposed to the proposal. One woman asserted that uniforms would be "a badge of service," and others complained that they would look like, variously, orphans, charity patients, paupers, and waitresses.

The battle over dress standards waxed and waned for the next four decades; although the specific terms of the debate changed over time, saleswomen at every point affirmed their preference for more relaxed standards. In 1913, for example, four-fifths of the saleswomen demanded the right to choose between black and white garments, on the grounds that "the management owed us the right to dress as we pleased." In 1930, saleswomen invoked their rarely used right to a store-wide referendum under the terms of the store's worker-participation plan; they voted twenty to one in favor of a broad standard prescribing only that they dress in "business-like styles and neutral shades." The justification this time referred not to their offended dignity or rights, but contained a barely veiled threat to management that saleswomen meant to practice what they preached to their customers. The women of one department warned that they could not sell effectively if they didn't feel that they were "dressed well and look[ed] smart." Management refused to bend the existing rules, but the choice could not have been a simple one: by continuing to require monochromatic dress, they were undermining not only their own efforts to have saleswomen think of their work as skilled and dignified, but also their attempts to spread the culture of consumption. The dilemma was endemic to the industry: a measure, like this one, designed to serve one of the retailer's goals frequently sabotaged other aspects of his management strategy.

Similar contradictions grew out of management's encouragement of skilled selling through suggestions and developing a clientele. Suggestion selling required the exercise of initiative and empathy in a deferential context, but in practice saleswomen often assumed a kind of equality with customers, to the distress of customers and managers alike.

> A smart-looking business woman, with an air of authority, approached the counter and asked to see a stylish and serviceable low collar. The girl put forward a collar that was a specialty of a leading firm.
> "Here's one that we are selling lots of to stenographers and typewriters, and lots of us girls have bought 'em, too," the girl explained.
> Harriet saw a shade of resentment pass over the woman's face, as she set her lips firmly, dropped the collar and started to turn away.

The complaint that saleswomen were too forward in imposing their judgment on customers is a staple of the retailing literature. Managers' attempts to encourage saleswomen to develop independent judgment, "good taste," and a fashion sense conflicted sharply with their desires to have the clerks display servant-like deference. A saleswoman firm in her conviction that she had the last word on fashion was prone to sneer at a customer whose dress or merchandise requests were less modish.

The issue of clientele was no less problematic. Saleswomen took the charge to develop a continuing relationship with a group of customers more literally than managers intended, and frequently refused to wait on, or at least to wait on effectively, a customer outside their charmed circle. Moreover, they served their clientele in ways that went far beyond management's definition of good service; saleswomen, for example, sometimes hid merchandise until it was ready for a markdown, at which point they would alert a favored customer. Managers wanted saleswomen who had the social skills to get along well with customers and to be able to advise them tactfully on fashion questions—but the women most skilled in these respects were likely to be equally independent and resourceful in dealing with their employers. Moreover, since managers constantly gave mixed messages about dignity and deference, it was not surprising that saleswomen had at best a mixed sense of loyalty to their bosses. By encouraging saleswomen to use their "womanly" skills of interaction and empathy on the job, managers set loose forces whose operation it was impossible to control closely.

Even more serious was managers' failure to break the grip of saleswomen's own ways of managing the selling floor. During the years when managers had allowed their sales forces to grow "like Topsy," the saleswomen had given their own brand of order to the selling floor. Observers throughout the period under consideration remarked upon the social order of the selling floor, but perhaps the definitive assessment of saleswomen's informal self-government came from George F. F. Lombard, who observed the children's clothing departments at Macy's in 1940, three decades after managers had begun to try to control the selling floor and the skill of its workers. Lombard concluded:

> Within the limits of the facilities themselves, the processes of control . . . allowed a very full elaboration of the values important to each of the groups and to many of the individual girls . . . [T]he salesgirls achieved this opportunity for the expression of self in what is often considered a restricted environment—a business organization—where the need for profits and the relative sameness of working conditions have seemed to many to offer little—and sometimes no— chance for self-expression. . . . These salesgirls, women of different ages, products of different cultures, had achieved for themselves a way of life whose effectiveness in terms of controlling behavior we can view only with great respect.

In the years when salespeople were haphazardly chosen and barely trained, if at all, saleswomen developed a de facto apprenticeship system whereby newcomers were initiated into the complex dynamics of the selling floor by their peers rather than by their superiors. When management tried to appropriate this function through training programs, saleswomen received the newly trained workers with reactions ranging from wariness to hostility; each had to be "retrained" on the selling floor according to the department's unwritten rules. Ways of relating to one another, to customers, and to management were firmly conveyed by precept and example to new saleswomen, and this informal training system was remarkably impervious to managers' initiatives.

Department store managers by and large failed to replace the shopgirl with a skilled saleswoman who met their complex and contradictory specifications. Three decades of efforts to train a skilled selling force left retail managers little more satisfied with the performance of the women behind their counters in 1940 than they were in 1910. One despairing writer opined, "In spite of the efforts of training departments, the standard of service remains mediocre . . . [F]ew clerks can be depended upon really to facilitate an intelligent choice." Managerial disillusion was reflected in the trade press: articles on the need for skilled selling increasingly shared the spotlight after 1940 with testimonials to the necessity of "self-selection" or "simplified selling"—both euphemisms for self-service. Dramatic changes in the nation's social and economic climate, which are beyond the scope of this discussion, reinforced store executives' sense that skilled selling could no longer be the foundation of their sales strategy. Reeling under the impact of the depression and World War II and painfully aware of the failure of their training programs, they embarked upon a new path that their successors still follow today.

The history of management policy toward department store saleswomen provides a useful case study that both revises and broadens our conceptions of business experience in the twentieth century. The path followed by department store managers was related to, though distinct from, that taken by their counterparts in factories. Rationalization in stores relied far less on scientific management than in factories, and far more on the skills of employees. . . .

The study of a specific industry, far from narrowing our perspective, greatly broadens it. Only by seeing how major trends and social forces interact in the crucible of a concrete situation can we grasp the full complexity of historical change. The study of department store management provides the opportunity to understand the ways in which larger business trends such as rationalization, personnel management, and the culture of consumption interconnected with, and sometimes contradicted, one another. Finally, it shows the way in which managers have responded to two of the most basic categories in our society: class and sex.

The
Gospel
of
Success

IRVIN G. WYLLIE

Culver Pictures

Easter Parade, 1902, on 5th Avenue, New York City

THE STERN GOD PURITANS PREACHED OF was replaced by a less severe God who smiled on the wealth of American society. In the following article, Irvin G. Wyllie describes how the Protestant clergy became apologists for those who worshiped both God and money. Leading ministers Henry Ward Beecher and Lyman Abbott were joined by popular writers who had left the ministry—Horatio Alger and Matthew H. Smith, for example—in promoting a gospel of success. The doctrinal basis of their gospel was the belief that God required every person to lead a financially successful and useful temporal life, as well as a successful spiritual life.

The clergy blessed business enterprise by approving the pursuit of wealth as an appropriate activity and by sanctifying the economic virtues of industry, frugality, and sobriety, the economic virtues that were essential to accumulate capital. The message from many pulpits, and from the novels of Horatio Alger, was that hard work would be materially rewarded. Business leaders responded well to these admonitions by taking an active part in church affairs. Wall Street titans stopped at Trinity Church on their way to work; successful entrepreneurs built churches; some industrialists even required their employees to attend prayer meetings. For the growing middle class, the message that wealth was a gift from God, a sign of His favor, was indeed comforting. However, for the poorer masses the verdict was less encouraging: poverty was a sign of God's displeasure with those who had been found wanting in virtue.

MATTHEW H. SMITH, who had a double career as a clergyman and a Wall Street journalist, spoke wisely in the year 1878 when he predicted that whoever wrote the history of American business would also have to write the history of religion. Having served both God and Mammon, Smith was conscious of their relationship and sensed that justice could not be done to one if the other were ignored. As it turned out, European not American investigators first explored the connection between capitalism and Protestantism. Thanks to Max Weber, Ernst Troeltsch, Richard Tawney and others, the complex relation of religion to the spirit of business enterprise has been carefully and critically examined. Thanks also to fruitless debates on whether Protestantism caused capitalism, or *vise versa*, the fact of their historic congeniality has too often been lost to view.

In nineteenth-century America religion and business were no less partners in common enterprise than they had been in seventeenth-century England. Both Weber and Tawney erred in assuming that in the eighteenth century religious and moral foundations of the get-ahead gospel had been swept away by secular currents. Weber, for example, looked upon Benjamin Franklin as a classic symbol of the secularization of the Protestant ethic, an ethic "without the religious basis, which by Franklin's time had died away." Tawney contended that by the nineteenth century the church possessed no independent standards to which economic practice was expected to conform, and that the church's customary warnings against materialism "wore more and more the air of afterthoughts." If this means that Russell Conwell had less power to enforce fair business practices in Philadelphia than John Calvin had in Geneva, the point must be conceded without debate. But if it means that Conwell and his clerical associates had no serious interest in the morality of success, and had nothing to teach in this sphere, the contention must be emphatically denied. Throughout the nineteenth century religious and moral precepts provided the foundation for the self-help creed, and clergymen who preached the gospel of success encouraged their business allies to behave in a conscionable manner. Their counsel was often ignored, but the fact of failure should not obscure the extent and vigor of the effort.

One of the impressive facts about the American cult of self-help is that many of its leading proponents were clergymen. The names of Henry Ward Beecher, Lyman Abbott, William Lawrence, Russell Conwell, and Horatio Alger were as familiar to readers of success tracts as to those who worshipped in the leading Protestant churches on the Sabbath. By teaching that godliness was in

THE GOSPEL OF SUCCESS   By Irvin G. Wyllie. Originally published under the title "God and Mammon." From *The Self-Made Man in America: The Myth of Rags to Riches.* Copyright © 1954 by Trustees of Rutgers College in New Jersey. Reprinted by permission.

league with riches such spokesmen put the sanction of the church on the get-ahead values of the business community. And by so teaching they encouraged each rising generation to believe that it was possible to serve both God and Mammon.

Like the businessmen whose careers they glorified, these clergy were of the Protestant faith. Fully 90 percent of the leading American businessmen of the early twentieth century were Protestant, and of the well-known clergy who pointed the way to wealth, none was a Roman Catholic. Despite Catholicism's numerical strength in the urban centers where the great fortunes were made, no eminent prelate wrote books or preached sermons urging young men to seek salvation along the road to wealth. The reasons for this negative performance are obvious. Since there were relatively few Catholics in the American business elite, probably never more than 7 percent prior to 1900, the Church had no special interest in glorifying this group. Furthermore, less than 10 percent of the nation's business leaders were foreign born. In ministering to immigrants in the years after the Civil War, and especially to those from southern and eastern Europe, the Catholic Church was working with men who had very little chance of achieving outstanding financial success. In addition, by standing aloof from the glorification of wealth, Catholic spokesmen upheld their church's traditional indictment of materialism.

Virtually all the leading Protestant denominations, with the exception of the Lutheran, produced at least one nationally known clergyman who honored the wealth-through-virtue theme. Most of these ministers, like the business leaders of the time, were natives of the New England and the Middle Atlantic states. Almost without exception they had pulpits in the financial and industrial centers of the North and East, and by virtue of their location, and the economic status of their congregations, they had easy contact with businessmen and business values. A substantial number were Calvinists: the Congregational church produced more prominent self-help publicists than any other denomination. How much this was due to theology, and how much to the church's dominant position in industrial New England no one can say, but there is a suggestion in the fact that rural clergymen did little to glorify the cult of self-help, while their urban brethren, Calvinists and non-Calvinists alike, preached it as true gospel.

Consider some of the nineteenth-century Congregational clergy who, by their utterances on success, proved themselves worthy successors to Cotton Mather. One of the earliest of these was John Todd, who lectured on *The Foundations of Success* in 1843, and subsequently wrote two self-help handbooks, *The Young Man* (1845) and *Nuts for Boys to Crack* (1866). Todd was no back-country preacher, though his pulpit was at Pittsfield, Massachusetts, in the extreme western portion of the state. The fact that Todd preached at Pittsfield when it was developing as an important shoe and textile manufacturing center probably had something to do with his interest in worldly success. Matthew H. Smith began his career as a Congregational clergyman in 1842 at Malden, Massachusetts, a boot and shoe center not far removed from Boston. After eight years in Malden Smith moved to New York where he began a new career as a Wall Street journalist. In addition to his address, *The Elements of Success* (1854), Smith wrote *Twenty Years Among the Bulls and Bears of Wall Street* (1870), and *Successful Folks* (1878). Francis E. Clark, nationally famous as the founder of the Christian Endeavor Society, was a Congregational minister in

Portland, Maine, the commercial metropolis of that state. His two self-help books, *Our Business Boys* (1884), and *Danger Signals, the Enemies of Youth from the Business Man's Standpoint* (1885), were based on ideas and information provided by Portland businessmen. Wilbur F. Crafts, who published *Successful Men of Today and What They Say of Success* (1883), occupied a pulpit in New Bedford, Massachusetts, a cotton manufacturing center, before moving to larger pastorates in Chicago and Brooklyn. Through *Seven Lectures to Young Men* (1844) Henry Ward Beecher had established himself as an expert on self-help long before he began to preach industry, frugality, and sobriety to the wealthy congregation of Brooklyn's Plymouth Church. Lyman Abbott followed in Beecher's footsteps, taking over the pastorate of Plymouth Church in 1887. His book, *How to Succeed* (1882), established him as a true prophet of the success cult.

Though Congregational ministers were most prominent in this line they had considerable competition from leaders of other faiths. The principal Episcopal self-help spokesman was William Lawrence, Bishop of Massachusetts and son of the industrialist Amos A. Lawrence. He memorialized success values in his *Life of Amos A. Lawrence* (1888) and in a famous essay on the "Relation of Wealth to Morals," published in *The World's Work* in 1901. William Van Doren, author of *Mercantile Morals* (1852) occupied a pulpit of the Dutch Reformed Church at Piermont, New York, the town that served as the first eastern terminus of the Erie Railroad. The leading Baptist spokesman was Russell Conwell, a self-made Yankee who built the Baptist Temple in Philadelphia, founded Temple University, and created a popular sensation with his success sermon, *Acres of Diamonds*. Methodism was represented by Daniel Wise, a one-time grocer's apprentice who filled many pulpits in the commercial and industrial towns of New England and New Jersey, and glorified the self-made man in his book, *Uncrowned Kings* (1875).

Of all the popularizers of self-help values none was better known to the post–Civil-War generation than Horatio Alger, who got his start as a Unitarian minister at Brewster, Massachusetts, in 1864. Like Matthew H. Smith before him, Alger abandoned both the pulpit and New England for a literary career in New York. He found his inspirations in the city, as did others who played upon the rags-to-riches theme. Unlike Smith, who reported the doings of Wall Street operators, Alger concentrated on boys who had not yet arrived. He invested his heroes with all the moral virtues honored by the cult of self-help, but even in this he was different, in that Ragged Dick and Tattered Tom won success by some sudden stroke, rather than by steady application to business. These features, together with his preference for the fictional form, set Alger apart from other leading writers in this field.

Even without Alger the success-minded clergy represented a numerous host, and one of great influence in the cult of self-help. They wrote many of the books of its bible, preached its gospel, tried to restrain its excesses, and protected it against the charge of godlessness and materialism. In nineteenth-century America, where the mass of men respected business and religion, the partnership organized by the clergy proved profitable to both.

II

The doctrine of the secular calling provided the foundation for the religious defense of worldly success. In proclaiming this doctrine American clergymen, like their European predecessors, argued that God required every man to lead a successful and useful temporal life as well as an acceptable spiritual life. Under this conception the calling was an exacting worldly enterprise in which man could conquer his own base nature and overcome the limitations of his social environment. The man who succeeded in his vocation proved that he deserved a high station in this life as well as salvation in the next. Since every man won salvation in his profession, and not outside it, God provided a suitable calling for all. As one authority explained, "The principle is, that however poor, ignorant, or prone to evil we are born, God gives to each a glorious opportunity. If true to him, and if rightly alive to our great advantages, we may make our fortune."

Throughout the nineteenth century clergymen and laymen alike insisted that business stood high on God's list of approved callings. Matthew H. Smith, writing for *Hunt's Merchants' Magazine* in 1854, asserted that God had ordained business as the great purpose in life. "The race were [*sic*] made for employment," Smith said. "Adam was created and placed in the Garden of Eden for business purposes; it would have been better for the race if he had attended closely to the occupation for which he was made." The man who chose business as a career did not have to fear that he would be cut off from opportunities for spiritual improvement, for the spiritual and the material were united in business. Theodore Parker emphasized this point when he described the merchant as "a moral educator, a church of Christ gone into business—a saint in trade . . . the Saint of the nineteenth century is the Good Merchant; he is wisdom for the foolish, strength for the weak, warning to the wicked, and a blessing to all. Build him a shrine in Bank and Church, in the Market and the Exchange . . . no Saint stands higher than this Saint of Trade." Despite the secularization of American thought in the latter part of the century, the theme of the God-appointed business calling did not lose its popularity with either clerical or lay writers. As the century closed, Orison Marden warned his readers against the "fatal error" of regarding the church as sacred and the warehouse as secular, for both were sacred and uplifting. In the year 1898, Charles P. Masden, a Methodist clergyman in Milwaukee, told a group of business college students that business was not just an occupation but a divine calling. "It is sacred," Masden declared. "It is a means of grace. It is a stewardship. It is building up for eternity, and laying up treasures in heaven."

This did not mean that God disapproved the laying up of treasures on earth. Far from it, for in the American cult of success, as in the Calvinist ethic, the pursuit of wealth became a positive religious duty. Reverend Thomas P. Hunt, one of the earliest writers on this subject, summarized the case for riches in the title of his work: *The Book of Wealth; in Which It Is Proved from the Bible that It Is the Duty of Every Man to Become Rich* (1836). Lyman Abbott rejoiced in the parable of the talents, and used it to justify his claim that Jesus approved the building of great fortunes. "He did not condemn wealth," Abbott declared. "On the contrary, he approved of the use of accumulated wealth to accumulate more wealth." Russell Conwell agreed, for in *Acres of Diamonds* he asserted that it was man's "Christian and godly duty" to seek wealth. Secular writers were especially pleased to have such friendly assurances from the clergy. Edwin T. Freedley, for one, argued that as long as religion sanctioned accumulation, no other sanction was needed.

If religion blessed business by approving the pursuit of wealth it doubled the blessing by sanctifying all the economic virtues essential to its accumulation. Of the virtues dear to the business community, religion exalted industry above all others. God required hard, continuous labor of rich and poor alike, not only as punishment for original sin, but as a constructive means of personal discipline. Labor kept man from sensuality, intemperance, and moral degeneration. It offered an opportunity to worship and glorify God through imitation of his creative labors. When combined with other virtues it allowed man to lay up treasures on earth as well as in heaven, and helped him win an earthly success which served as a measure of his heavenly salvation. Protestant clergy of all denominations agreed that labor had special honor in the sight of God, and that it formed an integral part of true religion. Daniel Wise, a Methodist minister, spoke for all religious prophets of success when he advised a group of young men that "Religion will teach you that industry is a SOLEMN DUTY you owe to God, whose command is, 'BE DILIGENT IN BUSINESS!'" The religious aspect of labor was emphasized so much in the nineteenth century that even secular-minded men sometimes talked of labor in religious terms. Andrew Carnegie, for example, once remarked that an honest day's work was "not a bad sort of prayer."

Frugality also had special honor in the sight of God, and was considered like labor, a positive religious duty. In the tradition of the Protestant ethic the man who aspired to success and salvation was supposed to live simply and frugally, avoiding luxury and ostentation. This tradition carried over into the American ethic of self-help, whose clerical prophets advertised frugality as "the good genius whose presence guides the footsteps of every prosperous and successful man." Through frugality God provided a way to wealth which was open to all, and one which all were supposed to travel. The great exemplar of frugality was none other than Jesus of Nazareth, who, after he had fed the multitude with loaves and fishes "commanded his disciples to gather up the fragments, lest anything should be wasted." Frugality led inevitably to sobriety, for the man who husbanded his means had nothing left to spend on the vices. "Drinking habits," Henry Ward Beecher observed, "take hold indirectly upon the whole framework of a man's prosperity. They lead to very many expenses besides the daily expenses of the cup."

According to the theology of success God always rewarded the industrious, the frugal, and the sober with wealth. One Episcopal clergyman argued that it would have been surprising indeed if God had not provided material rewards for the faithful practice of his appointed virtues. These rewards, said the cleric, "like all the profit of godliness, are to be gathered in this life as well as in that which is to come." According to this logic the possession of wealth made the possessor one of the elect. Wealth was a gift from God, an evidence of his favor, and a reward for faithfulness—comforting doctrine to substantial pew-holders in urban churches. Apologists who turned to the Scriptures noted that Abraham, Solomon and other Old Testament heroes received wealth from the Lord in token of his approval. "The Old Testament doctrine of wealth is frank and unmistakable," a Unitarian minister told his congregation in 1885. "It is a *blessing from the Lord*. It is a sign of the divine approval. . . ." Little wonder, in view of such assurances, that John D. Rockefeller brushed off his critics with the simple assertion that it was God who had given him his money.

In accounting for the superior prosperity of the well-to-do, clergymen invariably pointed to their superior morality. Russell Conwell insisted that ninety-eight out of every hundred rich Americans stood above their fellowmen in honesty. "That is why they are rich," he said. "That is why they are trusted with money. That is why they carry on great enterprises and find plenty of people to work with them. It is because they are honest men." If one were to accept the gospel of success at face value he would believe that virtually every rich man was a paragon of moral virtue. William Lawrence, Episcopal Bishop of Massachusetts, summarized the clerical point of view when he observed that "in the long run, it is only to the man of morality that wealth comes. . . . We, like the Psalmist, occasionally see the wicked prosper, but only occasionally. . . . Godliness is in league with riches."

Turned around, this doctrine meant that wickedness was in league with poverty. Those who were poor had no reason to reproach the Giver of Gifts, for they had been tested and found deficient in virtue. "It is no respect for persons that causes the Lord to make some rich and some poor," said one authority, "but it comes of His infinite love to all, and His effort to save all from the evils and corruptions of their own hearts." The man who complained against God's wise way of distributing wealth had the root of evil in him. "And is the young man aware, when repining at his penury, that he is reproaching his Maker, and charging Him indirectly with being stingy?" another clergyman asked.

By identifying the rich with the elect and the poor with the damned, clergymen provided strong religious and moral defenses for the well-to-do. He who attacked the rich, or urged a system of distribution favorable to the poor, automatically advertised himself as an enemy of God and of the moral order. Thanks to the religious defense of money-making, wealthy Americans of the nineteenth century knew the meaning of the assurance offered by one popular success handbook: "Heaven taketh notes of thy career, and the angels are guardian watchers and abettors of thy prosperity."

III

No one-way system of advantages characterized the partnership of God and Mammon. In return for the sanction of religion, businessmen were supposed to be sincerely religious, identifying themselves with the doctrines and activities of the church. Clergymen and laymen alike agreed that the way to wealth passed through the church. A Methodist minister, Daniel Wise, insisted that the qualities necessary for success appeared most often in those who embraced and faithfully followed the teachings of Christ. And William Speer, a lay writer, claimed it was more important for the young man to begin his business career with proper religious perceptions than with a diploma "certifying that he is master of all the 'ologies' of all the colleges." Since Bible-reading developed proper religious perceptions, businessmen were constantly advised to seek inspiration in the Scriptures, especially in Solomon's Proverbs. By the same token they were supposed to shun those intellectual influences which undermined faith. In the 1890s, after Darwinism, the higher criticism, and the social gospel had made inroads on traditional religion, Edward Bok warned prospective businessmen that one of the keys to success was strict adherence to the ancient creeds. The man who rejected the faith of his fathers invited disaster. "Without that faith, without that absolute conviction," Bok declared, "he will be hindered and crippled in whatever he undertakes." Except for Andrew Carnegie, the major post–Civil-War titans did not cripple themselves by straying off the paths of orthodoxy. And at the turn of the twentieth century the vast majority of American business leaders still identified themselves with the Episcopal, Presbyterian, Methodist, Baptist, and other respectable Protestant churches.

Mere affiliation was not enough, however. The responsible man of affairs attended church regularly, after the manner of J. P. Morgan, Jay Cooke, John D. Rockefeller, Peter Cooper, and a host of others. Even on weekdays periods of formal worship had their uses. J. P. Morgan sometimes left his office in mid-afternoon to go to St. George's Church, to pray and sing hymns, hour after hour. In the years after the Civil War, Wall Street capitalists paused on their way to the Exchange to seek the Lord's blessing in Trinity Church or stopped there at the end of the day to offer thanks for victories won. Nearby, at the old Dutch church, every day many of the most prominent men on the Street dropped their worldly cares at noon to commune with God through prayer. These worshippers probably agreed with another famous churchgoer, Daniel Drew, who observed that "When a man goes to prayer meeting and class meeting two nights of the week, and to church twice on Sunday, and on week days works at his office from morning till night, his life is made up of about two things—work and worship."

Sometimes these men also played an active role in the work of the church. In addition to attending Episcopal conventions as a deputy from New York, J. P. Morgan usually transported the leading church dignitaries to the convention city. Peter Cooper fulfilled his obligations to the Lord by serving as a Sunday School superintendent, while John D. Rockefeller taught industry, frugality, and sobriety to young men in a Baptist Bible class. Nor were these exceptional cases. Two close observers of the New York business community testified that the most prominent merchants and financiers could usually be found on Sabbath mornings in the churches intepreting the Scriptures. Making money was important but saving souls appeared to go along with it hand in hand.

If a man had no talents as an evangelist he could at least pay the way for those who did. Men of wealth were expected to support the local work of the church and to underwrite missionary activity in distant vineyards. Methodist ministers encouraged Daniel Drew to endow a theological seminary which would send men out to preach the gospel to a sinful world. The more common tactic was to ask for more magnificent houses of worship; the Astors, Vanderbilts, Rockefellers, Wanamakers, Morgans, Armours, Pullmans, and Mellons were all builders of churches.

Even in the conduct of business affairs there were opportunities to promote religion. In hiring clerks employers could give preference to those with religious connections; self-interest suggested such a policy anyway. They might also coerce clerks into participating in religious observances. Arthur Tappan was exceptional, no doubt, but he showed what could be done. Tappan required his clerks to attend prayer meetings twice a week and regular services twice on Sunday. Every Monday morning his employees had to report what church they had attended, the name of the clergyman, and the texts used as the basis of the sermon. Those employers who had no desire to police the religious activities of their employees could still promote religion by not requiring them to work on the Sabbath and by not asking them to perform deeds that violated their religious scruples. The wise businessman respected evidence of Christian living at all times. "Don't scoff at those . . . who are trying to lead Christian lives," one adviser warned, "and don't for a moment belittle the importance of their competition in the struggle for supremacy. The quiet, easy, smooth-spoken man who is looked upon as a milk-sop, may have in him all the elements of business success." William Van Doren, a Dutch Reformed minister, claimed that he knew one hard-hearted employer who rescinded a Sabbath working order when he discovered that his clerk was ready to sacrifice his job rather than violate the Lord's day. The employer "cared neither for God, heaven, hell, or worse, but he did care for a trusty clerk," Van Doren said. "He knew not the value of an interest in the Redeemer, but he did most accurately understand the value of one, whom nothing of pecuniary interest could tempt." The clerk who advertised that he had lost his job by refusing to work on the Sabbath was bound to receive many offers of employment, for according to the cult of success, church-attending employers always sought Sabbath-observing employees. Creditors also took notice of who went to church. This led one success tract to advise that "A good advertisement for a working man, is a seat in church."

By attending church, participating in its work, underwriting its expenses, and honoring its teachings, the businessman put his stamp of approval on religion. In so doing he reciprocated the application of religious sanctions to business, and sealed the partnership of God and Mammon.

IV

The application of these religious sanctions, however, was by no means automatic. Clergymen who identified themselves with the success cult did not hesitate to pass moral judgment on men and methods in business. Like other authorities on self-help they did not attempt to glorify notorious men like Jay Gould, Jim Fisk, or Daniel Drew, for they generally held that "No amount of money can make a highway robber or any other kind successful. . . . Even millions of plunder does not constitute success, which must include a good name." P. T. Barnum was denounced by Matthew H. Smith who claimed that in his race for wealth Barnum had operated on the principle that any tactic was legitimate so long as it was not criminal. "Humbug, tricks, deceit, low cunning, false stories, were stock in trade," Smith declared. And Henry Ward Beecher pointed from his Plymouth pulpit to "an old obese abomination of money" operating in Wall Street, and warned his congregation against worshipping such a man. "He has utterly defiled and destroyed his manhood in the manufacturing of wealth," Beecher charged; "he is a great epitomized, circulating hell on earth, and when he dies, hell will groan—one more woe."

In order to enjoy the approval of the church wealth had to be earned in an honorable calling, one that contributed to the social welfare. Saloon-keepers, speculators, gamblers, and others who rendered no useful service could not qualify. Merchants, manufacturers, and bankers were honored by the clergy as long as they kept in touch with the needs of mankind and provided the necessary capital, goods, and services. "When will you manufacturers learn that you must know the changing needs of humanity if you would succeed in life?" Russell

Conwell asked. "Apply yourselves, all you Christian people, as manufacturers or merchants or workmen to supply that human need. It is a great principle as broad as humanity and as deep as the Scripture itself."

The clergy knew that an honorable calling was not enough, however, for there were many dishonorable men in reputable vocations. Too many business-men agreed with the sentiment attributed to Daniel Drew. "A business man has got to get along somehow," he said. "Better that my hog should come dirty home, than no hog at all." Such men, even if they acquired wealth, did not have any honor among clerical writers of success tracts. "Riches got by fraud, are dug out of one's own heart and destroy the mine," said Henry Ward Beecher. "Unjust riches curse the owner in getting, in keeping, in transmitting." William Van Doren, who was aware of the questionable tactics of many New York businessmen, insisted that in all fortunes dishonestly acquired there was a curse which "sooner or later will break forth like a leprosy." To a widespread belief in the business community that the completely honest man was at a disadvan-tage in the quest for wealth, the clergy answered that whatever the short-term disadvantages, honesty brought the long-term gains. Though the wicked might enjoy a temporary prosperity, the laws of moral retribution would deprive them of permanent fortune.

Ministers constantly warned moneymakers of the moral dangers inherent in their quest. These warnings were not inspired by religious objections to wealth, but rather by the fear that the passion for money would lead men into sin. The only man who could seek wealth and remain morally upright was the one who was capable of the most rigorous personal discipline. "If you have entered this shining way, begin to look for snares and traps," warned Henry Ward Beecher. "Go not careless of your danger, and provoking it." While one rich man climbed into heaven, ten sank into the bottomless pit of hell. "You seek a land pleasant to the sight, but dangerous to the feet," Beecher declared, "a land of fragrant winds, which lull to security; of golden fruits, which are poisonous; of glorious hues, which dazzle and mislead."

All wealth-seekers ran the risk of making accumulation an end in itself. Religion warned her business partner against this deadly sin. "It is folly su-preme, nay madness," said William Van Doren, "to make the acquiring riches, and enjoying them, the chief end of life." The man who coveted wealth for its own sake was a mere beast of burden, who would go "toiling beneath his load, with gold on his back, and hell in his heart, down to destruction." Clergymen who taught that Jesus approved the quest for wealth also taught that Jesus scorned the man who loved the quest for its own sake. He who did not think beyond the problems of accumulation was hell-bent. "The man that worships the dollar instead of thinking of the purposes for which it ought to be used, the man who idolizes simply money, the miser that hordes his money in the cellar, or hides it in his stocking, or refuses to invest it where it will do the world good, that man who hugs the dollar until the eagle squeals," Russell Conwell warned, "has in him the root of all evil."

Since the twin of miserliness was prodigality, clergymen had to remind their business associates that God had not given them wealth just to live merrily and without care. In the eyes of the church it was a sin for the wealthy to waste their substance on luxurious clothing, lavish entertainment, great mansions, and other forms of ostentatious display. The rich man was meant to live simply and frugally, spending no more than necessary for his subsistence. Here, as elsewhere, moderation should characterize his actions; he should be neither miserly nor prodigal but follow instead a middle course.

The doctrine of the stewardship of wealth provided the clue to the right use of wealth. Since it was God who had made the rich man's lot different from that of his poor brother, his money was simply held in trust to be used in doing God's work. Thus it could not be used exclusively for his own benefit, but must be applied primarily to the benefit of others. In practice this meant support of schools, libraries, museums, orphanages, hospitals, churches, and similar beneficent institutions. As a onetime Unitarian minister, Ralph Waldo Emerson, explained, "They should own who can administer, not they who hoard and conceal; not they who, the great proprietors they are, are only the great beggars, but they whose work carves out the work for more, opens a path for all. For he is the rich man in whom the people are rich, and he is the poor man in whom the people are poor. . . ." By this reasoning the good steward could be considered as much a saint as any saint of the church and as deserving of religious honor.

The church's teachings on the subject of wealth provided the foundation on which secular writers built an elaborate body of doctrine concerning the ethics of success, but they also provided the businessman with a convenient rationale by which he could justify his superior position in society. It would be a mistake, however, to assume that all those who used the rationale either lived by its precepts or gave them a respectful hearing. Occasionally God and Mammon exchanged harsh words. In 1891 an English Methodist minister, Hugh Price Hughes, condemned Andrew Carnegie for piling up a fortune at the expense of his fellowmen. Carnegie, who never took the partnership of business and religion seriously, was so nettled by the attack that he hurled back into the minister's teeth the parable of the talents and the teaching of John Wesley, founder of the Methodist faith: "Gain all you can by honest industry." Clergymen, in time, grew weary of businessmen who quoted the Scriptures to suit their own purposes. It was no accident that the Episcopal and Congregational churches, which had led all others in providing spokesmen for the self-help cult before 1890, became the most productive of clergymen of the social gospel after that date. With the rise of the social gospel, ministers like Washington Gladden, George D. Herron, W. D. P. Bliss, Bouck White, and Walter Rauschenbusch tried to dissolve the partnership of God and Mammon.

Frank Lloyd Wright, the *Family,* and the Prairie House

ROBERT C. TWOMBLY

Robie House, 1907–1909, Chicago, by Frank Lloyd Wright

FRANK LLOYD WRIGHT is considered by many to have been the greatest American architect. The following selection is about a group of houses he designed in Chicago between 1901 and 1909—the so-called Prairie Houses—and about how their unique designs influenced the families that lived in them. Robert C. Twombly also explains how these particular styles of home design began to give a new look to the middle-class American house.

Twombly argues that the Prairie Houses emphasized certain values that Wright's clients found important. For example, the buildings reflected the growing detachment of individual families from the larger community by stressing privacy: overhanging roofs allowed people inside the house to look out but prevented those outside from looking in; doors were rarely visible from the street; yards were carefully enclosed. Also, the internal arrangement of the houses emphasized the developing intimacy *within* the family. The open floor plan that allowed all family members to know where everyone was and what he or she was doing demanded close, harmonious relationships. Finally, Twombly concludes that their external appearances made the houses seem like shelters in which people could be protected from the outside world and safe from the forces of disintegration that seemed to be threatening American society.

FRANK LLOYD WRIGHT'S CONTRIBUTION to architecture begins with the development of the "prairie house" at the turn of the 20th century. A departure from the various eclectic styles which dominated American design, it embodied, according to Wright, "a radically different conception" of how a residence should appear, what it should do, and what it should contain. The prairie house looked longer and lower than conventional dwellings, with its masses, terraces, portes-cochere and roof overhangs stretching out horizontally across the land, reflecting the earth-lines of the Middle West where Wright and most of his clients lived. Its interior space was more open than in other styles, with reception, living and dining areas flowing into each other, and with substantially increased fenestration merging indoors and out. Internal and external horizontal trim emphasized interpenetrating spaces, added to the feeling of sheltered intimacy, and unified the design around simple harmonies uncharacteristic in an era of architectural overstatement.

Many of Wright's admirers still maintain that the prairie house received a hostile reception. Contractors, bankers, the professional establishment and the general public supposedly ridiculed Wright and abused those brave clients who suffered indignities "in the cause of architecture." Actually, the new design was popular, the more so as it continued to depart from architectural tradition. From 1901, when he first announced it in the February *Ladies' Home Journal,* until September 1909 when he left his office to spend a year in Europe, Wright was commissioned to design approximately one hundred prairie houses, of which 64 were actually built. From 1901 through 1904 he erected a yearly average of six of nine residences, and from 1905 through 1909—when many projects were more startling than ever—eight of twelve, indicating that as his work evolved his following grew. He received consistently friendly coverage in the architectural press where he was frequently illustrated, and in 1902 and 1907 held widely acclaimed exhibitions under the auspices of the Chicago Architectural Club.

Wright's popularity can also be measured by the success of others who designed in his manner or drew on him for inspiration. Some had been trained in his own Oak Park, Illinois studio, some had worked with his mentor, Louis Sullivan, and others had seen his buildings depicted in the journals. Between 1902 and 1914 at least twenty young designers scattered in large and small Midwestern cities, collectively called the "Prairie," "Chicago" or "Western" School, achieved considerable prominence with their residential efforts. The

FRANK LLOYD WRIGHT, THE FAMILY AND THE PRAIRIE HOUSE   By Robert C. Twombly. Originally published under the title "Saving the Family: American Middle Class Attraction to Wright's Prairie House, 1901–1909." From *American Quarterly,* 27 (1975), pp. 57–72. Copyright 1975, American Studies Association. Reprinted by permission of the journal, the author, and the American Studies Association.

best of these—Walter Burley Griffin, George Elmslie, William Purcell, William Drummond, Barry Byrne, George Maher and Robert C. Spencer Jr.—injected new life into American architecture. Far from appealing to a tiny band of visionaries, Wright's "radically different conception" received enthusiastic endorsement among the bourgeoisie in middle America. . . .

The essential point about Wright's clients . . . is that they *do not* seem particularly different from other men and women of their socioeconomic class. Their significance lies not in their alleged uniqueness but in their very typicality. . . . They were upper-middle-class independent businessmen likely to own their own moderate-sized manufacturing firms, conservative Protestant Republicans who frowned on eccentric social behavior, liberal causes or protest literature. In a period of "progressive" reform, they clung to traditional values, and like others in the emerging metropolis felt themselves engulfed by sweeping changes not entirely to their liking. In the midst of rapid social reorganization and economic consolidation, the simpler world they had known was disappearing. It seems likely therefore that their attraction to the prairie house was as strongly emotional and psychological as it was conscious and rational, for Wright's designs satisfied needs and wishes murkily understood but deeply felt by large numbers of city dwellers, more directly, in fact, than conventional styles. The prairie house appealed to an apprehensive upper middle class by emphasizing in literal and symbolic ways the security, shelter, privacy, family mutuality and other values it found increasingly important in a period of urban dislocation and conflict.

Rapid industrialization and urbanization in late 19th century America created a disorienting situation. Armies of working class immigrants from Europe and from American farms and small towns contributed to dramatic social tensions and instabilities. Newcomers of all classes, having lost their roots, found their places of residence determined not by family tradition or landholding but by unpredictable and insecure job situations. Vast impersonal corporations assumed control over the lives of laboring men and their families, over white collar workers and executives, and over self-employed businessmen and professionals whose livelihoods depended on the whims of an incomprehensible and seemingly arbitrary economic system. The depression of the 1890s, the most devastating in American history to that point, exacerbated the general apprehension as even more people began to sense their helplessness. Few individuals could count on uninterrupted upward mobility, permanent employment or a happy future for their children. Even the upper middle class, especially people like Wright's clients who did not possess inherited wealth, faced the specter of possible downward mobility.

The expanding metropolis also weakened family connections. When parents no longer employed their offspring in their own enterprises, children were forced to make their way on their own. Success became dependent on market conditions, not personal skills. The individual on his own, not the family as a group, became the primary economic unit. The civic and social demands of the city further weakened kin ties, especially in the middle class. With the father absent from home most of the day, the mother involved in voluntary associations, and the children in school with access to great numbers of neighborhood playmates, the family's time together decreased. "The social literature of the last half of the nineteenth century abounded in references to the instability of the family," one observer notes, "and practically predicted the extinction of family organization, at least in its present form." In that kind of social climate, the family's physical encasement took on special importance for those whose wealth allowed the luxury of choice. "Home may be an *emotional bulwark* against the threats and insecurities of a too-big, too-fast, too-complicated world where one must compete, man against man, for his place in the sun," write Charles Abrams and John P. Dean. "The high-tension currents of the job and the fears of the future are transformed into an extra need for the 'home' as a security." Richard Sennett argues that in the unknowable and potentially dangerous urban situation of the late 19th century, the family became a retreat, a shield against the destructive impact of the bureaucratic, industrial city.

As much as any other American metropolis, Chicago experienced the crises and dislocations of maturing corporate capitalism. Indeed, its spectacular revival after the great 1871 fire may have exaggerated the growing pains felt everywhere. Jane Addams' Hull House, standing in the midst of some of the nation's worst slums, called attention to the immigrant's plight, to social injustice and economic privation. Chicago had witnessed some of the bloodiest and most protracted labor-capital disputes in American history: the Haymarket Riot of 1886 and the Pullman Strike of 1894 were still alive in local memories. At the crossroads of the Middle West, the city was a center of Populism, Socialism and Progressivism, and was of course the site of William Jennings Bryan's "Cross of Gold" Speech in 1896. United States Steel, the first billion-dollar corporation, formed the same year Wright announced the prairie house, dominated the eastern approaches to the metropolis at Gary, Indiana. At a time when the railroad had been popularly identified as the grasping octopus of business and politics, Chicago was the rail capital of the nation. And Upton Sinclair's *The Jungle*, published in 1906, exposed the venality, vulgarity and sheer horror of the local meat-packing industry. Chicago was the dynamo of America, an exhilarating but disconcerting fact for its residents.

Forty per cent of Wright's houses built between 1901 and 1909 were in Illinois, mostly in greater Chicago, and several others were summer homes for his urban clientele. Although it looked different from prevailing styles, the prairie house was familiar and reassuring in several important ways. The general public did not perceive Wright or his work as totally unique but saw them in the context of the Prairie School—itself rooted in architectural tradition, as Allen Brooks has shown—and in relation to other architects and other manners of expression. The artistically informed considered the prairie movement and its contemporary Colonial revival as equally legitimate avenues toward the creation of a distinctively American architecture, an objective that had concerned many for decades. In retrospect we can appreciate the special importance of Wright's work but at the time its social and cultural milieu had a certain homogenizing effect, reducing it for the client to one of several styles from which to choose. When the professional journals and local newspapers singled Wright out, it was as often for the beautiful surroundings he had created as for his innovative efforts.

Wright's façades were unmistakably novel, but he gave his clients conventional interior programs, consisting of a living room, dining room, kitchen, two or three bedrooms, servant quarters and, depending on special interest, a music room or a library. If . . . the typical Prairie School purchaser was unaware of what he was getting and remained oblivious to architectural sophistication, particularly the manipulation of interior space, then he was probably attracted to the many features prairie houses shared with other styles, even though the outside was obviously different from prevailing standards of taste. This conclusion complements the findings of a 1954 study undertaken by the International Council on Building Research in Paris that a family's judgment of its home was an overall assessment, not a compilation of reactions to specific factors like room size or traffic patterns. The outside of the house was apparently not of singular importance in the resident's assessment of its worth. It could have been that Wright's clients overlooked the unique to seize upon the familiar, that they hired him *in spite of* his unusual façades and subtle interiors.

Another set of familiar characteristics his homes shared with their contemporaries was an emerging "suburban norm," a selective combination of urban and rural architectural values. Studying residential development on Boston's fringes from 1870 to 1900, Sam Bass Warner observes that when the middle class moved to the suburbs it brought with it "standards first established by the grid street and frontage lot" of the city, including the 40-foot thoroughfare, the prominent façade, uniform building lines, setbacks and side yards, and a rough equality of light, air and access. Neighborhoods tended toward homogeneity, with dwellings similar in cost, in the owner's economic and social rank, and in well-tended and well-planted appearance. A middle class wanting buildings "which would contain both the tone of the rural ideal and the symbolic formality of town housing" found a replacement for the rowhouse in a detached dwelling on a lot two or three times larger than in the city, but not dependent on nature for effect. The new suburban norm combined country privacy and setting with urban dignity and uniformity, making conscious reference to the prosperity and individuality appropriate, Warner notes, in an era "so devoted to private money-making." In addition, most suburban builders were imitative, modeling their homes on those already erected or others depicted in builders' manuals and in popular magazines like *Godey's* or *Scribner's*. Variety and individual expression came only in detail and ornament. Like other architects, Wright challenged little and embraced most of this suburban ideal.

Wright described his new residential concept in 1901 as "the city man's country home on the prairie," a succinct formulation of the suburban norm. Believing that the "homeowner who fully appreciates the advantages which he came to the country to secure" was being cheated by the 50-foot lot, he proposed a maximum of four prairie houses on a site 400 feet square, each having "absolute privacy" from the others and from the community. Foliage and landscaping would be substantially increased to give the dwelling as much rural flavor as possible. (Wright used the word "country" three times to describe this suburban venture.) The prairie house was not conceived, however, as an isolated residence but as part of Wright's "quadruple block plan" in which four homes would be variations on the same design scheme, and in some versions connected by low garden walls, basically an urban concept in which the block gave definition to the house. But the basic assumption was, as landscape architecture critic J. B. Jackson has put it, "that man is always striving for freedom from society."

Many clients came to Wright because of another aspect of the suburban norm, the imitative nature of residential development. A significant number hired him because they were relatives or friends of earlier purchasers, lived nearby and saw his work, or knew that he was becoming fashionable, with the result that his houses began to cluster together and in one scholar's view to become formularized. There were five on the same road in Delavan Lake, Wisconsin, all summer homes for Chicagoans built within five years of each other. In Oak Park Wright erected or remodeled 29 structures between 1889 and 1909, including a dozen grouped near his own home. He received four commissions in Buffalo from executives of the Larkin Company, a mail-order business for which he had designed administrative offices in 1904, after erecting an Oak Park house in 1903 for W. E. Martin, brother of Darwin D. Martin, a company official. The Martins first went to Wright after seeing his own studio and then in 1905 rehired him to build their E-Z Polish Factory in Chicago. The list of those who met him at church or other civic functions, saw his designs when visiting their relatives, or discovered him through other informal connections is quite long. Mrs. Harvey P. Sutton put the matter concisely: "Having seen a plan you drew for Chas. Barnes, and being favorably impressed," she notified her future architect in 1905, "[I] write you to see if you can do something for me." There developed a kind of Wright coterie, a group who chose him because others had done so and because he had a certain vogue. It took no special bravery to buy plans similar to those of friends, relatives, neighbors or business associates.

Of course, there *was* something special about Wright's work, assuring it a place of historical preeminence. Part of his genius lay in offering to typical members of the upper middle class the very best version of what they most wanted. The central themes and symbols of his homes—the features that informed and defined them—represented values expressed by other styles. But Wright stated them more clearly. His importance lies not in his appeal to a select group of conscious or unconscious art patrons but in his ability to minister to the fears, needs and aspirations of members of his class at that time in the city. Wright was very much a product of his era, bound up with its worries, aware of its memories, uneasy in its swirling change. His work was an interpretation of the values of his contemporaries.

For all the eccentricity that characterized his later life, Wright was a dedicated suburbanite during his Oak Park years. Unlike Buckminster Fuller or Paolo Soleri today, he was not considered a strange or incomprehensible man but was, as an Oak Park newspaper put it, "held in high esteem by his neighbors." When he opened a drafting room in his home in 1893 he announced that "to secure the quiet concentration of effort essential to the full success of a building project," it had been necessary for him to leave "the distractions of the busy city," Six years later he admitted that Chicago's "hustle" had "somewhat hardened" him. Wright knew from experience the potentially destructive impact of urban life and though he depended heavily on Chicago he was also repelled by it. He was not unaware that middle-class families were retreating from urban disorder to make peaceful islands for themselves in the suburbs.

His own personal history further increased his inclination to strengthen family intimacy in the suburban home. By the time he was twelve he had lived in six towns in four states from Massachusetts to Iowa, moving nearly every two years. His family had been plagued by emotional distance between husband and wife and between father and children, by financial insecurity and internal instability. An important constant during those years, especially in the summers of 1871 and from 1878 to 1886 after which Wright moved to Chicago, was the Lloyd Jones clan, his maternal relatives in Spring Green, Wisconsin, a collection of aunts, uncles and cousins each in their nuclear households but actually functioning as a large extended family. The young architect emulated this model, not that of his parents Anna and William Wright, when he established his own home in suburban Oak Park in 1889. The close-knit, intimate group, confronting the social and physical unknowns of the frontier, was a cultural memory that the native American urban middle class was in the process of enshrining as national myth. This rural panacea for urban problems had been a part of Wright's own childhood, and for the new suburbanite who shunned contact with immigrants, feared the future of the metropolis and romanticized his own past, the traditional family of farm and small town became a seductive model upon which to base his expectations. Ultimately it proved a failure for Wright, who left his wife and children in 1911 to retreat to the country. But for a decade it informed the organization, the goals and the atmosphere of the prairie house.

One reason Wright eventually left Oak Park to settle in rural Wisconsin was lack of personal privacy, a high priority for him and for the American middle class at the end of the 19th century. Post-Civil War homes, Sam Bass Warner remarks, revealed a "strong contemporary interest in private family life," and Richard Sennett writes that the need for privacy was crucial "as a means of quelling the fear and uncertainty men experienced in these new urban places. . . . So the first bulwark against the industrial city lay in the conditions of privacy vis-à-vis the outer world and the non-private intimacy within the family itself." The prairie house fulfilled these needs perfectly, better in fact than other styles, for one of its most obvious themes was detachment from the community as a basis for close association among residents. Wright achieved the first part of this duality—privacy vis-à-vis the larger community—in a number of ways. Although the prairie house had more window space than its neighbors, it was protected by shelf roofs or overhanging eaves, difficult to see under but not restricting the view out. Doorways were usually placed behind walls, hidden in deep recesses or tucked around corners; rarely were they visible from the street, and the difficulty of finding them could discourage casual access. Terraces, gardens and verandas, themselves enhancing privacy, were often screened by strategic plantings, so that even the family's outside activities were shielded from prying eyes. Although prairie houses gained seclusion from nestling along the ground, their first floors were sometimes raised higher above grade than usual—occasionally living rooms were on the second level—enabling clients like Frederick C. Robie to "look out and down the street to my neighbors without having them invade my privacy." With openings and appendages guarded from actual and visual penetration, but with a clear view of surroundings—in fact, with increased vista due to greater fenestration—and with overhanging eaves and hovering roofs thematically emphasizing privacy, Wright's residences were like manor houses for an urban gentry, projecting an image closer to reserve than hospitality. Unlike his homes of the 1920s and

1930s, they did not turn from the street to face the interior of the lot, but neither did they invite the neighbors to call. With their guarded apertures their social statement differed from the large-windowed dwellings common in Victorian America where pulling the shades insulted the neighbors. The prairie house buttressed the newer suburban notions that home life was not to be intruded upon, that it was separate from though not totally withdrawn from the rest of the community, and that contact with the outside world should be at the residents' discretion.

Detachment from surroundings could well enhance, in Sennett's words, "non-private intimacy within the family," another major motif of the prairie house. "The fragmentation . . . of the many private worlds, experienced outside in the city," he notes, "was replaced by an overwhelming sense of intimacy within the house," by an increase in "absolute face-to-face relations with each other." Thus "someone uneasy in the large world found in the home a situation of the most direct and unimpeded contact with other people." Wright's prairie houses seemed purposefully designed to accommodate these relationships, placing an obvious premium on family togetherness. The "open plan" that became associated with his name merged living, dining and other common rooms, uniting the family more often than had been possible where each function was treated as a discrete entity. Wright generally made the entire first floor (excluding the kitchen) a single large space, separating the activities by suggestion and screening rather than walls and doors. This brought the family physically together more often: people could be seen and their presence felt from one end of the house to the other most of the time. Space became multi-purpose, minimizing the singularity of an event's location but increasing the importance of the time it was performed. With the open floor-plan children could not be isolated (except in their bedrooms, of course, or if there was a nursery) nor could functions be kept apart (a luxury in the metropolis where space is at a premium). The dining area might become a sewing room between meals and the parlor a noisy playroom all day. Uniting the family and its activities could work in two different but not exclusive directions: toward increased parental authority over children who were now easier to supervise, or toward greater mutuality and tolerance among family members who came together more. The fact that most prairie houses still serve as private homes 70 years later indicates successful adaptation to the more permissive post-World War II concepts of child-rearing. But even if they were intended to support a traditional family structure, they invariably increased contact among its members.

Wright's clients were undoubtedly attracted by the striking embodiment of shelter, strength and security in the prairie house. He had had the idea, he wrote in 1936 of his early work, that "*shelter* should be the essential look of any dwelling," so he covered his homes with low spreading roofs and generously projecting eaves. Lying close to the ground, stretching out as if to embrace as much land as possible, the prairie house was protected literally from the elements and symbolically from other dangers by its land and its plantings, its roofs and its overhangs. It was a conspicuously strong and sturdy edifice, its mass and materials conveying a sense of durability, an impression enhanced by the broad chimney staking it firmly to the ground. Anchored resolutely in place, looking as if nothing could rip it from its moorings, the prairie house offered a snug harbor to the family battered about on the uncharted seas of metropolitan life. Wright himself appreciated the "sense of shelter" in the look of it, he wrote years later in his autobiography. It is noteworthy that he used the phrase "sense of shelter" rather than "shelter" alone, for it was the tone and feeling of his buildings as well as their physical properties that appealed to upper middle class buyers. Low ceilings, protected doors and windows, narrow hallways, massive hearths and quiet recessed corners worked to create a warm, convivial atmosphere within. Architecturally shaped long vistas assumed a variety of dimensions only with human movement, and like the subtleties of interpenetrating spaces, could best be appreciated after extensive and intimate contact in a kind of symbiotic relationship between building and resident unavailable to casual visitors. Wright's vigorous houses seemed almost to reinforce egos, encouraging inhabitants to rise to their challenge. From the outside the complexities and power of the façade suggested that deep within a sturdy family approached life on its own terms. "The sense of architecture as human shelter is a very fine sense," Wright wrote, perhaps with his businessmen clients in mind, "common sense, in fact."

His buildings also appealed to members of the upper middle class through their literal and symbolic associations with nature and the land, a sought-for harmony Wright avidly encouraged. "The horizontal line [is] the line of domesticity," he wrote, that enabled his homes to "lie serene beneath a wonderful sweep of sky," avoiding a struggle between architecture and the environment in which the residence, particularly the eclectic revivals of the late 19th century, had become a battleground. Wright proposed a working partnership with nature, "a more intimate relationship with out-door environment." He increased the number of windows that even in the rain could stay open under overhanging eaves, casement windows that gave one a sense of regulating nature's impact. Emphatic horizontal trim, the antithesis of "artistic" embellishment, paid homage to and interpreted the lay of the land. Far-reaching eaves, terraces, wings, verandas and portes-cochere drew the outside into the perimeter of the house itself. Conspicuous urns and built-in window boxes made greenery a permanent part of the façade. Stained and waxed wood, brick, plaster and in a few cases rough-cut fieldstone replaced paint, varnish, wallpaper and other "unnatural" materials. Gentle hip roofs cherished the snow for its insulating value, and instead of gouging the earth with an excavation the cellarless prairie house left it essentially unscathed under its concrete slab foundation. All of this was intended to eliminate visual and psychological barriers between outside and in, to create harmony between the two so that man, nature and architecture might unite in peaceful oneness. "Any building for humane purposes should be an elemental, sympathetic feature of the ground," Wright explained, "complementary to its nature-environment, belonging by kinship to the terrain." As urbanization progressed and as society increasingly mythologized its agricultural past, people looked for ways to "get back" to nature. Moving to the suburbs was one way; purchasing a Wright house was even better.

Merging exterior with interior space was one of several methods Wright employed to achieve the goal of architectural unity, an ideal in part intended to alleviate urban confusions. The prairie house open floor-plan emphasized the mutuality of the household rather than the individuality of its members by uniting them more often in spaces which flowed together as a greater whole.

Wright insisted, furthermore, on landscaping the residence and designing all its furnishings; sometimes this meant table runners, carpets, draperies, and on one celebrated occasion even the clothing of his client's wife. His purpose was to create for the family the harmonious environment it lacked elsewhere, unified down to the last detail or, in the case of the "quadruple block," up to the entire neighborhood. His buildings embodied "a yearning for simplicity," he once wrote, a "search for quiet." Historian Vincent Scully observes that Wright's impetus toward unity was expressed in two opposite but very American ways: that emphasizing the permanence and stability that most men desire, seen in his solid blocklike forms which were sometimes massed as building cores; and that toward the movement, expansion and dispersal that typified the continent, stated in continuous trim, interpenetrating spaces, far-flung appendages and distant vistas. "In this synthesis of opposites," Scully concludes, "Wright's intention was to mesmerize the fragmented individual into a state of serenity and peace, the 'Great Peace' of sheltered but continuously expansive space to which he himself so often referred." Americans were restless but wanted roots, were adventuresome but approached the unknown cautiously, took risks to make money but were socially conservative, and were ruthless in business but loved their families. Somehow the prairie house embraced these behavior and value paradoxes in a symbolic, architectural and atmospheric synthesis that clients were able to grasp. This attempt at sense-making, at bringing simplicity out of confusion, at resolving conflicts among basic social values, made Wright's work especially comforting.

It is almost a commonplace that people who feel their institutions threatened sometimes elevate them to the highest moral plane, sanctifying them at precisely the moment they are least able to perform their traditional functions. Architectural historian Norris Kelly Smith has argued persuasively that certain aspects of Wright's work had the effect of sanctifying the family and its values. Exceptionally formal elements like the entrance hall of the 1893 William Winslow house, according to Smith, affirmed "the sacredness of hearth and home. . . . Behind a delicate wooden arcade, which carries with it something of the . . . flavor of a rood screen before an altar," is a fireplace alcove. Too large for everyday use, "it looks as if it were intended for the celebration of some solemn family ritual," Smith speculates, "affirming the sacramental nature of the institution of marriage." Other quasi-religious motifs concerned the matter of dining: "Wright consistently treats the occasion as if it were liturgical in nature," Smith observes. "His severely rectilinear furniture set squarely within a rectilinear context, makes these dining rooms seem . . . like stately council chambers. . . . They declare unequivocally that the unity of the group requires submission and conformity on the part of its members." A few of Wright's façades, furthermore, were precisely symmetrical, attesting to an exacting order and regularity for interior events. Even his infrequent use of these formal devices reveals his capacity for exalting certain family functions to the level of ritual and sacrament "in keeping," he wrote in the parlance of 1901, "with a high ideal of family life together."

Wright's flamboyant image obscures the fact that he was a product of Victorian America. Despite his futuristic architecture he was dedicated to preserving a pre-urban family. He was prefectly willing to provide it with startling new surroundings, not to change it in any fundamental way but to strengthen it against assault. Near the end of his life, in 1954 at age 87, he continued to speak nostalgically of the small-town family he himself had always believed ideal—

> Back in farm days there was but one big living room, a stove in it, and Ma was there cooking—looking after the children and talking to Pa—dogs and cats and tobacco smoke too—all gemütlich if all was orderly, but it seldom was; and the children were there playing around. It created a certain atmosphere of a domestic nature which had charm and which is not, I think, a good thing to lose altogether.

—a homey recapitulation of determining prairie-house characteristics: multifunctional interpenetrating spaces, an intimate atmosphere and family mutuality. Wright shared with other migrants to the city an inclination to protect the family from the real and imagined forces of disintegration rising from economic uncertainties and social reorganization in the new metropolis. Recreating the best of the past was as much his goal as anything else, and it was probably this familiar feeling, albeit in modern dress, that attracted his clients. With its occasional sanctification of the family; its provision for shelter, internal intimacy and group mutuality; its motifs of strength, security and durability; its dependence on familiar suburban and architectural standards; and its close association with nature and other cherished social and cultural values, the prairie house appealed to members of the upper middle class anxious about a way of life they had adopted but had not yet made their own.

COMMUNICATIONS

The
Telephone

SIDNEY H. ARONSON

Halbe Collection, the Kansas State Historical Society, Topeka

Central operator, Dorranee, Kansas, 1910

TECHNOLOGICAL ADVANCES OPENED UP ENTIRELY NEW OPPORTUNITIES for communication. "A Taste for Reading" and "The Penny Press," in the first volume of this anthology, detail how mass circulation dailies partially replaced books and pamphlets as the sources of ideas and news. New processes in printing and paper production that made newspapers more affordable were at the heart of this change. In the following account, Sidney Aronson details how Alexander Graham Bell's remarkable electrical toy found its own niche in the modern communication network.

When Bell invented the telephone, in March of 1876, the telegraph was the undisputed vehicle for passing information over distances. Telegraphic lines provided businesses with necessary data through the tickertape; automatic telegraphy permitted news to be transmitted to a number of places simultaneously; alarms used telegraphy to signal the location of fires. In fact, home signal boxes that translated Morse code were on the verge of bringing telegraphy into American households when Bell came up with something better.

In his effort to keep his financial backers interested while he worked out technical problems with his device, Bell first demonstrated his telephone by transmitting drama, music, and news, showing it as a commercial medium of entertainment. Later, Bell developed the switchboard and began to exploit the telephone as a superior tool for communicating. By 1878, Bell envisioned a system that could link by voice business offices in different cities and homes on opposite ends of the country.

A mass audience then had to be developed for the telephone. Although advertising circulars promoted the domestic advantage of being in instant communication with the grocer, butcher, and baker, it was businesses, not the domestic market, that paid the early expenses of telephone expansion. Americans quickly adopted the telephone as *the* means of communicating in business—and later accepted the telephone in domestic life—permitting the efficient transfer of information in far-flung enterprises as well as in rapidly suburbanizing cities.

THE TELEPHONE CAME TO AMERICA—and to the rest of the world—on March 10, 1876; on that day, as far as is known, Alexander Graham Bell became the first person to transmit speech electrically. The American response to that event included a mixture of wonder, confusion, and sheer disbelief. That spoken words could be converted into electrical waves, transmitted along wire, and then reconverted into sound at the other end of the line could not easily be comprehended even after the telephone had been widely described. Perhaps the best way to understand one of Graham Bell's incredulous contemporaries is to imagine how we would feel if we were told that a way had been devised to make extrasensory perception a means of communication.

Even after the telephone had been widely discussed and its principle had begun to be understood, for many the telephone—as remarkable as the idea seemed—had no obvious use. There is even evidence that some who should have known better did not immediately appreciate the possibilities of the amazing new device. Sometime in the late fall or winter of 1876–1877, Gardiner Greene Hubbard, Bell's future father-in-law and a partner in the telephone venture, offered to sell all the rights to the telephone patent to the Western Union Telegraph Company for $100,000. Western Union's president, William Orton, turned down that extraordinary opportunity to monopolize all electrical communications at a time when it had become customary for big business leaders to seek to dominate their entire industry. Orton apparently did not even think it was worth buying the patent just to keep the thing off the market. According to one of Bell's biographers, Orton dismissed the offer with the words, "What use could this company make of an electrical toy?" Thomas A. Watson, Bell's assistant, was disappointed at Western Union's rejection because he lost the chance to receive $10,000 for his share of ownership of the patent. This suggests that the future of the telephone was not evident from the mere fact of its invention, as $10,000 was a considerable sum in those days.

Furthermore, the officials of the British Post Office Department, who controlled the telegraph industry in England, also turned down the chance to purchase Bell's English patent.

Matthew Josephson, chronicler of the activities of the first generation of avaricious industrialists, attributed Western Union's blunder to "customary bureaucratic caution" and the reluctance to bear the considerable expense of substituting telephone equipment for the telegraph. Those reasons indeed suggest that Orton did not fully appreciate the telephone and that his legendary retort to the offer was shortsighted. He and his British counterparts were probably no different from most of those who grew up in the telegraph age and witnessed or read about one improvement in telegraphy after another. By 1876, it seemed that future developments would take place exponentially, as inventors who seemed to be congregated in Boston but were, of course, dispersed throughout the Western world were trying to strike it rich by adding to the techniques for instantaneously transmitting more and more messages. At the electrical shop of Charles Williams, Jr., on Court Street in Boston, a group of especially talented inventors, including Joseph B. Stearns, Thomas Edison, and Graham Bell himself, all vied at one time or another for the honor of making still another breakthrough in telegraphy that would bring a fortune.

What these and other inventors had devised by 1876 may help explain this initial indifference to Bell's invention by the telegraphists. By that year telegraphy had so developed that people were still marveling over a means of communication that had already been in operation for over forty years. Over 200 submarine cables had been laid and succeeded in making virtually every corner of the earth a link in a worldwide chain of communications. Direct service could be conducted by telegraph between points several thousand miles apart. Printing telegraphs recorded messages in Roman letters as early as 1841. The advantage of the telegraph over the telephone, as those who ran the telegraph industry saw it, was that telegraphy left a permanent record.

In 1876, a number of specialized telegraphs catered either to the public at large or to special interests. For example, telegraphs for financial and commercial offices provided investment houses and brokerage firms with the latest prices in stocks, gold, and merchandise printed on what came to be known as ticker tape. By that time, the fire alarm telegraph—first invented in 1851—was in use in seventy-five major cities and towns in the United States. Systems consisting of a series of locked signal boxes were placed at convenient intervals throughout a locality—New York City had 600—each containing a mechanism for transmitting a numerical signal along connecting telegraph lines that indicated which box had initiated the alarm. That device made it possible to dispatch fire-fighting equipment within a minute or two after the alarm. By 1871, W. B. Watkins improved the fire alarm telegraph so that the fire itself triggered the signal automatically. By 1870, district telegraphs, or signal boxes, were being placed in homes in virtually every major city in the United States and were connected telegraphically with a central station. By simply turning a crank at any hour of the day or night, a messenger or policeman could be instantly summoned or a fire alarm transmitted.

The speed of telegraph transmission was accelerating. Automatic telegraphy held the promise that the telegraph operator using a Morse instrument and painstakingly tapping out 25 words a minute would soon be eliminated by a set of devices that could send 800 words a minute. Automatic telegraphy also made it possible to send messages to many places simultaneously and was especially useful in sending large quantities of news in duplicate to various parts of the country.

One of the chief disadvantages of telegraphy was that a skilled operator had to decipher all messages; perhaps it does not sound too complicated a task to "read" Morse code, but it was generally regarded then as a highly skilled occupation. By 1874, however, autographic telegraphy—a process devised as early as 1848—allowed Americans to write a telegram on an ordinary piece of paper that could then be transferred to a metal plate for transmission. Some entrepreneurs expected that such a device would someday be placed in every American home and business.

Another disadvantage of the older means of communication was the limited capacity of the line. At first, telegraph wire could carry only one message in one direction at any one time. That limitation often meant telegrams were piled on tall mounds in telegraph offices, waiting hours to be sent and ultimately delivered. But the capacity of telegraph technology to transmit messages was continually improving as multiplexing allowed two or more messages to be transmitted simultaneously. The duplex telegraph, perfected around 1870, allowed operators at each end of a line to transmit simultaneously. Between 1871 and the time Alexander Graham Bell succeeded in transmitting speech over wire, Western Union used these methods to increase the working capacity of its lines by 25 percent, the equivalent of nearly 50,000 miles of wire at a fraction of the expense.

By 1876, the United States was criss-crossed by 214,000 miles of telegraph wire delivering 31,703,181 telegrams through 8,500 telegraph offices. Even these figures do not complete the story of the predominance of the telegraph, since they do not include telegraph companies organized for general commercial and business purposes, telegraph systems owned and operated by the various branches of the federal government, and municipal electric and police patrol systems. If all that were not enough, one of the most promising developments was the creation in 1877 of the Social Telegraph Association in Bridgeport, Connecticut. It installed instruments in subscribers' homes that could be connected, through a central switchboard, to one another so that subscribers could "speak" to one another through the Morse Code once they had been taught how. Those unwilling or unable to learn the Morse Code would simply have to wait for the autographic telegraph.

Bell himself, as well as his backers, for a time showed signs of being members in good standing of the society of telegraphists. This is not surprising because he discovered the telephone while working on the harmonic or musical telegraph. This device would have greatly increased the efficiency of telegraphy, since it would have permitted "thirty or forty messages . . . [to be] sent simultaneously" over the same wire.

Given the hold of telegraphy over communications in the America of 1876, it is not surprising that many could not see any immediate use for Bell's invention. The inventor and his backers thus faced the formidable task of inventing uses for the telephone and impressing them on others. What complicated that task is that many members of the public did not distinguish between the telephone and the telegraph, and when the terms were separated, the word telephone was often associated with the transmission of music. What further compounded the difficulty of finding uses for the telephone was the quality and character of the instrument in the early days of its existence.

In the experimental telephones used on March 10, 1876, when Bell first succeeded in talking to Watson over the telephone, the same mechanism was used alternately as a transmitter and as a receiver. Two-way conversation, however, could be done only on very short circuits. Furthermore, transmission and reception tended to be poor—in subsequent demonstrations it often did not work at all—and Bell decided to concentrate on developing the "membrane" telephone as a transmitter and the "iron-box" telephone as a receiver, with the result that sound was transmitted in one direction only. That limitation posed a serious problem for Bell. What possible use could there be for that kind of telephone—as extraordinary as it was— which would enable him and his backers to recoup their investment, let alone make money? How could such an instrument be made to pay off?

Bell's first attempts to deal with this problem can be seen in his early public lectures and demonstrations of the telephone. On May 10, 1876, at a meeting of the American Academy of Arts and Sciences in Boston, Bell disclosed his theory of the telephone and related something of its practice. Although he was not sufficiently confident to attempt the transmission of speech on his still primitive apparatus, he hinted about a possible use of the telephone. At that lecture he sent a telegraphic signal to a confederate who waited at a "telegraphic organ" in Bell's office at Boston University, a few doors away from the lecture hall. "To the astonishment of the audience" at the Academy, a box on the table emitted the melody "Old Hundred." At the Centennial Celebration of American Independence in Philadelphia in the summer of 1876, Bell left the judges and went to the other side of the exhibition hall where he had placed the transmitter. He proceeded to recite Hamlet's soliloquy verbatim. In his first telephonic transmission from Boston to New York in July 1876, Bell played "Yankee Doodle" on an organ and then asked the telegraph operator on the other end to name that tune.

Later that summer at the family home in Brantford, Ontario, Bell devised the "triple mouthpiece" to see if three persons could speak simultaneously over a single transmitter. Since the triple mouthpiece was relegated to the museum of phone fossils not long after it was devised, one may wonder what Bell had in mind. The answer seems to lie in the first use of the triple mouthpiece. Bell arranged for several performers in Brantford to sing into that curious device and to transmit their words and music a distance of several miles. Similarly, at a demonstration in Salem, Massachusetts, on February 12, 1877, Bell had Watson in Boston read the latest news from Washington.

The telephone's use to transmit music, drama, and news—what can now be called a radio concept of telephony—resulted from two sources. First, Bell and Watson had not yet sufficiently improved the telephone so that the same instrument could both transmit and receive effectively. That prevented Bell from putting the telephone into immediate commercial use doing what he intended it to do: to make conversation possible for people who were at a distance from one another. The demonstrations described—with the exception of the one in Salem—were done before the problem of two-way communication over long circuits was satisfactorily resolved. Yet Bell was under pressure to produce profits for his impatient backers, and he may have seen entertainment and enlightenment before paying assembled audiences as the immediate practical use of the telephone until such time as "long-distance" talks could be perfected.

Although Bell and Watson succeeded in improving the telephone so that they could hold a satisfactory two-way conversation by October 9, 1876, Bell continued to give radio-like performances. The reason was that Bell's years as an inventor had left him without a comfortable income. Demonstrating the telephone before large audiences would serve both to popularize the telephone and raise badly needed cash. Bell and Watson thus perfected the art of transmitting music, drama, and enlightenment, as Rosario Tosiello has amply documented.

The "lecture performances" began early in 1877; they lasted between two and two-and-a-half hours. Introduced by a prominent member of the community, Bell lectured on electricity and demonstrated his several instruments. Then he signalled for music—usually by telegraph in the early lectures because he did not yet trust the telephone as the sole means of intercommunication—and Watson, located at a distance from the lecture hall, would play the organ. His repertoire included popular, religious, and patriotic favorites such as "America," "Hail Columbia," and "Killarney." Then Bell and Watson would attempt a conversation. Watson would shout sentences such as "How do you do?", "What Do You Think of the Telephone?", and "Good Evening." For the more discriminating New York audiences, Bell engaged a professional singer, but the singer, who was reluctant to put his lips close to the transmitter, did not project his voice as well as Watson. In May of 1877, the opera singer Signor Brignoli sang selections over the telephone from the stage of a theater in Providence for transmission to Boston. Occasionally there was a brass band or a cornetist of renown. Seminar discussions, the state of the weather, the time of the day, and newspaper dispatches were also carried over the telephone. In April of 1877, another radio-type feature was added to the format of Bell's performances when Watson, situated in Middletown, Connecticut, transmitted his shouts, songs, and conversations to Skiff's Opera House in New Haven and to Robert's Opera House in Hartford—shades of the radio network.

It would be interesting to know what sense audiences made of these demonstrations; beyond the descriptions of their amazement and wonder, there is little information about the possible uses they attributed to the telephone. That Elisha Gray, who later claimed priority in the invention of the telephone, also took to the lecture circuit in 1877 to demonstrate his device may have added to any lingering confusion about the telephone, for Gray's telephone could not transmit articulate speech and could only be used to carry music over telegraph wire.

During his performances, Alexander Graham Bell never lost sight of the primary use of the telephone; he always set aside some time for the discussion of its future. He told his audience that he envisioned a central office system wherein telephones in various locations could be connected by means of a "switch." Soon rapid improvements in the quality of telephone transmission and reception, as well as the appropriation of the switchboard from telegraphy, made that prediction seem absolutely prophetic. These advances allowed Bell to be even more discerning. In a letter he wrote on March 25, 1878, to the "Capitalists of the Electric Telephone Company," a group organized to develop his invention in Britain, it was obvious that he had already conceived the true character of the telephone system:

> It is conceivable that cables of telephone wires could be laid underground, or suspended overhead, communicating by branch wires with private dwellings, country houses, shops, manufactories, etc., etc., uniting them through the main cable with a central office where the wire could be connected as desired, establishing direct communication between any two places in the city. Such a plan as this, though, impracticable at the present moment, will, I firmly believe, be the outcome of the introduction of the telephone to the public. Not only so, but I believe in the future wires will unite the head offices of the Telephone Company in different cities, and a man in one part of the country may communicate by word of mouth with another in a different place.

If Bell's vision of the future was prophetic, magazine and newspaper writers (surely among the better informed members of the public) were still not sure of its purpose and did not always distinguish between the telegraph and the telephone. Thus, *Frank Leslie's Illustrated Newspaper* in the summer of 1876 referred to Bell's device as an "electric speaking trumpet." A *Puck* cartoon of April 1877 placed the telephone at the front door suggesting that the magazine had confused the new device with a speaking tube. In a subsequent issue, *Puck* pictured a telephone connection consisting of a speaking tube extending beneath the Atlantic Ocean from Europe to New York. By December 1, 1877, *Puck* was improving its conception of the telephone although it was still drawn as a speaking tube. Moreover, the radio concept of telephony persisted. The *Boston Transcript* of July 18, 1876, speculated about the "wonderful results which are sure to follow" the improvements in "telegraphy" brought about by Bell's invention: "But if the human voice can now be sent over the wire, and so distinctly that when two or three known parties are telegraphing, the voice of each can be recognized, we may soon have distinguished men delivering speeches in Washington, New York or London, and audiences assembled in Music Hall or Faneuil Hall to listen."

Nature, on August 24, 1876, also associated Bell's telephone with what later became radio. Remarking on Bell's "notable improvement" on the electric telegraph, the article predicted that at some future date it would be possible to

> at a distance, repeat on one or more pianos the air played by a similar instrument at the point of departure. There is a possibility here . . . of a curious use of electricity. When we are going to have a dancing party, there will be no need to provide a musician. By paying a subscription to an enterprising individual who will, no doubt, come forward to work this vein, we can have from him a waltz, a quadrille, or a galop, just as we desire. Simply turn a bell handle, as we do the cock of a water or gas pipe and we shall be supplied with what we want. Perhaps our children may find the thing simple enough.

Gradually the concept of the "speaking" or "talking" telephone took hold, and notions about usage changed accordingly. The first telephones were installed between two places such as home and office and were known as "private lines." Under that arrangement a telephone subscriber could call only one other "party." By June 30, 1877, when the telephone was little more than a year old, 230 telephones were in use; by July that figure rose to 750 and by the end of August to 1,300. These were mainly substitutes for telegraph instruments used to communicate between two points. The telephone was becoming more popular, doubtlessly because it eliminated the necessity for the skilled telegraphist on private lines, but it was not too different from the previously existing system of private telegraph lines.

Even the introduction of the central office, which paved the way for modern telephony by breaking through the severe limitations of private lines, did not at first change usage. The first experimental telephone exchange was in operation in Boston on May 17, 1877, and connected Brewster, Bassett and Company, bankers, the Shoe and Leather Bank, and the Charles Williams Company. These "stations" were repeatedly interconnected, and many conversations were held.

Despite the operational success of that system, E. T. Holmes, who held the license to operate the telephone business in Boston, was not immediately aware of the most profitable use of the central exchange. Holmes did proceed to build a central office at which subscribers' lines terminated, but instead of providing customers with the opportunity to talk to one another, he used the system to receive orders which he retransmitted to a general express agency. Making money that way seemed to be assured, and it was along that line that the telephone was first developed in Boston.

Holmes was not the only one who used the telephone this way; it also seemed ideally suited for district telegraph systems, which were connected telegraphically to subscribers' homes and were used by the latter to summon a messenger. Although some district telegraph companies resisted substituting a telephone for a telegraph, others took to the new instrument. For example, in March 1878, the American District Telegraph Company of Missouri discontinued renting telegraphic signal boxes at $12 per year and instead rented telephones at $20 a year. The subscriber of a district *telephone* company found that he could not only call a central office for a messenger or other related service but he could also speak to other subscribers on the same line.

Early in 1878, the Bell Telephone Company directed its agents to urge district telegraph companies to switch to the telephone on grounds that they were logical places for establishing a central exchange system. By September, however, Hubbard was encouraging telephonic central exchange systems instead of district systems, for he had come to see the telephone system as distinct from the district telegraph and feared that the latter would retard the achievement of his goal of interconnecting all telephone subscribers.

If any single event deserves credit for demonstrating the value of exchange service and the utility of the telephone as a means of prompt communication, it was a railway accident at Tariffville, Connecticut, in January 1878. The first news of the disaster was wired to the Western Union office in Hartford, urging that as many surgeons as possible be sent. Fortunately, Isaac D. Smith, the proprietor of the Capitol Avenue Drug Store in Hartford, had obtained an agency of the New England Telephone Company in July 1877 and used it to organize a central telephone system whose subscription list was made up primarily of doctors and a livery stable. By November 1877, Smith had twenty-one subscribers who could all call one another on request.

On the night of the accident, the Western Union operator in Hartford immediately telegraphed Isaac Smith's drug store with news of the accident and relayed the plea for the doctors. The clerk, in turn, telephoned the twenty-one physicians, called the livery stable for an express wagon, and packed it with bandages, morphine, chloroform, and other first-aid equipment. Meanwhile the doctors were rushed to Tariffville by special train. This was the first example of the benefits that the telephone and the exchange system could provide in a catastrophe, and press coverage aroused public interest in the invention and its applications.

But the events of the Tariffville accident did not necessarily suggest to ordinary Americans to what use *they* could put Bell's marvel. It may be obvious now when the telephone often seems to be an appendage to the mouth and ear how many different uses (and misuses) it has, but those living in the telegraph age had to learn them. To convince Americans that they needed the telephone, they first had to be taught *how* to use the telephone and what to use it for. Although many of the lessons were taught informally by a flood of favorable articles in newspapers and magzines, it should come as no surprise that American entrepreneurs who took control of the business decided to advertise the new medium's possibilities.

The campaign began modestly and concentrated more on the "how" than on the "what for." In May 1877, Bell and his partners distributed a circular assuring the reader that using a telephone was not difficult: "Conversation can be easily carried on after slight practice and with occasional repetition of a word or sentence." Since the owners decided they would sell service only and retain title to the instruments, the circular referred to the uses of the phone only indirectly in connection with the costs for renting the telephones. "The terms for leasing two Telephones," the circular read, "for social purposes connecting a dwelling house with any other building will be $20 a year, for business purposes $40 a year, payable semiannually in advance." Thus, two broad categories of telephone usage were set forth. In a circular issued April 26, 1879, by the National Bell Telephone Company—a predecessor of the American Telephone and Telegraph Company—"social or club purposes" were defined as being "for use between residences . . . for social purposes exclusively" designed to serve neighborhood groups. Just how the telephone was to serve neighborhood groups was left to the imagination.

On October 27, 1877, a circular issued by a Bell licensee, Ponton's Telephone Central Service of Titusville, Pennsylvania, added a new aspect to the teaching of telephone usage. By that time, the exchange system was operating, and it was time to get people to shift from the private line to central service. Thus, Ponton's circular read:

> The system is extremely simple. All parties who wish to adopt to it must have a separate wire from their house, office, factory, hotel, store, bank or restaurant to a central switch room, where any one wire can instantaneously be connected with any other wire. Supposing that one hundred persons adopt this system, and that the average length of each wire is half a mile, it would give each person the privilege of using fifty miles of wire at less cost than it could be done with only one mile in the private line.

Then the circular described explicitly what a telephone connected to a central office could do for the subscriber. "In domestic life," it stated, "the telephone can put the user in instant communication with the grocer, butcher, baker." The circular went on to list 176 other occupations "and other places and persons too numerous to mention."

The American public did not always find these advertising appeals irresistible; in fact, the Ponton Company was out of business by January 1878. But the exchange did better in the larger cities and towns, perhaps because of the greater familiarity in such localities with the latest in telegraph technology. The district telegraph or messenger services had been used by many businessmen and had, moreover, educated others in the concept of the central office. Furthermore, as early as August 1867, a telegraph exchange was installed in Philadelphia and connected private telegraph wires through a central office. The subscribers to this system of intercommunication were the largest banking houses in that city and numbered fifty by 1872. The business of such central telegraph offices— New York had its first in 1869—was chiefly to report to each bank (by means of printing telegraphs) its daily debit and credit balance and to repeat to any bank messages received for it by wire from other banks. The wires of any two banks desiring communication, however, could also be connected together at a switch. Thus, the idea of intercommunication in telegraphy had begun to replace the concept of the telegraphed message.

American businessmen were beginning to learn the value of exchange *telephone* service; the directors of the *telegraphic* exchange companies began to replace the Morse instruments with telephones as early as 1878, and their subscribers started speaking to one another. Telephone exchanges were widely introduced in 1878—the same year Alexander Graham Bell told the British that they were not yet practicable—and quickly became an aid to commerce. They enabled conversation between points over distances "not exceeding 20 miles," a distance within which many, if not most, of one's business associates were located. The telegraph, with all its improvements, became a cumbrous means of communication compared to the telephone; confidence replaced the incredulity with which the business community had first regarded the telephone.

In its first decades, the telephone tended to be the monopoly of businessmen not only because they often simply substituted it for a telegraph, but also because they could afford AT&T's high rates better than most other Americans. At that time the Bell Company concentrated on the business community probably because company officials were still somewhat influenced by concepts that governed the telegraph industry; these saw that medium primarily as an aid to commerce and had given little priority to social telegraphy. Bell's bias toward businesses can be seen, for example, in the sixteen advertising appeals in its *National Telephone Directory* of 1897, which listed all subscribers connected to the long-distance lines. Half the advertisements were directed at the business community; the remainder could appeal to any user of the telephone.

The extent to which businessmen filled the ranks of telephone subscribers is also seen in the six-page Pittsburgh telephone directory of 1879; of the 300 telephones it listed, all but six were installed in business concerns. Even the six residential telephones were used for business rather than social purposes, since they belonged to anxious entrepreneurs who felt the need to keep in constant touch with their establishments.

In many other places practically all subscribers were businessmen. Tullahoma, Tennessee, had nine telephones in 1897; one was a public station, two were residential phones, two were connected to banks, one to a hotel, one to a flour mill, one to a factory, and one to a Western Union office. In that same year, Pawtucket, Rhode Island, had a total of 161 telephones in service; 3 were public phones, 25 were connected to municipal offices including police, fire, and school departments, 115 were business and professional phones, and only 16 were in residences. Two additional phones were connected to the homes of the chief of police and the commissioner of public works. Thus, only 11 percent of the phones in Pawtucket were residential, a pattern characteristic of the rest of the country.

This distribution suggests that most calls at that time were not retail orders from the public to retail establishments but were calls made from one business-man to another. Most communities had public telephones, however, and prac-tically every exchange had one or more offices at which nonsubscribers could make calls for ten to fifteen cents. Nonsubscribers could also use the telephone at a local drugstore where telephone use was free. In May 1879, D. M. Finley, a businessman in Providence, Rhode Island, advertised that he was the "first plumber and coal dealer whose establishment had been connected with the new telephone wires and that householders wanting coal the same day as ordered might telephone to the dealer from Mr. Leith's drug store."

The early history of telephone usage, then, is largely the story of how com-mercial and professional communities adopted the new means of communica-tion. That topic in itself could fill volumes, and only a few highlights of that usage can be suggested. At a time when raising money quickly and quietly was the key to corporate empire building, the telephone was ideally suited to the needs of the "robber barons"; it was simple to operate and left no written record, a decided advantage when the message often involved the violation of laws and values against monopolies. Banker George W. Perkins, an associate of J. P. Morgan, originated the "Perkins Plan" of "rapid transit telephony" in which a list of ten to thirty men were phoned in succession as quickly as the operator could reach them.

In the organization of industrial and manufacturing activities, the telephone's uses seemed unlimited. Factories installed internal telephone systems enabling the main office to keep in touch with shop foremen. Once long-distance service was available (development was underway by 1881), the main office could learn almost instantly the condition of any order in a main branch or factory. In the raising of skyscrapers, temporary wire was commonly strung vertically along the elevator shaft so that the architect on the ground could confer with a foreman sitting astride a girder hundreds of feet in the air, a system obviously superior to the whistles and messengers that had been previously used.

One of the first historians of the telephone, Herbert Casson, wrote: "To give New York the seven million electric lights that have abolished night in that city requires twelve private exchanges and 512 telephones." Casson was referring to the way those who directed the flow of traffic for power companies super-vised the distribution of electricity. In 1879, the Pennsylvania Railroad became the first railroad to install a telephone; by 1910, its own private telephone system had 175 exchanges, 400 operators, 13,000 phones, and 20,000 miles of wire. By the beginning of the twentieth century, the telephone was an intercom-munications system for a number of large-scale construction projects involving earthwork over extensive areas. In the construction of the Panama Canal and in reclamation projects for watering the arid regions of the West, an appropriate local telephone service was found to facilitate the handling of men and mate-rials. The infant telephone industry benefited from an 1877 Pennsylvania law that required the several hundred anthracite coal mines to have some means of oral communication between the interior and the surface.

In areas such as those surrounding developed water power, where the operation of factories, street car lines, and lights depended on electric power transmitted from a distance, the necessity of avoiding interruption was great. Defective conditions could be promptly reported and remedied if a telephone line was installed parallel to the power lines.

The telephone was also regarded as a boon for both the vacation industry and the tired executive who would have been reluctant to take a vacation in the pretelephonic age. Thus, the Special Census of Telephones of 1907 reported: "The last few years have seen such an extension of telephone lines through the various summer resort districts of the country that it has become practicable for businessmen to leave their offices for several days at a time and yet keep in close touch with their offices."

The role of the telephone in the hotel industry is especially interesting. Before its invention, the hotel depended exclusively on the messenger to satisfy the requests of its guests and to deliver instructions and receive information from employees stationed on each floor. When a guest wanted service he could signal a messenger who would have to make two trips, one to learn what the guest wanted and one to provide it. Under these circumstances the elevators and stairways were crowded with bell hops, and hotels had to employ many messengers. By 1900, practically every large and medium-sized hotel and many small hotels had telephones in every guest room. These provided for the interior needs of the hotel and also gave access to the local and long-distance lines. Hotels were able to make money on the charges received from customers.

By 1909, the hundred largest hotels in New York City had 21,000 telephones—nearly as many as the continent of Africa and more than Spain—which were averaging six million calls annually. The telephone system of the Waldorf-Astoria with 1,120 telephones and 500,000 calls a year (1904) constituted the largest concentration of telephones under one roof in the world. The guests of this American hotel used the telephone service freely but not for free; during the first month of the Waldorf-Astoria's installation, the business amounted to 30,000 calls exclusive of those made within the hotel.

The telephone was so important to business, commerce, and industry then that the fortunes of any Bell agency depended on proximity to concerns that could use the new medium. In the first few years, the Pacific Coast territory was a smaller field for telephonic development than the East Coast, because there were fewer manufacturing establishments or other concerns requiring communications between an office and the place where the work was actually being conducted. But if that meant little business for Bell agents in areas with few industries, businessmen's demands for the telephone in other places were greater than Bell's capacity to manufacture telephones; the company had a problem supplying instruments as early as 1877 and 1878.

The rapid inroads of the telephone into the industrial and commercial worlds reduced the cost of service and started the trend toward a telephone in every American home. Further, many new "independent" companies entered the telephone industry when Bell patents expired in 1894. As a consequence, the telephone became widely available to women and adolescents—two groups who, according to telephone folklore, distinguished themselves as talkers. Women could use the home phone for shopping, but the housewife did not always have to take the initiative in the new practice of shopping by telephone. In some localities, grocers would call their customers every morning to take the day's orders. Big-city department stores placed telephones at counters and advertised the telephone service that allowed a patron to call the salesman, who could generally perform the same services involved in a sale conducted across the counter.

Even small business owners, such as cobblers, cleaners, and laundresses, considered the telephone service necessary for keeping in touch with customers and reducing the amount of idle time. With early introduction of the private branch exchange in 1879, a separate line did not have to be run from the telephone company's exchange to every department in the store. Instead, a small switchboard, built and operated much like a central-office switchboard and attended by an operator, received all incoming calls and fed them to the appropriate department.

Although the telephone company early distinguished between business and social uses of the phone, it was vague about the nature of the purely social. Even shopping by phone does not clearly belong to that category since that always involved someone in business. Interestingly enough, Bell himself had a clear conception of an important social use of the telephone; he suggested during his lectures of 1877 that his invention would enable people to socialize at a distance. The time would come, he predicted, when Mrs. Smith would spend an hour with Mrs. Brown "very enjoyably in cutting up Mrs. Robinson" over the telephone; connection between the two women would be made possible by means of a central switching office. With the widespread diffusion of the telephone after 1894, such a use of the phone became commonplace.

Even with the advent of the independent telephone companies, the high cost of urban commercial service restricted it to the well-to-do. As early as 1882, a residential phone cost $150 a year in New York and $100 in Chicago, Philadelphia, and Boston. These initially high charges were to become even higher in the 1890s as improvements in telephone technology and the growth of the number of subscribers drove costs up. In some urban areas, the high rates frequently brought complaints. They were beyond the means of the average factory worker as well as the white collar employee.

But the *use* of a telephone was certainly not limited to the affluent. In its early days, as we have noted, some establishments such as banks and drugstores offered free telephone use to their customers. By the end of the century, the pay telephone was well established. In 1902, of the 2,315,000 telephones in the United States 81,000 (3½ percent) were "nickel-in-the-slot" (more accurately three nickels) phones. Most inhabited places in the United States had at least one public station, and in the larger cities and towns these might be found in every conceivable retail establishment from liquor stores to fish markets, from real estate offices to undertakers' parlors. Above all, the public phone was found in drugstores; although it would be impossible to tell whether every drugstore had a pay phone, it would not be far from the truth. Finally, those who had no phone might have a neighbor who would permit them to use it.

In discussing early patterns of telephone usage, we should take further note of what has been called the radio concept of telephony. Alexander Graham Bell gave up his idea of the telephone as a commercial medium of entertainment and enlightenment when he solved the problem of reciprocal communication over distances, but the concept developed just the same and in a number of ways. In many communities the first to transmit news were not professional reporters or broadcasters but the telephone operators themselves. It is likely that in the role of informal broadcasters, operators illustrated the possibilities of the telephone. By the time increased telephone traffic made it impossible for them to continue that service, it was relatively easy for the enterprising to see the direction that a new medium might take.

Thus, in the telephone's early days, the operators were accustomed to giving news about crises like fires and floods, missing persons reports, man-wanted bulletins, crimes, and so forth. Some of the information was of interest only to certain subscribers. For example, operators often took calls requesting the services of particular doctors who were out making home visits. These doctors would then "call in" for their messages.

The nature of telephone technology in its early days allowed the operator to eavesdrop. That obviously made it easier for her to cover her beat as a newscaster, but it also gave telephony one of its enduring characteristics—the absence of privacy.

Once it had become customary for operators to inform individual subscribers about local events, the latter came to feel that they had the right to receive such information when they called Central. The newscasting service of the operator started in city exchanges in the early days of telephony and then spread to the farm after 1894 when the independents and farmers' cooperative lines brought the telephone to rural America. The country operator continued to perform these services even after the introduction of radio, though it relieved much of the pressure to do so.

The radio concept of telephony ultimately took the form of the "telephone-newspaper," introduced in Budapest, Hungary, in 1898. . . . The telephone newspaper broadcast news, music, and theatrical performances. Similar telephone-newspapers were established in the United States. In Philadelphia, for example, the Bell Telephone Company arranged with the newspaper the *North American* for operators to give callers news summaries at any hour of the day and night.

Before long, in the larger cities and towns the large numbers of subscribers and the small number of operators made it virtually impossible to provide the personal service that continued to be rendered in rural regions. Company officials were aware of the changing nature of urban telephony as it grew, but they found it impractical to continue the previous kind of service. Increasing complexity, the size of the traffic, the nature of the equipment, as well as operating arrangements for handling the load demanded more formality in managing the calls. Furthermore, customers gradually came to regard telephone employees as impersonal representatives of the industry and to judge the service on a less personal basis than was customary in smaller localities. In cities most calls involved little of the unusual, and the main consideration was prompt, accurate handling. There was no need for the operator to comment or to raise questions. The customer's major requirement of the operator was an attentive and pleasing attitude. At times, of course, a more individual approach to the urban subscriber was required, but these were only a small percentage of all calls and were well within the capacity of an obliging operator. These involved requests for charges on toll calls, reports of service troubles, and emergency calls such as fires, accidents, and burglaries. They also included long-distance calls, especially those in which there was difficulty in locating the called parties.

The process of urban telephony's development thus depersonalized the service from the standpoint of the operator's acquaintance with the individual subscriber. This made it possible for her to sense urgency on any call while it also discouraged customers from seeking preferential treatment from an operator who had come to know them better. Nor was it easy for some customers to get acquainted with the operators and thus to make greater claims than less friendly subscribers. Thus, all calls and callers had to be treated alike, and it is reasonable to expect that since the operators could not, in most cases, know the importance of a particular call, they tended to handle each call as though it were urgent. This businesslike sense of urgency for each call contrasted with the situation in rural places where the operator not only could tell how pressing each call was—and therefore placed some before others—but also knew which callers merited personal consideration.

The tremendous growth in the number of subscribers connected to urban switchboards—the Cortlandt exchange in New York City had 5,000 lines in use in 1890 and 9,000 by 1900—obviously transformed the character of a job that had once provided much satisfaction for genial and helpful young women. In 1912, Caroline Crawford studied telephone operators in Boston and concluded that making connections at the switchboard was difficult. That operation required "constant employment of the muscles of the eye in different directions [and] constant use of the optic nerve." The ear, too, she asserted, "is obliged . . . to distinguish between a number of different voices, to ascertain at once, so as to avoid repetition, the number asked for, no matter how indistinctly or ill-pronounced the number may be; this necessitates constant alertness of the auditory nerve; while the vocal organs are scarcely less constantly in use in answering calls and such conversations as may be necessary." Under such circumstances and the pressure to complete 200 calls per hour, Crawford concluded that work in an exchange involved a tremendous strain upon the "mental constitution as well as upon the nervous system."

Crawford found particularly objectionable the job of the "allnight" operators. They went on duty at 7 P.M. and worked until midnight; they would then sleep on a cot in a rest room of the exchange until 6 A.M. when they returned to the switchboard for an hour. That really was not a six-hour day, according to Crawford, because "it is understood that their sleep may be interrupted whenever the number of calls becomes abnormal." Also reprehensible was the fact that the two girls—who might be no older than seventeen—who paired up at night in the exchange were locked up alone. "Think a little," Crawford wrote, "about what might happen while they are there." Also offensive were the "tests" or "listening in" of supervisors—often officious college graduates—regarded by the company as necessary to see that the operators attended strictly and efficiently to their duties. It had the opposite effect, according to Crawford, since it deadened the connection and subjected the operator to much extra strain. Furthermore, the tests overlooked the need of the operator to use "phrases not in the 'ritual,'" especially when talking to foreigners. Yet they were reproved for the slightest deviation from the set of words prescribed for them. Thorstein Veblen, the sociologist-critic of large-scale organizations such as the telephone company, later referred to such strict and self-defeating adherence to bureaucratic rules as "trained incapacity."

Crawford completes her critique of the working conditions of the operators by noting the frequent confrontation with subscribers who accused the operator of not working diligently to complete calls, of supervisors' incessant pressures to "hurry, hurry," of the difficulty of getting relief to go to the lavatory or to get a drink of water, and of bearing heavy apparatus on her chest. But perhaps the unkindest cut of all was the "split trick" which divided the operators' work time between two parts of the day and which involved either an extra carfare or the alternative of loafing around the city. Crawford cited the opinion of social workers who "say that a very real danger for girls lies in 'killing time' at the moving picture shows." Parts of the indictment were later repeated, and the frequent turnover of operators was later a major problem for the telephone company. . . .

Although this chapter has focused on usage, the more complicated and intriguing question is that of the impact of the telephone. Are we justified in assuming that the telephone actually changed the character of American society, that we are different because of it, and that the differences between a society that has an effective telephone system and one that does not are as great as those between literate and preliterate societies? But those are different questions that no doubt will receive their deserved attention now that social scientists have discovered the telephone, almost 100 years after Alexander Graham Bell did.

The
Department Store

GUNTHER BARTH

Macy's opening day, New York City, 1904

THE FOLLOWING SELECTION describes how the creation of the department store
turned shopping into a major leisure-time activity—a kind of new social art—
particularly for American women. Gunther Barth explains that the department store
grew along with the modern city and could not have existed without the enlarged retail
market, the improved communications systems, and the new building technology that
all developed late in the nineteenth century. The city brought together large numbers of
people, all of whom needed clothing, houseware, and other dry goods. The growth of
cities brought new means of mass transportation that allowed even more people access
to markets; it made possible the modern newspaper that refined advertising, and finally,
it accommodated new and larger buildings that could store and display vast quantities
of merchandise under a single roof.

The primary beneficiaries of the new department stores were women. Shopping was
a form of emancipation that enabled them to escape the incessant chores of their

homes. Shrewd department store owners tried to make shopping enjoyable by offering relaxation, luxury, service, and magnificence. The happier customers in turn stayed longer, and presumably bought more. The women benefitted psychologically, because the department store treated every female customer like a "lady." Unlike in the small urban specialty shops, all goods were openly displayed and easily accessible. All prices were clearly marked—there was no haggling, so no one was embarrassed to discover that an intended purchase was too expensive. Also, the store provided a range of services that made the customer feel important and valued—guarantees, credit, and special facilities such as restrooms, reading rooms, and nurseries. At the same time, the store made all women feel equal. Less affluent shoppers gained status simply by sharing a counter with more prosperous shoppers and by receiving the same treatment from clerks.

Perhaps most significant, the department store accentuated the importance of shopping by intensifying desire. Customers saw the latest and most fashionable goods on display; they saw what other people were buying and what society defined as desirable. Even people on the street could look into the massive plate glass windows and be persuaded to buy. The store also stimulated shopping by creating the "fashion cycle," the annual and seasonal changes of merchandise that created the desire to be up to date. In summary, Barth presents the department store as a stage set in which city dwellers came to act as discriminating shoppers, roles that utilized countless hours of newly available leisure time.

"HANGING ON THE SKIRTS, very literally, of indecision," a small boy wearily trailed his aunt through the splendor of the "ladies' great shop" in New York City in the early 1850's. Five stories high, A. T. Stewart's magnificent Marble Palace "bravely waylaid custom" on the Chambers Street corner of Broadway. It regularly interrupted aunt and nephew on their way home from a dentist's office on Wall Street, confronting them with displays of fashionable life familiar to the boy from reading *Godey's Lady's Book*, the first American women's magazine, while waiting his turn in the dentist's chair. Shopping gave his aunt "the familiar Stewart headache from the prolonged strain of selection" and exposed him to "the enjoyment of our city as down-towny as possible," Henry James recalled in his old age. Their experience reflected some of the impact of a new urban institution, the department store, on the residents of the modern city.

The modern city, providing the economic incentive and the physical setting for new enterprise, produced the department store. The city stimulated the expansion of the retail market, improved communications systems, and generated a new building technology. Swept along by the tide of progress, residents steadily expanded the range of their consumption beyond food and material for clothing; the ambience of the large city encouraged many people of modest affluence to aspire to an air of solid comfort, if not luxury. Changing life-styles engendered a new pattern of urban life. Making money absorbed men, while women sought to realize their growing expectations through the purchase of household furnishings, ready-made clothes, children's toys, and other fashionable goods. These new desires took all sorts of women into the heart of the city,

THE DEPARTMENT STORE   By Gunther Barth. From *City People: The Rise of Modern City Culture in Nineteenth-Century America*. Copyright © 1980 by Oxford University Press, Inc. Reprinted by permission.

hastening the emergence of a new kind of store, one that displayed conveniently a large variety of goods under one roof and served shoppers obligingly.

The department store was the focal point for a novel form of downtown life. Its imposing appearance lent dignity to other, smaller shops that had gained a foothold among wholesale establishments and warehouses, hotels and churches, banks and offices. Its alluring presentation of merchandise attracted legions of women. Horsecars, trolleys, and cable cars facilitated the invasion of what had been—with the exception of a trip to church on Sundays, an occasional visit to a dentist, or a carriage ride to the theater—predominantly the austere world of draymen, clerks, merchants, lawyers, and bankers.

The palace of merchandise towered over the parade of pedestrians and the lines of streetcars that discharged women on the sidewalks skirting it. Coachmen and cab drivers quickly recognized that the curb in front of the main entrance had a special significance for their passengers. It was the starting point for a successful shopping spree and the best place to pick up returning customers carrying bags and bundles. These activities projected some of the order and safety of the store interior onto the sidewalk, reassuring those women who felt ill at ease in the hustle of porters and messengers or under the stare of loafers and workmen. The extravagant size of the plate-glass display windows also bestowed an aura of security and splendor upon the downtown streets, making the clean, smooth sidewalks into a woman's world—even though the glass might be "easily shivered by a boy's marble or a snowball," as Philip Hone feared when he first saw Stewart's Marble Palace in 1846. . . .

The social dynamics of the modern city in the United States generated the momentum that brought the full-fledged department store into existence. This store not only sold great varieties of goods, constantly advertised in newspapers and conveniently displayed in an impressive building, but also served large numbers of women from all segments of society and made the presence of women a distinct attribute of the downtown section of the modern city. . . .

The department store made the new phenomenon of a feminine public possible. Its rise accompanied that of the modern city. In New York, which, with one million inhabitants, offered the largest department store market, in the 1860's and 1870's, the department stores that emerged during these two decades still accounted for almost half of the city's leading department stores a century later. The department store thrived on the concentrated urban markets that clamored for goods and on the industrial sector of the American economy, which eagerly sought new outlets for its products. It brought about the decline of many small retail shops that could not keep up with the systematic marketing of goods on a large scale. Railroad lines and urban transit speeded the flow of merchandise as well as the movement of people from their homes to stores that sold inexpensive products. The advance in building technology provided practical as well as lofty structures that permitted spacious displays and attracted attention as expressions of that boundless energy generated by the modern city. Slowly the metropolitan press became the primary medium for the advertisements of the department store.

In 1846, an anonymous pamphlet directed attention to the new mode of doing business in New York. Its author considered the kind of organizational genius and executive ability which A. T. Stewart represented indicative of "the paramount tendency of the age . . . to systematize." A commercial house, with "several heads properly organized, may divide its labor into various departments of buying, selling, and management," the author explained, and "become perfect in its adaptedness." In his view, Stewart carried out "what must be apparent to every reflecting mind the proper plan of business—to render a Dry Goods store a grand magazine." In the following year, *Hunt's Merchants' Magazine* expressed admiration for the departmental organization of a Philadelphia dry goods store which had perfected the new form of business organization. The management of any firm along departmental lines created "a beautiful thoroughness" that "is becoming more and more part of our national character," *Putnam's Monthly* stated in 1853.

The American national character, only vaguely defined in the first place and now being modified by the impact of large waves of immigrants, encouraged and accommodated new methods of selling and buying. "We are so busy in improving what the Past has bequeathed to us, that we forget we owe it anything," *Harper's* "Easy Chair" explained in 1854. The expansion of merchandise beyond the conventional limits of a dry goods store was accepted readily by New Yorkers who, accustomed to thinking of their city as a great clothing emporium fed by ready-to-wear factories, put everything "used for covering the human body" into the category of dry goods.

Although the sale of dry goods provided the start for most department stores, in some instances other products made up the core of the merchandise. A few major department stores developed from jewelry, crockery, and hardware shops, such as E. J. Lehmann's Fair in Chicago in 1875. At times a department store emerged because retailing on a big scale in a magnificent building seemed the most profitable way to use a downtown lot or a large structure. The Emporium in San Francisco grew out of a real estate speculation when first developed in 1896.

The extension of the circle of customers to include women from all walks of life occurred as a matter of course. The practice of calling any woman who might buy something from a merchant a "lady" coincided with the rise of new businessmen in the modern city. In 1825, A. T. Stewart, fresh from Belfast, offered his goods "for sale to the Ladies of New York" in the *Daily Advertiser*. With this extension of the term went the egalitarian assumptions that began to shape the relationships among customers in a store. "Testify no impatience if a servant-girl, making a six penny purchase, is served before you," Miss Leslie's *Behaviour Book* counseled in the 1850's. "In all American stores, the rule of 'first come, first served,' is rigidly observed."

In the late 1840's and early 1850's, women "squeezing toward the counter of the last new emporium" represented a familiar sight in the changing downtown scene. In his editorial accompanying the opening of Stewart's Marble Palace in 1846, *Herald* editor James Gordon Bennet stressed that "as long as the ladies continue to constitute an important feature of the community, the dry goods business must be in a flourishing condition." The Panic of 1857 convinced other segments of the public that the woman shopper had definitely arrived because the recession, in the language of *Hunt's Merchants' Magazine*, "brought us the lady buyer."

The financial crisis of 1857 drastically tightened the supply of money in the United States. The shortage drove shopkeepers to desperate measures in their attempts to raise enough cash to meet obligations. It sanctioned certain business practices that hitherto had been used only by reckless men to drum up business quickly. Cost sales, fire sales, shipwreck sales, distress sales, and panic sales succeeded each other, and the tumbling prices heightened the delight of shopping for women who used their time to look around extensively to find the best buy. At auctions, the stock of bankrupt tradesmen fell cheaply into the hands of more fortunate merchants who indiscriminately added the merchandise as new attractions to their repertories of goods. During the late 1850's, the "inevitable dry goods stores," which before the Panic had already been notorious in New York for crowding churches out of the downtown district, fostered a "rage for building superb business palaces" that filled "acres of brick with gorgeous marble and stone fronts and converted New York into a city of palaces."

Among these calico palaces, occupied by such firms as Lord & Taylor—whose name is still a household word—A. T. Stewart's new uptown store stood out as the epitome of a true department store. Erected between 1859 and 1862, the breathtaking building covered the entire block between Broadway and Fourth Avenue, Ninth and Tenth streets, and was separated by Astor Place from the Cooper Union, another New York landmark exhibiting and distributing through shows and lectures the practical accomplishments of the age. Various designations, such as "Stewart's Tenth Street Store" or "Astor Place Store," referred to the store by its location. However, no name did justice to the significance of the building as did "Stewart's New Store," which distinguished it from the Marble Palace, now clearly "old" after sixteen years of renovations and additions. That name also suggested, albeit unintentionally, the novel achievement embodied in one enormous building devoted to the sale of a great variety of goods to a large clientele of women.

Many features of the building bespoke the special nature of the store. A. T. Stewart, "an enthusiastic advocate of cast-iron fronts for commercial structures," often used to compare the iron front dressed in white paint "to puffs of white clouds." The cast-iron facade, with plain columns and molded arches in the Venetian manner of the Italian Renaissance, rose five stories in height, "arch upon arch," eighty-five feet above the sidewalk. The artistic economy of John Kellum, a New York architect with expertise in iron fronts, immediately touched the practical sense of the masses of people who daily thronged the store, "as they do an exposition," A. T. Stewart thought. Kellum's plain design shunned the hideous filigree work and elaborate pattern of fluted columns that had discredited the first iron fronts when they appeared in the 1840's. Instead, he reduced the four enormous walls of the store facing the surrounding city to rows and rows of windows that brought "ample light" into every corner of the building.

The merchant's conviction that "everybody will know it is A. T. Stewart's" kept the facade free from signs and advertisements and increased the distinction of the magnificent building. The purity of the cast-iron design also added a definite American note to the city's eclectic architecture, one contemporary commentator stressed. He felt that such "a chaste and airy edifice of iron" formed a happy contrast to the pretentious marble palaces and bulky brick offices that crowded the densely built-up business quarter. An observer standing "on any of the four corners of Stewart's immense dry-goods store," he argued, could not mistake its "lightness and grace for anything but iron," and iron he considered "emphatically an *American* building material."

Stewart's intimate knowledge of the urban scene inspired his choice of building styles. The "graceful dome" that rose ninety feet above the main hall of his old Marble Palace owed much to the splendid rotundas of two New York landmarks, City Hall and the Merchants Exchange. His use of a rotunda in department store construction in 1846 shaped commercial architecture for some time. Stewart himself may have been influenced by the wide publicity given fifteen years earlier in Frances Trollope's Graeco-Roman-Turkish Bazaar in Cincinnati, the only commercial building to use dome, rotunda, and stairway before the Marble Palace, as part of her concept of combining the dissemination of culture with the sale of merchandise. . . .

. . . [T]he rotunda's charm kept it a feature of department store architecture long after electricity and fire hazards had made it obsolete, as many buildings constructed in the 1880's and 1890's indicated. In 1896, the first San Francisco department store, the Emporium, opened with a central dome and kept the rotunda until 1957, through its reconstruction after the earthquake and fire of 1906. The most stunning example appeared in 1902, when Marshall Field & Co. in Chicago opened a new store, built by the firm of D. H. Burnham, with a gigantic Tiffany glass dome.

Stewart shaped the development of the department store in various ways. In building the New Store, he boldly defied conventions and flew in the face of the praise his contemporaries had heaped on the Marble Palace, which added distinction to a generally drab cityscape. Calling it a "white marble cliff" when marble was considered a singular "ornament to the city," New Yorkers regarded it as a "model" giving character to the city's architecture. Their enthusiastic approval launched the *palazzo* mode barely two years after the *North American Review* had proclaimed its greater virtue for American architecture over that of the Greek Revival.

With the design of his New Store, Stewart turned against the tide his Marble Palace had helped to create. The choice of iron, the hallmark of industrialization, over marble in the midst of the Civil War gained approval as a result of the general preoccupation with military technology, from cannons to trains and from ironclads to bridges. But behind his daring also stood sound economic sense, because the iron structure permitted wide windows that opened to all floors the daylight that cumbrous walls faced with marble had kept out of Stewart's downtown store.

Almost immediately Stewart's New Store fulfilled the promise its visual impression made. The efficient arrangement of the uniform interior highlighted the sense of purpose and expressed dedication to service. An enormous skylight admitted sunshine directly into the vast main floor. Its simple harmony of lines, formed by the individual panels of glass, did not obstruct the flow of light, correcting a shortcoming of the Marble Palace, where daylight had to struggle past the ornamentation of the rotunda and "the elegant lantern in the dome." The carefully arranged space, with counters and aisles symmetrically disposed, gave the ground floor and the open circle of upper stories the appearance of a utopian order that was a relief after the orderly anarchy of modern city life that engulfed the building.

In Stewart's New Store, a minor feature of Edward Bellamy's utopian vision seemed to have come true, a quarter of a century before *Looking Backward* appeared in 1888. There it was, a warehouse for an entire city, "where the buyer, without waste of time and labor, found under one roof the world's assortment in whatever line he desired." The novelty of the displays heightened the impression of boundlessness conjured up by the great variety of goods. Prefabricated household furnishings, ready-made clothes, mass-produced toys, fashionable stationery, and inexpensive books helped make Stewart's the largest retail store in the world. Its departmental organization ordered countless displays with "military precision," *Harper's Monthly* noted, the whole machinery working, "as it were, by electric touches."

Alexander Turney Stewart, to give at least once the full name that seems to have been used sparingly during his lifetime, kept strict discipline among his 2,000 employees. His absolute authority resulted from an intimate familiarity with all aspects of the business. An immigrant, a well-reared Ulster Scot holding a Dublin Trinity College degree, he had built up his organization methodically since the 1820's, when he began in a dry goods shop measuring twelve by thirty feet on lower Broadway. Although he seemed almost inaccessible, maintaining the granite-like reserve that often goes with a Scottish ancestry, he constantly managed to impress his clerks on the floor with his standards of service. His customers liked the bland friendliness he showed them. His honesty gained him their loyalty, which compensated for his shortcomings: he advertised extensively but poorly, and banned displays from his store's show windows and interior. His salesmanship stressing service was what attracted a steady stream of customers.

A shrewd trader, who sold on credit but always paid cash for his purchases, Stewart ran several eastern mills that manufactured woolen goods, cotton and silk, ribbons, threads, blankets, and carpets. He operated offices and warehouses in Great Britain, Ireland, France, Germany, and Switzerland to control his imports. His European buying organization, the outgrowth of annual trips he began in 1839, served as a model for other American retailers. The range of his business corresponded with his success, and in three years before his death in 1876, the combined wholesale and retail sales amounted to $203 million.

Stewart's careful business calculations undoubtedly contributed much to his accomplishment. However, his determination to keep abreast of general trends of urban and industrial growth made him also a brilliant entrepreneur. A sequence of daring moves revealed him as a good judge of human nature and urban expansion. Against the wisdom of the 1840's, he built his Marble Palace on a corner lot of the penny or shilling side of Broadway, where he could acquire real estate cheaply because most merchants preferred the other side of the street where pretentious stores attracted well-to-do customers. The spectacular store immediately drew the dollar trade across the street, with "the beautiful carriages of the millionaires stopping on the shilling side of Broadway to purchase dry-goods." When he located his New Store further uptown in the early 1860's, in another act of seeming folly, he had assessed the population movement of the surging metropolis correctly and found his customers already uptown.

The image of his business, the variety of his merchandise, and the organization of his enterprise provided the foundation for a full-fledged department store. In addition, the orientation of his services toward large numbers of women gave his store its cultural significance as the focus of a new community. The grief expressed in the faces of women listening to the announcement of Stewart's death in front of his New Store, captured by one of the best nineteenth-century American illustrators in *Harper's Weekly*, suggested the bond that linked them to the store. About forty years later, Gordon Selfridge, who had come to London from Chicago's Marshall Field in 1906 and started a department store, coined the phrase that explained the constant stream of women shoppers in such a store: "You know why they come here?" he asked. "It's so much brighter than their homes. This is not a shop—it's a community centre."

The social functions of the department store turned around the needs of women shoppers who emerged as directors of family consumption in the middle of the nineteenth century. These services, at first piecemeal accommodations rather than systematic programs, assured the popularity of the department store among women who regarded the new activity of shopping as a relief from the boredom of familial confinement or the drudgery of domestic routine. In a long-range perspective it can be seen that shopping actually provided the framework of a gilded cage keeping women from their share of freedom. However, in the 1860's and 1870's the ability to shop in the center of large cities seemed to the large number of women crowding the department store a form of real emancipation. It was a small but tangible token, like the independence Elizabeth Cady Stanton had urged on the wife of her Congressman in 1854, when she induced her to buy a much-needed stove without her husband's approval or company.

The attention the department store devoted to its female customers changed the urban environment and made downtown streets attractive to women. Clean and orderly sidewalks became an extension of the store. The displays in the large plate-glass windows added the diversion of window-shopping to the pleasures of the promenade. Women came downtown purposely to see and to be seen, to chance meeting a friend in the store's hospitable atmosphere, or to enjoy shopping in company. They arrived in numbers that continuously called for more services. In 1883, a cartoon facetiously labeled a group of window-shoppers a neglected class because the storekeeper had failed to make provisions for their comfort and they were forced to inspect the exhibits of a clothing store sitting on piano stools. Under these circumstances the department store and the upgraded downtown also furnished a setting that placed on an equal footing with each other women who might have suffered from a sense of inequality if they had visited one another at home.

Dreiser's Sister Carrie, who cringed when she compared her small flat with rich Mrs. Vance's apartment, managed to recover some of her equanimity during mutual shopping sprees, seeking "the delight of parading here as an equal." The department store also permitted fleeting identification with ladies from the upper crust of society who visited it as part of their carefully timed pursuit of pleasure. Women aspiring to the air of solid middle-class comfort could find it, at least temporarily, in the atmosphere and appearance of the new downtown center of their life.

The appearance of the department store heightened the illusion of shared luxury among the shoppers. In the form of a marble palace, a cast-iron show-place, a sprawling grand depot, or a masonry castle, it emphasized dedication to the ideal of shopping as an endless delight. The fact that no offices or other tenants crowded the building's upper stories signaled its commitment to a sole purpose. Rows and rows of large windows filled it with daylight and relieved the shopper's dependence on gas lighting for the many purchases that involved a decision about the colors of fabrics. Elevators accommodated customers who felt reluctant to climb more than one flight of stairs. These features symbolized prosperity and prestige. Above all, they emphasized convenience.

The arrangement and display of the merchandise reinforced the leisurely atmosphere the store sought to create. The division into departments assured easy access to goods, contrasting with the orderly confusion of the general store and the exclusive air of the specialty shop where gloves or shawls waited in boxes for the right customer to call. Clearly marked prices on wares attractively displayed on tables and counters made social equality an element of the convenience of a store catering to a cross section of the population; for pre-established prices eliminated the possibility of any embarrassment that might have arisen had the sudden disclosure of a price taxed the shopper's means excessively.

Haggling over prices had gradually disappeared from the retail scene in large cities during the first half of the nineteenth century, although the practice continued in smaller cities as a "regular and accepted part of retail buying," with formal discounts given to so many groups that "the occasional person who did not ask for a cheaper price paid too much for his goods." In large stores, however, where many sales were made by many clerks, bargaining was quite understandably passé—proprietors saw no way to entrust setting prices to the numerous and often inexperienced sales people on the floor. Furthermore, a department store management recognized that feature of human nature that aspires to get something for nothing—or, at least, for less than it seems to be worth. Thus came the introduction of the bargain table and the bargain basement, as stores catered to the economic as well as the psychological needs of some of their customers. In 1888, John Wanamaker created in his Philadelphia store a Bargain Room "into which our other rooms will empty all those goods that block their way to serving customers quickly with style and size sought." Edward Filene's Automatic Bargain Basement, a distinct innovation introduced in Boston in 1909, featured unsold goods at reduced prices in order to generate high turnover and to clear the other floors of distress merchandise.

Most stores backed extensively the claims they made to attract customers. They buttressed the policy of accurately advertised merchandise with money-back guarantees, if a customer was not satisfied. John Wanamaker summed up his attitude with a "trinity of square-dealing":

All goods to be sold openly,
All traders to be treated alike,
All fraud and deception to be eliminated.

Some stores, like Marshall Field in Chicago, gave short-term credits and billed monthly, occasionally offering discounts for cash. Others, like Macy's in New York, had no charge accounts at all for many years. All avoided excessive markups and instead sought profits on volume, selling at low prices and low margins. The key to a high stock turnover was extensive local advertising, coupled with price reductions on slow-moving items and extensive customer service. Rapid turnover provided the cash needed to buy in quantity the latest lines and thus to be responsive to ever-changing consumer demands.

The orientation of the department store toward service and mass merchandising was reflected initially in the spectacular selection and convenient arrangement of its merchandise. But new facilities became essential when large numbers of customers spent several hours in the building. Rest rooms and lounges led the way to restaurants and reading rooms. At the end of the nineteenth century, nurseries for customers' children, mail-order services, complaint and credit counters, check-cashing windows, post offices, and ticket agencies quite naturally joined the features of the department store because women wanted these services.

Customer service became the credo of department store personnel. "Public service is the sole basic condition of retail business growth," John Wanamaker emphasized in 1900, while in 1916 the designer of a model store called it a "Service Store," because "every detail has been laid out with the customer's convenience in view." As different as their approaches to retailing and management may have been, most of the legendary builders of great stores—Aristide Boucicaut, William Whiteley, A. T. Stewart, Rowland H. Macy, Isidor and Nathan Straus, Potter Palmer, Marshall Field, Gordon Selfridge, John Wanamaker, Jordan Marsh, and Edward Filene, to name the better known among them—made service a tenet that they upheld meticulously during their regular walks through the aisles of their stores. Through example and exhortation, with fines and dismissals, they impressed the staff with their determination to carry out the policy of service. Their routine rounds and sudden appearances drove the point home to clerks and customers alike.

At such moments, shoppers saw their yearnings to be served answered by a patrician merchant who personified the store's written policies. Clerks saw the owner's art of salesmanship giving dignity to their own skills in a society that considered waiting on people a menial task, somewhat below the dignity of free men and women. A millionaire who greeted his customers and responded to the grievances of a shopper on the crowded floor of his store elevated an obsequious act to the level of a public service, well respected and highly regarded in a professedly democratic society. The Chicago novelist Ernest Poole recalled that as a boy shopping with his mother, he would stare at a "cold-souled courtly merchant" with "a low voice and charming manners," as "he moved about the store with bright observing smiling eyes": Marshall Field, "the richest man in Chicago and ace merchant of the West."

In the 1870's and 1880's, Marshall Field stood out among Chicago merchants who sought to make their department stores servants of the public. He followed approaches to the "carriage trade" and the "shawl trade" that had been laid out by Potter Palmer, his one-time business partner. Field used equality of service to create a social no-woman's-land that allowed upper- and lower-class women to shop together. He made both groups essential actresses in the drama of shopping and spending. A poor woman's self-esteem was elevated by her ability to share a display counter with a rich woman, who in turn achieved her satisfaction from the admiration of clerks and customers. Field's salesmanship made easier the use of the "pecuniary canons of taste," Thorstein Veblen's term for the basis of a new gentility that considered all people equal who had the money to acquire certain goods, indicating they knew which possessions mattered. Although Field at times handled customer-store relationships on the floor of his emporium and actually saw to it that the lady got what she wanted, his skillful displays of merchandise and well-timed promotional campaigns ensured that his customers "wanted things and services that money alone could buy." These things and services he sold.

Field's success depended to a great degree on making his store "irresistibly attractive" to customers. He, and the other great retail merchants, incorporated personality into their cult of public service. Before marketing research made retailing a science, they knew instinctively that not only the quality and price of the merchandise, but also the image and identity of the enterprise, attracted people to shop a particular store. Each was the personification of his store, and because they could not wait on every customer personally, they relied on the store image they created to convey the impression that they were indeed serving their public.

If this magic failed, floorwalkers stood ready to reinforce the elusive sense of the owner's presence with a touch of managerial involvement. They substituted diligence for those features of the owner's style they were unable to copy. They also extended the doorman's measured greetings cheerfully into the more remote departments where they served as "a politely convenient living directory." The notion of public service they maintained pervaded the entire house and also extended to the store detectives, who discreetly dealt with thievery as an accident best kept out of earshot because the sight of one apprehended thief could conjure up the fear of pickpockets everywhere and undermine the harmonious ritual of buying and selling.

The great number of well-categorized employees made that harmony possible, but most remained hidden from view. The sales clerks, the group most directly in contact with the customers, served the public in the most literal way. Although they waited on individual customers for ten hours a day and for roughly six dollars a week in the 1890's, they considered themselves not as servants, but as friendly counselors who provided information about materials, comments about quality, and advice about style to untutored women shoppers.

Increasingly, women assumed the role of sales clerk as the opportunities of the city lured men elsewhere. By 1900, due to the wide range of better-paid jobs open to men, women became the dominant sex behind the counters. Most managerial jobs were closed to them, although Margaret Getchell rose from cashier to superintendent in Macy's during the 1860's and became one of the first women to attain an executive position in American business. On the other hand, management and customers welcomed women clerks as especially competent sales people. Unlike men, who only tolerated the changes in retailing, young women adjusted quickly to the new ways of selling because the department store represented an economic start for them. They cherished being in urban surroundings that removed them further from domestic chores than did waiting on tables in a restaurant or sewing clothes in a sweatshop. Here, they did not rely on tips, but earned wages. They were able to experience something of the glamor of the big city and meet interesting people. The seasonal help even endured wholesale dismissals preceding the slack months and came back willingly when needed.

Furthermore, the female sales force fit better than men into this new kind of store that replaced the hard sell with an emphasis on service. They easily accepted the novel requirement of attention to the orders of all superiors, essential to the operation of a store no longer run by a single proprietor. They adapted smoothly because they did not bring to the job the burden of outdated practices. To them, strict regulations and disciplined operating procedures were not impersonal or degrading but primarily new, because they had no memories of "the good old days" in the life of a "real clerk." To be sure, they resented some rules, particularly the store's demand that they stand continuously during their long working hours, and they managed to bypass other edicts they found unreasonable. Massie, "a deep-tinted blonde, with the calm poise of a lady who cooks buttercakes in a window," one of the 3,000 clerks in O. Henry's "Biggest Store," chewed tutti frutti "when the floor-walker was not looking" and "smiled wistfully" when he did.

Quite naturally, female clerks also meshed smoothly with the department store's female clientele. They knew what these shoppers wanted because they themselves desired similar possessions. The customers, for their part, found it easier to share their intimate desires with them than with men. Fitting new garments was also simplified with the help of sales people of the same sex. Constantly exposed to fashionable goods and demanding customers, the clerks themselves became models of stylish elegance, smartly dressed like O. Henry's Miss Claribel Colby, who personified the "thousand girls from the great department store." When they needed a new gown, like Maida in "The Purple Dress," they skipped meals or starved on skimpy diets and, with the encouragement of management and employee discounts, they spent an inordinate amount of their meager salaries on their wardrobes.

Shopping as a new social art and the department store as a new social institution rose simultaneously, complementing one another. The personnel's commitment to service, the atmosphere of ease and luxury, and the magnificence of the building awed many customers unfamiliar with the idea that they, too, were entitled to service. Under these novel circumstances, they felt relieved, as well as flattered, by the attention and assistance they received. But many people who were pretending to be as affluent as they craved to be lacked experience in shopping for the luxury goods of the new manufacturers, particularly dress goods and household furnishings that came ready-made from the factories. While the specialty shops carried these lines too, the department store strove to take the lead with the newest items. Its lavish displays, conveniently arranged and clearly priced, also provided a wide range of choices in one location, allowing customers unfamiliar with such objects to absorb information about goods just by wandering through the store, without revealing their ignorance as could have happened in an exclusive shop where a haughty sales clerk might have taken any inquiry as an admission of social inferiority. Women shoppers who went into the department store with one purchase in mind invariably left it with many new ideas. Thus clerks and customers learned that shopping as a social art involved acquiring a share of the better life in the future by dreaming of it in the present, both savoring the moment when the purchase actually took place.

Indeed, the buying stage of shopping appeared as the most widely visible sign of female emancipation in the modern city. A Chicago *Herald* political cartoon, reprinted in other newspapers of the Midwest, portrayed that concept in a comment on the presidential campaign of 1892. A young woman representing *the* American shopper briefly interrupts her window-shopping at a dry goods store in order to straight-arm William McKinley into what in that year seemed political oblivion, with an imperious gesture that clearly indicates she is not buying.

In their daily lives, women also responded alertly to the dictates of necessity and the lure of opportunity, and some may even have followed consciously Elizabeth Cady Stanton's advice to "Buy, Buy" as a welcome expansion of their domestic routine. For the most part, they spent the salaries of white-collar workers, professional men, and small entrepreneurs, who had begun earning just enough money to keep the cash tubes of the department store humming with pouches of coins and to keep the women busy making change in the basement cashroom. Buying on credit was not a common practice among these people who were just learning to buy things they did not need, but had not yet discovered that they could do so with money they did not have.

There were of course ladies among the ranks of customers who could afford the purchases they made in the new department stores. Their presence and style set standards of behavior that raised the expectations of women from less affluent homes and led them to buy some new item as the most direct way to prolong the association with the rich which the store induced. Much of the store's success depended on the intensification of desire through the shopping process that helped create this identification. The consideration with which A. T. Stewart and Marshall Field welcomed enormously wealthy ladies to their stores indicates that they appreciated the fact that the visits of these influential people induced vast numbers of other customers to patronize their stores.

Window displays and store decorations also played a major role in stimulating demand. The department store, growing with the new technology of construction, new forms of management, and new systems of communication, quickly utilized these innovations to influence people. The activities of pioneer owners soon swept aside A. T. Stewart's restraints. Potter Palmer, originally an upstate New York merchant who once had bought his goods wholesale from A. T. Stewart, opened his Chicago store with fanfare. His window of gloves and hosiery, black silk and white cotton, skillfully arranged against a background of crepe shawls, stirred the city in the fall of 1852. Novel phosgene lamps illuminated the display at night and radiated their brilliant light onto the murkey street. In 1878, in his Philadelphia "Grand Depot," a rambling old freight depot of the Pennslyvania Railroad converted into a huge dry goods and men's clothing emporium. John Wanamaker first used electricity to light an entire store "as in daytime." At the time of the Chicago World's Fair in 1893, Marshall Field & Co. had blended displays and exhibits into such an artistic achievement that advertisements could declare the entire store "an exposition in itself."

Advertising had previously been drawn into the service of the department store, but it took John Wanamaker's genius for promotion to make it a major force. His messages telling consumers to buy the latest item appeared on every fence, construction site, and empty building in Philadelphia; even the curb-stones advertised his offerings. Before he opened his store in 1861, he littered the city with a series of handbills that built up curiosity. He took in $20.67 on his first day of business, and promptly spent $20 on advertisements in the Philadelphia *Public Ledger* announcing a sale of complete men's suits for $3— since he had suddenly acquired the stock of a bankrupt ready-to-wear maker of men's suits. Within ten years he ran the largest men's retail clothing operation in the United States, an accomplishment announced in 100-foot-long signs along the train tracks leading into the city. He marshaled parades, gave a suit to everyone who returned one of the large balloons he released, and sent costumed employees through the steets blowing hunting horns from tallyho coaches that were pulled, not by four horses as was customary, but six.

John Wanamaker went all the way with his promotional campaigns, and he did the same with newspaper advertising. Most early department stores advertised modestly, but regularly, in newspapers. In New York, after the Civil War, Lord & Taylor and Macy's moved into double-column-width advertisements, a long step away from the tiny display ads used extensively by A. T. Stewart and Arnold Constable & Co.; but Wanamaker outdid them by advertising daily, using more space on a newspaper page than his competitors, and enlivening the descriptions of goods with hints about their usefulness. His first full-page advertisement appeared in 1879. By 1890 other stores were copying his methods so liberally that they furnished Wanamaker with additional publicity, enabling him to accompany his messages with announcements such as the following: "17 quotations found in the East and the whole advertisement copied bodily in the West."

Wanamaker understood that truncated messages about new merchandise in the advertising sections of a newspaper could not systematically make casual readers regular shoppers in his store because women also liked to hear the story behind the new dress coats or kitchen utensils. He therefore sponsored advice columns about style, etiquette, and fashion trends that subtly prepared readers for the next novelties to appear in his exhibits. His store talks in newspapers informed his customers about the latest innovations in the store to make shopping easier, detailing the functions of service centers or providing instruction on how conveniently a novel safety catch could be installed on an apartment door. Soon these messages began spilling over into regular advertisements and helped to make advertising more literate as well as more honest. In 1896 Wanamaker acquired Stewart's New Store. Its magnificent building had for years been defaced by hideous slogans and gaudy banners that the executors of Stewart's estate had used in a vain attempt to save their declining business. The modest tablet Wanamaker placed at the main entrance reflected his intelligence as well as his integrity as advertiser. It read:

> JOHN WANAMAKER
> FORMERLY
> A. T. STEWART AND CO.

The work of John Wanamaker reflected yet another aspect of the sophistication of retailing, one which shaped the department store as well as the shopper. His use of display advertising and paid newspaper columns helped educate the consumer and thus contributed to the rise of the knowledgeable downtown shopper who ultimately freed the department store from its dependence on the wholesale side of the business, which had filled the orders traveling salesmen drummed up in country stores and provided some of the support for the lavish extension of the retail operation. Creating large groups of customers, new concepts of shopping and selling expedited the expansion of a store like Macy's in New York, which in the 1860's, without the support of a wholesale operation, grew from a small clothing and fancy dry goods store into a department store by adding different lines and acquiring adjacent shops.

Advertising messages and advice columns awakened large numbers of women to the art of calculated shopping based on deliberation and selection. Women who supplied their families' needs by buying in the department store came to rely on these forms of publicity for keeping in touch with the latest styles and offerings. Department store newspaper advertising also introduced women shoppers to a concept of obsolescence that merchants considered quite acceptable. The fashion cycle kept alive the demand for merchandise without violating the ethics of the business *vis-à-vis* the quality of goods. Changes in taste shortened the life span of a garment or a lamp much more effectively than the use of cheap material or shoddy craftsmanship could have done, without stirring suspicion of creating resentment among customers, who greeted "something new" with delight.

The fashion cycle, which sustained the rising department store by making shopping a perpetual social drama, received its impetus from the freedom of modern city life, which abrogated the political, social, and economic restraints that in the pre-modern age had curbed extensive social use of fashion. It did away with innumerable ordinances and conventions that had once governed life from cradle to grave. . . .

The economic opportunities of the modern city vastly expanded the range of participants in the fashion cycle, and the tempo of life accelerated the speed with which one style succeeded another. More and more people strove to outdo one another in their attire, and as soon as one style became established, new ones emerged. The less impressive people's position or family background was, the more they relied on fashionable appearance as a credential. Jane Addams explained the sound economic sense behind a working woman's spending most of her income on appearance: "Her clothes are her background and from them she is largely judged."

Men and women on the make swelled the ranks of stylishly dressed people, and their numbers increased the chance that the vogue of any particular fashion would have an abrupt end. In the free air of the modern city, anyone with money could aspire to become a social aristocrat by staying just ahead of the next turn of the fashion wheel, while anyone not rich but intent on getting ahead in life could draw closer to the leaders by acquiring a ready-made version of the made-to-order dress or suit of a style-setter. "There is a tide in the affairs of (wo)men that, taken at the flood, leads on to Fashion," an advertisement for a St. Louis department store explained in the 1890's, tying the fashion cycle directly to a department store—"That Kind of Flood is Always at Barr's." In Philadelphia, Wanamaker's emphasized: "What the public *desires*, we must *do*."

The democratization of the fashion cycle through the department store depended also on new, practical components that gained significance as the number of participants continually expanded. The days of owning one working dress and one Sunday suit became numbered as modern city life created more and more social pressures. The promenade required different attire from the parlor; shopping called for one dress, a social call another. The office and the theater each made different demands on one's wardrobe. People who wanted to belong needed to know what was appropriate for a specific occasion, so that at least their dress, their furniture, or their food would indicate that they had arrived or showed promise of being part of the charmed circle of insiders. The department store selling these status-conferring accouterments provided guidance by means of displays, advertisements, and advice columns that, in turn, increased the demand for the goods.

Dress requirements were correlated with the seasons, particularly in the field of ready-made clothes, and thus added new complexity to the female shopping expedition. Spring, fall, summer, and winter emerged as divisions of the fashion year promulgated by the department store. Each signaled the automatic beginning of a new fashion cycle. Christmas and Easter became high points of fashion, as did the summer vacation and the opening of school in the fall. Colors, cuts, and trimmings changed with them. Wool gave way to silk, and silk again to wool. Full-page advertisements in the Sunday papers of the metropolitan press eliminated any possible confusion for people tied to the wheel of fashion. "It wasn't a cyclone! Nor a 'landslide' that took St. Louis by storm last week and set all the Ladies to talking," the announcement of "Barr's Grand Value-Reducing Sale" clamored. "OH, NO! It was an Avalanche of New Spring Goods," which produced "the greatest sacrifice" of "strictly first-class fine wool dress goods."

The time-honored device of the sale quickened the tempo of style changes. By the 1890's new features had been added to the repertoire of inducements used in the 1840's. "Miss January" and "Mr. Merchandise" came out in costumes at Wanamaker's in January 1888, and launched their sale as "The White Occasion." The sensational language of the advertisements and that of the news columns of the metropolitan press reinforced each other. Nouns like "bomb" and "crash" and adjectives like "desperate" and "solid" spoke not only of the social conditions of the 1890's but also of the department store sales of the period, which fluctuated between "slaughter" of prices and "sacrifice" of goods. Shipwreck sales diminished when big stores moved inland, but trainload sales increased, and grand anniversary sales and white sales were institutionalized. An emphasis on great selections of goods and on low prices, and a lack of restraint, characterized most promotions. In 1893, a St. Louis department store proclaimed itself, on the occasion of a spectacular sale, "by popular vote the headquarters of the North American Continent, both as regards to variety and low prices."

Sales and seasons produced a constant succession of changes. Highlighted through new displays in store windows and on bargain tables, and introduced with advertising campaigns in the newspapers, the frequent turns of the fashion cycle camouflaged in a superficial way social and cultural divisions among the residents of the modern city. The cycle encouraged the egalitarian activity of department store shopping, and thus steadily increased membership in the society of consumers and stimulated identification across social classes. The process also established a distinct urban identity, because access to downtown shopping facilities was essential for participation in the latest fashion trends.

The department store made shopping itself fashionable. It gave status to what had been drudgery and added an element of diversion to the lives of women who could afford to play the game. "Fashionable Shopping in New York" was the caption of a large woodcut illustration of Stewart's Marble Palace in a *Herald* advertisement in September 1846, on the occasion of the store's opening. The department store captured an audience of women shoppers who found a female enclave amid splendid settings and constantly changed scenes which matched well the ever-changing modern city.

By its very nature, shopping in a department store became a public act that educated people for living in the city. Successful participation demanded that the shopper possess not only money but also the poise to assess shrewdly the offered goods. It involved familiarity with the ways of the world and knowledge of the value of things. Buying, the culmination of shopping, constituted yet another measure of success. Though the goods people bought reflected well-established divisions among them, the egalitarian features of shopping diminished these inequalities and linked shoppers as an interest group. Through their shopping and buying activities women acquired not only a knowledge of what to buy but also the power to determine what was sold. Women's consumer's leagues began using that power in the 1890's, when the spread of the department store enabled them to touch all the major retail outlets with one boycott.

Most women welcomed the adventure of downtown shopping, which for many was not only a fashionable activity but also a truly urban one. They went window-shopping, strolled through the stores, gazed at the displays and each other, chatted with friends, listened to clerks' explanations, assessed the articles and other shoppers, bought something they considered a bargain, and under fortunate circumstances went home with the feeling that they had not only done something women were supposed to do, but had actually enjoyed doing it. This experience, repeated almost daily, intensified their identity as modern urban women.

This new identity also engendered stress. At the beginning of the twentieth century one observer, sketching her impressions of "typical American women on a typical shopping tour," discovered "the anomaly that the longer they take to shop, the less they actually buy." She saw women "poorly clad, pale and irritable from fatigue," moving from counter to counter, "fingering, pricing, commenting, passing on, hour after hour," with "an ice-cream soda in the basement" as their "only lunch." This was followed by a "complete rearrangement of hair in the 'Ladies Parlor,'" and "a slow stroll through the Art Department," in a routine common to "tens of thousands of our women in every city in the Union."

The identity of the modern urban woman acquired its distinct character through her relationship with the department store. In response to the lure of shopping, women became a presence in the downtown section of the modern city. As shoppers, they exercised daily control over the household budget; this not only gave them a growing measure of independence but also earned them the special attention of merchants, who recognized their purchasing power as the sine qua non of large-scale retailing. Moreover, though the women who worked as sales clerks may have earned low salaries and worked long hours, this form of employment opened up a major female avenue into the male-dominated urban job market. The total effect was to introduce women as a new social force in city life.

. . . [T]he department store freed large numbers of women from the isolation of domesticity and chained them to a novel form of servitude—shopping as a social obligation. With the feminization of shopping, the department store turned a chore into an elaborate process that oriented most residents of the modern city toward money as the common denominator of urban life.

Shopping also reinforced the separation between two spheres of life, leaving the acquisition of the funds for shopping to men while making the task itself a woman's affair. Ultimately, shopping and increased consumption may also have shaped the subtle relations between some men and women in an age that reinforced the ideal of middle-class marriage with layers of convention. In Dreiser's *Sister Carrie*, Mr. G. W. Hurstwood enjoyed himself thoroughly in Philadelphia during a brief escape he had engineered from the demands of his Chicago home life. On his return the whole incident was glossed over, "but Mrs. Hurstwood gave the subject considerable thought. She drove out more, dressed better and attended theaters freely to make up for it."

Both men and women felt the social impact of the department store in other realms as well. They witnessed the transformation of the center of the city, which, during working hours at least, had been almost exclusively a male domain, into a downtown area where clean sidewalks enticed women to linger in front of store windows without fear of being harassed by draymen and crowded by office boys. The department store brought into the bustle of downtown the civility that most men had reserved for those aspects of city life they considered properly the social sphere. Thus the store added a new charm to the modern city by opening the city center to the civilizing influences of women and visitors from out of town, making urban life, in the words of Henry James, "so much more down-towny."

Much of that new urban charm stemmed from the substitution of a shopping district for a wholesale or business district as the core of the city. Magnificent buildings and attractive sidewalks introduced into the downtown section the same sense of spatial order that the department store had brought to large-scale retailing. In a world barely touched by concepts of city planning, this innovation expressed the promise of an ordered urban life. In addition, as the destination of large numbers of women shoppers the department store furnished a focal point for expanding urban transit systems. This validated the downtown district as the center for the flow of people as well as of goods. As the heart of the modern city this district sought to create and attempted to satisfy in the most concentrated form the population's infinitely expanding demands for goods and services.

With its far-ranging utility, the department store reflected the culture of the modern city. It constantly assessed people's hopes for a better life and responded to their dreams. As a creative social force, the department store sustained the shared experience of shopping, produced a new form of communal life, and provided links among heterogeneous people. Ultimately, the department store gave urban life a downtown focus, not only bestowing charm and civility but also evoking democratic qualities that enriched the urbanity of the modern city and reaffirmed its egalitarian nature.

The Poor Man's Club

JON M. KINGSDALE

Brown Brothers

Chuck Connor's saloon on the Bowery, 1905–1910

THE URBAN WORKING-CLASS SALOON was not unlike the colonial coffeehouse and multifunctional frontier saloon. According to Jon M. Kingsdale, the differences are differences only in time and place, not in fundamental significance. Like the coffeehouse and the frontier saloon, the "poor man's club" performed social, political, and economic services for its clientele.

In some ways, the workingman's saloon was a second home, a sort of private club, in which a man could pick up mail, meet friends, and cash checks. In fact, it was a place to *escape* the crowded, dirty, unpleasant physical conditions of urban tenement life; a man could relax and be sociable as he could not at home. In addition to drinking, the saloon provided recreation and amusement—newspapers, cards, live entertainment, and pool tables. The patrons came together as members of a neighborhood, bound by their ethnic backgrounds and even by their friendships with the bartender.

The saloon was also a key setting for urban politics. As the local gathering place for dozens of men, it was a logical place to organize political machines; ward captains and precinct bosses could create alliances and do favors for individuals, thereby earning votes.

Kingsdale maintains that the saloons helped the workingman economically. Some of these establishments were hangouts for members of a particular occupation, and so men of similar skills and abilities were drawn together. As a result, saloons became a kind of informal unemployment office where information about job openings was passed around. Also, in an era of open hostility to unions, the saloons frequently provided a place for union locals to hold meetings cheaply and safely.

HISTORICAL STUDIES OF THE PERIOD 1890 to 1920 generally refer to the saloon in connection with urban machine politics or Temperance, yet often ignore the saloon's social and cultural functions. But an analysis of the urban saloon is important to an understanding of working-class social history in this period. Saloons seem to have exercised a significant influence upon the values and behavior of the urban working class; certainly they were central to the workingman's leisure-time activities. The saloon provided him a variety of services and played three significant roles in a growing urban industrial environment: it was a neighborhood center, an all-male establishment and a transmitter of working-class and immigrant cultures.

In the middle of the 19th century, as America's cities were experiencing the first shocks of industrialization and "new-stock" immigration, the saloon came to replace colonial taverns and corner grocers as the urban liquor dispensary, par excellence. The saloon became an increasingly popular institution: by 1897 licensed liquor dealers in the United States numbered over 215,000, and unlicensed "blind pigs" or "blind tigers" represented an estimated 50,000 additional outlets. Most brewers—the brewing industry being highly competitive at the close of the 19th century—sponsored as many outlets as possible, as exclusive retailers of their own beer, thus saturating cities with saloons. In Chicago, for instance, saloons were as numerous as groceries, meat markets and dry goods stores counted together. Cities without effective restrictions were deluged with saloons: in 1915 New York had over 10,000 licensed saloons, or one for every 515 persons; Chicago had one licensed saloon for every 335 residents; Houston had one for every 298 persons; San Francisco had a saloon for every 218 persons. The skewed distribution of saloons within cities and the large number of unlicensed retailers meant that many an urban working-class district had at least one saloon for every 50 adult males (fifteen years of age and older). Reflecting both the growing popularity of saloons and a switch from distilled spirits to beer, alcoholic beverage consumption increased steadily after 1850. While consumption of distilled spirits fell by half, adult per capita consumption of beer rose from 2.7 gallons at mid-century to 29.53 gallons per year in the period 1911–15.

THE POOR MAN'S CLUB   By Jon M. Kingsdale. Originally published under the title "The 'Poor Man's Club': Social Functions of the Urban Working-Class Saloon." From *American Quarterly,* XXV (1973), pp. 472–88. Copyright 1973, American Studies Association. Reprinted by permission of the journal, the author, and the American Studies Association.

Of the saloon's popularity there can be little doubt: in one day half the population of a city might visit its saloons. A survey of Chicago found that on an average day the number of saloon customers equaled half the city's total population. In Boston, with a total population of less than half a million in 1895—including women and children, most of whom did not frequent saloons—a police count numbered 227,000 persons entering the city's saloons. Many of those counted were suburban commuters not included in the city's population, as well as customers entering for a second or third time that day; nevertheless, considering the size of Boston's adult male population, the count is surprisingly high.

Part, but not all, of the saloon's attraction was alcoholic. Certainly the liquor was an integral and necessary element, as the failure of most temperance substitutes in America proved. But saloons did a great deal more than simply dispense liquor. The alcoholic "stimulation"—the neurological effects of alcohol are actually depressant, producing a diminution of inhibitions and thus a reduction in reserve and distance in social gatherings—cannot readily be distinguished from the social aspects of the saloon. The bartender, as "host" in his saloon, knew as well as the middle-class hostess of today that alcohol is an excellent icebreaker. . . .

Despite city ordinances regulating location and levying high license fees, it was relatively easy to open a saloon. With $200 to start, one could easily find a brewer willing to provide financial backing and find a location. The brewer paid the rent, the license fee, a bond if necessary, and supplied the fixtures and the beer. The saloon-keeper agreed to sell no other brand of beer and reimbursed his brewer by means of a special tax added on to the normal price of each barrel of beer. Four-fifths of Chicago's saloons were estimated to be under such an arrangement with brewers in 1907, as were 80 to 85 per cent of New York's saloons in 1908.

Although an appealing and easily accessible occupation, saloon-keeping was often an unprofitable business enterprise. The competition was tremendous; many saloons closed after only a few months in operation. In the lean years, 1897–1901, a third of Chicago's saloons closed down or sold out—in one and a half blocks of Chicago's 17th ward eighteen saloons opened and closed in as many months. Some saloons flourished as fancy establishments or well-known hangouts for politicians, athletes and other notables. But many saloons failed, and of those which stayed on, most merely continued to do a steady quiet business with neighborhood regulars.

Urban saloons of the late 19th and early 20th centuries did not conform to a single pattern. Saloons varied greatly in appearance, atmosphere and character of the clientele they served. Yet a majority of urban saloons may be subsumed under a single prototypic description. Usually situated on a corner for maximum visibility, the typical workingman's saloon was readily recognizable by its swinging shuttered doors and wrought iron windows cluttered with potted ferns, posters and bottles of colored water. Inside was a counter running almost the length of the room, paralleled by a brass footrail. The floor was covered with sawdust. Across from the bar were perhaps a few tables and chairs backed up by a piano, pool table or rear stalls. Behind the bar and over an assortment of lemons, glasses and unopened magnums of muscatel, port and champagne hung a large plate-glass mirror. The other walls would sport a number of murals, posters, photographs and brewer's advertisements. As common as the plate-glass mirror was the presence of at least one chromo reproduction of a disrobed siren reclining on a couch. The posters and photographs were often of sports heroes: about 1890 a picture of John L. Sullivan would have been found in most saloons. A few men might be leaning over the bar, clustered about the saloon-keeper—in his white starched coat or vest, moustache and well-oiled hair; a few more might be playing pool or sitting at tables talking over a beer, reading or playing cards. Beer for five cents and whiskey for ten or fifteen were the staples. The whiskey was drunk straight—to do otherwise would be considered effeminate—followed by a chaser of water or milk to put out the fire.

The typical workingman's saloon experienced rather slow business through the day until about seven or eight o'clock, except on weekends when it was generally crowded from Saturday noon to early Monday morning. The morning in most saloons began at about five or six o'clock and was spent mostly in cleaning up and preparing the free lunch for the noontime crowd and teamsters who would drop in throughout the afternoon. But in the evenings things picked up as workingmen gathered in saloons to enjoy each other's company.

Though by far the most common, the working-class saloon described above was not the only type of urban saloon. There were suburban beer gardens, downtown businessmen's saloons, and waterfront dives and barrel-houses serving sailors, tramps, petty criminals and the very poor. Jacob Riis, in *How the Other Half Lives*, described the lowest of the low in a New York tenement slum: in a dark clammy hovel were grouped ten or fifteen tramps and petty criminals seated on crates and broken chairs around a keg of stale beer. The dregs from used beer barrels lying out on the sidewalk awaiting the brewer's cart were drained off and doctored up to be served in old tomato cans to the less than distinguished clientele. But this was an extreme case. William Cole and Kellog Darland of the South End House in Boston described a typical waterfront dive as small, dirty and inhospitable. It was lighted by unshaded flickering gas jets revealing a gaudy mirror, foul beer-soaked sawdust on the floor, and no tables, chairs or inviting free lunch to encourage patrons to linger at their ease.

At the other end of the spectrum, the business districts contained a large number of well-appointed saloons catering to professionals, businessmen and the middle and upper classes in general. Here the bars were of mahogany, the pictorial art of a better class, and some even had orchestras. These saloons were often used as meeting places for business purposes, especially by sales representatives and buyers who might complete a transaction over a beer in an oak table alcove. In the suburbs could be found old homes of solid decor, converted to roadhouses for the use of travelers and suburban residents. Also in the suburbs as well as in town were German-model beer gardens providing good food and open spaces in which to relax while listening to a symphony orchestra.

With this perspective in mind, let us turn to an analysis of the social functions of the working-class urban saloon. The workingman's saloon was a leisure-time institution playing a large part in the social, political, even the economic, aspects of his life. It performed a variety of functions, major and minor: furnishing the cities' only public toilets, providing teamsters with watering troughs, cashing checks and lending money to customers, in addition to serving as the political and recreational focus of the workingman.

In its most encompassing function the saloon served many workingmen as a second home. If the middle-class male retired to his living room after dinner to relax, the workingman retired to the corner saloon to meet his friends, relax and maybe play a game of cards or billiards. Many workingmen thought of and treated the corner saloon as their own private club rather than as a public institutuion. They used it as a mailing address; leaving and picking up messages, and meeting friends there; depositing money with, or borrowing from, the saloon-keeper. Workingmen played cards, musical instruments and games, ate, sang and even slept there. Even today, "home territory" bars are characterized by a familiarity among patrons and hostility or suspicion toward newcomers.

For slum residents, especially in immigrant ghetto and tenement districts, the neighboring saloons were inevitably more attractive than their own over-crowded, dirty, noisy, ugly, poorly lighted and ventilated flats. For many immigrants their new homes in America were merely places to sleep and eat—life moved out of the flats into the streets and saloons. Large numbers of lodging-house boarders adopted saloons as surrogate homes, their own quarters being cramped, filthy and dull. Compared to cheap boarding houses that slept men dormitory style in long rows of bunks, the corner saloon was by far the more hospitable place to spend the evenings. Some saloon habitués even slept there—a place on the floor at night cost five cents.

Saloons also functioned as food suppliers. The "free lunch" fed thousands of men in each city. There was usually something on hand in saloons to munch on at any time, but from about eleven o'clock in the morning to three in the afternoon a special buffet lunch was served free to customers—who were, of course, expected to buy at least one beer. If a saloon did not serve a free lunch it often served a "businessman's lunch," which for ten to twenty-five cents was better than most restaurants could offer. The accent in the free lunch was on salty and spiced foods to provoke a thirst, but for five cents the workingman got a better lunch than most ten cent restaurants served, plus a beer and more attractive surroundings in which to enjoy it. Saloons could afford the free lunch because the brewer supplied the food at cost, having purchased it cheaply in quantity.

Saloons that sold lunches and some large saloons that offered free lunches provided quite a feast. One saloon in the 17th ward of Chicago, a working-class district, offered in its free lunch a choice of frankfurters, clams, egg sandwiches, potatoes, vegetables, cheeses, bread, and several varieties of hot and cold meats. Employing five men at the lunch counter, it gave away between thirty and forty dollars' worth of food a day: 150 to 200 pounds of meat, 1 to 2 bushels of potatoes, 50 loaves of bread, 35 pounds of beans, 10 dozen ears of corn and $2 worth of other vegetables. This was not the typical fare in a workingman's saloon, but even the average free lunch in an Eastern city—the free lunches in the East were usually less generous than those of the West and South, due perhaps to higher food prices and less competition among saloons of the East—was sufficient for noontime needs. In Boston, New York, Philadelphia or Baltimore a typical free lunch would consist of bread or crackers, bologna or weinerwurst, sliced tomatoes, salad, pickles, onions, radishes and perhaps soup or a hot meat stew. But even this, considering that cheap restaurants in Boston charged five cents for a sandwich, a piece of pie, two doughnuts, or a glass of milk, ten cents for a meat pie and twenty-five cents for a full dinner, was a bargain.

The free lunch fed a large portion of the working class and the middle class. Probably half or more of the cities' saloons offered a free lunch. In some cities, such as Boston, saloons were required by law to offer free food, if not exactly a meal, though in others, Atlanta for instance, they were forbidden by law to offer food. In Chicago, at the end of the 19th century, 92 of the 157 saloons in the 19th ward, and 111 of the 163 saloons of the 17th ward, both working-class districts, offered a free lunch. Along a distance of four miles on Madison Street, which ran through working-class residential and business districts of Chicago, 115 saloons offered a free lunch, compared to three restaurants offering a 5¢ lunch, five 10¢ restaurants, twenty 15¢ restaurants and twenty-five restaurants charging 20¢ to 35¢.

Saloons were also the most important source of recreation and amusement for the urban working class. They provided both recreational facilities and a general atmosphere which encouraged informal, spontaneous group activities. They catered to a larger clientele in a greater variety of ways than any other leisure-time institution, until athletics, films, the automobile and radio achieved a dominant position in recreational activities in the 1920s. In Boston, to take one example, the relatively extensive system of outdoor swimming facilities drew an attendance of just over 2 million in 1899—an attendance which Boston's saloons surpassed in nine days. Poolrooms in Boston drew a daily attendance one-tenth as large as the saloons attracted; coffee rooms did less well than poolrooms; and reading rooms in Boston drew a daily attendance less than one-twentieth of the saloons' patronage. While there was always a saloon just down the street or around the corner, city parks were usually located at such a distance from working-class residential districts that they were of little value to workers except on Sundays and holidays. In Boston the parks nearest working-class areas were far beyond walking distance. In Manhattan parks were conspicuous by their absence from tenement areas. Chicago's fine system of parks was located primarily in the suburbs. Public and private athletic facilities, reading rooms, clubs, labor union recreational halls, etc., were not plentiful at the turn of the century, nor were they desired by the working class nearly so much as saloons. They often catered to the values of a sponsoring philanthropist, whereas saloons tried to give the workingman exactly what he wanted.

Saloons offered a variety of amusements and recreational facilities, such as newspapers, cards, movies, a gramophone or live entertainment—usually a violinist, singer or vaudeville show—billiards, bowling, and sporting news relayed by ticker tape. Tables and chairs, cards and billiards were the most common and widely used facilities, though for an evening's entertainment at least one saloon offering a burlesque show was usually within easy reach of any working-class neighborhood.

The quality and quantity of amusements varied from one city to the next, and from one section of the country to another. In the East facilities were often limited due to strict government regulations which either explicitly prohibited certain forms of recreation in saloons, or kept the number of saloons in a city low enough that there was little competitive incentive to sponsor amusements in order to attract customers. In Boston, for example, pool tables in saloons were permitted only in rare instances; tables, chairs and cards were rare;

prostitution and gambling were totally divorced from the saloons. Gambling machines, billiards, bowling and similar games were prohibited in Philadelphia's saloons. Recreational facilities were more plentiful in the West. The great majority of saloons in St. Louis had tables, chairs and cards; many had billiard tables, and some had pianos. Tables, chairs, cards, billiards, gambling machines and games, and prostitution were common in the saloons of San Francisco. In Chicago, of the 320 saloons in the 17th and 19th wards, 183 had tables and chairs, 209 provided newspapers, 102 had pool tables and several saloons ran small gymnasiums, provided handball courts, music halls and/or gambling.

More important than the actual facilities was the air of relaxed, informal sociability which pervaded saloons. Saloon names like "The Fred," "Ed and Frank's," "The Club" and "The Poor Man's Retreat" promised a warm, friendly atmosphere. Patrons of a saloon often had something in common with each other—neighborhood ties, similar interests or a common occupation or ethnic background—to stimulate group feelings and camaraderie. Neighborhood ties and a common ethnic background most often united the group. Sometimes formal groups patronized saloons: singing societies, lodge chapters and neighborhood committees often met in saloons or adjoining rooms. Boxers and other athletes opened saloons which attracted fellow sportsmen and spectators. Saloons such as the "Milkmen's Exchange" and the "Mechanic's Exchange" attracted workingmen of the same occupation.

Alcohol, by virtue of its inhibition-releasing effect, stimulated feelings of social familiarity, group identification and solidarity and was, itself, a focus of group activity. The custom of treating was nearly universal: each man treated the group to a round of drinks, and was expected to stay long enough to be treated in turn by the rest of the group—which made for much happy backslapping, sloppy singing and drunken exuberance. If things were going slowly the saloon-keeper might treat the house to a round in order to stimulate fellowship and, hopefully, a few more paying rounds. The saloon-keeper often played the part of a host, keeping the "guests" happy—and somewhat orderly—and keeping the "party" going.

Singing seems to have been fairly common, both by groups and arising spontaneously. The songs, like the conversation, were often highly sentimental, lamenting the fallen girl or the drunk, idolizing motherhood, patriotism, the nobility of the workingman, the righteousness of working-class causes, or almost any other highly emotional subject. Such songs as "A Boy's Best Friend is His Mother," "Always Take Mother's Advice" and "A Flower From My Angel Mother's Grave" typify the sentimentality of saloon singing. But the saloon could be subdued and relaxed as well as loud and exuberant. Men might sit over a single beer for hours in earnest conversation, quietly playing cards or discussing politics.

Being central to the workingman's leisure-time activities, saloons came into contact with almost all aspects of his life; they touched the life of the cities at many points, from crime and poverty to politics and work. Crime, poverty, prostitution and machine graft flourished in the city and fed off saloons. Though the causes of these evils were deep-rooted and complex, the saloon was often pictured—in an overly simplified view—as the sole or main force responsible for the cities' problems. The saloon symbolized that threat which the lower-class immigrant, caught up in the harsh urban-industrial explosion after the Civil War, posed to traditional American morality.

Evils were ascribed all too simply to saloons, and the evils manifest in saloons were often exaggerated. As E. C. Moore, professor of sociology and social worker at Hull House, testified, saloons generally did not stand for intemperance and vice. In two hundred visits to saloons in Chicago's working-class districts he saw only three drunken men. Only 2 of the 157 saloons in Chicago's 19th ward were known to police as hangouts for thieves; one was known as a house of assignation. In Boston and Philadelphia gambling and prostitution were completely divorced from the saloons. But in many cities the connection did exist. The Raines Law in New York, prohibiting all liquor retailers except hotels from opening on Sunday, the biggest day of business, turned hundreds of saloons into brothels, or so-called Raines Law hotels. In certain well-defined sections of Chicago, St. Louis, San Francisco, Denver, Buffalo, Baltimore and many more cities prostitution and gambling were rife in the saloons. Chicago's Vice Commission of 1911 found saloons to have been the most conspicuous and important element in connection with prostitution aside from the brothels themselves. Prostitutes were tolerated by some saloon-keepers for the added business they were expected to attract. Sometimes the proprietor contracted with the girls to pay them a commission on drinks bought for them—a commission the saloon could well afford since it charged twenty-five cents for a beer in the rear stalls, and often served the girls soft drinks when they ordered distilled liquor. Sometimes waiters were expected when they took a job to bring their own prostitutes or bar girls with them to solicit drinks. Most saloons in almost every city were also guilty of consistently breaking laws regulating their closing hours and forbidding sales on Sunday. The fighting and drunkenness endemic to slum life was found as much in the saloons as on the streets and in tenements—perhaps more so, despite the fact that most saloon-keepers refused to serve drunks and tried to maintain order in their saloons, out of self-interest if for no other reason.

In assessing the relationship of crime, poverty and insanity to saloons, one is handicapped not so much by a lack of information as by a plethora of contradictory statistics, reflecting the bias of the surveyor as well as the reluctance of subjects to be completely frank. When data do seem reliable and statistical correlations are strong and positive, still, nothing is revealed of the causal relationship. Nevertheless, for what it is worth, the correlation of intemperance with pauperism, crime and insanity seems to have been very high. What this says about saloons is unclear since intemperance was not dependent solely upon saloons, nor did it disappear with Prohibition. As for the allegation, commonly made by temperance advocates, that the liquor bill was a drain on the family budget, it would seem to have been the cause, in itself, of very few cases of poverty. Liquor consumption averaged not more than 5 per cent of a workingman's family budget.

Saloons became involved even in the occupational concerns of the working class. Men of the same occupation would gather at certain saloons, and unemployed co-workers would go there for news of job openings and perhaps some relief. Employers in need of laborers might apply to the saloon-keeper. Prior to the existence of the International Longshoremen's Association dockworkers were usually hired by saloon-keepers—and sometimes forced to spend their wages in the contractor's saloon.

The unions had mixed feelings about saloons. Though union members were overwhelmingly anti-prohibitionist, union organizers and officers often feared the dulling effect of alcohol on working-class consciousness. Thus, although locals of the Union of Bakers and Confectioners met in saloons before the establishment of a national office, an officer of the national union stated his opposition to saloons, "especially when a 'Baker's Home' is connected therewith. When possible we establish employment offices ourselves, to give work free of charge to our members." The Knights of Labor and the Brotherhood of Locomotive Firemen refused membership to saloon-keepers. The United Garment Workers, the Journeymen Tailors and the United Mine Workers, to name only a few, tried whenever possible not to hold meetings in halls connected with saloons. But saloons welcomed unions and offered their rooms at prices below market level for chapter meetings, at a time when many unions were hard pressed to find any halls open to them. At the turn of the century half or more of the United Brewery Workers, the Wood Carvers' Association, the Amalgamated Wood Workers, and the Brotherhood of Boiler Makers and Iron Shipbuilders met in saloons or halls connected with them. In Buffalo, at the turn of the century, 63 of the city's 69 labor organizations held their meetings in halls connected with saloons, and in many other cities the dependence on saloons was nearly as great.

In politics, too, saloons played a major role. The liquor industry as a whole was thoroughly involved in politics, and saloons in particular were often associated with urban machine politics. Saloons provided politicians a means to contact and organize workingmen, and the political machine sold favors to saloons. In the former case, saloons were especially useful at the ward level. The ward leader was the backbone of the political machine, his club the bastion of political power in the ward. He built his following out of the ward club, called them together at the club for special occasions and kept them happy there. The club was a pleasant place where leaders and followers could find relaxation at a billiard table or a bar, and chew the political fat. It served as a social institution, a center for recreation and camaraderie, and a refuge from wife and family. The ward leader needed to be friendly, generous and thoroughly knowledgeable about his neighborhood. Saloons fitted the needs of the machine politician perfectly. Saloons could, and did, easily double as ward clubs, and the type and extent of the saloon-keeper's contact with his neighborhood was a valuable political asset. Being a working-class social center, the saloon provided a natural stage for politicians and an excellent base for organizing the vote. Plus, saloons were a good source of bums, drunks, petty criminals, hoboes and anyone else who might sell his vote for a few dollars in cash or in liquor. Half the Democratic captains of Chicago's first ward at the beginning of the 20th century were saloon proprietors. One-third of Milwaukee's 46 city councilmen in 1902 were saloon-keepers, as were about a third of Detroit's aldermen at the end of the 19th century. Tweed's "Boodle Board" of aldermen was composed in half of saloon-keepers or ex-saloon-keepers; in 1884 nearly two-thirds of the political conventions and primaries in New York City were held in saloons; and in 1890 eleven of New York City's 24 aldermen were saloon-keepers.

If the saloon was a natural center for political activity and a boon to the machine politician, the combination of early-hour closing laws and strong competition among saloons made the crooked politician and his favors indispensable to saloon-keepers. Proprietors were forced to pay the police and the political machine in order to stay open late at night, as well as for prostitution and gambling. In Chicago's first ward the annual Democratic Club Ball cost every saloon-keeper fifteen to twenty-five dollars in fifty-cent tickets, not to mention the routine monthly payments. Thus was cemented the bond between saloon and politician. The saloon was as often the victim as it was the springboard of the machine politician—in either case the relationship was intimate.

Not surprisingly, the saloon was itself a major, perhaps the major, issue in urban politics and reform. Sunday closing laws and their enforcement were a perennial, often highly emotional and important, campaign issue, which elicited from saloons an active and organized response. For instance, the Keep Your Mouth Shut Organization, centered in Detroit, supported, out of assessments on its member saloons, political candidates favorable to the liquor interests. The Detroit Liquor Dealers Protective Association was founded in 1880 with the intention of challenging "unfair" liquor legislation in the courts and aiding any of its 400 members charged with violations of the closing laws. At the end of the 19th century both retailers and brewers organized fraternal orders to promote their interests and protect themselves from temperance legislation. The Royal Ark organized Detroit's saloons into wards, each with a captain to look after the interests of the saloons in his ward. It also distributed to its members a list of endorsed candidates who would not enforce Sunday, holiday and early-hour closing laws. This was known as the "Saloon Slate."

If, then, the saloon affected the workingman's life in a variety of ways, what significant role did it play for the working class? The urban workingman's saloon served three major functions. First, saloons served as a major social focus of the neighborhood. The saloon was a local institution in an economy well on its way to production and consumption en masse. It was a neighborhood center in an urban environment which denied its residents that sense of community and stability inherent in an earlier, small-town America. Although some working-class saloons clustered about industrial enterprises, feeding off factory workers during the day, or depended on nightly entertainment and prostitution to draw patrons from a wide radius, these types were common only in certain slum, business and industrial areas of a city. Most saloons in residential districts—urban and suburban—drew a steady crowd of neighborhood regulars. And most city blocks had at least one "neighborhood" saloon. Indeed, the corner saloon may have been the most neighborly institution in the city. While children played in the street and women talked on tenement stoops, the men went to a saloon.

The saloon-keeper, himself, was often an important figure in the neighborhood and claimed a large place in the hearts of his regular customers. If a new saloon opened or an old one changed management the whole neighborhood would know of it in a matter of hours and come in to size up the new proprietor. The saloon-keeper often fostered community ties, for commercial reasons or otherwise. He might open connecting rooms for the entertainment of a local boys' club, or provide them with a club room for a small price. He might be the favorite local "pharmacist," prescribing stale beer for a gaseous stomach, a sloe gin fizz for clearing morning-after headaches, and other mixtures for chest colds, cramps, etc.

Saloons mirrored the character of the surrounding neighborhood, helped to shape it and tried to serve it. One could speak of the typical Jewish saloon on the lower East Side where the signs and conversation were all in Yiddish, of an Italish café-style saloon, the Irish-American stand-up saloon, or the German beer garden which attracted not only neighboring males, but their families as well. Whatever the ethnic background, saloons offered their services to the community. In a survey of Chicago's saloons they were noted to offer furnished rooms free or for a small charge to local men's clubs, musical societies, fraternal orders, small wedding parties and neighborhood meetings. As the surveyor stated, "The saloon is, in short, the clearing house for the common intelligence—the social and intellectual center of the neighborhood."

In a second aspect of its role, the saloon was a male institution in a culture still predominantly male-oriented, but loosing ground quickly to the concept of female emancipation and equality. Although some women drank in restaurants and beer gardens, the social and legal injunction against women drinking in, or even entering, working-class saloons was generally observed, except by prostitutes. The saloon was a thoroughly male institution with the appropriate atmosphere, from the sawdust on the floor to the pictures of athletes on the walls to the prostitutes in the backroom stalls. The saloon supported and reinforced a stereotypically masculine character and a self-sufficient all male culture separate from the prissy world of women and the constraints of family. Judging from barroom conversation and behavior, women were valued primarily as sexual objects. Otherwise they were pictured as a nuisance, superfluous at best, downright troublesome at worst. The ideal as represented in the decor and personified by the saloon-keeper was the strong male, unfettered by domestic chains and enjoying the camaraderie of his fellows with a carefree sociability. As children often gathered at saloon doorways, excited by the noisy scene within, the saloon probably played a part in the process by which many boys formed their values as American males. That happy, boisterous, uninhibited scene was a powerful model for the American male. As Jack London put it: "In the saloons life was different. Men talked with great voices, laughed great laughs, and there was an atmosphere of greatness. . . . Terrible they might be, but then that only meant they were terribly wonderful, and it is the terribly wonderful that a boy desires to know." Drink was the badge of manhood, the brass rail "a symbol of masculinity emancipate."

It seems likely that some sort of bachelor subculture existed prior to Prohibition and has since waned. The proportion of singles among the male population has declined significantly since the end of the 19th century: of males aged fifteen and over, the proportion single declined from 42% in 1890 to 33% in 1940, and to less than 25% in 1950. The thousands of men in any large city who lived in lodging houses, spending their days at work and their evenings in saloons and pool halls, had little real contact with women other than prostitutes. The saloon was particularly important as a social center for this group of workingmen. Many saloon-goers were, of course, married, but in some saloons the patrons were noted to be mostly over thirty and single. Clark Warburton, in his study of the effects of Prohibition, estimated that more than half of working-class drinking was done by single men. Certainly many of the heavy drinkers, saloon regulars, were bachelors: although only 45% of Boston's male population aged fourteen or over was single, 60% of a study sample of arrested drunks in Boston in 1909 were unmarried.

For married men the saloon was an escape from wife and family. The workingmen at McSorley's—of John Sloan's painting, "McSorley's Saloon"— looked "as if they never thought of a woman. They were maturely reflecting in purely male ways and solemnly discoursing, untroubled by skirts or domesticity." For married men, free for only a few hours, as well as for young "stags" and older bachelors, the saloon was an escape, a bastion of male fellowship and independence.

Abstainers, too, seem to have understood the self-sufficient masculine character of saloons. Saloons were often pictured by Prohibitionists and middle-class women as competitors to home and family. Feminists heartily supported the Temperance movement. The Women's Christian Temperance Union was a leading temperance organization, also strongly committed to female suffrage and feminism. The Anti-Saloon League, though it tried to stay clear of all causes other than Temperance, apparently felt that the link between prohibition and woman suffrage was so strong that the League could hardly afford to ignore the latter. For the Temperance movement was in part a reflection of a public desire, especially strong among women, to curb the self-assertive, boisterous masculinity of the saloon, to support and protect the family, and to return the husband—immigrant workingmen in particular—to the home. Even moderate temperance advocates felt that the nation needed and Prohibition might start "a new awakening to the values of the home . . . broadened into a contagion that shall cover the country."

Third, the saloon was symbolically and functionally alien to that traditional American ethic rooted in a largely Anglo-Saxon, Protestant population heavily influenced by its Puritan antecedents. The Yiddish saloon on the lower East Side, as much as the intoxicated "nigger" in the South, was perceived as a threat to the traditional culture and social fabric. The saloon was not only the symbol of a predominantly urban, new-immigrant, working-class life-style alien to the traditional American ascetic ethic of work, frugality, self-control, discipline and sobriety; it served as an alternative, a competitor, to the traditional pattern. Content to waste his time and money in saloons and take his sodden pleasures in near absolute leisure, the urban immigrant worker lacked the ability and incentive to boot-strap himself up into the middle class. In the eyes of the temperance advocate, it was the saloon that kept him down, thus impeding the process of cultural assimilation and slowing down America's march to material bliss.

Rather than aid immigrant groups to assimilate, rather than encourage the working class to adopt middle-class manners and aspirations, the working-man's saloon tended to conserve and reinforce ethnic and class ties. Saloons in immigrant districts usually attracted and catered to a single ethnic group, according to the character of the neighborhood and the nationality of the saloon-keeper. As a highly adaptive local institution, the saloon tended to reflect and serve the character of its clientele: drinking habits, games, newspapers, language—all reflected the ethnic milieu. Immigrants also used their saloons for ethnic group meeting halls and for the celebration of their national occasions. Moreover, the saloon provided immigrants, Eastern and Southern Europeans especially, the kind of informal, relaxed, slow moving social setting many had been accustomed to in the old country. As for class ties, the workingman's saloon was oriented toward relief from work and toward the weekend binge: the absence of time limits, the stimulus to uninhibited self-expression, the lack of any goal-oriented activity in saloons made them a purely nonproductive leisurely institution, reflecting working-class values in general and a lower-class tendency to divorce work and enjoyment in particular.

The ethnic and class orientation of saloons was clear. They were most dense in immigrant neighborhoods and most frequented by the working class. The working-class saloon was central to a way of life engendered by large-scale immigration and a growing urbanism and industrialism, and appropriate to a relatively newly formed proletariat. Providing ample opportunity for relaxation, supporting immigrant groups in their efforts to retain ethnic identity, harboring vice, gambling, criminals and machine politicians, the saloon was alien to Puritan America and efficiency minded Progressives alike.

The saloon, then, was a community center tending to give some coherence to neighborhoods by focusing the attention of male residents upon the people and events of the area. It was a male institution reinforcing stereotypically masculine qualities and catering to the social needs of that large segment of men who remained bachelors. It was a form of amusement that encouraged the working class, immigrants especially, in the retention of their cultural identity and retarded the movement to assimilation into the American middle class.

MANAGING THE ENVIRONMENT

Designing Places
for
Mechanized Leisure

ROBERT E. SNOW AND DAVID E. WRIGHT

Luna Park, Coney Island

AMERICANS HAVE SHAPED AND RESHAPED THEIR ENVIRONMENT with each successive generation, a process that has cleared forests and transformed settlements into metropolises. The selections in the first volume of this anthology detail how Europeans changed the landscape that the Indians had molded to their social and economic needs into a landscape that conformed with the settlers' way of life. Then, people of later generations promoted the development of city parks in response to the problems of overcrowding, lack of proper sanitation, and the loss of the beauty of Nature. In the following selection, Robert Snow and David Wright detail how the creation of modern amusement parks along the beach front of Coney Island in the late 1890s and early 1900s brought about another environmental transformation—in this case, one in which the mechanization of the industrial revolution was used not to build factories, but to power leisure-time activities.

Coney Island developed first as an isolated beach resort and later, with improved transportation to New York City, it became a major center of vacation hotels for the middle and upper classes. When F. L. Olmsted developed plans for Brooklyn, he envisioned Coney Island as a natural area where people could escape from the frenzy of city life. But instead, Coney Island turned into the location of a cluster of amusement parks and home to mechanized rides and a sea of electric lights. People came because the stimulating atmosphere allowed escape from the dull worries of daily urban life. Many came to the parks because they were attracted more by the wonders of mechanical technology than by the aesthetic beauty of the existing urban parks.

The family atmosphere at such amusement parks as Steeplechase and Dreamland was the result of conscious planning. The architectural themes were unified, and the grounds were landscaped and clean. Strict rules of conduct also helped to keep order in the tumultuous environment. This formula worked for over three quarters of a century; millions of New Yorkers flocked annually to Coney Island, neglecting it only in the 1960s when wear and tear had destroyed the illusion of neatness and order.

To SAY THAT AMERICAN LIFE has been radically altered by mechanization in the last one hundred fifty years seems, at first, to belabor the obvious. We have accepted these changes more or less happily, certainly in housing and transportation, if not always in our jobs. But in one major area of life—leisure—where mechanization is not clearly prescribed by economic necessity or social custom, there is controversy over its virtues and disadvantages. Snowmobilers and crosscountry skiers, powerboaters and sailors, motorhomers and backpackers argue, usually good-humoredly but sometimes acrimoniously, about their methods of enjoying snow, water and wilderness. It sometimes seems we are divided into two camps: the purists who reject mechanized leisure, and the mechanists who warmly embrace it. Involved in this conflict is the clash of two very different systems of values between which are significant aesthetic, psychological and moral differences and, of course, very different conceptions of man's proper relationship to nature.

Why this division of opinion? What are the popular images and mythologies associated with mechanized and non-mechanized leisure? And perhaps most basically, how does mechanization affect popular culture and, conversely, how do popular ideas affect the implementation of new technologies? In the development of Coney Island as America's first and probably still most symbolic commitment to mechanized leisure, we have a fascinating case study which reveals this interaction between popular culture and technical change and affords us the opportunity to begin answering some of our questions.

Our procedure in studying Coney Island, which also provides the format for this article, was to begin by writing an interpretive popular and technical history of Coney Island depending as much as possible on nineteenth and early twentieth century sources close to Coney's development and the ensuing debate. From these sources we tried to sort out various attitudes toward the mechanization of Coney and to search for their origins in the aesthetic, moral and psychological beliefs of the time. We also looked at the economic status of

DESIGNING PLACES FOR MECHANIZED LEISURE   By Robert E. Snow and David E. Wright. Originally published under the title "Coney Island: A Case Study in Popular Culture and Technical Change." From *Journal of Popular Culture* 9 (1976), pp. 960–74. Reprinted by permission.

workers and the changes in technology during the period to ascertain how these factors affected the development and popularity of Coney.

In this early example of mechanized leisure there are a series of suggestive relationships between popular culture and technical change. The working classes, those most affected by the increasing pace and increasing mechanization of life, accepted mechanized Coney most readily. For reasons discussed in the second half of the paper, the extroverted, fast-paced, time-structured, sensuous and sensual experience of Coney appealed to them. The opponents of mechanized Coney, on the other hand, were the educated and affluent whose station allowed them to escape the most deleterious effects of mechanized life. Due largely to their religious and aesthetic beliefs, leisure was viewed ideally as an opportunity for spiritual "re-creation" spent in introspective activities preferably involving close contact with nature.

One of the most important aspects of Coney's history was the way this conflict was partially resolved by Coney's great entrepreneurs with the creation in the late 1890's and the early 1900's of the modern amusement park: enclosed, morally policed, architecturally unified and moderately educational. Our study of Coney Island, joined with other case studies we are currently pursuing, leads us to speculate that when new technologies upset traditional patterns of work, play, transportation and living in general, a debate is generated within popular culture which is partially resolved by implementing the new technology in a way that makes concessions to popular myths and ideals. In turn, elements of the popular myths and ideals are modified, accommodating themselves to the technology and thereby imbuing it with positive attributes. This certainly seems to have happened at Coney.

Finally, we discuss Coney's decline. In the end Coney became a victim of its own success and of the technologies which created its great appeal. But it also appears that the formula developed by Coney's entrepreneurs has, using new technologies, survived in the Disneylands and Cedar Points of today.

Coney Island's history as resort and amusement area can be divided into four periods: the Beach Era, 1829–1875; the Hotel and Midway Era, 1876–1896; the Enclosed Amusement Park Era, 1897–1910; and a long period of increasing crowds and eventual deciine, 1911–present. Coney's appearance and the experience of its visitors changed remarkably during these years—and actually the major changes took place in a much shorter time, from 1865–1905—as the island evolved from a quiet beach resort to a nocturnal, mechanized fantasy land where the beach was all but obscured from view. These changes were produced by the complex interaction of technological, social and political changes, or, put another way, through the interaction of popular culture and technical change.

The Beach Era began in 1829 when the Shell Road (constructed with sea shells) connected Long Island and a desolate sand bar known to Gravesend farmers as Coney (pronounced in the 19th century like "looney") Island. A few wealthy patrons began traveling from Brooklyn by coach to stay at the island's first hotel, The Coney Island House. They sought the resort for its solitude, its salt air which was thought to aid cholera victims, and for its sublime vistas. The visitors strolled the beautiful beach, enjoyed both the soon-to-be-famous Coney clam dinners served with local ale and the solitude which was broken only occasionally by local residents digging clams or shooting snipe.[1]

In the 1850's two events began to change Coney's complexion: first, mixed bathing (which had theretofore been considered improper) was popularized by the rich at Newport; and second, it began to be possible to reach the island by public transportation, although the horsedrawn street cars from Brooklyn ran irregularly and were slow and dirty.[2] Small hotels, numbering about twelve by 1866, and their bath houses sprang up along the beach.[3] The middle and working classes began coming out to Coney on Sundays for swimming and relaxation. With them came the "vicious classes," the gamblers, con artists, and prostitutes, drawn to Coney because it was outside New York City and Brooklyn police jurisdiction and because there were crowds with money to spend on leisure.[4] These "gentlemen of uncertain business occupations" and the "ladies of the demi-monde" staked out a claim to the westernmost portion of the island from which they were not dislodged by reformers until well after the turn of the century.

By the early 1870's steamers were plying the waters of New York harbor bringing visitors from the city to Coney; on land, the horsedrawn cars had been supplemented by steam railroads. Attendance had increased from the "hundreds" who visited Coney only on Sundays in the mid-sixties to the many "thousands" who now came several days a week.[5] Yet despite these changes, Coney was still a sandbar with small hotels and bath houses scattered along the shore. One observer noted that there were "few attractions" on this "low, unpicturesque . . . dreadfully sandy" island, but that the beach and the swimming were superb. Further, despite the increasing bustle, Coney retained until the early seventies an almost rural ambiance. One traveler, arriving at the beach, encountered a sign reading: "Bathers Without Full Suits Positively Prohibited By Law." Under the signpost were the carcasses of a horse and a dog.[6]

Yet the rapid improvements in the quality and quantity of public transportation and the huge crowds made the further development of Coney too attractive to be foregone by entrepreneurs.[7] The resulting effort to provide new attractions, distractions and services to Coney's patrons ushered in the next period: The Hotel and Midway Era, 1876–1896.

This second historical period was characterized by the addition of more than a dozen huge structures (of three different types) to Coney's theretofore rather barren landscape. First, three large hotels, the Manhattan Beach, the Oriental, and the Brighton Beach were erected between 1877 and 1880.[8] The Manhattan Beach and the Oriental were situated on the previously undeveloped eastern end of Coney known as Manhattan Beach. They were massive structures featuring landscaped lawns, verandas, flag-tiped cupolas, and opulent dining and sitting rooms. These hotels, serviced by their own railroads from Brooklyn and separated by an unimproved expanse of sand from Coney's main resort section, catered to the upper classes who began to return to the island in force. (They had been gone since the 1850's when "common" people overan the beach.) The third hotel, the Brighton Beach, was built just to the west of this exclusive strip. It catered to the larger middle class and was appropriately bigger than the Manhattan Beach or the Oriental. In fact, when it was completed, the 450 ft. x 120 ft. Brighton Beach Hotel was advertised as the largest resort hotel on the Atlantic.[9]

Interestingly, when these hotels were completed, Coney Island provided a linear, visual study in American class structure. On the western end of the island, at Norton's point, were the "vicious classes." The center-west portion, which came to be known as West Brighton and which was becoming the major amusement section, was patronized mostly by the working and middle classes. Just further east was middle-class Brighton Beach. And finally, aristocratic Manhattan Beach occupied the eastern tip of the island. Perhaps equally symbolic was the ease with which these classes mingled, at least for short periods. Middle and upper class men went "slumming." Gamblers and prostitutes were not infrequently seen on the back stairways of the lavish hotels. And middle class families trudged up the sandy beach for dinner at the Manhattan and a chance to be temporarily part of the elite.

The second group of buildings to rise into Coney's skyline came from the dismantled Philadelphia Centennial Exposition. In 1877 and 1878, the Japanese and Brazilian Pavilions and the U. S. Government building were moved and reassembled in West Brighton where they served more mundane functions as beer hall, dairy, and hotel-restaurant.[10] In 1881, the Philadelphia Exposition Observation Tower arrived. At 300 feet, it was, we believe, the tallest structure in greater New York. Visitors, who ascended via the steam driven elevator, described an awe-inspiring view of seascape, harbor and city.

The third category of buildings included two doubled decked steel piers, a giant wooden elephant, an aquarium, a 200 ft. diameter balloon hanger, and a 2,500 seat amphitheatre.[11] These buildings demonstrate the increasingly diversified and the more technologically dependent entertainment on the island. Although several steamship lines docked there, the steel piers, which stretched over one thousand feet into the Atlantic, served several other functions. They housed hotels, shops, restaurants, and 1,200 changing rooms for swimmers. Bands played continuously for dancers in the roof-top pavilions.

The 175 foot high wooden elephant, a minor technical wonder, housed a hotel, a restaurant, and shops in its legs and body.[12] The aquarium offered the public the first of a long line of wild animal and fish exhibits on the island.[13] A Professor King would send the brave a fifth of a mile into the heavens in his balloon which, tethered by a steel cable, was launched from his circular hanger.[14] The amphitheatre, built at Manhattan Beach, was packed when British pyrotechnic (firework) specialists, Pain and Brock, staged "Defeat of the Spanish Armada" and similar performances which included rapidly changing scenes and a cast of hundreds.[15] (Sometimes Professor King would assist by dropping fireworks from his balloon.) John Philip Sousa and Gilmore also used the amphitheatre for musical extravaganzas. Importantly, in these spectacles, followed later by horse racing and prize fights, Coney made its first commitment to technically sophisticated, mass entertainment. Tacky side show booths featuring electricity and lung testing machines, the camera obscura, jugglers, and freaks of all descriptions also appeared during this period.

The bigger crowds and the combination of all these new buildings began to produce the tactile and sensory experience for which Coney Island became famous, but which was very different indeed from the original experience of the quiet beach resort. Boisterous crowds mingled on paved concourses by the sea.

Flags from every nation, which for some reason became one of Coney's trade-marks, adorned every hotel and high building. The cries of barkers, the seductions of prostitutes, the strains of twenty or thirty different bands, and the laughter of the crowds filled the salt air. Significantly, by 1892, Coney drew more patrons by night than by day.[16]

The tempo and atmosphere of the island were monitored and regulated by one man, John Y. McKane, who made possible Coney's remarkable growth and prosperity during the Hotel and Midway Era. McKane began as a clam digger and a carpenter in Gravesend. In that latter capacity he got in on the ground floor of the post Civil War boom in small hotels and bath houses. His contacts helped elect him constable of Gravesend in 1867. By 1884, the ambitious McKane had become a one-man government. He simultaneously held office as Police Chief, Police Commissioner, Town Supervisor, Superintendent of Sunday Schools, Head of the Town Board, the Board of Health, and the Excise Commission. "His various offices enabled him to initiate legislation, pass it, award contracts, audit bills, reward friends and punish enemies."[17] The Chief, who sported a gold-handled cane and a diamond studded police badge, could throw the Gravesend and Coney Island vote to whomever he chose, and by huge majorities. In 1884 Coney supported the Democrat, Cleveland, by a lopsided margin; and in 1888 they elected the Republican, Harrison (who was running against Cleveland), by an equally large majority.[18]

McKane, whose only vice was the love of power, was sympathetic to the vices of others. He tolerated equally the illegal land deals by Coney's entrepreneurs and the prostitution and gambling, so long as none of it got out of hand and so long as the public kept coming back happy. "After all," he is said to have remarked, "this ain't no Sunday school."

So long as McKane ruled, Coney prospered in nonchalant indifference to the howls of critics in the New York press and clergy, who wanted the island cleaned up and its Bowery, or "Gut," replaced by a park.[19] But by the early 1890's, history was running against McKane for reform slates were winning elsewhere in New York. Finally, when he jailed poll watchers who had been impowered by the State Supreme Court, telling them, "injunctions don't go here," McKane made a fatal mistake.[20]

McKane left Coney for Sing Sing in 1894.[21] This and two other events ended the Hotel and Midway Era. Second, dating from the mid 1880's, severe storms eroded Manhattan and Brighton Beaches. In 1888 six railroad engines were used to drag the huge Brighton Beach Hotel back 450 feet from the disappearing shore.[22] But the era of the big hotels was over, and the respectable classes were leaving Coney again. Third, in 1893 and 1895 major fires swept the heart of the midway district in West Brighton.[23] These events ended the second of Coney's historical periods and laid the groundwork for the third: the era of the Enclosed Amusement Parks 1897–1910.

It was inevitable that Coney Island would become a major recreational area for New York City, but there was nothing inevitable about the form and nature of the recreation experience. In the early 1870's Frederick Law Olmsted included as part of his Prospect Park plan an Ocean Parkway designed to link Prospect Park with the Coney Island beach.[24] Other than a concern to provide for the leisure needs of New York citizens, the activities which came to characterize McKane's Coney had nothing in common with Olmsted's vision of providing peaceful "recreation" for the inhabitants of the frenzied city.[25] Clearly, Coney Island did not develop as Olmsted would have wished.

Mechanized leisure became firmly established as a major part of Coney during the 1870's and 1880's. The first technological spectacular was the 300 foot observation tower erected in 1881 but a more significant event had occurred a number of years earlier. Sometime in the 1870's a merry-go-round was erected on Coney's sands. It was the first and one of the mildest of a long series of mechanical rides which were to become the symbol of Coney. The formula behind the success of most of these rides was a combination of thrill plus some sort of intimacy with sexual overtones.[26] Perhaps this was best symbolized by the sign near one roller coaster:[27]

WILL SHE THROW HER ARMS AROUND YOUR NECK?
WELL, I GUESS, YES!

From the vantage point of our sophisticated age the gentle carousel seems far removed from the formula of thrill and intimacy, but in the 1870's before our senses had been jaded by so much exposure to speed and to flesh, that was not necessarily the case. The glimpse of a well turned ankle as the carousel steed was mounted and the stately revolution of the device was stimulation enough for many.

Many more mechanical rides were to follow. In 1884 the first of many variants using tracked railways appeared. Called the switchback railroad it was a mammoth thing, 600 feet long. Cars coasted over an undulating track from the beginning to the far end of the structure. They were then raised mechanically to the top in order to undulate their way back to the starting point. The next year a mutant form of the switchback was built in which the ends of the tracks were joined to form a circular and continuous ride; the American version of the roller coaster was born. Soon tunnels and caves were added to the roller coaster and it was re-christened the scenic railroad.[28] In 1894 George Tilyou, perhaps the greatest of the Coney Island entrepreneurs, brought the first Ferris Wheel to the beach.[29] 125 feet high, it was a direct imitation of the giant wheel which had dominated the Chicago Columbian Exhibition the previous year. It is important to note that the Chicago Ferris Wheel was America's answer to the Eiffel Tower. When challenged to produce a spectacular engineering triumph to match the Eiffel Tower, which had recently been the center of attraction at a Parisian exposition, Ferris responded with his wheel. Powered by two steam engines each of 1,000 horse power, it was 250 feet high, weighed 1,400 tons and could carry more than 2,000 passengers in its 36 cars. The Chicago Ferris Wheel like the Eiffel Tower represented in its day the ultimate in structural engineering. Tilyou, who had grown up on Coney Island, had a shrewd sense of what would appeal to the Island crowds. His importation of the engineering spectacular from Chicago was an immediate success.

Three years later Tilyou scored an even greater triumph when he opened Steeplechase, the first modern amusement park. The time was ripe for Steeplechase. McKane had been in Sing Sing for three years but the reformers who had hoped to clean up the gambling and prostitution in the gut had been only partially effective. Periodically, a hue and cry was raised as solid citizens sought to have the amusement area swept clean and turned into a park complete with green grass and benches. Tilyou also wanted to find a way to exclude the rowdy element and to attract families to his amusement devices which were now scattered over an area of several blocks in the heart of the gut. His solution, the enclosed amusement park, ultimately proved to be fabulously successful. Tilyou incorporated the rides, the side shows, the bands, the noise and constant motion which had come to characterize the Coney Island experience and brought them together within a unified architectural theme. To the auditory and tactile elements which had been long a part of the Coney Island scene Tilyou added a visual dimension and in the process provided clean, neat, landscaped, educational and respectable family entertainment. And yet the sensual element was still there. More surprisingly, the spate of magazine articles and newspaper feature stories which appeared in the next few years praising Tilyou and his park were unanimous in declaring that where the reformers had failed, Tilyou had won. Entertainment aimed at the whole family had triumphed over vice; and the gut, if not 99 and 44/100 percent pure, had changed significantly.[30]

Even more spectacular than Steeplechase was Luna Park which opened in 1903.[31] Luna utilized to the fullest the newly mature technology of electricity employing 250,000 light bulbs, at the time the greatest number ever concentrated on a single site. On opening night 43,000 paid admission in the first two and a half hours. Its attractions included a Grand Promenade, Eskimo Village, Shoot-the-Chutes, Trip to the North Pole, German Village, Old Mill, Grand Ballroom, Canal of Venice, Electric Tower, Dragon's Gorge, Helter Skelter and Trip to the Moon.[32] It was entertaining, educational, flamboyant, and even sophisticates were impressed by the spectacle of Luna's lights. Maxim Gorki wrote:

> With the advent of night a fantastic city all of fire suddenly rises from the ocean into the sky. Thousands of ruddy sparks glimmer in the darkness, limning in fine, sensitive outline on the black background of the sky shapely towers of miraculous castles, palaces and temples. Golden gossamer threads tremble in the air. They intertwine in transparent flaming patterns, which flutter and melt away, in love with their beauty mirrored in the waters. Fabulous beyond conceiving, ineffably beautiful, is this firey scintillation.[33]

The next year a third amusement park opened. It was Luna Park plus! If Luna counted 250,000 electric lights, Dreamland boasted of 1,000,000. Despite the competition Luna drew 4,000,000 visitors in 1904.

The owners of the amusement parks, especially Tilyou, continued to innovate developing new rides. From 1905 to 1910 the *Scientific American* ran a number of articles describing the new rides while lauding the mechanical ingenuity and engineering sophistication which they displayed. The editors' favorite apparently was a ride called the Witching Waves which rated a cover story in 1908[34] but close behind was the Leap Frog Railroad and a variety of centrifugal devices.[35] While there was much at Coney Island and within the amusement parks which owed little to contemporary technology, it was the mechanical ride which had come to symbolize fun on the beach.

The brief history of Coney Island's development from beach resort to exotic amusement park reveals the complex interaction of technological, social, moral and esthetic forces and ideals. Any many of the "interactions" were, in fact, acrimonious clashes, for there was a great, though one-sided, argument over mechanized Coney's sins and virtues. Coney's admirers and patrons, who came principally from the working and business classes, were not polemicists; they debated with their feet and wallets. We know the intensity of the midway's appeal for them through Coney's phenomenal attendance figures and huge revenues.[36] But, because they were largely silent, we have to speculate about their motivations. On the other hand, Coney's detractors, who tended to be educated, middle or upper-class, relatively affluent, and reform-minded, were outspoken and specific. Interestingly, examination of the motivations and arguments of both of these groups prefigures our modern debate on the mechanization of leisure.

Before Tilyou's park made the midway more acceptable to them, critics rejected Coney on social, moral and aesthetic grounds. First, the wealthier class devoted themselves to historically aristocratic leisure activities, no doubt as an emblem of their caste. Significantly, Manhattan Beach preserved the landscaped lawns, the verandas and the ocean vistas of the beach resort era long after the beach at West Brighton had been all but obscured by rides and booths.

Second, reformers associated mechanized leisure with moral depravity and only partly because Coney's mechanized amusements were in the "gut" which was also the haven of gamblers and prostitutes. These reformers correctly understood that the speed, the power, the sexual overtones, and the general sensory bombardment ran very much counter to their contention that the proper role of leisure was moral and spiritual "re-creation," and not mind dulling amusement.

Third, the alternatives to Coney which the reformers proposed reveal their aesthetic biases. They had backed the development of Central Park in New York City and Prospect Park in Brooklyn completed in the 1860's and 1870's respectively, and they wanted to replace Coney's West Brighton area with another park. Central and Prospect parks, sculpted to picturesque ideals by landscape architect Frederick Law Olmsted, were to the reforming eye, "conspicuous" for their "moral" and "spiritual" effect on visitors. They hoped that a park at Coney would "cultivate among the community loftier and more refined desires." This is, obviously, an educated reaction to nature. Sitting in a park, or gazing at a seascape is a reflective, unstructured experience. It would naturally appeal to those schooled in the aesthetics of the picturesque and the sublime, or put another way, to those who "knew" how to look at nature.[37] Further, the experience would appeal to those used to leisure time and for whom introspection would not conjure up images of slum dwellings and long hours of labor at meager pay. Ironically, the civil engineering which undergirded the construction of Central and Prospect Parks represented a much more massive use of technology than Coney's roller coasters and ferris wheels.[38]

On the other hand, the throngs who packed the steamers and railways for the lights of Coney were not interested in aesthetic theories. Most of them, whether from the working or business class, whether immigrant or native American, had rural backgrounds. Having fought the land for a living, or having come to the city to make their fortunes, they did not see close contact with nature as a "spiritual necessity" as the Romantic aestheticians did. They did visit Central and Prospect Parks but their reasons for going and their experiences, though unrecorded, were probably very different from those of Coney's critics.

People probably enjoyed Coney for a number of reasons. First, the experience of the rides and the bustling midway was structured, fast-paced and extroverted. It allowed ordinary people to leave their cares momentarily behind and to escape into a fantasy land. Second, the atmosphere was sensuous and sensual. The crowds, the bands, the lights, the food and drink were seductive in themselves; but the rides and amusements also offered the promise of sanitized sex. Air jets in the funhouses lifted girls' skirts, couples were squeezed together by the force of the rides, and the promise of the sign by the roller coaster that, "she will throw her arms around your neck," was not lost on the crowd.

Third, the increasing pace and increasing mechanization of life may have made solitude and introspection unwelcome strangers to workers and business people alike. Mechanized, time structured leisure may simply reflect mechanized time structured lives.[39] Fourth and finally, Coney's technological wonders allowed people to participate vicariously in the myth of progress, and to use technology for escape—as a contrast to their common experience of growing constraints and frustrations imposed upon daily life by the engine of technical change.

In summary, Frederick Law Olmsted and Chief McKane represent the polarities of the debate on the mechanization of leisure at Coney. For Olmsted, the design of Central Park and Prospect Park was an intensely self-conscious effort to provide an environment within the city which would meet the emotional and psychic needs of the urban dweller cut off from rural vistas. Olmsted's version of "re-creation" embodied a cluster of values shared by many of the participants in the elite culture of the period. Needless to say, the values embodied by Chief McKane and the entrepreneurs of the gut were often antithetical to those of the elite. The gut provided amusement rather than recreation and it was a kind of amusement that was often perceived to be at odds with conventional versions of virtue and leisure. But, as the attendance figures show, it was popular.

Perhaps Tilyou's most important stroke of genius in the design of Steeplechase was in mediating between these two diverse value clusters. By enclosing his park, Tilyou was able to exclude the prostitutes and gamblers, the gross sexuality and vulgarity while still retaining the thrills and sensuous ambience that had come to characterize Coney. Tilyou had his own group of "enforcers" to see that rowdy behavior was dealt with promptly. The morals of women and children were protected by a strict rule prohibiting entertainers from using even mildly vulgar language;[40] to break the rule meant instant dismissal and one has the feeling that Tilyou had his own efficient version of "due process." There was a sexual element with the enclosed parks but it was largely limited to the public jostling generated by the amusement rides. It is even possible that the allure of this sanitized sex was counterbalanced in the eyes of the reformers by the educational value of the amusement park. The smiling faces of anthropology, geography, and zoology were presented to the children of the city streets as they viewed Eskimo or German Villages, sailed the Canals of Venice or rode the Camels and Elephants which were often a feature of the parks. While the aesthetic values of Steeplechase or Luna were not within the tradition of the picturesque, the parks did provide a unified architectural theme, landscaped grounds, and cleanliness which was in stark contrast to the disordered and disheveled collage of the gut. Much of Tilyou's achievement lay in his creation of a new vehicle for high density urban amusement which was able to attract patrons from a wide range of socio-economic levels.

Perhaps 1910 marked the high point of Coney Island's career as the world's most famous amusement center. The next year Dreamland burned never to be rebuilt. Although higher and faster and more terrifying rides continued to be built, the editors of *Scientific American* apparently felt that they were not worth reporting. Coney Island was beginning to fall off the crest of the entertainment wave it had created as the spring of technical inventiveness which had marked its glory years was transformed into the mindless repetition of a formula. As the public became increasingly inured to speed, one disgruntled islander commented, "Nowadays you have to half kill them to get a dime."[41]

When the massive use of electrical lighting became commonplace and the automobile began to replace the railroad as the dominant form of transportation, Coney Island progressively lost its aura of excitement and began to assume more the shabby atmosphere of the small town carnival. Even in its heyday it was easy for the unsympathetic critic to look behind the facade of burlap, lath and plaster that gave form and shape to Dreamland, Luna, and Steeplechase. Despite his apparent genuine captivation with the spectacle of Coney's evening skyline, "a fantastic city all of fire," Gorki could see only human emptiness and sham on closer examination. After describing in detail his experiences in one amusement park attraction, "A Trip to Hell," Gorki added sardonically that "hell is very badly done."[42]

While the creative spirit faded, the transportation system which had meant so much to the development of the Island continued to improve until, in 1920, the subway reached Coney putting it within reach of virtually all of New York City for no more than a nickel. The crowds and the noise which had always been such an important part of Coney Island began to become unbearable. The subway clientele wanted their amusement at subway prices and the ever versatile entrepreneurs were ready to oblige; the slide towards the tawdry and the raucous accelerated. Attendance figures continued to climb reaching a remarkable 1,500,000 one sweltering day in 1952; but the magic was gone. By the early 1970's one writer could compare the hump-back skeletons of obsolete amusement rides to the remains of dinosaurs from the ancient past, fossilized relics from another era that time had passed by.[43]

In many ways Coney Island was a victim of the very factors which once made it great. Wedded to a technology of entertainment and amusement which no longer had the power to captivate, it was overwhelmed finally by the sheer growth of the city which had first nourished it. In a remarkable way, however, the formula pioneered by Steeplechase, Luna Park, and Dreamland is still with us. Dependent upon the new transportation technologies of the interstate highway system and jet transports, and exploiting to the full the entertainment potential of electronics and plastics, Walt Disney has given us an updated Dreamland which is "clean, neat, landscaped, educational and respectable family entertainment." Tilyou would have loved it.

NOTES

[1] There are two good anecdotal histories which contain a substantial amount of information of interest to students of Coney Island. These are *Good Old Coney Island* by Edo McCullough (New York: Scribner, 1957) and *Sodom by the Sea: An Affectionate History of Coney Island* by Oliver Pilat and Jo Ranson (New York: Doubleday, Doran & Company, Inc., 1941).

[2] Foster Rhea Dulles, *A History of Recreation: America Learns to Play*, 2nd. ed. (New York: Appleton-Century-Crofts) pp. 152–153.

[3] *New York Times*, 10 July 1866, p. 5, col. 2 (Hereafter cited as *NYT*).

[4] *NYT*, 21 July 1868, p. 5, col. 4; *NYT*, 31 Aug. 1874, p. 8, col. 1. The *New York Times* reporters writing in the 1860's and early 1870's take an almost proprietary interest in the growth of Coney. They scold the rich for going elsewhere when "they might spend just as much stabling their horses and dining at Coney Island as at Saratoga or Newport." The reporters view the sea as "the old Democrat" who erases class distinctions among bathers. Finally, they continually insist, even while reporting increases in gambling and prostitution, that crime on Coney's sands is about to be eradicated.

[5] *NYT*, 14 July 1873, p. 2, col. 7.

[6] *NYT*, 29 Aug. 1870, p. 8, col. 1.

[7] *NYT*, 6 May 1877, p. 10, col. 5.

[8] *NYT*, 13 Aug. p. 8, col. 1; *NYT*, 20 Aug. 1877, p. 5, col. 5. The reports say that the miraculous Manhattan Beach Hotel now stands where only "howling wilderness existed a year before."

[9] *NYT*, 9 Mar. 1878, p. 8, col. 2.

[10] *NYT*, 1 May 1878, p. 8, col. 1.

[11] *NYT*, 24 June 1878, p. 2, col. 5.

[12] *NYT*, 21 Feb. 1884, p. 8, col. 4; *NYT*, 30 May 1885, p. 8, col. 3.

[13] *NYT*, 20 Aug. 1877, p. 5, col. 5; *NYT*, 25 July 1880, p. 7, col. 2.

[14] *NYT*, 30 June 1879, p. 8, col. 4.

[15] *NYT*, 20 Mar. 1882, p. 8, col. 4.

[16] Clearly, many citizens approved of the changes at Coney. *The New York Times* of 18 July 1880 editorialized: "Probably no great business enterprise combining in so large a degree public benefit and private profit has ever been conducted in a more liberal spirit or with a greater intelligence than the transformation of Coney Island from a *dreary waste* (emphasis supplied) to a summer city by the sea."

[17] Oliver Pilat and Jo Ranson, *Sodom by the Sea: An Affectionate History of Coney Island*, (New York: Doubleday, Doran & Company, Inc., 1941) p. 36.

[18] The degree to which McKane's slight of hand confused the public can be seen in reporters' attempts to explain the many shady land deals at Coney. See *NYT*, 22 Aug. 1879, p. 8, col. 6; and Oct. 3, 5, 6, 7, 8, 10, 12, 14, 1882.

[19] The 13 July 1885 edition of the *Times* describes one of McKane's infrequent vice raids which, because it was announced three days in advance, netted few offenders.

[20] But McKane's power and influence is indicated by the fact that he was under grand jury indictment as early as 1887 (*NYT*, 31 Mar. 1887, p. 4, col. 1). Yet despite this and scathing attacks by the New York press he stayed in power six years longer.

[21] *NYT*, 8 May 1894, p. 4, col. 4.

[22] *NYT*, 3 Apr. 1888, p. 2, col. 3; *NYT*, 4 Apr. 1888, p. 8, col. 2.

[23] *NYT*, 7 Jan. 1893, p. 1, col. 5; *NYT*, 18 June 1893, p. 9, col. 7; *NYT*, 17 May 1895, p. 8, col. 1.

[24] Frederick Law Olmsted and Calvert Vaux, *Report of the Landscape Architects and Superintendents to the President of the Board of Commissioners of Prospect Park, Brooklyn, 1868*, in *Landscape into City Scape*, ed. Albert Fein (Ithaca: Cornell University Press, 1967) p. 158.

[25] Frederick Law Olmsted and Calvert Vaux, *Preliminary Report to the Commissioners for laying out a Park in Brooklyn, New York: Being a Consideration of Circumstances of Site and other*

Conditions Affecting the Design of Public Pleasure Grounds, 1866, in Fein, pp. 95–127. See especially pp. 100–102.

[26]To our knowledge, the thrill plus sex interpretation of the Coney Island rides was first suggested in an article appearing in the August 1938 issue of *Fortune*. The article was titled "To Heaven by Subway." Accompanying the article was a series of paintings by Robert Riggs, several of which emphasized the sensual aspects of the formula. See also the illustrations accompanying an article by Peter Lyon, "The Master Showman of Coney Island," which appeared in the *American Heritage* of June 1958, pp. 14–21, and pp. 92–95.

[27]Jannette Bruce, "Where the Fun Was," *Sports Illustrated*, 28 August 1967, p. 70.

[28]A useful history of the development of mechanical rides is provided by William F. Mangels in *The Outdoor Amusement Industry* (New York: Vantage Press, 1952). For 50 years Mangels manufactured equipment for the amusement operators at Coney Island and for their imitators around the world. He also dreamed of establishing a museum dedicated to his style of recreation. The August 1938 issue of *Fortune* reported that he had collected some 3,200 separate items and was trying to raise $75,000 to acquire a building to house his collection ("Mr. Mangels' Museum," p. 18). The same article also reported that the planners of the New York World Fair were using part of his collection in their search for amusement devices for the Fair. We are unaware of the final disposition of Mangel's collection but his enthusiasm enabled him to write a substantial chronicle of the development of outdoor amusements in Europe and the United States. A more recent and useful book is *Step Right Up Folks* by Al Griffin (Chicago: Henry Regnery Company, 1974).

[29]An excellent study of Tilyou is the article by Peter Lyon cited in note 26.

[30]That vice still flourished outside of Tilyou's controlled environment is demonstrated by articles in the *Times* from 1897 to 1902 such as "Adjie Costello arrested for immoral dancing," "D. A. tries to close illegal shows at Coney," "Streets of Cairo at Coney," and "Grand Jury on Coney."

[31]*NYT*, 17 May 1903, p. 2, col. 4.

[32]William F. Mangels, *The Outdoor Amusement Industry* (New York: Vantage Press, 1952) p. 44.

[33]Maxim Gorki, "Boredom," *Independent*, 8 Aug. 1907, p. 309.

[34]"Mechanical Joys of Coney Island," *Scientific American*, 15 Aug. 1908, pp. 108–110.

[35]"Leap-Frog Railroad," *Scientific American*, 8 July 1905, pp. 29–30; "Mechanical Side of Coney Island Where the Imaginative Inventor Holds Sway," *Scientific American*, 6 Aug. 1910, pp. 104–105.

[36]The three tables in Appendix I provide some statistical information about the economic and demographic conditions which set the stage for the growth of Coney Island. Of particular importance is the almost 30% rise in the standard of living between 1880 and 1895 and the phenomenal growth of New York City during the same period.

[37]For seminal readings in 19th century landscape aesthetics and for incisive introductions to these see John Conron's critical anthology, *The American Landscape* (New York: Oxford University Press, 1974). For background on the city park movement see Peter Schmidt's *Back to Nature: The Arcadian Myth in Urban America* (New York: Oxford University Press, 1969).

[38]See *Frederick Law Olmsted's New York*, edited by Elizabeth Barlow (New York, Praeger, 1972) for a series of drawings and photographs which graphically suggest the magnitude of the project. Pages 74–80 are particularly relevant. The text accompanying these pages mentions that ten million horse cart loads of earth were moved into and out of Central Park during its construction.

[39]Provocative but sketchy discussions of the relationship between work and leisure in pre-industrial, industrial and post-industrial societies may be found in *Mass Leisure*, edited by Eric Larrabee and Rolf Meyersohn (Glenco, Ill.: Free Press, 1958). See especially the articles by Greenberg, Clarke, Pieper, Lynes and Reisman. E. P. Thompson in his important article, "Time, Work-Discipline, and Industrial Capitalism," also raises some fascinating questions concerning the psychic capacity of workers in industrialized nations to respond to increased leisure time (*Past and Present*, No. 38, Dec. 1967, pp. 56–97).

[40]On page 15 of the article by Peter Lyon cited in note 26 there is a reproduction of a notice from the backstage area of the Steeplechase auditorium. The notice states: "Performers playing in this house are requested not to use any *Vulgarity* or *Slang* in their act and to kindly omit the words *Damn* or *Liar* or any saying not fit for *Ladies* and children to hear. This means an immediate Discharge on the first offence, so kindly save us the trouble of such an unpleasant thing to do, as our audiences are mostly ladies and children, and what we want is only *Polite Vaudeville*."

[41]"To Heaven by Subway," *Fortune*, Aug. 1938, p. 106.

[42]"Boredom," *Independent*, 8 Aug. 1907, p. 312.

[43]Keith D. Mano, "Coney," *National Review*, 13 Oct. 1972, p. 1140.

Log Cabins
and
Lone Prairies

JAMES O. ROBERTSON

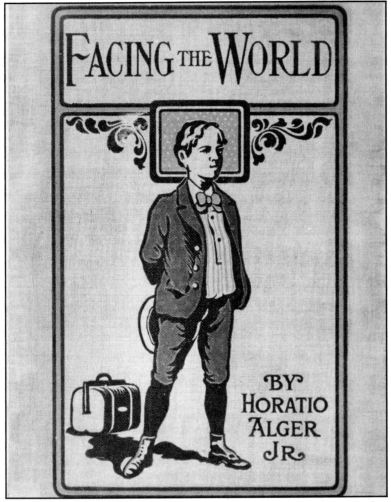

Brown Brothers

Horatio Alger book cover

A HERO IS AN INDIVIDUAL who represents what the society perceives as admirable and worthwhile. So, as society changes, the conception of heroes and the heroic changes.

As the United States became an urban, industrial nation, rural, agrarian heroes gave way to heroes more fitting the new age. In the next selection, James O. Robertson shows how Horatio Alger, Andrew Carnegie, Abraham Lincoln, and the cowboy each represented the new era. Earlier heroes, men like George Washington and Daniel Boone, symbolized the establishment of the nation. The new heroes, on the other hand, symbolized the future of the nation. Robertson notes that since America was in a state of transition, these new heroes served to reconcile the contradictions between organized, urban, industrial work and the independent, democratic, simple virtues of yeoman farmers and pioneers.

The Horatio Alger stories, for example, translated rural, agrarian values for urban Americans. Alger's heroes were hard working, self-denying, competitive, friendly, and reliable. They were not so different from earlier heroes in their values, but they *were* different in their settings. They lived in cities, and they worked in institutions, but they continued to respect the traditional values of the previous generations of Americans who lived in the country and who worked on the farm.

Unlike the heroes in Alger's books, the cowboy did not altogether accept the imposition of the urban, industrial world on the rural, agrarian frontier. Although the cowboy was reminiscent of Daniel Boone, Kit Carson, and Davy Crockett, he was not an independent, solitary figure as they had been; he was usually part of a larger group—the round-up or the posse. Also, he was not an independent entrepreneur; he was an employee, "a hired hand." But, like the Alger characters, the cowboy supported the idea that an employee could become a hero. This idea was crucial in a society made up largely of wage-earners.

SHORTLY BEFORE THE CIVIL WAR, the American economy started to take off toward a modern industrial economy. Throughout the late nineteenth century, cities grew larger and new cities were built. A national market was created by railroads and the telegraph. In that market, after the Civil War, the giant factories, the armies of workers, and the sprawling sales forces of big business grew. The value of industrial goods produced in America exceeded by ever-increasing percentages the value of the produce of American agriculture. Within little more than a single generation the United States changed from an essentially rural and agricultural nation into a rapidly modernizing urban and industrial nation.

Most people in America's first industrial generation after the Civil War had grown up believing that America's mission was to civilize the wilderness, to bring freedom, democracy, and *farms* to the forests and plains of America. Their heroes were pathfinders, frontiersmen, and pioneers who found their way into the wilderness and there created rural towns and producing farms. Their ideal of properly American behavior, of a true American life, was expressed in stories and images of the sturdy independence of yeoman farmers who fought off the Indians, tilled their own hard-won land, sold their crops and made some profit, got along with their fellows in cooperatively built communities, and sometimes rose to fame and fortune with the approbation, votes, or help of their fellows. The myths which shaped the beliefs and behavior of the first industrial generations were not those of an industrial or urban world. How did Americans who believed in pioneers and farms and rural democracy come to accept—in their beliefs as well as the patterns of their behavior—living in cities and being employed in great factories and huge offices? How did they come to give up the wilderness, and with it the rugged frontiersmen and the sturdy yeomen, and accept, in their own minds, the modern industrial world?

A great part of their acceptance of the strange new world in which they lived came because their myths were transformed, transformed in ways not obvious to them at the time, but ways which seemed to reconcile the old ideals with the new realities. There were new storytellers and new heroes to be told about; but

HORATIO ALGER, ANDREW CARNEGIE, ABRAHAM LINCOLN, AND THE COWBOY   By James O. Robertson. From *The Midwest Quarterly*, XX (1979) 241–57. Reprinted by permission of *The Midwest Quarterly*.

the new wore the same clothes as the old, possessed the same virtues, sought success and democratic popularity just as the old had done. Buffalo Bill dressed in buckskins like Daniel Boone, he fought Indians and hunted the wild game of the wilderness like Daniel Boone. Abe Lincoln had worked hard and educated himself; he rose to fame and the Presidency just as Andy Jackson had. General Custer was the greatest Indian fighter of them all. The new industrial world did not lack for heroes in the traditional American mold. Yet the myths had been transformed.

By the 1880's, millions of Americans, not all of them young, were reading the stories of Horatio Alger, Jr., one of the most prolific of the new storytellers. Alger's heroes were obviously American young men, fierce democrats, independent, eager to work hard and make their own ways to success. Their stories did not contradict the yeoman, agrarian ideal; indeed, they seemed to reinforce it.

One of Alger's stories opened in a small town named Groveton in wintertime. An ice-skating race for the boys in the local school was taking place. The prize for the winner of the race was to be "a Waterbury watch, of neat pattern." The leading contenders in that race were: "first, in his own estimation, Randolph Duncan, son of Prince Duncan, president of the Groveton Bank, and a prominent town official. Prince Duncan was supposed to be a rich man, and lived in a style quite beyond that of his neighbors. Randolph was his only son, a boy of sixteen, and felt that in social position and blue blood he was without a peer in the village. He was a tall, athletic boy, and disposed to act the part of a boss among the Groveton boys." After Randolph Duncan "came a boy similar in age and physical strength, but in other respects, very different." He was "Luke Larkin, the son of a carpenter's widow, living on narrow means, and so compelled to exercise the strictest economy." Luke was the janitor of the school as well as a student. "He had a pleasant expression, and a bright, resolute look, a warm heart, and a clear intellect, and was probably, in spite of his poverty, the most popular boy in Groveton. In this respect he was the opposite of Randolph Duncan, whose assumption of superiority and desire to 'boss' the other boys prevented him from having any real friends." Luke should have won the race, but he lost because one of the other boys, a "toady" of Randolph's, tripped him. Randolph won, and so had two watches, a silver one and the new Waterbury.

This novel, *Struggling Upward; or Luke Larkin's Luck*, was first published as a serial in *Golden Argosy* in 1886, part of the magazine's "Way to Success" series. It was aimed at young people who lived in the new urban and industrial world, and it transformed—as did all of Alger's stories—the myths of American individualism and success from a rural to an urban setting. It seems unlikely that Alger's readers were aware of any transformation; they were Americans and they lived in the industrial world. The opening scene of *Luke Larkin's Luck* was a contest, in good American competitive spirit, in a typically American small town. The outcome of the contest was decided the way the outcome of successful American competition was always decided—on what you could "get away with." The contestants were traditional American [who were locked in a struggle between] good and evil.

Alger defined the evil first, to make the contrast clearer. Every phrase and word used to describe Randolph Duncan was calculated to rub against the grain of American democratic values. Duncan's name itself smacked of British and Virginian "aristocracy," and to make the meaning perfectly clear,

Randolph's father's name was "Prince." Randolph's father was described as a "bank president," a "prominent official," and a "rich man"; all expressions calculated to rouse distrust in "common" Americans who had acquired their democratic souls from the ideals of Andy Jackson's day. Yet Prince Duncan's positions could have been earned; they could have been the results of American success. They were not necessarily descriptions of evil. The evil was made clear, in both Randolph and his father, by a phrase like "lived in a style quite beyond that of his neighbors," along with the distasteful aristocratic connotations that accompanied "only son," "social position," "blue blood," "peer," and "boss." The wealth and achievement of the Duncan family were thoroughly tainted by antidemocratic behavior. It would naturally follow, in American belief, that the position they had achieved must have been gained by evil means. The story later makes it clear that such, indeed, was the case.

Luke Larkin's very name, in contrast to Randolph Duncan's was "common." Luke's good democratic origins were clear: he was the "son of a carpenter's widow," "living on narrow means," "exercising strict economy," a "janitor" who worked at "sweeping" and "making fires." The position, duties, and economies of a poor man of the people were vivid. So were the virtues which accompanied them: "pleasant expression," "bright, resolute look," "warm heart," and "clear intellect." While Luke was poor, poverty itself was not a virtue. It was "in spite of his poverty" that Luke had already achieved one aspect of American success: he was "the most popular boy" in town.

As Alger's story made its complicated progress, Luke was accused of a crime he did not commit. He was saved from being convicted (in a court run by Randolph's father, who was the local judge as well as the local banker) by "a tall, dark complexioned stranger" who then took Luke to New York City, bought him two suits and a silver watch "superior even to a Waterbury," and put him on the path to his fortune. Through the stranger, Luke met a Mr. Armstrong, from whom some bonds had been stolen. Armstrong was immediately taken with Luke: "'A thoroughly good boy, and a smart boy too!' said Armstrong to himself. 'I must see if I can't give him a chance to rise. He seems absolutely reliable.'" Armstrong sent Luke on a journey to the West. Luke had a series of adventures, with con-men in Chicago and in gold mining camps in the Black Hills. He eventually returned with evidence which convicted banker Duncan of stealing the bonds from Armstrong. Duncan, in disgrace, was allowed to return the bonds, but his own dishonesty and mismanagement had ruined him. He "saved a small sum out of the wreck of his fortune, and with his family removed to the West." In the West, the Duncans "were obliged to adopt a very different style of living." Randolph became "an office boy at a salary of four dollars a week," and he was "no longer able to swagger and boast as he has done hitherto."

The conclusion of the story was success for Luke. The father of Luke's best friend became the new President of the Groveton Bank. Luke received a reward, and Mr. Armstrong took Luke "into his office" in New York City "at a liberal salary." And so, Alger wrote, closed "an eventful passage in the life of Luke Larkin." Luke had "struggled upward from a boyhood of privation and self-denial into a youth and manhood of prosperity and honor." There had been "some luck about it," Alger admitted, "but after all," he concluded, Luke was "indebted for most of his good fortune to his good qualities."

Every character in the story of Luke Larkin was a town dweller. The leading paternal characters were affluent city businessmen. None of the characters was identifiably rural, and farmers were never mentioned in the story. Alger's heroes lived in towns and they were going to the city. They looked to the cities for economic opportunity and success. Luke found his honor and prosperity, along with a "place" in an office and a salary, in the city. Urban America supplied the keys and symbols of success in all of Alger's stories. The West, the wilderness and the frontier, had long been the place where Americans sought opportunity and success. Not Alger's heroes. It was barely twenty-five years since Horace Greeley had made the advice, "Go west, young man, and grow up with the country," popular, but Luke Larkin did not seek his fame and fortune in the West, although he had gone west. The West, in Alger's stories, was where people went to "prove" themselves. The West was the well-spring of democracy, where those who had fallen, like the Duncans, could get "another chance" or where the arrogant, like Randolph, were "taken down a peg." The Duncans had needed to be "recycled" into genuine Americans. Alger sent them west. Alger's West was a place which produced democratic virtue and strengthened moral character, but it was not the scene of progress nor the environment for economic success. Success and progress were to be found in the city. As the older frontier heroes had gone west, Horatio Alger's heroes went to the city.

Luke Larkin's good qualities which earned him success were those of the older American sturdy, democratic yeoman. Luke was hard-working, self-denying, competitive, friendly, and reliable. The environment of his heroism had changed. And something else had changed, too. Not for Luke the sweating struggle on his own land to win profit and independence for himself and his family. Nor was he an independent entrepreneur, building his business on a shoestring and hard work. Luke Larkin was an employee. He worked in a town or a city—he even went west—as an employee.

And the setting of Luke's work was institutional. He was hired by an individual, but he worked for an "organization." He was a school janitor; then he was a bookkeeper in an "office," and finally successful, he was employed in an "office" at a liberal salary. Alger's heroes, undoubtedly like most of Alger's readers, worked for an office, an organization, a corporation or company or factory. They worked their way "up" on "ladders of success" which were the organizational structures of modern urban businesses and industries. Alger's heroes did not rise to the "top" of the ladders of success. Rather, like Luke, they started low—or off the ladder altogether—and ended "comfortably off." They did not go "from rags to riches," but from self-denial to comfort. Far from being anachronistic in the modern urban, industrial world, Alger's stories provided a mythical paradigm for the modern "organization man." The Alger hero's aspirations and successes were those of the urban white-collar worker. More than 50 million Americans bought, and yet more probably read, the stories of Horatio Alger.

Alger's were not the only success stories being told of new heroes in the latter third of the nineteenth century. Aside from the many who told similar fictional tales of urban and industrial success, there were tales being told of real people— stories more fabulous, in their reality, than any of Alger's fables. The new industrial society created undreamt-of wealth in America, which was the background which lent reality to Alger's stories. That wealth was sometimes the property of men who had started poor and "worked their way up," real men who really lived and worked and succeeded in America.

Andrew Carnegie was one such man. He had come to the United States as a poor immigrant boy. He worked himself "up" from sweeper to messenger boy to partner, and then to owner, operator, and organizer of a giant steel business. When the United States Steel Corporation was formed, in 1901, Carnegie sold his business and retired from active business life. He was paid nearly four hundred million dollars for his steel interests, and his income thereafter was in the neighborhood of twenty-three million dollars a year. Carnegie's success was a wild, impossible dream. His income amounted to $63,000 a day, more than most wage earners in America could hope to earn if they worked for sixty years. He earned in an hour twice as much as the average clerical worker, or government employee, earned in a year—and four times as much as the average industrial worker. Carnegie was the impossible dream, but he was a real person. Luke Larkin's success was much more believeable—as were the successes of most of Alger's heroes—than Carnegie's was.

Carnegie, the greatest of all "self-made" men, the "rugged individualist" *par excellence*, was a business organization man. He had not started the steel business, he had worked his way up in the steel business. Actually, he had worked his way up in another business, and then jumped into steel. He had spent all his early years as an employee. Stories about Carnegie were probably as widely circulated as Alger's stories. There were newspaper articles and stories, magazine stories about the great industrialist. Carnegie himself made lecture tours, and wrote books. He told young listeners that it wasn't enough simply to do your job for your employer—if you only did that then you would stay in the same job forever. No, he said: "The rising man must do something exceptional . . . . HE MUST ATTRACT ATTENTION" ("The Road to Business Success," *Empire of Business* . . .).

There was little difference between Carnegie's "attracting attention" and Luke Larkin's "luck." Carnegie believed that a man could create some of his own luck, that he must push if he were to be a "rising man." Such men were rising in a world where a young man would be working in a special department, in an organization, for an employer. It was a world, as Carnegie saw it, in which one specialized. The advice not to put all your eggs in one basket was "all wrong," according to Carnegie. "I tell you," he said, "put all your eggs in one basket, and then watch that basket!"

The complex overlapping of myth and reality in the stories told by men like Alger and in the stories told by and about men like Carnegie helped create a mythology of the American urban and industrial world. That mythology was made up of hundreds of stories, told again and again, which provided images, analogies, attitudes, and models which seemed to reconcile the contradictions between time-conscious, complexly organized, urban, industrial work, and the ideals and realities of the independence, democracy, and simple virtues of yeomen farmers and pioneers.

But what of the old heroes of the wilderness?

> When Daniel Boone goes by, at night,
> The phantom deer arise
> And all lost, wild America

Is burning in their eyes.
(Stephen Vincent Benét, *Selected Works*, I, 402)

How had the world in which Daniel Boone still walked abroad in daylight, and the deer were real venison on the hoof—the world in which Abraham Lincoln grew up—been transformed, in American minds, into the worlds of Andrew Carnegie and Horatio Alger?

Abraham Lincoln had been born when Daniel Boone was an old man. The stories of Lincoln's youth and his rise to the Presidency were told—after the Civil War—to the same people at the same time as the stories of Luke Larkin and Andrew Carnegie. The stories about Lincoln bridged the gap between the old wilderness world and the new industrial world. Lincoln's father had been a backwoodsman, moving as the frontier had moved, a man who cut down forests to make farmland, who lived in rude shelters in primitive conditions and helped start frontier communities. Lincoln himself had acquired the skills of the pioneer farmer; he was a rail-splitter, a plowman, and a ferryboat operator. And he had sought out "civilization:" he read books before the fire, walked miles to school, worshipped his mother, became a storekeeper and then a lawyer. He entered politics, and, ultimately, he was elected President of the United States. He boarded a train in Springfield and went to Washington City. There, as Civil War President and the Great Emancipator, he became a hero to his countrymen. He was assassinated, and "went home" finally in a long, sombre funeral train. It was the railroad, the locomotive with its giant machinery, its hissing steam and its piercing whistle, which took Lincoln out of the prairie to the city with all its busy-ness, took him to the midst of a great war fought with guns, railroads, telegraphs, and millions of men, and then brought him back again dead, shot as that war ended. The railroad was both the potent symbol and the reality of the industrial age, an age of steel and machinery and organized, machine-like masses of human beings. The railroad marked the death of the wilderness, as it marked the death of Lincoln. "I hear the whistle of the locomotive in the woods," Emerson wrote in 1842, "Wherever that music comes it has its sequel. It is the voice of . . . the Nineteenth Century saying, 'Here I am'". . . . Lincoln's assassination was the symbolic assassination of the frontiersman, the pioneer farmer, and the agrarian world they created out of the wilderness.

The railroad created its own heroes—Casey Jones, the "brave engineer" of the Illinois Central, or John Henry, the "steel drivin' man" of the Appalachian railroads. They were heroes of an industrial world, which, with the railroads, was spanning the continent and destroying the wilderness as it went. Wilderness America and the frontier life did not simply retreat before the railroads as they had before the backwoodsmen and the old wilderness roads; they were penetrated by the railroads and overrun; they finally disappeared. By the late nineteenth century there were few frontiersmen left in America. Like Lincoln, most of them were dead. No longer were stories of the frontier living stories about the present, the here-and-now, for Americans; they were stories about the past.

The only living men who resembled the frontiersmen were cowboys, and the stories being told about them were legion. In June, 1860, a few months before Lincoln was elected President, the first "dime novel"—an adventure story based in the "wild West"—was published. By 1865, when Lincoln was shot, nearly five million dime novels had been sold. The protagonist of the dime novel, and the dominating hero of the wild West ever since, was the "cowboy." The cowboy was the direct descendent of the backwoodsman, through Daniel Boone, who crossed the Mississippi in his old age and settled there, and Kit Carson, who, as a "mountain man" and a "pathfinder" became one of the earliest popular heroes of the "wild West." Carson, at some point in his mythical career, had mounted a horse—the backwoodsmen had been trackers in leggings and mocassins (like Leather Stocking and Daniel Boone). Kit Carson became, on that horse, in legend at least, one of the first cowboys.

While the cowboy, like the backwoodsman, was often a "loner," he was also found in bunches, in the round-up, in the outlaw's "gang," and in the sheriff's posse. The cowboy was often rowdy, as Mike Fink had been, and Davey Crockett and Jim Bowie. He was uneducated (or, if heroic, he hid his education), rough, "low," and usually dirty. His clothes were no longer the by-now-romanticized buckskins—although cowboy heroes like Buffalo Bill or General Custer often affected buckskins of extreme design, both in reality and in legend—but rather dirty "jeans" or "levis," which only much later generations would make as romantic as buckskins. And the rifle of the backwoodsman and the trapper became, in the hands of the cowboy (thanks to Samuel Colt, the Texas Rangers, and the Civil War), the "six-gun," the revolving, mankilling modern pistol. The cowboy-hero of legend and story was usually not a rancher, or a farmer, or a miner, all of which were his real contemporaries in the opening and settlement of the wild west. The few cowboy heroes of wild west stories who were ranchers did not, in the stories, work their ranches. The cowboy was not the descendent of the sturdy pioneer, carving out his own "place" on the Plains. He was not an entrepreneur, either, in the sense that most prospectors, ranchers, and farmers were. Ordinarily, in story and reality, the cowboy worked for someone else.

The cowboy was, like Alger's heroes, an employee. He herded cows for a rancher, or, as was frequently the case, for a ranch corporation. He might be a trail boss or a herd boss or a straw boss or a foreman, but whatever position he held, he was a hired hand. Kit Carson worked for a fur company. Buffalo Bill gained his reputation as a supplier of meat for the Union Pacific Railroad. And the "real" cowboy, or cowpoke, was a skilled technician hired to do the boring, and often dangerous, business of "working" cows. The people who read the cowboy stories, like those who read Alger's stories, probably did not notice that cowboys were employees. Most of the readers were employees themselves. The cowboy showed how an employee could be a hero.

The cowboy hero was a gunman. In the old stories of the pioneers, the rifle had become symbolic of "civilization," and, of course, a gun was a symbol of the armed and therefore independent citizenry of the United States. In the years after the Civil War the gun also became symbolic of the battle against "evil men" who opposed "progress" and destroyed freedom. So the revolver (which was more specifically a man-killer than the rifle had been) like the horse and employee status, became an inseparable part of the imagery of the cowboy.

"Cowboys and Indians" became—and remains—a favorite game of American children, and a favorite story for books and movies. In games and movies, it is a ritual re-enactment of the "winning of the West." On the one side are "the good guys"—the cowboys, the "settlers" with their covered wagons, the Cavalry, and miscellaneous miners, ranchers, farmers, railroads, stage lines, pony express riders, and towns and damsels in distress; on the other side are "the bad guys"—the Indians, the outlaws, the renegades, the evil agents, and the villains. In the stories and games, the conflicts between "good" and "evil" are battles: ritualistic duels between two, or a few, individuals, or pitched battles between numbers of people. They are military contests, in short, and, with triumphant trumpets blaring, the U.S. Cavalry very often comes charging to the rescue. The cowboy was, perhaps, the most important "good guy" in the wild west, but the Cavalry was a close second. In the "logic" of wild west mythology, cowboy and Cavalry were often interchangeable. Both represented good, both fought ritualistic "battles," and both were necessary to the "winning of the west." The Cavalry was the cowboy organized, regimented, and, as the Civil War had demonstrated, effective in bringing about the great ends of progress and reconstruction. Together, the Cavalry and the cowboy brought "law and order," civilization and progress, to the West.

On June 25, 1876, just a few days before America's Centennial Fourth of July, George Armstrong Custer and elements of the Seventh Cavalry Regiment fought their "last Stand." They died with their boots on near the Little Bighorn River in what is now southern Montana. One of the largest fighting forces of Indians ever assembled in the West defeated, and killed to the last man, 262 officers and men of the U.S. Cavalry. Within a month of the publication of the reports of Custer's last stand, Custer was an American hero—and he has remained so ever since. Custer's defeat did not lose General Terry's campaign against the Sioux, nor did it lose the war against the Plains Indians. Both, in the end, succeeded. Custer and his men had given up their lives, much as the cowboy hero sometimes did, in order to save civilization. It was the military way of "riding off into the sunset"—to die with your boots on fighting the Indians. The imagery of "dying with your boots on" in the wild West is a cowboy image: those boots are high-heeled and pointed-toed.

Custer and those like him were not needed by the civilization of railroads, cities, and industry, which had finally triumphed over the wilderness of the new world. Although Custer was killed, the Indians were defeated; civilization was saved, progress inevitably came, and there was no further need for Custer, the Cavalry, or the cowboy. Custer was not, like that other great hero Robert E. Lee, the defender of a Lost Cause. Custer was, for nineteenth century Americans, the symbol of the victory of civilization and progress over the wilderness and all its heathen denizens. At the same time, he was the symbol of the demise of the backwoodsmen, the frontiersmen, the mountain men, the cowboys, of all the pioneers.

Fourteen years after Custer died at the Little Bighorn, the United States Bureau of the Census announced that the frontier had disappeared from America. In the same year, the Army, at the "battle" of Wounded Knee, fired at a large group of Indians for the last time. Three years later, in 1893, Frederick Jackson Turner, a perceptive young historian, made a name for himself with a paper entitled "The Significance of the Frontier in American History." The frontier was history. Like Lincoln, the cowboys, Custer, and the Indians they had fought all belonged to the ages. They were part of the past, not part of the booming, progressing new industrial world of cities and factories, railroads and electricity. The stories of the wilderness and of the men and women who pioneered and fought in the wilderness were told over and over again in that new world. The stories became ritualistic, formulaic, little-changing; the cowboy always rode off into the sunset; the Cavalry died with its boots on; the frontiersman moved on to greener pastures. They became the endlessly repeated charter myths of an America which had conquered its storied wilderness.

For nearly three hundred years, from the founding of the colony at Jamestown to the end of the nineteenth century, progress in America had meant bringing civilization into the wilderness, and Americans had tried to pattern themselves on the heroes of that wilderness. But by the end of the nineteenth century, progress had moved to the cities; its cutting edge was made up of railroad networks and factory systems and great bureaucracies. Armies of employees were the mark of the new progress—not armies of frontiersmen or pioneers, or even cowboys, but armies of employees peopled with heroes created by Horatio Alger, organized and led—not by Daniel Boone, nor by Abraham Lincoln, nor by George Armstrong Custer—but led by industrial organizers like Andrew Carnegie and John D. Rockefeller.

The new Americans believed themselves to be like the old: still pathfinders, still pioneers, still carrying civilization into some wilderness. But the old wilderness was dead. So were its heroes. The patterns for Americans had been changed into something new.

PART FOUR

LIFE IN MODERN AMERICA

The daily lives of Americans have changed dramatically since 1920. By 1980, three-quarters of the population consisted of urban dwellers, living in an environment that had been reshaped by the automobile. The crowded, densely populated cities of the early twentieth century are now sprawling metropolises whose suburban populations live near freeways that stretch dozens of miles from the heart of downtown. The automobile has affected not only the landscape Americans enjoy, but also their leisure time; the motorized population has access to different shopping and recreating centers that have helped to shape their daily activities.

"The Family and the City" describes now the modern metropolis has placed greater burdens on family life. Because the world is larger and more impersonal, the family has the sole responsibility for supporting emotional life, raising children, and fulfilling leisure needs. For example, the overall effect of the automobile on the city has been to diminish the opportunity for personal interaction; sidewalks where people stroll and talk have been abandoned in favor of throughways where individuals in cars hurry to their next destination; cafes and restaurants where people gather for casual conversation are outnumbered by fast-food and drive-in emporiums. And even though the family remains a retreat from the city, individuals still wonder if it can provide for all of the human and personal needs of Americans.

The size and layout of American houses reflect the general assumption that these needs *will* be satisfied within the traditional family. "Awakening from the Dream" points out that most homes have been designed for a family made up of a husband/wage earner, wife/homemaker, and several unmarried children. The split-level home in a suburb, which is generally the house design that is at the heart of the American dream, may not be ideal for single-person or single-parent households or for two-wage-earner families; modern house designs do not meet the needs of millions of people. And, since homeownership is beyond the means of a third of the population, there is widespread alienation and frustration for those who find that their lives do not measure up to the American dream. The problem for modern Americans is not only that they need new housing forms, but, more fundamentally, that they need a new dream in which individual happiness is more broadly conceived.

For many Americans there are other places to retreat from the rush of everyday life. The neighborhood tavern, where artisans go to drink and play cards, shuffleboard, and other games, is such an oasis. "Social Life in a Working-Class Tavern" describes a gathering place for a group of blue-collar aristocrats. This country club for skilled craftsmen is a place where men share comaraderie, where they arrange hunting and fishing trips, and where they escape from both the tensions of work and the cares of family life.

The shopping mall is the epitome of a public place in modern America. "The Mall" explains how this new Main Street has become a one-stop center for entertainment and how many use the malls to define their identities. The new malls are almost cities in themselves—they are totally self-contained environments with stores, banks, theaters, offices, condominiums, and even amusement parks. Shoppers are offered a controlled setting in which the undesirable poor and the rowdy are kept out. Since the malls are easily accessible, they have generated their own urban development. High-rise office buildings and hotels ring many malls, creating new downtowns within sprawling metropolitan areas. Besides home and work, Americans spend more time in malls than anywhere else. People from all walks of life frequent them, and many earlier Main Streets with their boarded-up stores testify to the power of the mall in modern America.

The mall is also an important element in the restructuring of the environment of late twentieth-century American life. The dense arrangement of stores in the mall's interior is not a re-creation of a real Main Street or a small town—complete with second-hand stores and the customers who frequent them—but rather, it is a kind of replication of the sanitized pedestrian throughfares of Disneyland.

"Constructing Make-Believe Cities" explains how another place for leisure activity, the actual amusement parks, can reshape the environment on an even larger scale than the mall. It is the second generation Disneyland, Disney World in Florida, in which a new town has been created in an area twice the size of Manhattan. Americans come to experience a fantasy world that is supported by advanced urban services that are the envy of cities elsewhere in the United States. Disney World shows that a clean, ordered urban environment is within the grasp of our technology, even though most visitors are unaware of the service systems that make their visits so pleasant.

Americans spend a great deal of their leisure time at home watching television. "Window to the World" describes how TV has become the medium through which people experience the events of their time. From national tragedies, such as the assassination of President John F. Kennedy and the explosion of NASA's space shuttle, to sports extravangazas, such as the World Series and the Superbowl, television brings viewers to the scene of activity, while recognized experts help to explain and to interpret the events. National and local news present dramatic footage of events around the world in a format that is designed to be entertaining. Americans have taken to this late twentieth-century medium as enthusiastically as New Yorkers did to the penny press of the 1830s or as those in the late nineteenth century did to the telephone. TV is the link most people have to a larger world.

On a day-to-day basis, the waking time of most adults is spent at work. In the workplace, Americans are subjected to the stresses of competitive capitalism—from which many flee to the refuge of family, to the shopping malls, or to the taverns. But for many, work becomes the most important thing in their lives. "The Corporate Person" details how managers are socialized into the ways of the company by making it their primary interest. By requiring long hours, extended business trips, and frequent transfers from place to place, young executives are taught to put the corporation's interests above their own—if they don't, they probably won't get promoted.

For many Americans, work is a primary source of identity. The loss of a job is both a financial and an emotional crisis. "When to Retire" describes the effects of the combination of mandatory retirement, Social Security, and company pension plans on the elderly. For those who were forced to retire at sixty-five or seventy, Social Security and pension plans reduced the economic strain, but the loss was still a source of emotional stress. The push to eliminate mandatory retirement would, it seems, be a response to the elderly who claim that they should be able to decide when to retire. But this initiative is also the result of the enormous costs of retirement programs in a world where many more Americans are living longer lives.

The schoolhouse is the place in modern America in which children are prepared to be productive members of society. "The High School" describes how the lessons that teenagers learn come from the stifling environment just as much as from the rhetoric of the classroom. Dress codes and hall passes represent the control that the school has over minute aspects of students' lives; the most important lesson to be learned from the regimentation is that getting ahead means playing by the rules that have been set by others. For those who respond favorably, there is social mobility, appropriate credentials for the next stage in the journey of life. But there is also social stratification for those who rebel. They are made to feel inferior for their failure to conform and are given up as troublesome individuals who will have great difficulty succeeding in the world.

Despite the diversity in modern America, there is much to give citizens a sense of a common culture. "A Secular Faith" describes how we have another common bond, a civil religion, that gives all Americans a sense of unity. Our common rituals include the annual activities of national holidays, Thanksgiving and the Fourth of July, the extraordinary celebrations of the Bicentennial and the rededication of the Statue of Liberty, and the commemoration of such national heroes as George Washington and Martin Luther King, Jr. Our common faith is a belief in democracy and free enterprise.

The heroes in modern America are not just the political leaders of the past. "Heroes on the Playing Field" shows how sports figures in the 1920's came to epitomize traditional American values. In a world that was rapidly changing from agrarian to urban, many found themselves disoriented and confused. Sports heroes who rose to fame and fortune by natural ability and hard work, including Babe Ruth, Red Grange, and Jack Dempsey, showed that it was possible to succeed with old fashioned values in a complex new world. We continue to create new sports heroes for each successive generation, a continuing demonstration of the potency of the American dream of success.

The daily lives of Americans have been transformed during the course of the twentieth century, but they continue to be linked to the forms and experiences of earlier generations. Even in a world reshaped by the automobile, airplane, and television, people follow a routine of growing up, earning a livelihood, and growing old that resembles the pattern of the lives of those in the eighteenth and nineteenth centuries. Our belief in progress, and our certainty that the United States is a land of opportunity, is still as strong as it was two centuries ago. Americans in the twenty-first century will undoubtedly lead lives that are different from ours, but they will continue to be influenced by the institutions, traditions, and beliefs that have shaped us and our ancestors.

The
Family
and the
City

PHILIPPE ARIES

Family transportation in the 1950s

AS WITH EARLIER SELECTIONS IN THIS ANTHOLOGY, the following article maintains that during the nineteenth century, Americans used the home as a retreat in which to pull back from the outside world. Yet, the articles on "The Companionate Family" (in Volume I) and the family as "Utopian Retreat from the City" consider only the withdrawal from public life. In contrast, Philippe Aries claims that while the family was developing as a private world, a new public world was also developing—in the form of the urban cafe or the restaurant. The family and the cafe provided Americans with both a new setting for private activities and a new location for public life. Also, the family and the cafe were two of the domains seemingly outside the control and regulation of the ever-present, ever-powerful state.

The world of the cafe collapsed in the twentieth century because of changes in the nature of cities. People have moved to the perimeter of cities and suburbanization has deconcentrated the population. At the same time, cities have become divided into small islands, each inhabited by similar economic and ethnic groups. The automobile has added to this segregation by making it easier for people to move from one island to another. Together, these developments helped to replace the cafe and restaurant with the fast-food emporium and the drive-in. The public domain of the cafe has disappeared because the street and the sidewalk have become places for rapid locomotion instead of casual social interaction.

With the upheavals in the public sector, people have increased the domain of the private, thereby extending the role of the family. According to Aries, the extension of the family has so overburdened that institution that it is now close to collapsing. The family crisis of modern society thus results from an urban crisis—the collapse of the public world. Aries concludes that the way to solve the general problem of the family is to re-create the public world of the city and remove some of the burdens that have been placed on the family in the last century and a half.

. . .[WHEN] THE CITY (and, earlier, the rural community) deteriorated and lost its vitality, the role of the family overexpanded like a hypertrophied cell. In an attempt to fill the gap created by the decline of the city and the urban forms of social intercourse it had once provided, the omnipotent, omnipresent family took upon itself the task of trying to satisfy all the emotional and social needs of its members. Today, it is clear that the family has failed in its attempts to accomplish that feat, either because the increased emphasis on privacy has stifled the need for social intercourse or because the family has been too com-pletely alienated by public powers. People are demanding that the family do everything that the outside world in its indifference or hostility refuses to do. But we should now ask ourselves why people have come to expect the family to satisfy all their needs, as if it had some kind of omnipotent power.

LIFE IN TRADITIONAL SOCIETIES

First of all, let us take a brief look at Western traditional societies from the Middle Ages to the eighteenth century, that is, before they had been affected by the Enlightenment and the industrial revolution. Every individual grew up in a community made up of relatives, neighbors, friends, enemies, and other people with whom he had interdependent relationships. The community was more important in determining the individual's fate than was the family. When a young boy left his mother's apron strings, it was his responsibility to make a place for himself within the community. Like an animal or a bird, he had to establish a domain, a place of his own, and he had to get the community to recognize it. It was up to him to determine the limits of his authority, to decide what he could do and how far he could go before encountering resistance from the others—his parents, his wife, his neighbors, and the community as a whole. Securing a domain in this way depended more on the skillful use of natural talents than on knowledge or savoir-faire. It was a game in which the venture-some boy gifted in eloquence and with a dramatic flair had the advantage. All

THE FAMILY AND THE CITY   By Philippe Aries. From *Daedalus*, Journal of the American Academy of Arts and Sciences, *The Family*, 106 (1977), Cambridge, MA.

life was a stage: if a player went too far, he was put in his place; if he hesitated, he was relegated to an inferior role.

Since a man knew that his wife would be his most important and faithful collaborator in maintaining and expanding his role, he chose his bride with care. On her part, the woman accepted the domain she would have to protect along with the man with whom she would live. Marriage strengthened the husband's position, as a result not only of his wife's work, but also of her personality, her presence of mind, her talents as player, actress, story-teller, her ability to seize opportunities and to assert herself.

The important concept, then, is that of *domain*. But this domain was neither private nor public, as these terms are understood today; rather, it was both simultaneously: private because it had to do with individual behavior, with a man's personality, with his manner of being alone or in society, with his self-awareness and his inner being; public because it fixed a man's place within the community and established his rights and obligations. Individual maneuvering was possible because the social space was not completely filled. The fabric was loose, and it behooved each individual to adjust the seams to suit himself within the limits set by the community. The community recognized the existence of the empty space surrounding people and things. It is worth remarking that the word "play" can mean both the act of playing and freedom of movement within a space. Perhaps, by the act of playing, the free space to play in was created and maintained. The state and society were forces that intervened in a person's life only infrequently and intermittently, bringing with them either terror and ruin or miraculous good fortune. But for the most part, each individual had to win his domain by coming to terms only with the men and women in his own small community.

The role of the family was to strengthen the authority of the head of the household, without threatening the stability of his relationship with the community. Married women would gather at the wash house; men at the cabaret. Each sex had its special place in church, in processions, in the public square, at celebrations, and even at the dance. But the family as such had no domain of its own; the only real domain was what each male won by his maneuvering, with the help of his wife, friends, and dependents.

THREE IMPORTANT CHANGES IN THE NINETEENTH AND TWENTIETH CENTURIES: A NEW WAY OF LIFE

In the course of the eighteenth century the situation began to change. It is necessary at this point to analyze what the major trends were that produced this change. I find at least three important phenomena that caused and directed it. The first of these stemmed from the fact that, in the eighteenth century, society—or, more properly, the state—was loath to accept the fact that there were certain areas of life beyond its sphere of control and influence. Earlier, the situation had been just the reverse: such free areas were allowed to exist, and adventurous individuals were permitted to explore them. In American parlance, we might say that the community had a "frontier"—or rather several frontiers—which could be pushed back by the audacious. But following upon the Enlightenment and industrialization, the state, with its sophisticated technology and organization, wiped out those frontiers: there was no longer an area beyond which one could go. Today, the state's scrutiny and control extend, or are supposed to extend, into every sphere of activity. Nothing is to remain untouched. There is no longer any free space for individuals to occupy and claim for themselves. To be sure, liberal societies allow individuals some initiative, but only in specific areas, such as school and work, where there is a pre-established order for promotion. This is a situation totally different from the way things were in traditional society. In the new society, the concepts of play and free space are no longer accepted; it must be too well regulated.

The second phenomenon that produced this change is directly related to the first: this is the division of space into areas assigned to work and areas assigned to living. The working man now leaves what had been his domain in traditional society, the place where all his activities had taken place, to go to work far away, sometimes very far away, in a very different environment, where he is subject to a system of rules and to a hierarchy of power. He enters a new world, where he may, for all we know, be happier and more secure, and where he can become involved in associations with others—for example, through trade unions.

This specialized place devoted to work was invented by the new society in its abhorence of the void. Running industrial, commercial, and business enterprises requires systems of tight control. Free-enterprise capitalism has demonstrated its flexibility and ability to adapt. But this flexibility has nothing in common with the old concept of free space; rather it depends on the precise functioning of the unit as a whole. Although enterprises in a free-market economy may not be controlled by the state, they are no less controlled if by society at large.

One could reasonably argue that this displacement of workers was a form of "surveillance and punishment," . . . similar in nature to the locking up of children in school, madmen in asylums, and delinquents in prison. In any case, it was certainly, at the very least, a means of maintaining order and control.

The third and last important phenomenon that affected the transformations of the eighteenth and nineteenth century is of a very different order than the first two; it is psychological in nature. But the chronological correlation with the other two is nonetheless impressive. The era witnessed not only the industrial revolution but an emotional revolution as well. Previously, feelings were diffuse, spread out over numerous natural and supernatural objects, including God, saints, parents, children, friends, horses, dogs, orchards, and gardens. Henceforth, they would be focused entirely within the immediate family. The couple and their children became the objects of a passionate and exclusive love that transcended even death.

From that time on, a working man's life was polarized between job and family. But those people who did not go out to work (women, children, old men) were concerned exclusively with family life. Nor was the division between job and family either equal or symmetrical. Although there was no doubt some room for emotional involvement at work, the family was a more conducive setting; whereas the working world was subject to constant, strict surveillance, the family was a place of refuge, free from outside control. The family thus acquired some similarities to the individual domain in traditional society, but with an important distinction: the family is not a place for individualism. The individual must recede into the background for the sake of the family unit, and especially for the sake of the children. Furthermore, the family had become more removed from the community than it was in earlier times, and it tended to be rather hostile to the external world, to withdraw into itself. Thus, it became *the* private domain, the only place where a person could legitimately escape the inquisitive stare of industrial society. Even now, industrial society has not given up trying to fill the gaps created by the decline of traditional society; it does, nevertheless, show some respect for the new entity—the family—which has grown up in its midst as a place of refuge.

Thus, the separation of space into work areas and living areas corresponds to the division of life into public sector and private sector. The family falls within the private sector.

NEW FORMS OF SOCIAL INTERCOURSE IN THE NINETEENTH CENTURY: THE CITY AND THE CAFE

These, then, were the main features of the new way of life. They evolved slowly in the industrialized West, and were not equally accepted in all places. Two important periods must be distinguished: the nineteenth century before the automobile conquered space, and the first half of the twentieth. The difference between these two periods lies in the degree of privacy that people enjoyed and in the nature of the public sector.

During the first period, roughly the whole of the nineteenth century, family life among the bourgeoisie and the peasantry was already much as it is today, that is, it was a private domain. But—and this distinction is very important— only women (including those who worked) were affected by the increased privacy; men were able to escape at times, an outlet they no doubt considered a male prerogative. Women and children had virtually no life outside the family and the school; these comprised their entire universe. Men, on the other hand, had a lively meeting place outside their families and jobs—to wit, the city.

I would like at this point to focus my attention on the city, disregarding those peasant societies where age-old tradition and the innovations of the industrial era are so intertwined that it is difficult for the analyst to distinguish between them. Still, it should be noted that historians today agree that, thanks to the agricultural prosperity in Western Europe during the nineteenth century, a flourishing rural civilization developed there. This was no doubt true of the United States as well. Is it not said that in certain regions of the Midwest immigrants have maintained traditions which have long since disappeared in their original homelands? These flourishing subcultures testify to the enormous vitality of the peasant communities at a time when privacy, the family, and the school were making great inroads upon them. . . .

The long nineteenth century marked a high point in the development of the city and its urban civilization. No doubt urban populations had already increased to frightening levels; the poor immigrants who descended en masse upon them from the villages appeared as a threat to the bourgeois property-owners, who watched them encamp in their towns, and viewed them as an army of criminals and rebels. But this image born of fear need not deceive us today. To be sure, the large city was no longer what it had been in the seventeenth century, that is, a group of separate neighborhoods or streets, each constituting a community with a character of its own. In eighteenth-century

Paris, the arrival of a transient population without a fixed placed of residence upset this way of life. Traditional patterns of social intercourse based on neighborhoods and streets began to disappear. But new ones replaced them that maintained and developed the city's basic functions.

Central to these new patterns were the cafe and the restaurant, public meeting places where conversation flowed as abundantly as food and drink—the cafe was a place for discussion, an invention of the late eighteenth century. Previously there had been eating places, inns, and hostels, places to serve meals in the home or to provide food and lodging for transient guests. There were also taverns and cabarets where people went to drink, and often for the low life to be found there. But they were places of ill-repute, sometimes brothels. Cafes, on the other hand, were something completely new and different. They were strictly an urban phenomenon, unknown in rural areas. The cafes were meeting places in cities, which were growing very rapidly and where people did not know one another, as they had before. In England the cafes were enclosed like cabarets, but the name "pub" describes their function well. In continental Europe, cafes opened onto the street and came to dominate them, thanks to their terraces. Cafes with their large terraces were in fact one of the most striking features of nineteenth-century cities. They were all but non-existent in the medieval and Renaissance sections of the old cities, such as Rome, but made up for it by being very much in evidence in those same Italian cities around the large public squares that owe their existence to Cavour's vast urbanization and Italian unity. In Vienna, too, cafes were, and still are, the heart of the city. In Paris the opening of the cafes was probably the reason behind the shift of public life from closed places, like the famous gallery at the Palais Royal, to the linear, open space of the boulevard, the center of the city's night life.

Cafes no doubt originally served the aristocracy, rather than the bourgeoisie. But they were quickly popularized and extended to all classes of society and to all neighborhoods. In nineteenth-century cities, there was not a neighborhood without at least one cafe, and more often several. In working-class neighborhoods, the small cafe played a vital role; it enabled communication that would otherwise have been impossible among the poorly housed residents who were often away at their jobs: the cafe served as message center. That is why the telephone became so immediately accessible after its advent. The cafe became the place where steady customers could make and receive telephone calls, leave and receive messages. It is easy to understand Maurice Aguilhon's surprise at the extraordinary number of small cafes in a city like Marseilles, each with its little network of neighbors and friends gathered around the counter and the telephone. The number and popularity of these cafes suggest that a new public sector had spontaneously developed in the nineteenth-century city.

Needless to say, the state's desire for control extended even to this new public sector. The state immediately understood the danger represented by the cafes and sought to limit it by establishing and enforcing codes or regulations. But it never completely succeeded. In addition, self-righteous people, concerned with order and morality, were suspicious of the cafes, which they considered to be hotbeds of alcoholism, anarchy, laziness, vice, and political wrangling. In France even today urban planners relegate cafes to shopping districts in residential areas and at a good distance from any elementary or secondary schools. But the mistrust of the authorities and of the self-righteous has still failed to diminish the popularity of the cafes. In the nineteenth century, civilization was based on them.

Now let us compare the role played by the cafe in that era to that played by the family. The family was a private place; the cafe a public one. But they had one thing in common: they both managed to escape society's control. The family did so by right; the cafe in actual fact. These were the only two exceptions to the modern system of surveillance and order which came to include all social behavior. Thus, alongside the growing privacy of the family during the nineteenth and early twentieth centuries, a new and lively form of social intercourse developed in even the largest cities. This explains why the cities of the era were so full of life, and why the increased amount of privacy did not weaken the forms of social intercourse, at least among males.

THE DECAY OF THE CITY IN THE TWENTIETH CENTURY

Toward the middle of the twentieth century in Western industrialized societies, these forms of social intercourse began to break down. The social and socializing function of the city disappeared. The more the urban population grew, the more the city declined. I am reminded of the words of the comedian who suggested moving the cities to the countryside. That, in fact, was exactly what happened.

Immense continuous urban areas have developed in all countries, but especially in the United States where they have replaced the city. There, cities have ceased to exist. This phenomenon, one of the most important in the history of our society, must be seen in the light of what we know about the family and the ways it has changed. I should like to show how the decay of the city and the loss of its socializing function have affected contemporary family life.

From the late nineteenth century, even before the advent of the automobile, rich city-dwellers began fleeing from the crowded cities, considering them unwholesome and dangerous. Far from inhabited areas, they sought purer air and more decent surroundings. En masse they began to settle in those neighborhoods on the outskirts of cities that were still sparsely populated, such as the sixteenth and seventeenth arrondissements in Paris near the greenery of the Parc Monceau and the Bois de Boulogne. Later, thanks to the railroad, the streetcar, and, in time, the automobile, they pushed farther and farther out. This well-known phenomenon applies to all Western industrialized societies, but it is in North America that it developed most fully and reached its most extreme proportions, so we shall examine it there.

Neighborhoods are segregated not only by social class but also by function. Thus, just as there are rich, bourgeois neighborhoods and poor, working-class ones, so, too, there are business districts and residential ones. Offices, businesses, factories, and shops are found in one location, houses and gardens in the other.

The means of transportation most often used to get from one place to the other is the private car. In this scheme of things there is no longer room for the forum, the agora, the piazza, the corso. There is no room, either, for the cafe as meeting place. The only thing there is room for is the drive-in and the fast-food outlet. Eating establishments are to be found in both business and residential districts; depending on their location, they are busy at different times of the day. In business and industrial districts, they are humming with activity at lunchtime; in residential neighborhoods they do most of their business at night. During the off-hours, in both places, they are empty and silent: the only sign of life amidst the furniture and electric lights is the bored face of the cashier.

What is truly remarkable is that the social intercourse which used to be the city's main function has now entirely vanished. The city is either crowded with the traffic of people and cars in a hurry or it is totally empty. Around noontime, office workers in business districts sometimes take an old-fashioned stroll when the weather is nice, and enjoy a piece of cake or an ice cream cone in the sun. But after five o'clock the streets are deserted. Nor do the streets in residential neighborhoods become correspondingly crowded, except around shopping centers and their parking lots. People return to their homes, as turtles withdraw into their shells. At home they enjoy the warmth of family life and, on occasion, the company of carefully chosen friends. The urban conglomerate has become a mass of small islands—houses, offices, and shopping centers—all separated from one another by a great void. The interstitial space has vanished.

This evolution was precipitated by the automobile and by television, but it was well underway before they had even appeared, thanks to the growth of the cult of privacy in the bourgeois and middle classes during the nineteenth century. To people born between 1890 and 1920 (now between 50 and 80 years old), the green suburb represented the ideal way of life. They wanted to escape from the bustle of the city and to live in more rural, more natural surroundings. This shift to the suburbs, far from the noise and crowds of city streets, was caused by the growing attraction of a warm private family life. In those areas where private family living was less developed, as in the working-class areas along the Mediterranean, i.e., in societies dominated by obstinate males, community life fared better.

During the nineteenth and early twentieth centuries, the results of the increased privacy and the new family style of living were kept in check, it seems, thanks to the vitality of community life in both urban and rural areas. A balance was achieved between family life in the home and community life in the cafe, on the terrace, in the street. This balance was destroyed and the family carried the day, thanks to the spread of suburbia as a result of the unexpected help it received from the new technology: the automobile and television. When that happened, the whole of social life was absorbed by private, family living.

Henceforth, the only function of the streets and cafes was to enable the physical movement between home and work or restaurant. These are no longer places of meeting, conversation, recreation. From now on, the home, the couple, the family claim to fulfill all those functions. And when a couple or a family leave the house to do something that cannot be done at home, they go in a mobile extension of the house, namely, the car. As the ark permitted Noah to survive the Flood, so the car permits its owners to pass through the hostile and dangerous world outside the front door.

Not long ago I found myself in Rome at midnight in the working-class neighborhood of Trastevere. There were still crowds of people in the streets, but there were no adults, only *ragazzi* of 18 or 20. They were mostly boys, because people there have not yet gotten into the habit, at least in working-class neighborhoods, of letting girls run around at night. Although children and adults are content to sit in front of the television, adolescents are more interested in the life around them, in personal, spontaneous experiences. The young people of Trastevere were greeted by the marvelous Roman street, still the warm, picturesque setting of their daily life. But what about places where the setting no longer exists? Where do adolescents gather then? In the basements of houses, in underground garages, in the rooms of friends. They are always enclosed. They may very well reject their families, but they still retain their tendency to seek seclusion. Today's frontier is this internal wall: it continues to exist even though it no longer has much to protect.

CONCLUSION

In the so-called post-industrial age of the mid twentieth century, the public sector of the nineteenth century collapsed and people thought they could fill the void by extending the private, family, sector. They thus demanded that the family see to all their needs. They demanded that it provide the passionate love of Tristan and Yseult and the tenderness of Philemon and Baucis; they saw the family as a place for raising children, but, at the same time, as a means of keeping them in a prolonged network of exclusive love. They considered the family a self-sufficient unit, though at times they were willing to enlarge the circle to include a few close friends. In the family they hoped to recover the nostalgic world of Jalna and to experience the pleasures of family warmth; from the private fortress of the family car they sought to discover the world outside. And they cherished the family as a place for all the childish things that continue even beyond childhood. These trends were intensified by the baby boom. Since then, the family has had a monopoly on emotions, on raising children, and on filling leisure time. This tendency to monopolize its members is the family's way of coping with the decline of the public sector. One can well imagine the uneasiness and intolerance that the situation has created.

Although people today often claim that the family is undergoing a crisis, this is not, properly speaking, an accurate description of what is happening. Rather, we are witnessing the inability of the family to fulfill all the many functions with which it has been invested, no doubt temporarily, during the past half-century. Moreover, if my analysis is correct, this overexpansion of the family role is a result of the decline of the city and of the urban forms of social intercourse that it provided. The twentieth-century post-industrial world has been unable, so far, either to sustain the forms of social intercourse of the nineteenth century or to offer something in their place. The family has had to take over in an impossible situation; the real roots of the present domestic crisis lie not in our families, but in our cities.

The
High School

EDGAR Z. FRIEDENBERG

© J. Berndt/The Picture Cube

High school students well adapted to the regimentation of schedules

AS THE THREE EARLIER ARTICLES ON RAISING CHILDREN DEMONSTRATE, changes in methods of education have reflected larger transformations within society. The narrow sectarian focus of Puritan teaching in the seventeenth century was replaced in the nineteenth century by a more secular emphasis on striving for success in business. Also, responsibility for instruction and supervision slowly shifted from the family to society as parental influence over the lives of their children declined. By the early twentieth century, children were being required to attend school for part of each year, and other organizations, such as the Boy Scouts and the YMCA, were developing programs to occupy young people after school and on the weekends.

In this selection, Edgar Friedenberg focuses on the modern high school in which, he argues, students learn much about the nature of American democratic society. Here again, the lessons are learned not in civics classes but in the regimen of the school day. From his interviews with students at two representative working-class and middle-class high schools, Friedenberg describes in detail how completely the behavior of teenagers is controlled within the school environment. Regulations, from requirements for hall passes to dress codes, represent the control by authority figures that prolongs the dependency of childhood, arrests development, and makes possible the youth culture of modern adolescence. In Friedenberg's view, high school is the place where students learn to be minors, where they experience firsthand the restraints on freedom that the state can impose, and where they recognize that getting ahead means playing by the rules. The personal discipline of Puritan parents in the eighteenth century has been superceded by the less personal, but just as rigid, control exerted by the family surrogate, the school.

NOT FAR FROM LOS ANGELES, though rather nearer to Boston, may be located the town of Milgrim, in which Milgrim High School is clearly the most costly and impressive structure. Milgrim is not a suburb though it is only fifty miles from a large and dishonorable city and a part of its conurbation. Comparatively few Milgrimites commute to the city for work. Milgrim is an agricultural village which has outgrown its nervous system; its accustomed modes of social integration have never even begun to relate its present, recently acquired inhabitants to one another. So, though it is not a suburb, Milgrim is not a community either.

Milgrim's recent, fulminating growth is largely attributable to the extremely rapid development of light industry in the outer suburbs, with a resulting demand for skilled labor. But recent demographic changes in the area have produced a steady demand for labor that is not so skilled. In an area not distinguished for racial tolerance or political liberalism, Milgrim has acquired, through no wish of its own, a sizable Negro and Puerto Rican minority. On the shabby outskirts of town, a number of groceries label themselves Spanish-American. The advanced class in Spanish at Milgrim High School makes a joyful noise—about the only one to be heard.

Estimates of the proportion of the student body at Milgrim who are, in the ethnocentric language of demography, non-White, vary enormously. Some students who are clearly middle-class and of pinkish-gray color speak as if they were besieged. But responsible staff members estimate from 12 to 30 percent. Observations in the corridors and lunchrooms favor the lower figure. They also establish that the non-Whites are orderly and well behaved, though somewhat more forceful in their movements and manner of speech than their light-skinned colleagues.

What is Milgrim High like? It is a big, expensive building, on spacious but barren grounds. Every door is at the end of a corridor; there is no reception area, no public space in which one can adjust to the transition from the outside world. Between class periods the corridors are tumultuously crowded; during them they are empty; but they are always guarded with teachers and students on patrol duty. Patrol duty does not consist primarily in the policing of congested throngs of moving students, though it includes this, or the guarding of

THE HIGH SCHOOL By Edgar Z. Friedenberg. From *Coming of Age in America.* Copyright © 1963, 1965 by Edgar Z. Friedenberg. Reprinted by permission of Random House, Inc.

property from damage. Its principal function is the checking of corridor passes. Between classes, no student may walk down the corridor without a form, signed by a teacher, telling where he is coming from, where he is going, and the time, to the minute, at which the pass is valid. A student caught in the corridor without such a pass is taken to the office where a detention slip is made out against him, and he is required to remain at school for two or three hours after the close of the school day. He may do his homework during this time, but he may not leave his seat or talk.

There is no physical freedom whatever at Milgrim. That is, there is no time at which, or place in which, a student may simply go about his business. Privacy is strictly forbidden. Except during class breaks, the toilets are kept locked, so that a student must not only obtain a pass but find the custodian and induce him to unlock the facility. My mother, who had a certain humor about these matters unusual in her generation, had a favorite story about a golfer who, in a moment of extreme need, asked his caddy to direct him to the nearest convenience. The poor boy, unfortunately, stuttered; and the desperate golfer finally interrupted him, sadly, saying, "Never mind, now, son; I've made other arrangements." How often this occurs at Milgrim I do not know, but when it does, the victim is undoubtedly sent for detention.

Milgrim High's most memorable arrangements are its corridor passes and its johns; they dominate social interaction. "Good morning, Mr. Smith," an attractive girl will say pleasantly to one of her teachers in the corridor. "Linda, do you have a pass to be in your locker after the bell rings?" is his greeting in reply. There are more different kinds of washrooms than there must have been in the Confederate Navy. The common sort, marked just "Boys" and "Girls," are generally locked. Then, there are some marked "Teachers, Men" and "Teachers, Women," unlocked. Near the auditorium are two others marked simply "Men" and "Women," intended primarily for the public when the auditorium is being used for some function. During the school day a cardboard sign saying "Adults only" is added to the legend on these washrooms; this is removed at the close of the school day. Girding up my maturity, I used this men's room during my stay at Milgrim. Usually it was empty; but once, as soon as the door clicked behind me, a teacher who had been concealed in the cubicle began jumping up and down to peer over his partition and verify my adulthood.

He was not a voyeur; he was checking on smoking. At most public high schools students are forbidden to smoke, and this is probably the most common source of friction with authority. It focuses, naturally, on the washrooms which are the only places students can go where teachers are not supposed to be. Milgrim, last year, was more liberal than most; its administration designated an area behind the school where seniors might smoke during their lunch period. Since, as a number of students explained to me during interviews, some of these students had "abused the privilege" by lighting up before they got into the area, the privilege had been withdrawn. No student, however, questioned that smoking *was* a privilege rather than a right.

The concept of privilege is important at Milgrim. Teachers go to the head of the chow line at lunch; whenever I would attempt quietly to stand in line the teacher on hall duty would remonstrate with me. He was right, probably; I was fouling up an entire informal social system by my ostentation. Students on hall patrol also, when relieved from duty, were privileged to come bouncing up to the head of the line; so did seniors. Much of the behavior Milgrim depends on to keep it going is motivated by the reward of getting a government-surplus peanut butter or tuna fish standwich without standing in line for it.

The lunchroom itself is a major learning experience which must make quite an impression over four years' time. There are two large cafeterias which are used as study halls during the periods before and after the middle of the day—the middle three or four are lunch shifts. The food, by and large, is more tempting than the menu; it tastes better than it sounds. The atmosphere is not quite that of a prison, because the students are permitted to talk quietly, under the frowning scrutiny of teachers standing around on duty, during their meal—they are not supposed to talk while standing in line, though this rule is only sporadically enforced. Standing in line takes about a third of their lunch period, and leaves plenty of time for them to eat what is provided them. They may not, in any case, leave the room when they have finished, any more than they may leave class in the middle. Toward the end of the period a steel gate is swung down across the corridor, dividing the wing holding the cafeterias, guidance offices, administrative offices, and auditorium from the rest of the building where the library and classrooms are. Then the first buzzer sounds, and the students sweep out of the cafeteria and press silently forward to the gate. A few minutes later a second buzzer sounds, the gate is opened, and the students file on to their classrooms.

During the meal itself the atmosphere varies in response to chance events and the personality of the teachers assigned supervisory duty, especially in the corridor where the next sitting is standing in line. The norm is a not unpleasant chatter; but about one teacher in four is an embittered martinet, snarling, whining, continually ordering the students to stand closer to the wall and threatening them with detention or suspension for real or fancied insolence. On other occasions, verbal altercations break out between students in the cafeteria or in line and the *student* hall patrolmen. In one of these that I witnessed, the accused student, a handsome, aggressive-looking young man, defended himself in the informal but explicit language of working-class hostility. This roused the teacher on duty, who walked over toward the boy and, silently but with a glare of contempt, beckoned him from the room with a crooked and waggling finger and led him along the corridor to the administrative office: the tall boy rigid in silent protest; the teacher, balding and duck-bottomed in a wrinkled suit, shambling ahead of him. The youth, I later learned, was suspended for a day. At some lunch periods all this is drowned out by Mantovani-type pop records played over the public address system.

What adults generally, I think, fail to grasp even though they may actually know it, is that there is no refuge or respite from this: no coffee break, no taking ten for a smoke, no room like the teachers' room, however poor, where the youngsters can get away from adults. High schools don't have club rooms; they have organized gym and recreation. A student cannot go to the library when he wants a book; on certain days his schedule provides a forty-five-minute library period. "Don't let anybody leave early," a guidance counselor urged during a group testing session at Hartsburgh, an apparently more permissive school in our sample. "There really isn't any place for them to go." Most of us are as nervous by the age of five as we will ever be; and adolescence adds to the strain; but one thing a high school student learns is that he can expect no provision for his need to give in to his feelings; or to swing out in his own style, or to creep off and pull himself together.

The little things shock most. High school students—and not just, or even particularly, at Milgrim—have a prisoner's sense of time. They don't know what time it is outside. The research which occasioned my presence at Milgrim, Hartsburgh, and the other schools in the study required me to interview each of twenty-five to thirty students at each school three times. Just before each interview, the student was given a longish description of an episode at a fictitious high school to read as a basis for our subsequent discussion, and I tried to arrange to be interviewing his predecessor while he was reading the descriptive passage. My first appointment with each student was set up by the guidance counselor; I would make the next appointment directly with the student and issue him the passes he needed to keep it. The student has no *open* time at his own disposal; he has to select the period he can miss with least loss to himself. Students well adapted to the school usually pick study halls; poorer or more troublesome students pick the times of their most disagreeable classes; both avoid cutting classes in which the teacher is likely to respond vindictively to their absence. Most students, when asked when they would like to come for their next interview, replied, "I can come any time." When I pointed out to them that there must, after all, be some times that would be more convenient for them than others, they would say, "Well, tomorrow, fourth period," or whatever. *But hardly anyone knew when this would be in clock time.* High school classes emphasize the importance of punctuality by beginning at regular but uneven times like 10:43 and 11:27, which are, indeed, hard to remember; and the students did not know when this was.

How typical is all this? The elements of the composition—the passes, the tight scheduling, the reliance on threats of detention or suspension as modes of social control—are nearly universal. The complete usurpation of any possible *area* of student initiative, physical or mental, is about as universal. Milgrim forbids boys to wear trousers that end more than six inches above the floor, and has personnel fully capable of measuring them. But most high schools have some kind of dress regulation; I know of none that accepts and relies on the tastes of its students. There are differences, to be sure, in tone; and these matter. They greatly affect the impact of the place on students.

Take, for comparison and contrast, Hartsburgh. Not fifteen miles from Milgrim, it is an utterly different community. It is larger; the school district is more compact and more suburban, more of a place. First impressions of Hartsburgh High are almost bound to be favorable. The building, like Milgrim, is new; unlike Milgrim, it is handsome. External walls are mostly glass which gives a feeling of light, air, and space. There is none of the snarling, overt hostility that taints the atmosphere at Milgrim. There are no raucous buzzers, no bells of any kind. Instead, there are little blinker lights arranged like the Italian flag. The green light blinks and the period is over; the white light signals a warning; when the red light blinks it is time to be in your classroom. Dress regulations exist but are less rigorous than at Milgrim. Every Wednesday, however, is dress-up day; boys are expected to wear ties and jackets; the girls, dresses rather than skirts and sweaters. On Wednesday the school day ends with an extra hour of required assembly and, the students explain, there are often outside visitors for whom they are expected to look their best.

Students at Hartsburgh seem much more relaxed than at Milgrim. In the grounds outside the main entrance, during lunch period, there is occasional horseplay. For ten minutes during one noon hour I watched three boys enacting a mutual fantasy. One was the audience who only sat and laughed, one the aggressor, and the third—a pleasant, inarticulate varsity basketball player—was the self-appointed victim. The two participants were portraying in pantomine old, silent-movie-type fights in slow motion. The boy I did not know would slowly swing at Paul, who would sink twisting to the ground with grimaces of anguish; then the whole sequence would be repeated with variations, though the two boys never switched roles. In my interviews with Paul I had never solved the problems arising from the fact that he was eloquent only with his arms and torso movements, which were lost on the tape recorder, and it was a real pleasure to watch him in his own medium. This was a pleasure Milgrim would never have afforded me. Similarly, in the corridors at Hartsburgh I would occasionally come upon couples holding hands or occasionally rather more, though it distressed me that they always broke guiltily apart as they saw me or any other adult. One of my subjects, who had completed the preliminary readings for his interview and was waiting outside for me to finish with the previous subject, was dancing a little jig by himself in the corridor when I got to him. This is all rather reassuring.

It is also contrary to policy. There is a regulation against couples holding hands and they are punished if caught by the kind of teacher who hates sexuality in the young. The air and space also, subtly, turn out to be illusions if you try to use them. Hartsburgh High is built around a large landscaped courtyard with little walks and benches. I made the mistake of trying to conduct an interview on one of these benches. When it was over we could not get back into the building except by disturbing a class; the doors onto this inviting oasis can only be opened from the inside, so nobody ever goes there. Since the courtyard is completely enclosed by the high school building this affords no additional protection from intruders; but it does sequester a possible place of informal refuge. The beautiful glass windows do not open enough to permit a body to squirm through and consequently do not open enough to ventilate the rooms, in which there are no individual controls for the fiercely effective radiators. Room temperature, at Hartsburgh, is a matter of high policy.

Teachers do not hide in the washrooms at Hartsburgh, but the principal recently issued to all students a letter warning that any student caught in the vicinity of the school with "tobacco products" on him would be subject to suspension; students were directed to have their parents sign the letter as written acknowledgment that they were aware of the regulation and return it to school. Staff, of course, are permitted to smoke.

A former teacher, promoted to assistant principal, is now a full-time disciplinarian, but students are not dragged to his office by infuriated teachers as sometimes happens at Milgrim. Instead, during the first period, two students from the school Citizenship Corps go quietly from classroom to classroom with a list, handing out summonses. The air at Hartsburgh is less rancorous and choleric than at Milgrim, and there seem to be more teachers there who like teaching and like kids. But the fundamental pattern is still one of control, distrust, and punishment.

The observable differences—and they are striking—are the result almost entirely, I believe, of structural and demographic factors and occur despite very similar administrative purposes. Neither principal respected adolescents at all or his staff very much. Both were preoccupied with good public relations as they understood them. Both were inflexible. But their situations are different.

At Milgrim there is a strong and imaginative district superintendent who takes cognizance of educational problems. He likes to have projects going on that place the district in the national eye, particularly in research and guidance. Guidance officers report through their chairman directly to him, not to the building principal; and the guidance staff is competent, tough, and completely professional. When wrangles occur over the welfare of a student they are likely to be open, with the principal and the guidance director as antagonists; both avoid such encounters if possible, and neither can count on the support of the district office; but when an outside force—like an outraged parent—precipitates a conflict, it is fought out. At Hartsburgh, the district superintendent is primarily interested in keeping a taut ship with no problems. To this end, he backs the authority of the building principal whenever this might be challenged. The guidance office is rudimentary and concerned primarily with college placement and public relations in the sense of inducing students to behave in socially acceptable ways with a minimum of fuss.

In these quite different contexts, demographic differences in the student bodies have crucial consequences. At Milgrim, the working-class students are not dominant—they have not got quite enough self-confidence or nearly enough social savvy to be—but they are close enough to it to be a real threat to the nice, college-bound youngsters who used to set the tone of the place in their old elementary or junior high school and who expect to go on dominating the high school. The working-class influx has left many middle-class students feeling engulfed by the rising wave of lower-status students, as they see it; while the lower-status students, many of whom are recent migrants and even high school transfers from the city, can remember schools in which they felt more at home.

The result is both to split and to polarize student feeling about the school, its administration, and other students. Nobody likes Milgrim High. But the middle-class students feel that what has ruined it is the lower-class students and that the punitive constraint with which the school is run is necessary to keep them in line. In some cases these middle-class students approach paranoia; thus, one girl, in commenting on the mythical high school described in our research instrument, said, "Well, it says here that the majority of the students are Negro—about a third!" (The actual statement is "about a fifth.")

The working-class students are hard-pressed, but being hard-pressed they are often fairly realistic about their position. If the Citizenship Corps that functions so smoothly at Hartsburgh went about its duties as smugly at Milgrim, actually turning people in and getting them in trouble, they would pretty certainly receive some after-school instruction in the way social classes differ in values and in the propensity for nonverbal self-expression. At Milgrim, the working-class kids know where they stand, and stand there. They are exceptionally easy to interview, for example, because it isn't necessary to be compulsively nondirective. Once they sense that they are respected, they respond enthusiastically and with great courtesy, but they do not alter their position to give the interviewer what they think he wants, or become notably anxious at disagreeing with him. They are very concrete in handling experience, not given to generalization. Most of them seem to have liked their elementary school and they share the general American respect for education down to the last cliché—then one will add, as an afterthought, not bothering even to be contemptuous, "Of course, you can't respect *this* school." They deal with the situation it presents them with in correspondingly concrete terms. Both schools had student courts last year, for example, and Hartsburgh still does, though few students not in the Citizenship Corps pay much attention to it. Student traffic corpsmen give out tickets for corridor offenses, and the culprits are brought before an elected student judge with an administrative official of the school present as adviser. But Milgrim had a student court last year that quickly became notorious. The "hoody element" got control of it, and since most of the defendants were their buddies, they were either acquitted or discharged on pleas of insanity. The court was disbanded.

The struggle at Milgrim is therefore pretty open; though none of the protagonists see it as a struggle for freedom, or could define its issues in terms of principle. The higher-status students merely assent to the way the school is run, much as middle-class white Southerners assent to what the sheriff's office does, while the lower-status students move, or get pushed, from one embroilment to the next without ever quite realizing that what is happening to them is part of a general social pattern. At Hartsburgh there aren't very many lower-status students, and those that there are can easily be dismissed by their middle-class compeers, who set the tone, as a "hoody element." There are not enough of these and they are not sufficiently aggressive to threaten the middle-class youngsters or their folkways, but, for that same reason, they do not force the middle-class youngsters to common cause with the administration. The administration, like forces of law and order generally in the United States, is accepted without deference, as a part of the way things work. In America, one doesn't expect authority to be either intelligent or forthright; it looks out for its own interests as best it can. Reformers and troublemakers can only make it nervous and therefore worse; the best thing is to take advantage of it when it can help you and at other times to go on living your own life and let it try to stop you.

This is what the Hartsburgh students usually do and, on the whole, the results are pleasant. The youngsters, being to some degree Ivy, do not constantly remind the teachers, as the Milgrim students do, that their jobs have no connection with academic scholarship. Many of the teachers, for their part, act and sound like college instructors, do as competent a job, and enjoy some of the same satisfactions. The whole operation moves smoothly. Both Milgrim and Hartsburgh high schools are valid examples—though of very different aspects—of American democracy in action. And in neither could a student learn as much about civil liberty as a Missouri mule knows at birth.

What is learned in high school, or for that matter anywhere at all, depends far less on what is taught than on what one actually experiences in the place. The quality of instruction in high school varies from sheer rot to imaginative and highly skilled teaching; but classroom content is often handled at a creditable level and is not in itself the source of much difficulty. Generally speaking, both at Milgrim and Hartsburgh, for example, the students felt that they were receiving competent instruction and that this was an undertaking the school tried seriously to handle. Throughout our sample of nine schools—though not necessarily in each of them—more than four-fifths of our pretest sample, aggregating nearly one thousand students, agreed that the following statements applied to their school:

> There are teachers here who, when they tell you your work is well done, you know it is good.

> Many of the teachers know a great deal about things other than what they cover in their subject in class.

> Some teachers surprise you by getting you interested in subjects you'd never really thought of before.

But important as it is to note that students generally recognize academic quality in the schools, and particularly the contributions of exceptional teachers, serious questions remain as to how the school affects the students' conception of either academic mastery or of themselves. For more than 80 percent also agree that:

> You have to be concerned about marks here; that is, if you are going to get anywhere and be anything.

> The school doesn't expect students to wear expensive clothes, but they do have to be neat and clean. Clothes that are too sporty or sexy are "out."

> The student newspaper here is pretty careful not to report things in such a way that they might make trouble for the school with other people.

> Keeping everybody quiet when they're in the library is a regular cause with the librarians here.

> A girl who went too far here and got into trouble would be suspended or expelled.

In my judgment, the kind of tutelage and status that the high school assigns students affects their lives and subsequent development far more crucially than the content and quality of formal instruction. What is learned most thoroughly by attendance at Milgrim or Hartsburgh is certain core assumptions that govern the conditions of life of most adolescents in this country and train them to operate as adult, if not as mature, Americans. The first of these is the assumption that the state has the right to compel adolescents to spend six or seven hours a day, five days a week, thirty-six or so weeks a year, in a specific place, under the charge of a particular group of persons in whose selection they have no voice, performing tasks about which they have no choice, without remuneration and subject to specialized regulations and sanctions that are applicable to no one else in the community nor to them except in this place. So accustomed are we to assuming that education is a *service* to the young that this statement must seem flagrantly biased. But it is a simple statement of what the law provides. Whether this provision is a service or a burden to the young—and, indeed, it is both, in varying degrees—is another issue altogether. Compulsory school attendance functions as a bill of attainder against a particular age group, so the first thing the young learn in school is that there are certain sanctions and restrictions that apply only to them, that they do not participate fully in the freedoms guaranteed by the state, and that, *therefore, these freedoms do not really partake of the character of inalienable rights.*

When services are to be provided to an individual whom the law respects as it does the agency providing the services the normal legal instrument is, of course, a contract, which defines the rights and obligations of both parties and provides each with legal remedies against the contract's breach.

Compulsory school attendance, however, is provided by a law which recognizes no obligation of the school that the students can enforce. He cannot petition to withdraw if the school is inferior, does not maintain standards, or treats him brutally. There are other laws, certainly, that set standards for school construction and maintenance, the licensing of teachers, technics of discipline, and so forth; and proceedings under these may be invoked if the school does not abide by them. But they do not abate the student's obligation to attend the school and accept its services. His position is purely that of a conscript who is protected by certain regulations but in no case permitted to use their breach as a cause for terminating his obligation.

Of course not. The school, as schools continually stress, acts *in loco parentis*; and children may not leave home because their parents are unsatisfactory. What I have pointed out is no more than a special consequence of the fact that students are minors, and minors do not, indeed, share all the rights and privileges—and responsibilities—of citizenship. Very well. However one puts it, we are still discussing the same issue. The high school, then, is where you really learn what it means to be a minor.

For a high school is not a parent. Parents may love their children, hate them, or, like most parents, do both in a complex mixture. But they must, nevertheless, permit a certain intimacy and respond to their children as persons. Homes are not run by regulations, though the parents may think they are, but by a process of continuous and almost entirely unconscious emotional homeostasis, in which each member affects and accommodates to the needs, feelings, fantasy life, and character structure of the others. This may be, and often is, a terribly destructive process; I intend no defense of the family as a social institution. Salmon, actually, are much nicer than people: more dedicated, more energetic, less easily daunted by the long upstream struggle and less prudish and reticent about their reproductive functions, though inclined to be rather cold-blooded. But children grow up in homes or the remnants of homes, are in physical fact dependent on parents, and are too intimately related to them to permit their area of freedom to be precisely defined. This is not because they have no rights or are entitled to less respect than adults, but because intimacy conditions freedom and growth in ways too subtle and continuous to be defined as overt acts.

Free societies depend on their members to learn early and thoroughly that public authority is *not* like that of the family; that it cannot be expected—or trusted—to respond with sensitivity and intimate perception to the needs of individuals but must rely basically, though as humanely as possible, on the impartial application of general formulae. This means that it must be kept functional, specialized, and limited to matters of public policy; the meshes of the law are too coarse to be worn close to the skin. Especially in an open society, where people of very different backgrounds and value systems must function together, it would seem obvious that each must understand that he may not push others further than their common undertaking demands or impose upon them a manner of life that they feel to be alien.

After the family, the school is the first social institution an individual must deal with—the place in which he learns to handle himself with strangers. The school establishes the pattern of his subsequent assumptions as to which relations between the individual and society are appropriate and which constitute invasions of privacy and constraints on his spirit—what the British, with exquisite precision, call "taking a liberty." But the American public school evolved as a melting pot, under the assumption that it had not merely the right but the duty to impose a common standard of genteel decency on a polyglot body of immigrants' children and thus insure their assimilation into the better life of the American dream. It accepted, also, the tacit assumption that genteel decency was as far as it could go. If America has generally been governed by the practical man's impatience with other individuals' rights, it has also accepted the practical man's respect for property and determination to protect it from the assaults of public servants. With its contempt for personal privacy and individual autonomy, the school combines a considerable measure of Galbraith's "public squalor." The plant may be expensive—for this is capital goods; but nothing is provided graciously, liberally, simply as an amenity, either to teachers or students, though administrative offices have begun to assume an executive look. In the schools I know, the teachers' lounges are invariably filled with shabby furniture and vending machines. Teachers do not have offices with assigned clerical assistance and business equipment that would be considered satisfactory for, say, a small-town, small-time insurance agency. They have desks in staffrooms, without telephones.

To justify this shabbiness as essential economy and established custom begs the question; the level of support and working conditions customarily provided simply defines the status of the occupation and the value the community in fact places on it. An important consequence, I believe, is to help keep teachers timid and passive by reminding them, against the contrasting patterns of commercial affluence, of their relative ineffectiveness; and to divert against students their hostilities and their demands for status. Both teachers and students, each at their respective levels, learn to regard the ordinary amenities and freedoms of middle-class life as privileges. But the teacher has a few more of them. He hasn't a telephone, but he may make calls from a phone in the general office, while, in some schools, the public pay phone in the hallway has a lock on it and the student must get a key from the office before he can dial his call. Where a hotel or motel, for example, provides in its budget for normal wear and tear and a reasonable level of theft of linens and equipment and quietly covers itself with liability insurance, the school—though it may actually do the same thing—pompously indoctrinates its students with "respect for public property," "good health habits," and so forth before it lets them near the swimming pool. In a large city, the pool may have been struck out of the architect's plans before construction began, on the grounds that it would be unfair to provide students in a newer school with a costly facility that students in older schools do not have.

If the first thing the student learns, then, is that he, as a minor, is subject to peculiar restraints, the second is that these restraints are general, and are not limited to the manifest and specific functions of education. High school administrators are not professional educators in the sense that a physician, an attorney, or a tax accountant are professionals. They are not practitioners of a specialized *instructional* craft, who derive their authority from its requirements. They are specialists in keeping an essentially political enterprise from being strangled by conflicting community attitudes and pressures. They are problem-oriented, and the feelings and needs for growth of their captive and disfranchized clientele are the least of their problems; for the status of the "teenager" in the community is so low that even if he rebels the school is not blamed for the conditions against which he is rebelling. He is simply a truant or juvenile delinquent; at worst the school has "failed to reach him." What high school personnel become specialists in, ultimately, is the *control* of large groups of students even at catastrophic expense to their opportunity to learn. These controls are not exercised primarily to facilitate instruction, and, particularly, they are in no way limited to matters bearing on instruction. At several schools in our sample boys had, for example, been ordered by the assistant principal—sometimes on the complaint of teachers—to shave off beards. One of these boys, who had played football for the school all season, was told that, while the school had no legal authority to require this, he would be barred from the banquet honoring the team unless he complied. Dress regulations are another case in point.

Of course these are petty restrictions, enforced by petty penalties. American high schools are not concentration camps; and I am not complaining about their severity but about what they teach their students concerning the proper relationship of the individual to society. The fact that the restrictions and penalties are petty and unimportant in themselves in one way makes matters worse. Gross invasions are more easily recognized for what they are; petty restrictions are only resisted by "troublemakers." What matters in the end, however, is that the school does not take its own business of education seriously enough to mind it.

The effects on the students of the school's diffuse willingness to mind everybody's business but its own are manifold. The concepts of dignity and privacy, notably deficient in American adult folkways, are not permitted to develop here. The high school, certainly, is not the material cause of this deficiency, which is deeply rooted in our social institutions and values. But the high school does more than transmit these values—it exploits them to keep students in line and develop them into the kinds of people who fit the community that supports it.

A corollary of the school's assumption of custodial control of students is that power and authority become indistinguishable. If the school's authority is not limited to matters pertaining to education, it cannot be derived from educational responsibilities. It is a naked, empirical fact, to be accepted or controverted according to the possibilities of the moment. In this world power counts more than legitimacy; if you don't have power it is naïve to think you have rights that must be respected; wise up. High school students experience regulation only as control, not as protection; they know, for example, that the principal will generally uphold the teacher in any conflict with a student, regardless of the merits of the case. Translated into the high school idiom, *suaviter in modo, fortiter in re* becomes "If you get caught, it's just your ass."

Students, I find, do not resent this; that is the tragedy. All weakness tends to corrupt, and impotence corrupts absolutely. Identifying, as the weak must, with the more powerful and frustrating of the forces that impinge upon them, they accept the school as the way life is and close their minds against the anxiety of perceiving alternatives. Many students like high school; others loathe and fear it. But even these do not object to it on principle; the school effectively obstructs their learning of the principles on which objection might be based; though these are among the principles that, we boast, distinguish us from totalitarian societies.

Yet, finally, the consequence of submitting throughout adolescence to diffuse authority that is not derived from the task at hand—as a doctor's orders, or the training regulations of an athletic coach, for example, usually are—is more serious than political incompetence or weakness of character. There is a general arrest of development. An essential part of growing up is learning that, though differences of power among men lead to brutal consequences, all men are peers; none is omnipotent, none derives his potency from magic but only from his specific competence and function. The policeman represents the majesty of the State, but this does not mean that he can put you in jail; it means, precisely, that he cannot—at least not for long. Any person or agency responsible for handling throngs of young people—especially if it does not like them or is afraid of them—is tempted to claim diffuse authority and snare the youngster in the trailing remnants of childhood emotion, which always remain to trip him. Schools are permitted to infantilize adolescence and control pupils by reinvoking the sensations of childhood punishment, effective because it was designed, with great unconscious guile, to dramatize the child's weakness in the face of authority. In fact, they are strongly encouraged to do so by the hostility to "teen-agers" and the anxiety about their conduct that abound in our society.

In the process, the school affects society in two complementary ways. It alters individuals: their values, their sense of personal worth, their patterns of anxiety and sense of mastery and ease in the world on which so much of what we think of as our fate depends. But it also performs a Darwinian function. The school endorses and supports the values and patterns of behavior of certain segments of the population, providing their members with the credentials and shibboleths needed for the next stages of their journey, while instilling in others a sense of inferiority and warning the rest of society against them as troublesome and untrustworthy. In this way, the school contributes simultaneously to social mobility and social stratification. It helps to see to it that the kinds of people who get ahead are those who will support the social system it represents; while those who might, through intent or merely by their being, subvert it are left behind as a salutary moral lesson.

When

to

Retire

WILLIAM GRAEBNER

© Patrick Ward/Stock, Boston

Sun City, Arizona, exercise class

IN RECENT YEARS, Americans have recognized that "ageism" is a form of prejudice, as is racism or sexism. In fact, some people even believe that this change in attitudes toward older people has led to an improvement in their conditions. As evidence for this argument, one may point to the passage of a federal law in 1978 that raised the age of mandatory retirement from sixty-five to seventy—this can be considered an improvement if one assumes mandatory retirement meant Americans did not appreciate the contributions of older people.

In the following selection, William Graebner questions whether the change in retirement age actually does show a change in attitude. Graebner makes his point by examining the history of retirement in the twentieth century; he argues that retirement policies have not been shaped by a concern for the elderly at all, but rather by a concern for larger social problems. For example, in the early part of the century, some employers favored establishing pension plans and retirement systems to diminish economic and social conflict between employer and employee. Employers also considered pension plans a way to reduce labor turnover, attract the young and talented, and maintain order by giving workers a sense of security and stability.

Graebner also suggests that the most important pension plan in the country—Social Security—was *not* established only for the benefit of older workers. He points out that the Social Security system contains a retirement qualification; in order to receive benefits, a person must have retired. The system therefore functions as a way to help younger workers by forcing older people out of the labor market and making more jobs available.

Over time, the development of pensions and retirement programs has created a new problem—how to pay the enormous costs of these programs. According to Graebner, this new concern has eased mandatory retirement laws; decisions about the proper age for retirement are again being made in the interest of the general welfare, not in the interest of older Americans. If Graebner is right, older citizens are still being discriminated against, and there has been no significant improvement in society's attitude.

IN 1978 A FEDERAL statute made it illegal for most employers to impose mandatory retirement on workers under seventy. The new law was widely touted as yet another triumph of twentieth-century enlightenment. For, after all, was not compulsory retirement a relic of an era when the abilities of the elderly were not fully appreciated?

It would be comforting, perhaps, to believe that we have indeed progressed. But viewed through the lens of history, our present retirement policy appears to be a step backward, a regression—in time, at least—to a nineteenth-century world based solidly on the work ethic. More important, a glance into the past makes clear that significant changes in policy have always been made to serve broad economic and social needs rather than those of elderly people.

"Retirement," of course, means something very different now from what it did in the nineteenth century. In fact, retirement as we have understood the term since 1950—either as something forced upon us or as a great block of leisure time granted as the reward for years of labor—did not exist to any appreciable extent in 1900 or even in 1935.

Today, despite recent inroads on the institution, for most of us retirement calls up a montage of images of how we expect to spend a span of years. Retirement is late breakfasts, a thoroughly read newspaper, watching the Cubs at Wrigley Field on a Tuesday afternoon, framing pictures down in the base-ment or doing needlepoint in the living room, Meals On Wheels, getting by on Social Security, moving to St. Petersburg.

For turn-of-the-century Americans, retirement was something altogether dif-ferent. The common lot of the elderly was work, not leisure. Aside from judges and railroad men, very few employees were subject to mandatory retirement. Even ordinary pension plans were rare, with coverage being limited to Civil War veterans, public employees in major cities, and a handful of workers in private industry.

WHEN TO RETIRE   By William Graebner. Originally published under the title "When Should We Retire?" From *American Heritage*, 34 (April, 1983): 100–105. © 1983 William Graebner. Reprinted by permission of William Graebner.

In the absence of pension plans and Social Security, workers who were neither required to retire nor could afford to do so stayed on to staff the nation's shops, factories, offices, government bureaus, and professions. In 1903, for example, 114 employees of the Treasury of the United States, representing nearly 2 percent of its staff, were between the ages of seventy and seventy-nine, while another 12 were more than eighty years old. In 1913 the Protestant Episcopal Church maintained 406 clergymen who were seventy or older, and 41 who were eighty or older. In that year, more than one-eighth of the church's total salary payments went to clergymen above sixty-five. A decade later the Chicago school system employed two eighty-three-year-old principals and six principals and teachers over seventy-five.

Most of these older people labored as hard, and presumably as productively, as their younger colleagues. Others, usually with the approval of their employers, combined work with "on-the-job" retirement. Federal employees who were also Civil War veterans were, according to one source, "permitted to hold their present positions without disturbance, irrespective of the work done by them." Some "government paupers"—a term commonly used to describe aged employees—came to work on crutches or in wheelchairs. A 1904 report on Chicago's police department found "incapacitated men tucked away in every corner, guarding schools when there is no necessity . . . doing messenger duty when there is no necessity. . . ." In 1911 the New York Factory Investigating Commission discovered that the critical occupation of factory inspector was being used as an informal retirement mechanism. "There are a great many inspectors," one witness testified, "who have reached that age, where it is very hard for them to do practical inspection work; that is, to climb the stairs, to go out on fire escapes, and to go down into dark basements. . . ." Many corporations and government agencies transferred older workers to less demanding tasks and even tolerated special arrangements. In Philadelphia, for example, an elderly teacher twice a day left her class in charge of a student monitor while she took a nap.

While, to us, this on-the-job retirement may seem flawed by a tolerance for inefficiency or even corruption, the system was in some ways workable and humane; it allowed thousands of older people to receive a dependable, if somewhat reduced, source of income through an arrangement made on the basis of personal ties between employee and supervisor. And these ties often, if by no means invariably, ensured that workers would be treated as individuals, with special needs and abilities.

In the early years of the twentieth century, when mandatory retirement was being debated, it was a bitterly controversial political issue—on the same order as, say, railroad regulation, the trusts, the tariff, conservation, and other staples of the Progressive Era. The furor was most violently provoked by William Osler, a Canadian who had served as physician-in-chief of the Johns Hopkins Hospital for sixteen years. In 1905 Osler gave a valedictory address at Johns Hopkins before leaving to become Regius Professor of Medicine at Oxford. During his triumphant tenure in Baltimore, he had reaped rewards as teacher, medical scholar, administrator, and man of letters. The shocking lesson he had drawn from this varied experience was that creativity, energy, and achievement were inversely related to chronological age. Before a large audience Osler characterized his departure as akin to retirement, and he went on to suggest the need for institutionalizing early retirement as a means of maintaining an active and productive medical faculty. Without a hint of humor, the fifty-six-year-old physician spoke of the "uselessness of men above forty years of age" and referred—with a touch of levity this time—to novelist Anthony Trollope's vision of a "peaceful departure by chloroform" at the age of sixty-one.

Osler's valedictory provoked a storm of indignation. One prominent critic was Sen. Chauncey Depew of New York. Interviewed by a reporter from the Baltimore *American*, the seventy-one-year-old Depew cited several examples of successful older people and went on to provide hour-by-hour details of his own strenuous schedule of speeches and travel. Throughout the country, newspapers carried essays extolling the achievements of men over forty: Franklin, Hawthorne, Webster, Lincoln, Gladstone, Disraeli, Lew Wallace. "Dr. Osler declares that men are old at 40 and worthless at 60," the Washington *Times* observed tartly. "There must be an age at which a man is an ass. What is the Doctor's age, anyhow?"

In raising the issues of aging and retirement and linking them to productivity, Osler had touched a raw nerve. Corporations and government agencies had begun to question and to deprecate the contributions of workers over forty. An increasingly mechanized and industrialized America began to value youth as never before. A Springfield, Ohio, printer attributed the growing interest in youth in his business to the new Mergenthaler typesetting machines. Because of the "intense productivity" of these machines, he said, "no longer can the mechanic in the printing craft— nor in any other, for that matter—look forward to a long career in his chosen profession. Twenty-five to thirty years can safely be placed as the limit. So far as the mechanic is concerned, Osler's theory is a fact."

In the military, too, the value of youth was emphasized. Shortly after Osler's blast, Adm. George Dewey warned that the nation would "assuredly meet with disaster in a naval war unless younger men are given command of the ships of our navy." (Dewey himself was sixty-eight at the time.)

During the decades following Osler's valedictory, ageism and retirement became weapons in a national crusade for efficiency, productivity, creativity, and progress itself. Retirement was not conceived of as a simple reward, nor was it synonymous with leisure. It had purposes and functions. It was part of what some called the "labor question," and it would soon become a part of the repertory of the new practitioners of industrial relations. George W. Perkins captured the expectations surrounding retirement in a 1914 letter to Coleman du Pont, who had asked the retired banker for advice on setting wages. "I never heard of any plan except one," Perkins wrote, "that would assist in regulating salaries, and that is a pension plan. . . . The right sort of pension plan comes pretty near being a panacea for most of the ills that exist between employer and employee."

The belief that economic and social problems would wither away when tapped with the magic wand of deferred compensation in the form of pensions may strike us as hopelessly optimistic. But it seemed reasonable to a generation committed to the gospel of efficiency preached by Henry Ford and Frederick W. Taylor, whose stopwatch had by 1910 become a familiar sight in American machine shops. . . . Thus the pension became one of several devices adopted by corporations to "rationalize" and reduce burgeoning labor turnover in the decade after 1910. The pension would encourage workers to forgo higher wages elsewhere; at the same time, it would discourage the "floaters" who undermined stability in the urban labor markets. Meanwhile, both in higher education and in churches with stagnating memberships, advocates of retirement defended the pension as a means of attracting the young and talented to professions that were losing the flower of youth to business and law, where they could make more money.

In public schools, where pensions were common by 1920, efficiency was used time and again to justify mandatory retirement programs. In 1919 a House committee considering a District of Columbia pension bill heard a teacher named Rebecca Shanley defend a provision that would allow compulsory retirement at sixty-two. "We felt," said Shanley, "that at that age the teacher who had been in the schoolroom with 40 or 50 children for so many years will have lost much of her efficiency. . . . We felt that a teacher . . . at the age of 62 ought to be retired for the good of the service." For employers, retirement programs served another purpose: they could save money by retiring higher-salaried teachers and replacing them with younger—and cheaper—ones.

On another level, retirement was seen as an effective new means of controlling unrest within a society that felt threatened by anarchism, socialism, and the "new immigrant." "The present social unrest among all classes of people— especially the ignorant," the Springfield, Massachusetts, superintendent of schools had written in 1891, required a new breed of teacher—well-rewarded, secure, capable of making a forceful impression on "the minds of the vulgar and the innocent." In short, teachers were expected to turn out good, conservative citizens. The Carnegie Foundation for the Advancement of Teaching was established in 1905 with a similar end in mind. The foundation administered a retirement program for college professors. The director, Henry S. Pritchett, believed, that once professors were organized in such a program, they would gain a heightened sense of their place in the social order—a greater feeling of "responsibility"—and this, in turn, would have a benign effect on the content of their teaching. A narrower case for the pension as an instrument of social control was made in a 1905 essay by a banker named Frank A. Vanderlip. He attributed the railroads' interest in the "straight" pension—under which employers provided the entire sum—to their justifiable desire to establish "military discipline" among workers. For the sake of a pension, an employee would, Vanderlip believed, "sacrifice much of his personal liberty, including his right to strike for better wages and shorter hours."

Vanderlip, Pritchett, Perkins, and Osler were all involved in the same enterprise: the transition from one system of security (or dependency), based on the workplace, to another, which was based on money payments. The wrenching experience involved in this transition is illustrated by events in the federal agencies following the passage of the Civil Service Retirement Act in 1920.

Many of the first retirees were angry and frightened by what was happening to them. They felt that they had been deprived suddenly of job, friends, and income.

In Washington, D.C., one bureaucrat wrote "GOODBYE, PAY ROLL: Wail of a Retired Federal Clerk" for a new magazine called the *Annuitant*. One verse began, "Friends in office I adore, but love the pay envelope even more."

High-level bureaucrats in charge of administering the law were divided about how it should be enforced. Although most employees were to be retired automatically at age seventy, they could apply for a two-year "continuance," to be awarded on the ground of efficiency. In evaluating whether a worker should be granted a continuance, some officials—defenders, if you will, of the old system of security—took personal problems into consideration, such as debts, mortgages, health, and the number of relatives dependent on the worker. ("This woman," one report noted, "was unfortunate in her marital relations, and the earning capacity of her husband is not a very large factor in the maintenance of the home, and he makes no contribution at all towards the payments on this property.")

Compassion, however, was on the way out. The future belonged to men like Gaylord Saltzgaber, commissioner of pensions in the Interior Department and a staunch advocate of the new system. Eighty-eight persons in his jurisdiction applied for continuance; he refused to grant even one. "I do not believe there is one [older person in the pension bureau]," he wrote, "whose work may not be better done by a younger person and generally at a lower initial salary; consequently I do not see how I can honestly certify that the continuance of any of them would be advantageous to the public service." Saltzgaber and his ilk could now retire aging clerks with a comparatively good conscience, secure—as the clerks themselves were not—in the knowledge that the federal pension insured their survival.

It was not the elderly themselves, then, who provided the initial impetus for retirement (although most older workers, as much from necessity as choice, supported the new retirement systems). It was, rather, the efficiency experts seeking to meet the competitive pressures posed by the eight-hour day, the industrial relations experts engaged in labor-force control, the bureaucrats like Saltzgaber for whom older workers were obstacles in the quest for cost-effective government. Fundamentally, retirement was a product of the needs of American business.

Perhaps because some workers had clung to the work-based, nineteenth-century system of security, or because retirement had not proved to be the panacea some had expected it to be, on the eve of the Great Depression the modern system of retirement had yet to take hold. As of 1932, less than 20 percent of American workers were covered by pension plans.

The Depression, curiously, helped gain widespread acceptance of the new system. At a time when jobs were so hard to find, thousands of older workers willingly sacrificed their own work lives and retired to open up jobs for the young.

In the ten years after 1930, the percentage of males over sixty-five in the labor force dropped a full ten points. More important, the decline was not only related to the Depression, for many older workers stayed out of the labor market through the boom years of the Second World War. By the early 1950s, when corporations began to support benefit increases, retirement had replaced work as the general experience of older Americans.

Two factors accounted for retirement's final triumph. The first was the Social Security Act of 1935. Drafted by the Committee of Economic Security, appointed by Roosevelt in 1934, the act reflected the industrial relations outlook of the committee members. The program was designed to facilitate—but also to ensure—the ouster of older people from the work force. It included what is called the "retirement test"—fifteen dollars per month being set as the maximum one could earn without losing benefits. Although those who drafted the act were doubtless concerned with providing economic security to retired persons, there was never any question that they had to be retired—removed from the labor market—to receive benefits. As one committee member recalled later, "We *never* called these benefits anything but retirement benefits."

The second factor contributing to the triumph of retirement was the "selling" of leisure. If the new system of retirement was to become dominant, more older workers had to "choose" the life of leisure. Thus life insurance companies—and others deeply involved in the pension business—began marketing retirement to the public. In a speech delivered to the National Industrial Conference Board in 1952, vice-president H. G. Kenagy of the Mutual Life Insurance Company urged his audience to prepare employees for retirement at fifty. "Just recently," he said, "house organs that are coming to my desk have been doing a splendid job of selling the idea . . . that old age can be beautiful, and that the best of life is yet to come. . . . That is done by constant stories of happily retired people telling what they do, but still more, of course, emphasizing what they did to get ready for the life they are now living." A host of new magazines for the retired, from *Lifetime Living* to *Modern Maturity*, boosted retirement as a nirvana of travel, hobbies, and petty capitalism. Most major corporations and labor unions developed retirement "preparation" programs, designed as much to condition employees to accept a fundamentally functionless old age as to plan financially for it. The state of Florida, hoping to lure the retired from the chilly North, held out the vision of retirement as an adventurous combination of work and play, emphasizing in its promotional literature the "endless opportunities to start small services and business ventures." While academic sociologists of the 1960s praised retirement as a form of "disengagement" or "inevitable mutual withdrawal," their colleagues in the new discipline of leisure studies argued that if the elderly found retirement difficult, this was because they had not yet learned how to enjoy themselves on what David Riesman called the "frontier of consumption." When Americans learned to play, retirement would come naturally.

They did learn to play. But even as they learned to frolic in the sun, the whole edifice of retirement began to show signs of stress. A combination of economic and social incentives had convinced millions of older workers that they could afford to retire and that they wanted to. Unfortunately, maintaining an aging population in year-round leisure—even in moderate discomfort—was proving to be an expensive proposition. And while the cost of funding Social Security began to seem prohibitive, raising the tax rates to keep the system sound was a politically risky business. A significant sector of the political and business communities became convinced that the nation, as a productive unit, could no longer tolerate retirement policies that were based on simple age classifications rather than on ability. Mandatory retirement, created in the name of efficiency, was now regarded as inefficient.

One result of these pressures was a spate of proposals to raise the eligibility age under Social Security. Another was the Retirement Act of 1978, which raised the permissible mandatory retirement age from sixty-five to seventy in most public and private employment. This denouement was, perhaps, inevitable; after all, the nation has some economic problems, and if a rollback of retirement would help to solve them, so be it.

Yet while this recent twist, or turn-about, is understandable, there is something disturbing about the manner in which legislators and the public at large were able to conveniently forget why mandatory retirement had been instituted in the first place and what its role in society had been. Overnight, it seemed, what had been created and accepted as a functional instrument of social engineering was transformed into a curious relic reflecting nothing but prejudice, stereotypes, and ignorance. Overnight, too, the alluring concept of leisure was replaced by a new—or rather centuries-old—concept: work. In place of the idyllic postwar vision of retirement, Jimmy Carter offered the vision of an active and "inspiring" old age, trotting out as evidence his seventy-eight-year-old mother, who a decade before had served in the Peace Corps in India. And liberal senator Jacob Javits, apparently oblivious to all the effort that had once gone into ensuring that older people would *not* work, now hailed his own antiretirement measure as "a new Magna Carta for older people."

If elderly people of the turn of the century could compare notes with those of us approaching this century's end, the two generations might well conclude that, whatever else has changed, the fate of the elderly remains the same: to serve the needs of other age groups and to be retired, or put back to work, in the interest of someone else's conception of the general welfare.

The
Corporate Person

DIANE ROTHBARD MARGOLIS

© *Ellis Herwig/The Picture Cube*

Group portrait for an annual stock report

MILLIONS OF AMERICANS earn their livelihood in modern corporations. In the following selections, Diane Rothbard Margolis describes how managers are socialized in the ways of corporate life. Just as rural workers had to be trained for the discipline of the factory, so middle-class candidates for managerial positions in the modern corporation have to be initiated into the ways of the organization. While blue-collar workers have specific duties, managers must *become* the corporation by learning the unspoken duty to act in the interest of the company.

Novices are transformed into company people by responding positively to the demands of long hours, extended business trips, and frequent transfers. In this way, the budding executives become people who are loyal to the corporation, sometimes to the exclusion of families and communities. For example, frequent transfers from city to city subjugate the needs of the family in favor of the needs of the business by curtailing extended family ties, severing friendships, and limiting community involvement. The long hours required of rising executives also help to place business first; typically managers spend 70 hours a week at work, leaving little time for family activities. The expenditure of time is taken as a demonstration of loyalty to the company Those who fail the test by putting the needs of the family above those of the corporation are not likely candidates for promotion; those who pass become successful corporate managers. For the modern manager then, work is turned into a principal source of satisfaction, even more important than family, friends, and community.

. . . Here is one manager's detailed description of his years at Global Products, Inc. Al Corelli was in sales. A man in merchandising might have spent most of his time at headquarters; one in production, personnel, or finance might have moved neither so far nor so fast; but, in general, this man's career was typical:

> Right now I'm a regional sales manager. I've been in the sales area for the entire twelve years. I started out as a sales representative in Cleveland. The salesman is basically calling on retail stores, trying to get them to display your products and price them properly. So my job was to make sure they order it, and make sure they order more than they need. Make sure it's priced right, and on the shelf right, enough space. Yeah, cover up your competitor when you can. I spent almost two years there.
>
> The next level I went to was account manager. I had to move to Columbus, and I had accounts there and in Dayton. There I called on the buyers, the guys who make decisions for the chains. You're really dealing across a desk instead of in the stores, although I still retained some retail responsibilities but very little.
>
> I spent on the account manager job, I think it was a year and a half, and then I became a sales supervisor and my responsibility was for the Syracuse area, so I traveled around upstate New York a great deal. That job was supervising salesmen to make sure the salesmen were trained properly to cover retail stores and get our products displayed. That's about the first level of management. I was there about a year.
>
> Then I went on the same job to Philadelphia, with a bigger market. I spent about a year there doing the same thing, but there I had people who had headquarters accounts reporting to me too. I didn't have the large customers, I had the smaller customers. I had about nine men and three of them had accounts, so I got involved in supervising accounts, supervising men who had accounts, which was another experience. GPI is a series of experiences. I was there about a year and a half, which seems to be the magic number.
>
> I was moved then to headquarters into what they call a staff assistant, who is kind of in training for district manager. It gives everybody in headquarters an opportunity to see how this guy thinks. He does some jobs that are questionable. Analysis, administrative detail work that really nobody wants to do but somebody has to do. And in the process of doing these jobs which are really not very important, it gives all the people who are important an opportunity to look at this guy and see how he thinks. I wasn't there that long, only for half a year as it turned out.

Usually it was supposed to be like a year or a two-year duty, so I came in and started to do my thing and before you knew it they needed a district manager and they said, "Corelli, you're it!" So that was kind of nice. We were living in Portchester then. We had bought a home and everything, because the guy I replaced had been there two years. There's no way of knowing, and neither was I given any indication that it would be a short time. They told me it would probably be a year or two years and before you knew it somebody quit and a guy in Texas got promoted and they offered me the Texas district. And I was happy to go because that's what I wanted, a district manager's job.

That was another new experience because that's a broker territory, strictly brokers. I was district manager in Texas for about fifteen months and then I went to San Francisco and was district manager there. I had a district sales force there. I covered basically northern California and a little bit of Nevada. I had Lake Tahoe and that area up there, but I really didn't get up there that much. My basic business was in the Bay Area and Sacramento; that's where my direct sales force was. I was there for two years and then I came to headquarters again as region manager.

Region manager is the guy who supervises the district managers.

In his twelve years with GPI, Corelli had held eight different positions. Each was in a different part of the country from the one previous, each therefore required his family to move, and each presented Corelli with new and more demanding training. Through that training he had changed from the innocent tyro he presumably had been twelve years earlier to the seasoned corporation man he was when interviewed. Though Corelli spoke of his career dispassionately, as an orderly and uneventful stepwise progression, those years of climbing the corporate hierarchy were for him, and for most managers, an all-consuming experience culminating in a transfer to headquarters.

Corelli was the son of a semiskilled factory worker. As was the case with nearly all the managers, his career path was determined by his blue-collar origins. These were not men born to be chief executives. Corporate leaders are generally chosen from the ranks of the upper class and the upper middle class, from among those who have attended select preparatory schools, elite colleges, and a handful of leading business schools. There is at the corporation a noticeable difference between the career paths of such men and the paths of ordinary graduates of state universities or denominational colleges.

To illustrate what a difference one's background could make, a manager in finance told a story about a Harvard Business School graduate he knew:

You know the degree is worth something when you see who the people are that get ahead. Like there was one fellow whom I thought was extremely bright and then I found out that he went to Harvard Business School. I said, "Gee, he doesn't impress me as being a guy who went to HBS." Normally they have an air about them and this fellow just didn't have it. You were able to talk to him. He just didn't put you down all the time. The others tend to get a little bit snippy once in a while. But this fellow was struggling along in his capacity and finally (I don't know if he made a conscious decision but I have to think that he did) he became area director for contributions to Harvard Business School. And Harvard picks this up right away and has him put his picture in our weekly paper. Well, I have to tell you this, from that day forward his career has just taken off. He jumped twice and has got quite a responsible position now in one of the new divisions. You know it can't be coincidence—it just can't be. There he was for three years and nobody knew the poor guy existed; he was doing a good job but all of a sudden, once it became generally known, he just took off. You know, when you read your bulletins on people who are getting the promotions, well, Ivy League schools and a Harvard MBA are just so prominent; they're the people who are really getting the promotions.

Without such credentials a manager's chances of reaching the top are slim. That is so, management experts argue, not because the leaders of industry are snobbish exclusionists, but because the managerial job is amorphous; training for it has more to do with learning attitudes and values than with the actual learning of knowledge and skills. According to Rosabeth Moss Kanter, "Conformity pressures and the development of exclusive management circles closed to 'outsiders' stem from the degree of uncertainty surrounding managerial positions." Bureaucracy, many contend, reduces uncertainty, yet within large corporations the higher the rank the greater the number of situations where people, rather than impersonal procedures, have to be relied upon. Thus it is that the higher the rank the more likely the position will be open only to individuals whose social backgrounds match the elite backgrounds of those already in the highest places.

Which is not to say that the highest ranks are the exclusive preserve of those with elite backgrounds. There are too few of the latter to fill all of the former. However, if the elite socialization necessary to a captain of industry has not been part of a man's upbringing, he will have to make up for the lack with much effort and decades of resocialization, so that eventually he will think, feel, and act like those raised to command.

Because some of the highest positions at a corporation must be filled by those from lower classes, most managers are treated as if they are in training for the top. And because as he rises in the corporation his work becomes less predictable and therefore less easy to control by rules, a manager's training is not simply a matter of learning skills, but one of learning a corporate attitude, of taking on corporate values as his own. It is an initiation.

Initiations are not peculiar to giant corporations. They are found in every society as processes by which an individual assumes a new status. Rites of passage, the tribal ceremonies that induct an adolescent into adulthood, are the prototypical form of initiation. Generally they include a series of ordeals during which the initiate is critically altered. The processes whereby people are inducted into specialized occupations in industrial societies are analogous to rites of passage.

Through both the tribal and the industrial initiation new members are indoctrinated into their social roles: they learn new languages; they share new values with other group members; they assume new identities; they develop new associates and new loyalties; and they internalize new emotional responses. Thus, through initiations, social institutions shape new members into the institutional mold. Cloning not being possible, initiations are the way older members and leaders can replicate themselves.

There are, of course, important differences between the initiations of preindustrial and industrial societies. In their transport from one kind of society to the other, initiations have lost their apparent ceremony, some of their intensity, and they have become more drawn out. They have also become more varied. In primitive societies there are, in addition to the rites of passage marking adult status, only one or two other initiations into specialized secret functions such as those of the hunter or the shaman. In societies with extensive divisions of labor, on the other hand, a large number of specializations offer individual initiations.

In the army it is basic training; in medicine, internship; and for lawyers there is a period called clerkship. At the corporation there is no name for it. Managership is a new kind of employment and giant corporations are a new kind of social institution. Their ways are changing and are not yet standard enough to be codified and named. Some corporations, but not GPI, have training programs. These are part of, but not the entire, initiation. The conditions that characterize an initiation can often extend through a manager's entire career. Such a long initiation period is unique to the corporation.

Though all specialized roles require training, they do not all require initiations. In most cases the simple acquisition of a new skill is all that is required. At giant corporations, for example, blue-collar workers need not endure initiations. Unlike managers, their exchange with the corporation is strictly economic—duties and wages are precisely specified in advance. But between the manager and the corporation, reciprocity is more subtle; it is a social and political exchange. The blue-collar worker works *for* the corporation; the manager, as a result of his initiation, becomes a part *of* the corporation. The corporation, like all social institutions, has no existence outside the successive generations of people who, as members of the institution, give it life. It is because managers, if they become top executives, will be the life of the corporation that they must undergo an initiation. They must learn to think for the corporation; the corporation's interests must become their own.

Given these goals, it is not surprising that many aspects of a corporate initiation are comparable to those of religious conversions. Peter L. Berger and Thomas Luckmann have described the ingredients that go into those total transformations they call "alternations":

> A "recipe" for successful alternation has to include both social and conceptual conditions, the social, of course, serving as the matrix of the conceptual. The most important social condition is the availability of an effective plausibility structure, that is, a social base serving as the "laboratory" of transformation. This plausibility structure will be mediated to the individual by means of significant others, with whom he must establish strongly affective identification.... The plausibility structure must become the individual's world, displacing all other worlds, especially the world the individual "inhabited" before his alternation. This requires segregation of the individual from the "inhabitants" of other worlds, especially his "coinhabitants" in the world he has left behind. Ideally this will be physical segregation.
>
> ... Such segregation is particularly important in the early stages of alternation (the "novitiate" phase). ...

That is the "recipe" for "alternations." But, as Berger and Luckmann point out, socializations to work roles are only partial transformations. "They build on the basis of primary internalizations and generally avoid abrupt discontinuities within the subjective biography of the individual." It is not necessary that the trainee abandon or repudiate all alternative realities. A reordered emphasis is all that is usually required. For example, the army recruit who has been taught not to kill in his primary socialization has also been taught to be loyal, obedient, and patriotic. During basic training the latter lessons will be reinforced enough to enable the recruit to overcome the former. Similarly, in the development of the manager the values of primary socialization seldom need to be repudiated or replaced. Instead, out of the plethora of often contradictory values and interpretations of reality that mark an industrial society, the junior manager will be guided toward a world view in which some values assume absolute priority while others are allowed to atrophy.

In the process, most of the ingredients of an "alternation," usually in a modified form, will be present. The corporation itself is the laboratory; the manager's boss, or rather, succession of bosses, is the significant other; and the combination of long hours, business trips, and transfers serves to segregate novitiate managers from the inhabitants of other worlds.

A transfer is a change of job within the corporation, usually a promotion, which involves a move from one corporate location to another. As the managers step from job to job, their families follow, living in many communities. A corporation transfers its managers for several reasons. The most apparent is that it has a position to be filled at one location and a person who is able to fill it at another. A vice-president (of another corporation) . . . described the following series of transfers:

> We have somebody in the Philippines we're going to replace. This situation has triggered five moves. The man in the Philippines is being let go because he's not doing the job. A man in Hong Kong will be moved to the Philippines. A man in Singapore will go to Hong Kong. One in Thailand will be transferred to Singapore and a man somewhere else in Asia, we haven't decided who yet, will replace the man in Thailand.

Although not all locations are so exotic, the chain effect is a common characteristic of transfers. When a large corporation recruits only for lower positions and fills its higher positions through internal promotions, it is not unusual for one transfer to trigger a half dozen or so more. Most giant corporations think of their "personnel pool" not as scores of separate bodies each at a different facility, but instead as a single entity encompassing all corporate salaried employees. When a position needs to be filled in one location, the supervisor does not restrict himself to those already stationed there, but instead he sends a message to a central personnel office where a computer is programmed to find those ready to fill the opening, no matter where they are stationed. A GPI manager explained the process:

> I guess obviously an opening has to appear. Normally someone leaves a position and they're looking around for someone to fill it. Then the supervisor will ask for the file of people who are ready for that individual position and they will send the cards to him. Then the ones who will make the decision will screen the cards and pick two or three people that they seem to like and they will interview these three people and choose from them.

At the simplest pragmatic level that is all there is to a transfer: a job has to be filled and the most qualified manager at the corporation is chosen to fill it. Geographical considerations are irrelevant. Yet, in terms of the manager's training, geography—the need for a man to move through several locations—is critical. Corporate spokesmen readily acknowledge the use of transfers "to broaden the man's experience, season him, [and] groom him for future and greater responsibilities." They are not generally as aware of or as outspoken about the process by which transfers play a key role in the psychological initiation of managers.

That process points to the emotional and ideological changes that are meant to occur in the manager during his acculturation to the company. Not only do transfers separate managers and their families "from the inhabitants of other worlds," but they are, among all the components of a corporate initiation, the most ritualistic. They have the clearest symbolic overtones.

Arnold van Gennep, the turn-of-the-century ethnographer who coined the term "rites of passage," distinguished in those ceremonies the recurring themes of death and rebirth:

> The life of an individual in any society is a series of passages from one age to another and from one occupation to another. . . . Progression from one group to the next is accompanied by . . . ceremonies whose essential purpose is to enable the individual to pass from one defined position to another.
>
> [The] dramatic representation of death and rebirth . . . is suggested or dramatized in rites of puberty, initiation, pregnancy and delivery. . . . The "logical idea" behind these [ceremonies of] . . . transition from one state to another is literally equivalent to giving up the old life and "turning over a new leaf."

At the corporation, with its many transfers, death and rebirth are played out not just once, but often as the leitmotif of the initiation. From the moment that the man first becomes aware of stirrings at the corporation (when he is called to some distant location for an interview), a transfer carries with it overtones of both birth and death. His announcement to his wife that a transfer is in the offing is similar, especially in the early years of his career, to her announcement of a pregnancy. There is the exhilaration of an approaching new life somewhere else, the joy of success, and the reward of promotion; and there is the excited planning for the happy event. Betty Corelli, the wife of the manager whose career took the family to eight different places in twelve years, told how she felt about her moves:

> Each move was in a sense like going out to the next adventure. I hated leaving but then I was excited about going.

It is only later, when there have already been several moves, that the husband's announcement of yet another transfer calls forth a rueful response. Then the excitement of new places, of finding a new house and decorating it, of growing familiar with a new community and meeting new people, is overpowered by the sadness of leaving, with its emptying of the home and its partings from friends and neighbors.

A woman . . . who had been moved fourteen times in as many years, said:

> Just moving gets to be quite a chore, especially when you do it every eleven months or so. Once you know you're going to go, you live geared to the fact that you're going to go. You don't participate in anything that's going on in town. You say, "Well, why should I get involved in town politics, why should I care about the town taxes? I won't be here anyway to pay them." And you say, "Why worry about making too many friends? I won't be here." I know that every time we have actually known that we were going to have to move, you get yourself

ready to move by shutting off what you've got. You turn off and start thinking in terms of "This is where I am going" and start thinking, "I am moving and this is where I am going to live." And right away you have to start cutting the ties where you are.

My daughter said to me that this is one of the things she always did when we moved: she began thinking about all the bad things she was leaving and all the good things about where she was going to go. You get yourself into that, you're going to go and actually once you know you're going to go, the sooner the better, because it's sort of something that's hanging over your head all the time then.

Many people approaching death have noted that others tend to shun them. Persons about to be transferred reported the same sort of withdrawal. The woman continued:

If people know you're going to move, they themselves start to disengage themselves from you, too. It's very noticeable that when people find you're going to move, you find them backing off. You'd think they'd say, "Gee, we haven't much time left together, let's do this and let's do that." But that's not what happens at all. You start finding out that they're not there anymore. They're busy. And they're busy with things they know they're going to be doing without you so they start doing them without you even before you've left. You notice it and it's just a feeling you get. It's not just all of a sudden, slice, you're cut off. But you do notice people starting to draw back. And the kids, I know, would say that they couldn't get any friends to come and play. The other kids would suddenly be busy with somebody else, even though they'd always been with them. Their friends were starting to find somebody else because after all, "she's leaving."

The similarity between death and transfers highlights precisely that quality of the transfer which makes it such an important ingredient in the indoctrination of the manager. The transfer separates people. In this, the first transfer is most critical, for it is the one that removes the manager and his family from the places and persons of his primary socialization. It calls a halt to the daily conversations (and the possible criticism of his new behavior) that might reinforce early training, and it leaves the young manager open to new ideas and values. Away from the people of his youth, he can develop into a corporation man without the need to defend his changing self.

Through the initiation the small-town or ghetto youth is transformed so that he no longer resembles the people of his early years. They might be proud of his "success" but they are also likely to be resentful as he becomes different from them. If he were to stay in his hometown there would be a daily tug-of-war over him between the corporation and the members of his primary community. The first transfer makes possible a circumvention of such difficulties.

Beyond that, the first move teaches the young couple that they can live successfully without the people and communities that nurtured them. Release from old associations seemed to the GPI managers and their wives to represent a newly found independence. Actually, however, most men and women did not become autonomous; instead they transferred their needs for security, nurture, and community from family and friends to the corporation. Partly because they were so taken up by their nascent careers and partly because they were so closely associated with the corporation that it could readily fill the gap left by their initial separation, the men reported no feelings of either anxiety or release as a result of the first transfer. Their wives, on the other hand, pointed to the first move as the most difficult and also the one which made all subsequent moves easy. One young women said:

> It was a big move for us to move east, but now it doesn't seem like anything at all and now I would go to Florida or the Philippines or anywhere my husband wanted to go, and he would be willing to, too. Our first big move was going to New Jersey and after that it wasn't a big hassle.

Another made more of the difference between her reaction and her husband's:

> I don't find moving difficult now. At first I did because we had lived all our lives, both of us, in Detroit, and when he took this job I don't think we realized, maybe he did and I didn't, what it would involve. I think the first move was the hardest, moving from Detroit to Battle Creek only three hours away and we could get in often, but just breaking the family ties was difficult for me. It wasn't for him. I guess it never is for a man; they're not as close to their families as women are. After that I really got to enjoy it, meeting people and seeing the country and traveling around. But it took a while to adjust to it and each move had its adjustments because it's a new situation, but we've always made friends and I've enjoyed it.

After the first move, subsequent transfers serve to prevent the man and his family from developing extracorporate relationships. Human associations take time to develop. Although transients become adept at striking up instrumental relationships—friendships geared to mutual help or to parallel play—they seldom in adulthood develop the feeling or caring relationships they enjoyed in high school. The prevention of deeply felt relationships outside of the corporation was not recognized by any of the managers or corporate officers as one of the functions of transfers. In other organizations that transfer their personnel, however, it is an acknowledged purpose of the transfer. Herbert Kaufman in his study of the U.S. Forest Service notes that the Service would transfer rangers who became too closely involved with their communities. In addition, it moved its men regularly to prevent any community attachments that might compete with loyalty to the Service:

> Transfer of personnel is treated in the Forest Service as a device for "the development, adjustment and broadening of personnel"; consequently, men are deliberately moved a good deal, particularly during their early years in the agency. The Service does not merely wait until vacancies occur; it shifts men to replace each other in what looks like a vast game of musical chairs . . . the impact of rapid transfer is more profound than training alone; it also builds identifications with the Forest Service as a whole. For during each man's early years, he never has time to sink roots in the communities in which he sojourns so briefly. . . . He barely becomes familiar with an area before he is moved again. Only one thing gives any continuity, any structure, to his otherwise fluid world; the Service. . . . Loyalties to the agency are so well nurtured that they offset competing loyalties to other groups and symbols.

When it was suggested to some of the managers that their transfers at the corporation might have had the same motive as transfers did in the Forest Service, they were surprised. Nonetheless, when talking about their community activities, most of them mentioned their transfers as one reason they had not become involved in their communities. One man explained:

I've never been a joiner. I think you'd have to say, though, that there hasn't been one community I've lived in while at Global Products where I expected to establish any roots. Not one. I fully expected to progress out of an assignment, and that would mean a move. After you've been in a place, say a year, you finally begin to understand what it has to offer and you can begin to pick and choose what you want to do and you really are just getting settled at that point. I guess we were only in two places, Chicago and Syracuse, for as much as two years.

A woman gave a similar explanation of her husband's lack of participation in community activities:

My husband has never gotten involved in the community. He was never here. We were either moving in and he was getting established or we were moving out and he was already gone. He hardly lived anywhere for a full year. It takes about a year to get settled in before you can get terribly involved. So he almost never was active in the community. The few places where we were there more than two years or a little bit longer, he got involved. He was always very involved with the family but spreading it out beyond that, no. After all, when you move so much, you have to give a lot more to your family because you have to help the children get established and help them find their level and their friends. As for myself, I was a Girl Scout leader in California.

Many found friendships not much easier to form in a short time than community attachments. A manager talked about his loneliness:

Superficially you might not be alone but realistically you are. Superficially people may be friendly with you because you are a neighbor and you'll probably be invited to a local neighborhood party or something like that.

It's hard to say what makes a relationship superficial. I've never been anywhere long enough for me to sit back and analyze it. I think you can generally see if someone is genuinely interested in you. At this point, I'm not sure I have a close or even a semiclose relationship with any of the men here.

Men at the corporation were aware that the social and emotional difficulties caused by transiency had been the subject of adverse criticism in recent years. Combining their faith in the benevolence of the corporation with a belief, quite prevalent in the sixties and early seventies, that the discovery and analysis of any problem is tantamount to its solution, many considered transfers to be already a thing of the past. The remarks of a manager in his early fifties were typical:

Talking to younger people you'd have a different set of situations than you would have talking to me, because the times have changed. I find now, for example, that people are reluctant to move where that was not the case fifteen or twenty years ago when we started this rat race. I find that big corporations, specifically GPI, are much more reluctant to move people now. Not just expense-wise, although that's important these days, but because I do think it upsets people. They don't seem to think it's as necessary as it used to be.

A man about a decade younger concurred:

I'd have to say we're doing a better job in Global Products now, of not moving people around as much. I think that there's a couple of reasons. You could say that it's expensive to do that and we're in an austerity year, or have been for the last couple of years. But I think it's beyond that. I think that there's managers now like myself who were moved around a lot who have decided that it didn't make any sense, not only for themselves but for the organization. There was no continuity. Nobody was there in a job long enough to really understand it, let alone make it move forward. For instance, we have now a forty-three-year-old group vice-president who also sits on the board of directors who, by his own admission, was never in a job long enough to understand it or really know it. He is the ultimate product of that system. Very successful, very bright, but he's concerned that he doesn't know how to manage anything because he's never spent any time long enough in one place to do that. The corporation has finally said, "Hey, we've got to slow something down; we're not learning from our mistakes, plus nobody really has had to live with their mistakes."

Nonetheless, by 1978 there was no firm evidence that the rate of transfers had declined or that managers were any less willing to take a transfer that enhanced career opportunities. On this score accounts in the popular press based on isolated instances of managers' resistance to transfers have tended to contradict evidence from more careful studies that corporations continue to demand transfers and that managers continue to be willing to move. . . .

If transfers break up extended family and community relationships, long hours spent at work warp relationships within the nuclear family. Extensive corporate demands upon the young manager's time separate him not only from his friends and neighbors but from his wife and children as well. Of course, isolating the man from others is not the ostensible purpose of overwork at the corporation. As in the case of transfers, isolation is a seemingly unintended by-product. Nonetheless, the excessiveness of work at the corporation, along with its frequent absurdity and arbitrariness, points to its function as part of the initiation.

How much did the men at GPI work? Not many reported as few as fifty hours a week. More commonly, the men put in from sixty to seventy hours. Most left for work around seven thirty in the morning and did not return home for eleven or twelve hours. Usually they brought back with them two or three more hours of work. This homework typically involved catching up on correspondence or on business periodicals and trade journals, but occasionally it included report writing or communications with fellow workers. One man reported regularly receiving business-related telephone calls until eleven o'clock at night.

An average manager's Monday-through-Friday time chart might look like this:

Commuting to and from work	10 hours
Working at desk or in conference and group meetings	40 hours
Business lunches and dinners	8 hours
Homework, reading periodicals, etc.	12 hours
Total work time	70 hours

In addition most managers traveled. Many reported being out of town regularly from Tuesday through Friday.

Weekends were different. Most managers thought of weekdays as corporation time and weekends as family time. If they wanted to spend more time with their families during the week, they slept less or skimmed more quickly through their periodicals. On weekends, though, except for the four to eight hours of work they generally brought home, their time belonged to the family.

Beyond GPI and their families, few of the men had other interests. A couple were hunters. One had a basement filled with decoys he had carved, and in the fall he rose at dawn and went to nearby lakes to shoot ducks before work. The other hunter chased bigger game on weekend jaunts. Two carried into adulthood their schoolboy interest in basketball; a few others were weekend tennis players. As for the rest, none seemed to have any deep or developed avocations. There was among them not one camera buff, not one Sunday painter, not one amateur musician, although two collected antiques. By and large, these were not the men around whom the currently burgeoning leisure-time industry is being built. They did not flit from hobby to hobby seeking ways to fill empty hours. They had few empty hours. And that was the way it had to be if by the end of their initiation the corporation were to become their supreme interest.

Nowhere was this so apparent as in their role as citizens and community members. To be sure, one man was a member of Fairtown's Democratic Town Committee, another was president of the neighborhood association in his subdivision, an additional three were once members of the Jaycees. But that was the extent of the GPIers' community participation. Although most of the men said they thought they should be more active, they all explained their default in terms of the demands of work. One said:

> I think it would be very tough to attend a meeting, particularly when you travel. Because that would be kind of unfair to your wife, to come home and say, "Well, I'll see you, I'm going to a meeting." That would be very tough. I won't always be traveling, and when I'm not traveling, I think I'll have more time to devote to that and it's something I think I'd enjoy.

A woman whose husband had joined a GPI subsidiary in his late forties, after working for smaller firms in the Midwest, compared his current situation with his previous activities:

> He was on the finance committee of the school board in Indianapolis but he doesn't have time now. He'll vote, hopefully, if he's in town, but I don't think now he'd have time for the meetings. If he had a job where he was home every night at five o'clock, he would be a very active person. I can remember when Jimmy was small and Bob was basically working then eight to five and not traveling. He was gone to meetings every night then.

Travel and long hours were not all that inhibited participation. Many of the men felt that too deep an involvement in community activities would be disapproved of at work.

When asked what their corporation's attitude was toward community participation, half the men answered that GPI had no attitude. The other half thought the corporation had a position, but they were not united on what it was. Some believed the corporation encouraged only top executives to participate. Others felt that the corporate message was ambiguous. One of them explained:

> There's a corporate policy—they encourage you, okay? Now there's another theory and I thought it was a pretty good one, you know, being maze-bright or

maze-dull, okay? To be maze-bright in a situation like this, you sort of suspect—
if you're going to be successful in a corporation you've got to devote a lot of
time to being successful in a corporation. Then, fine, they like to see you as
president of the American Red Cross in your community, but they don't want
you to devote that much time to it. So the object is to join the organization, get
to be president, and do as little work as you possibly can and hang on for as long
as you possibly can, and devote the time to GPI as a corporation. Whereas the
maze-dull individual would take them seriously and he'd be in there slugging
away helping them raise money every year and he'd be a worker and never get
into the executive branch of the organization where he could just slough off and
not really do anything for them.

So I would tend to agree that this is what GPI is really encouraging their
people to do—go through the ranks of an organization outside as fast as you
can and not really devote that much time to it. They want that time for GPI.

The managers understood corporate priorities and adopted them as their
own. They stayed away from community affairs and devoted their time and
energies to GPI. Only a few men complained about the exclusive demands the
corporation made on their time. One finance manager granted the corporation
the right to call upon him for extra hours, if absolutely necessary, but when
such requests seemed arbitrary, he grumbled:

There are certain times of the year where financial people have to work Satur-
days and Sundays. Like I have to work Good Friday. Because of the nature of
finance, there are times in the year when it has to be done and people in finance
look on it almost like a cop who has to work on Christmas day.

It's different when it's not warranted, when it's somebody's whim. They say,
"Gee, I'd like to see something by tomorrow," and it's five o'clock. They don't
even think of you as a person sometimes. It's not as if he's deliberately treating
you like a machine—he just doesn't know any better. For instance, if they want
you to go on a trip or something and you say, "Geez, it's Easter Sunday," they'll
say, "Oh, yeah, I guess so, I guess you'll want to be home, huh?" They never
even think, "He wants to be home with his family on Easter Sunday." They just
say, "Do this." It doesn't even enter their mind that they're infringing on you.

The idea of corporate infringement had not, in fact, entered the minds of
most GPIers. . . . When it did, a wife, not a manager, was usually the one airing
a grievance. Yet two key aspects of overwork at the corporation were its
frequent meaninglessness and its intrusion into all spheres of a managerial
family's life.

Overwork, indeed overwork to the point of exhaustion, is part of many
initiations in industrial societies, but generally it is required only briefly as part
of an initial training period. In the army, recruits are forced through long
marches during basic training. Medical interns and residents endure work
schedules that "sometimes require them to put in 100 hours of duty a week,
including on occasions fifty hours or more without a break." Such overwork
has the effect of lowering the novice's resistance, of making him submissive. It
has much the same effect that seclusion, flagellation, or intoxication has on the
adolescent initiate in tribal societies: it anesthetizes him. As Arnold van Gennep
notes, "The initiate's anesthesia is an important factor in the rite of initiation. . . . The purpose is to make the novice 'die,' to make him forget his former
personality and his former world." In the case of soldiers and doctors, what
needs forgetting is former aversions—to killing or to multilation.

At the corporation, overwork is rarely extreme enough to induce stupefying exhaustion, nor is the desired alteration in attitudes so drastic. What is to be accomplished is not a total change in the young man's values or attitudes but merely their reordering. The priority of the corporation must be established. For that to happen, exhausting workloads are less strategic than work situations that put the corporation into competition with other institutions or persons who might lay claim on the man. These competitions, which always have the appearance of accidents, are in fact intentional enforcers or tests of the man's loyalty to the corporation.

However, they are seldom viewed as such by commentators on corporation life. On the contrary, the conflicts occasioned by the corporation's work demands are considered to be not an integral part of the organization's training program but pathological aberrations. Wilbert Moore, for instance, distinguishes between "routine managers" and "leaders." The latter, he claims, are "dangerous [men] at the corporation," in part because in the exercise of their leadership they are likely to stage competitions for subordinates' energies and loyalties on noncorporate turf.

> Under the guise of leadership, . . . the leader who extracts heroic performance from his followers may be thereby interfering in their normal involvements in all sorts of nonoccupational but proper uses of time and energy. His leadership may involve imperialistic forays into neighboring territories and consequent border disputes.

Such an analysis overlooks two aspects of the corporation's "imperialistic forays into neighboring territories." First, the corporation seldom loses more than one or two border disputes over a single man without shortly thereafter severing its relationship with him; and second, such forays are not a rarity at the corporation, but a common occurrence.

True, few men or their wives complained about "infringements." But that indicates not that the complainers were rare victims of unusual bosses playing "leader," but rather that only a few still recognized territories that ought to have been inviolable. What set such men off from the rest was the continued vitality, for them, of the worlds of their primary socialization. In general, they tended to be more deeply religious than the rest and to have avoided transiency. They also, as a rule, were earning less and were in a less advanced position than were other men their age.

The family has a sacred place in the American scheme of things and it cannot be openly attacked. Instead, competitions between the family and the corporation must have the appearance of accidents. Business trips scheduled on religious holidays, last-minute demands for seemingly unnecessary reports when an anniversary dinner or a child's birthday party is scheduled, requests for information as the young manager is about to leave for home at the end of the day—these do not have the appearance of planned contests. Indeed, the superior who makes such demands may be unaware that he is staging a contest. Moreover, if the conflict is brought to his attention and if the young manager chooses the claims of family over those of the corporation, the supervisor is likely to acquiesce and withold overt disapproval. After all, in this culture he must at least give lip service to the prior claims of the family. Some other time, however, in some other context, perhaps at the young manager's yearly evaluation, the boss will question the young man's "attitude." The complaining finance manager, Bob Hogan, describes the process:

> The man who works from nine to five is the man who will make his $14,000 a year and no more. And he might really be brilliant in some respects and still make only $14,000. Because the company, as it starts promoting you, does indirectly say to you, "You owe me more than nine to five. You owe me Saturdays and you owe me nights and you owe me weekends." They don't say it directly but you get that message. Four thirty in an afternoon an executive will say, "Gee, I'd like to see the, ah, the K, P, and L lines for the last five years on Global Products measured against the profit plan. Can I get that first thing in the morning?" It's now four-thirty and he wants it by nine. You have a choice. You can tell him, "Well, by the time I get in at nine it won't be ready till noontime." He might say, "Okay." But he gave you the message, see, the message was there. "I'd like it first thing in the morning." You've got to know that the guy means around nine o'clock—he doesn't mean around noontime. Now you make a choice. You've got to make a choice. He's not telling you to stay. Some of them do but let's say the subtler ones—it's usually subtle.
>
> Now the man who resists, who says, "I'll have it by noon," will be labeled "uncooperative," "not willing to extend himself for the corporation," and I think he would be considered "not dependable." Then when a promotion comes up and he's being considered, they'll touch bases and ask all around about him. Then somebody will say, "You know that guy; what do you know about him?" And the one who asked you to stay will say, "Oh, he's got a lousy personality. Every time I see that guy he's got a frown on his face. Am I going to have to put up with him again?" That'll kill you right there. There's a man who has an opinion about you. You can make a choice but you're not making it in a vacuum, you know damn well what you're doing to yourself. They won't fire you but you'll get bypassed when promotions come up.

The man who chooses family over corporation is failing the test, and the family that puts too much pressure on the man is failing, too. In that crucial moment, when the young manager phones his wife to announce that his boss wants him to stay late, he must show his strength and withstand the expression of her disappointment. Eventually her complaints will be muted. Hogan explained that process, too:

> What happens is this. You fit your family around the corporation. You do it this way. You say, "You always have to be available and if I'm called on then everything revolves around it." I do it and then the family life adjusts. They adjust their life or their recreation to the corporation. The family will change its style. It will learn to be less hurt about the canceled weekend. Maybe I shouldn't say it that way. It will get like a punching bag. When the husband says, "I have to take a trip," or "I have to work the weekend" and we cancel the weekend or we cancel the dinner or we cancel going out, and the family says, "Okay, take one more belt, I'm a punching bag anyway, so just hit me again." And it hits and it hurts, but they take the role that I'm here to get kicked around. Maybe it doesn't hurt any less but it sort of takes the guts out of the family and stuffs it with cotton. The family gets kicked around and then it sort of says, "Kick me around."

Of all the ways the corporation establishes its dominance over the family, perhaps the most insidious is through the work the manager brings home with him. Then he is "home," but not with the family. The wife is forced to hush the children and train them that they are "not to disturb Daddy while he has work to do." By turning the manager into a father and husband who is there but not available, the corporation can create a subtle wall of rejection between the man and his family that will strain family relationships. Then, the corporation can become the most satisfying world to him, and all other worlds can lose their importance.

A
Secular Faith

WILL HERBERG

© Ken Robert Buck/The Picture Cube

The flag as an object of worship

THE DIVERSITY OF RELIGIOUS PRACTICE that characterizes today's American society contrasts with the more homogenous Protestantism of the eighteenth- and early nineteenth-century populations. In the following selection, Will Herberg details the characteristics of today's so-called civil religion—the ideals, rituals, and symbols that provide Americans with a sense of unity. This secular faith, held in common by practitioners of diverse religions, reflects the established trends of American religious and political historyy.

Puritanism and Revivalism, described in Volume I of this anthology, each contribute to the modern civil faith. Puritanism, divorced from the concept of sin, advocates a strenuous, idealistic, and moralistic character. Revivalism advocates activity, spectacles, and pragmatism. Applying these beliefs to national life and culture results in the creation of a common set of rituals and symbols that people of all religions can share. Our rituals include the celebration of national holidays, from the traditional fireworks displays on the fourth of July and the traditional turkey dinners on Thanskgiving to the annual Memorial Day parades. Saints are Washington, Lincoln, and, more recently, Martin Luther King, Jr. Doctrines include a belief in a supreme being, an idealism and moralism in civic affairs, a faith in the power of education, and an abiding trust in democracy and free enterprise. Although Americans in the twentieth century continue to be divided along sectarian lines, Herberg concludes that they share a civil religion that fuses elements of their religious and political history.

WE GET OUR NOTION of civil religion from the world of classical antiquity. In the world of ancient Athens and Rome, "the state and religion were so completely identified that it was impossible even to distinguish the one from the other. . . . Every city had its city religion; a city was a little church, all complete, with its gods, its dogmas, and its worship." In recent years, many observers of American life have come to the conclusion that this country, too, has its civil religion, though not generally recognized as such, but fully operative in the familiar way, with its creed, cult, code, and community, like every other religion. On this there is wide agreement; but there are considerable differences among historians, sociologists, and theologians as to the sources of America's civil religion, its manifestations, and its evaluation in cultural and religious terms. These are precisely the matters I should like to discuss in the following paragraphs, with the hope of reaching some tentative conclusions on the subject.

"Every functioning society," says Robin Williams, in his influential work, *American Society: A Sociological Interpretation* (1951), "has, to an important degree, a common religion. The possession of a common set of ideas, [ideals], rituals, and symbols can supply an overarching sense of unity even in a society otherwise riddled with conflict." This we might call the *operative* religion of a society, the system of norms, values, and allegiances actually functioning as such in the ongoing social life of the community. And, of course, the operative religion of a society emerges out of, and reflects, the history of that society as well as the structural forms that give it its shape and character. If we ask ourselves what is this system of "ideas, [ideals], rituals, and symbols" that serve as the "common religion" of Americans, providing them with an "overarching sense of unity," it is obvious that it cannot be any of the professed faiths of Americans, however sincerely held; I mean Protestantism, Catholicism, or Judaism, or any of the many denominations into which American Protestantism is fragmented. What is it, then, that does serve that all-important function? What is it in and through which Americans recognize their basic unity with other Americans as Americans? What is it that provides that "overarching sense of unity," expressed in the system of allegiances, norms, and values functioning in actual life, without which no society can long endure? It seems to me that a realistic appraisal of the values, ideas, and behavior of the American people leads to the conclusion that Americans, by and large, find this "common religion" in the system familiarly known as the American Way of Life. It is the

---

A SECULAR FAITH   By Will Herberg. Originally published under the title "America's Civil Religion: What It is and Whence It Comes." From *American Civilization*, eds. Russell E. Richey and Donald G. Jones, Harper and Row (1974) 78–88. Reprinted with permission of Donald G. Jones and Russell E. Richey.

American Way of Life that supplies American society with its "overarching sense of unity" amid conflict. It is the American Way of Life that Americans are admittedly and unashamedly intolerant about. It is the American Way of Life that provides the framework in terms of which the crucial values of American existence are couched. By every realistic criterion, the American Way of Life is the operative religion of the American people.

This is the civil religion of Americans. In it we have—slightly modifying Fustel de Coulanges's classic formulation—religion and national life so completely identified that it is impossible to distinguish the one from the other. I want to make it clear that when I designate the American Way of Life as America's civil religion, I am not thinking of it as a so-called common-denominator religion; it is not a synthetic system composed of beliefs to be found in all or in a group of religions. It is an organic structure of ideas, values, and beliefs that constitutes a faith common to Americans as Americans, and is genuinely operative in their lives; a faith that markedly influences, and is influenced by, the professed religions of Americans. Sociologically, anthropologically, it is *the* American religion, undergirding American national life and overarching American society, despite all indubitable differences of ethnicity, religion, section, culture, and class. And it is a civil religion in the strictest sense of the term, for, in it, national life is apotheosized, national values are religionized, national heroes are divinized, national history is experienced as a *Heilsgeschichte*, as a redemptive history. All these aspects of the American Way as America's civil religion I will illustrate and document. But, first, I want to call attention to the notable difference in structure and content between America's civil religion and the civil religion of classical antiquity, or even the civil religion as conceived of by Jean-Jacques Rousseau. It is a difference that reflects not only the vast difference in historical context, but especially the separation between the culture of pre-Christian antiquity and the culture of Western Christendom, especially America, so thoroughly permeated with Jewish-Christian visions of redemptive history, messianism, and messianic fulfillment.

Let us try to look at the American Way of Life as America's civil religion in the same objective way, in the same detached yet not unfriendly way that an anthropologist looks upon the religion and culture of the primitive society he is studying. I say, let us try; it is a question whether we, as Americans, can really scrutinize ourselves, as Americans, with any very high degree of objectivity. For that, we may need another Tocqueville, though preferably not another Frenchman.

America's civil religion has its spiritual side, of course. I should include under this head, first, belief in a Supreme Being, in which Americans are virtually unanimous, proportionately far ahead of any other nation in the Western world. Then I should mention idealism and moralism: for Americans, every serious national effort is a "crusade" and every serious national position a high moral issue. Among Americans, the supreme value of the individual takes its place high in the spiritual vision of America's civil religion: and, with it, in principle, if not in practice—and, of course, principle and practice frequently come into conflict in every religion—the "brotherhood" of Americans: "After all, we're all Americans!" is the familiar invocation. Above all, there is the extraordinarily high valuation Americans place on religion. The basic ethos of America's civil religion is quite familiar: the American Way is dynamic;

optimistic; pragmatic; individualistic; egalitarian, in the sense of feeling uneasy at any overtly manifested mark of the inequalities endemic in our society as in every other society; and pluralistic, in the sense of being impatient with the attempt of any movement, cause, or institution to take in "too much ground," as the familiar phrase has it. Culturally, the American Way exhibits an intense faith in education, significantly coupled with a disparagement of culture in the aesthetic sense; and, characteristically, an extraordinarily high moral valuation of—sanitation! This is a good example of how what would appear to be rather ordinary matter-of-fact values become thoroughly religionized in the American Way as civil religion. A printed placard displayed in hundreds, perhaps thousands, of restaurants all over the country reads: "Sanitation is a way of life. As a way of life, it must be nourished from within and grow as a spiritual ideal in human relations." Here cleanliness is not merely next to godliness; it is virtually on the same level, as a kind of equivalent.

But, of course, it is the politico-economic aspect of the American Way as America's civil religion that is most familiar to us, as, indeed, in its own way, it was in the civil religions of the ancient world. If America's civil religion had to be defined in one phrase, the "religion of democracy" would undoubtedly be the phrase, but democracy in a peculiarly American sense. It exalts national unity, as, indeed, every civil religion does. On its political side, it means the Constitution. I am reminded of Socrates' deification of the Laws of Athens in the Platonic dialogue, the *Crito*. On its economic side, it means "free enterprise." On its social side, an egalitarianism which, as I have indicated, is not only compatible with, but indeed actually implies, vigorous economic competition and high social mobility. Spiritually, it is best expressed in the very high valuation of religion, and in that special kind of idealism which has come to be recognized as characteristically American. But it is in its vision of America, in its symbols and rituals, in its holidays and its liturgy, in its Saints and its sancta, that it shows itself to be so truly and thoroughly a religion, the common religion of Americans, America's civil religion.

But a word of caution. I have listed a number of aspects of the American Way that do not seem, at first sight, to be religious in a certain narrow sense of the word. But that is exactly the character of a civil religion; it is the religionization of the national life and national culture. You may be sure that the great annual Panathenaic Procession from the lower agora to the Acropolis, in which the youths of seventeen or eighteen received their arms and became adult citizens, entering the Athenian armed forces, would have seemed to us, accustomed as we are to the idea, though not to the reality, of the separation of national life and religion, to be really a political ceremony. But it was the archaic image of Athena that was carried at the head of the procession, and the procession moved on to the Parthenon, the temple of Athena. Do you want the contemporary equivalent of this symbolization? Then think back to the presidential inauguration ceremony of 1973. Who came forward as the intensely prestigious figures symbolizing this great civil ceremony of ours? The Warrior and the Priest, the soldier and the clergyman. Here is the perfect synthetic symbol of our civil religion, thoroughly traditional and immensely potent—and, if I may say so, not altogether unlike the Panathenaic Procession of ancient Athens.

But let us get back to what I would take to be the culminating aspects of this account of America's civil religion—its view of America, its Saints and sancta, its redemptive history. What is America in the vision of America's civil religion? Look at the reverse of the Great Seal of the United States, which is on the dollar bill. You see an unfinished pyramid, representing the American national enterprise, and over it the all-seeing eye of God. Most impressive are the mottoes, in Latin naturally: "Annuit Coeptis," "He (God) has smiled upon our beginnings"; and "Novus Ordo Seclorum," "A New Order of the Ages." That is America in America's civil religion: a new order, initiated under God, and flourishing under his benevolent providence. Could the national and the religious be more combined; is it at all possible to separate the religious and the national in this civil religion, any more than it was in ancient Greece or Rome?

It is this vision that gives substance to American history as redemptive history in America's civil religion. For this we can borrow the felicitous phrase of Oscar Handlin, "Adventure in Freedom." That is how Americans see the ultimate meaning of American history.

A redemptive history has, of course, its messianism. And so does America's civil religion. Over a century ago, in 1850, in an impassioned outburst in *White Jacket*, Herman Melville formulated this messianic vision in these tremendous words:

> God has predestined, mankind expects, great things from our race; and great things we feel in our souls. The rest of the nations must soon be in our rear. We are the pioneers of the world, the advance guard, sent on through the wilderness of untried things to break a new path in the New World that is ours. . . . Long enough have we debated whether, indeed, the political Messiah has come. But he has come in us. . . . And, let us remember that, with ourselves, almost for the first time in history, national selfishness is unbounded philanthropy.

One recalls Pericles' celebrated funeral oration, given by Thucydides.

Similarly Charles Fleischer, at the turn of the twentieth century, observed: "We of America are the 'peculiar people,' consecrated to the mission of realizing Democracy, [which] is potentially a universal spiritual principle, aye, a religion." Or Hugh Miller, in 1948: "America was not created to be supreme among the 'great powers.' It was created to inaugurate the transition of human society to just society. It is a missionary enterprise, propagating a gospel for all men."

With its redemptive history and its messianism, America's civil religion has its liturgy and its liturgical year. The traditional Christian year and the Jewish religious year have been virtually eroded in American popular religion, reduced to Christmas and Easter on the Christian side, and to Passover and the High Holy Days on the Jewish side. But, as W. Lloyd Warner tells us, "all societies, simple or complex, possess some form of ceremonial calendar. . . ." In America it is the ceremonial calendar of America's civil religion, our yearly round of national holidays. Lloyd Warner explains:

> The ceremonial calendar of American society, this yearly round of holidays and holy days, . . . is a symbol system used by all Americans. Christmas, [New Year,] Thanksgiving, Memorial Day, [Washington's and Lincoln's birthdays,] and the Fourth of July are days in our ceremonial calendar which allow Americans to express common sentiments . . . and share their feelings with others on set days preestablished by the society for that very purpose. This [ceremonial] calendar functions to draw all people together, to emphasize their similarities and

common heritage, to minimize their differences, and to contribute to their thinking, feeling, and acting alike.

Recall Robin Williams's characterization of civil religion as the common religion of a people that is quoted at the outset of this essay.

America's civil religion, too, has its Saints—preeminently Washington and
Lincoln—and its sancta and its shrines—think of Washington, D.C. and Hyde
Park. Some examination of the Saints of our civil religion is, I think, in place
here. I turn to Lloyd Warner again. He is describing, as an anthropologist
would, a Memorial Day service in Yankee City. First, as to the religio–national
function of Memorial Day: "The Memorial Day ceremonies and subsidiary
rites . . . are rituals which are a sacred symbol system, which functions periodically to integrate the whole community, with its conflicting symbols and its
opposing autonomous churches and associations. . . . Memorial Day is a cult
of the dead which organizes and integrates the various faiths, ethnic and class
groups into a sacred unity." That is what a civil religion is about. And then he
continues, quoting the chief Memorial Day orator at the ceremony he is reporting: " 'No character except the Carpenter of Nazareth,' this orator proclaimed,
'has ever been honored the way Washington and Lincoln have been in New
England. Virtue, freedom from sin, and righteousness were qualities possessed
by Washington and Lincoln and, in possessing these qualities, both were true
Americans. . . .' " It will not escape notice, I hope, that Washington and Lincoln
are here raised to superhuman level, as true Saints of America's civil religion.
They are equipped with the qualities and virtues that, in traditional Christianity,
are attributed to Jesus alone—freedom from sin, for example. And they are
endowed with these exalted qualities simply by virtue of the fact that they
were—true Americans! I don't know any more impressive illustration of the
deeply religious nature of America's civil religion.

What are the sources of America's civil religion? Only in the most general
way need we refer to civil religion in the ancient world, or even to the clearly
articulated notion of civil religion projected by Jean-Jacques Rousseau as the
civil religion of his ideal society so carefully described in his *Social Contract*.
First, we must recognize, and I want to repeat, that, in Robin Williams's words,
"Every functioning society has, to an important degree, a common religion, . . .
a common set of ideas, [ideals,] rituals, and symbols. . . ." And then we have to
look to American history and American experience for the sources of the particular form and features of America's civil religion as the American Way of
Life. After careful study and scrutiny I have come to the conclusion that the
American Way of Life, and therefore America's civil religion, is compounded of
the two great religious movements that molded America—the Puritan way,
secularized; and the Revivalist way, secularized. The legacy of Puritanism has
endowed us with its strenuous, idealistic, moralistic character; but deprived,
through pervasive secularization, of the Puritan sense of sin and judgment. The
Revivalist legacy has given us its active, pragmatic, what I might term its promotional, character; the slogan "Deeds not creeds!" comes not from John
Dewey, but from mid-nineteenth-century revivalism; but again, through drastic
secularization it is a pragmatism, a promotionalism, an expansivism no longer
"in the cause of Christ."

We do not know how against what earlier background, if any, the civil
religion of Athens or Rome emerged into historical times; but we can see the

emergence of America's civil religion out of the earlier Protestant Christianity some time toward the middle of the nineteenth century. Here we may be guided by Sidney Mead. "What was not so obvious at the time," Professor Mead writes, referring to the second half of the nineteenth century,

> was that the United States, in effect, had two religions, or at least two different forms of the same religion, and the prevailing Protestant ideology represented a syncretistic mingling of the two. The first was the religion of the [Protestant] denominations. . . . The second was the religion of the American society and nation. This . . . was articulated in terms of the destiny of America, under God, to be fulfilled by perfecting the democratic way of life for the example and betterment of mankind.

In these percipient words, we can recognize the outlines and substance of America's civil religion.

These words suggest that there have been various stages in the emergence of civil religion in America and in the varying relations of this religion to the more conventional religions of Christianity and Judaism. Unfortunately, this aspect of the problem of the development of America's civil religion has not yet received adequate study. Yet we are in a position to distinguish very generally certain phases. There is, first of all, the emerging syncretism to which Mead refers in the passage I have just read. After that, apparently, comes a very explicit and unembarrassed religionization of the American Way. And finally, some time in this century, the explicit exaltation of the American Way, or democracy, as the super-religion, over and above all other religions. Consider these two statements. The first is from J. Paul Williams, a distinguished scholar and professor of religion: "Americans must come to look upon the democratic ideal (not necessarily the practice of it) as the Will of God, or, if they please, of Nature. . . . Americans must be brought to the conviction that democracy is the very Law of Life. . . . The state must be brought into the picture; governmental agencies must teach the democratic idea *as religion*. . . . Primary responsibility for teaching democracy as religion must be given to the public schools." The civil religion as established religion with the public schools as its seminaries. But it is Horace M. Kallen, the well-known philosopher, who has put the matter most clearly and most strikingly. "For the communicants of the democratic faith," Kallen proclaims, "it [democracy] is the religion *of* and *for* religions. . . . [It is] the religion of religions; all may freely come together in it." America's civil religion, democracy, is the overarching faith, in which the particular religions may find their particular place, provided they don't claim any more. Think of the Roman overarching civil religion with its Pantheon, and with the niches in the Pantheon so generously awarded by Rome to the particular ethnic religions, so long as they did not come into collision with the overarching faith of Rome.

How shall we envisage the relation of America's civil religion to the various versions of Christianity and Judaism professed by Americans? This was a problem for the world of classical antiquity as well. Romans and Greeks of those days had at least four different kinds of religion in coexistence: (1) the very ancient Indo-European religion of the high gods, the Olympian deities for the Greeks—the religion of Zeus-Jupiter; (2) the domestic religion, compounded of the cult of ancestors and the household gods, the *lares* and *penates* of Rome;

(3) the so-called mystery religions, the personal salvationary cults, largely though not entirely of foreign, oriental origin; and, finally, (4) the great civil religion of the *polis* and the *civitas*, expanded into empire. We know, from unfortunately too fragmentary data, that the relations among these coexisting religions were always uneasy, sometimes hostile. In the Rome of the late republic and early empire, repeated attempts were made to outlaw the oriental salvation cults as incompatible with "true Roman piety," but to no effect. Even when the various bans were lifted or fell into disuse, however, the relations remained far from cordial.

In this country today, there seems to be, for the great mass of Americans, no sense of conflict, or even of tension, between America's civil religion and the traditional religions of Christianity and Judaism professed by almost all Americans. The civil religion is, of course, affirmed as the American Way, but is neither seen nor denominated as a religion by the great mass of Americans; and that makes coexistence all the easier. Yet there are some points of tension, perhaps even of conflict, at the periphery, what I have elsewhere called the "hold-out groups." There are, first, here and there, groups of incompletely enculturated—that is, incompletely Americanized—immigrants; quite naturally they stand on the margins of the American Way, and therefore have not yet come under the coverage of America's civil religion. It would not be difficult to specify names and places, but that is hardly necessary. These groups are very small, and are rapidly diminishing.

Second, there are what are sometimes called the "old-fashioned" churches, churches with a strong creedal or confessional tradition, which tend to look askance at some of the manifestations and expressions of America's civil religion. But this attitude, too, is rapidly eroding, and will not, I think, last very long. Finally, among the "hold-out" groups are the theologians and theologically inclined laymen, a rather small group in this country, but the group from which the various attempts to identify, examine, and criticize America's civil religion have mostly come. All in all, however, these "hold-out groups" comprise a very small proportion of the American people. By and large, the great mass of Americans are not aware of any tension, or friction, or conflict between America's civil religion and their professed faiths, whatever they may be.

I come now to the last, and perhaps most difficult, question that I have set myself in examining this problem of civil religion. And that question is double: how are we to evaluate America's civil religion culturally, on the one hand, and theologically, on the other? Some of my friendly critics, such as Sidney Mead and Andrew Greeley, gently upbraid me for treating America's civil religion too harshly. I plead Not guilty, and I will try to make my case. First, I, of course, regard America's civil religion as a genuine religion; and so was the Athenian civil religion and the Roman—in fact, all the various civil religions of the ancient world. The fact that they were, and America's civil religion is, congruent with the culture is no argument against it; all religions, even the most sectarian, are embedded in, and display some congruence with, some concretion of culture, simply because all religions, in their human dimension (and they all possess a human dimension) must necessarily reflect some aspects of human society and social life. Furthermore, America's civil religion, as it has emerged during the past two centuries, strikes me as a noble religion, celebrating some very noble civic virtues. But so was the Roman civil religion in its best period, and so was Confucianism turned into religion in classical China. On its cultural side, I would regard the American Way of Life, which is the social face of America's civil religion, as probably the best way of life yet devised for a mass society— with the proviso that even the best way of life, if it is the way of life of a mass society, will have its grave defects. And, if Abraham Lincoln, for instance, is to be taken as an exemplar of our civil religion, then we can see what a powerful strain of genuine Christian spirituality, in this case Calvinist, has entered into it. So I certainly would not want to disparage America's civil religion in its character as religion.

But, if it is an authentic religion as civil religion, America's civil religion is not, and cannot be seen as, authentic Christianity or Judaism, or even as a special cultural version of either or both. Because they serve a jealous God, these biblical faiths cannot allow any claim to ultimacy and absoluteness on the part of any thing or any idea or any system short of God, even when what claims to be the ultimate locus of ideas, ideals, values, and allegiance is the very finest of human institutions; it is still human, man's own construction, and not God himself. To see America's civil religion as somehow standing above or beyond the biblical religions of Judaism and Christianity, and Islam too, as somehow including them and finding a place for them in its overarching unity, is idolatry, however innocently held and whatever may be the subjective intentions of the believers. But this is theology, which I have discussed elsewhere, and which I have tried to avoid here. In this essay it has been my intention to set down my thinking, and some of the conclusions I have reached, on the nature, sources, purposes, structure, and functioning of America's civil religion, and to call attention to some of the questions that need urgent attention for a clarification of the overall problem. To some degree, I hope, I have contributed to this end, so important for a real understanding of our culture, society, and religion.

Awakening from the Dream

DOLORES HAYDEN

© *Peter Vandermark/Stock, Boston*

Tract houses in Florida

THE TWO ARTICLES ON HOUSING in Volume I of this anthology interpreted houses as markers of success and as reflections of family structure. In this volume, the previous article on housing looked at the houses of Frank Lloyd Wright as a response to changes in the relationship between individual families and the community. The next selection shifts focus slightly. Instead of considering why houses took a particular form, Dolores Hayden looks at some of the results of that form.

Hayden begins by pointing out that American houses have generally been designed to satisfy a set of circumstances that no longer exist. For example, the houses reflect the assumption that almost all American families are young, white, and nuclear, consisting of an adult male who works outside the home, an adult female who works only inside the home, and their unmarried children. This is no longer the dominant pattern. A large proportion of American households is made up of two wage-earners; many others are single-parent families; still others—the fastest-growing segment—are single-person units. Hayden maintains that this fact has not been recognized by the housing industry, and that many have been forced to live in housing inappropriate to their lives. The problem has been particularly severe for women working outside the house. They have been burdened by housing that requires them to fill two jobs—one inside the home—in order to keep it well maintained—and one outside the home—in order to pay for it.

These houses have also been ecologically wasteful. Standardized floor plans have ignored climatic considerations, requiring excess heating and air conditioning. Individual appliances have been required in each dwelling, adding to the glut of non-recyclable waste. Individual lots have increased the size of our cities, forcing working-people to drive great distances, in turn necessitating the importation of petroleum and the construction of nuclear power plants, thereby creating additional ecological and international dangers.

Even though our houses are inappropriate for many people, Hayden notes that almost all Americans have been socialized into desiring a single-family detached house. One result of this dream has been alienation and frustration for the third of American families not able to afford it. In addition to economic frustration, during the post-World War II period many Americans were excluded from home-ownership by race, class or gender. During the 1960s and 1970s, equal opportunity laws helped many Americans purchase a home, but the increasing number of people able to buy houses drove up the price to levels affordable by an even smaller number. The problems of housing highlight the shortcomings of the American dream. For many Americans, not owning a house is a sign of personal failure.

THE PERSONAL HAPPINESS and economic potential of many Americans have been thwarted by the design of housing and public space, yet few of us employ the language of real estate development, architecture, or urban planning to trace the contours of loneliness, boredom, weariness, discrimination, or financial worry in our lives. It is much more common to complain about time or money than to fume about housing and urban space. In part this is because we think of our miseries as being caused by personal problems rather than social problems. Americans often say, "There aren't enough hours in the day," rather than "I'm frantic because the distance between my home and my work place is too great." Americans also say, "I can't afford the down payment to live in Newton," or in Marin County, or in Beverly Hills, rather than "I'm furious because only the affluent can live in a safe and pleasant neighborhood." Together, space, time, and money intersect to establish the physical settings where all the events of life will be staged. Whether they are harmonious or discordant, residential neighborhoods reverberate with meaning, and disappointments about them affect women and men of varied ages, income levels, ethnic groups, and racial groups.

The house is an image of the body, of the household, and of the household's relation to society; it is a physical space designed to mediate between nature and culture, between the landscape and the larger urban built environment. In this sense the dwelling is the basis of both architectural design (as

AWAKENING FROM THE DREAM   By Dolores Hayden. Originally published under the title "The Future of Housing, Work, and Family Life." From *Redesigning the American Dream*, W. W. Norton & Company, Inc. Copyright © 1984 by Dolores Hayden.

archetypal shelter) and physical planning (as the replicable unit used to form neighborhoods, cities, and regions). Because the form of housing carries so many aesthetic, social, and economic messages, a serious misfit between a society and its housing stock can create profound unrest and disorientation. . . . Today the problems of a housing strategy based on suburban dream houses underscore the conflicts of class, gender, and race that characterize our society.

OUTGROWING OUR PRESCRIPTIVE ARCHITECTURE

The United States is a society of diverse cultures and diverse household types, yet for the last four decades most American space has been shaped around a simplistic prescription for satisfaction. American cities and American housing have been designed to satisfy a nation of predominantly white, young, nuclear families, with father as breadwinner, mother as housewife, and children reared to emulate these same limited roles. While prescriptive literature in the form of sermons, housekeeping guides, and etiquette manuals has always been available to describe and define the ideal middle-class Christian family in our society, our post–World War II cities mark the triumph of a prescriptive architecture of gender on a national scale.

Today only a small percentage of American families include a male breadwinner, a nonemployed housewife, and two or more children under eighteen. The valiant World War II heroes and their blushing brides have now retired. Their children have grown up. The predominant family type is the two-earner family. The fastest growing family type is the single-parent family, and nine out of ten single parents are women. Almost a quarter of all households consist of one person living alone, be they young singles or the elderly. Yet Americans have not acknowledged that the cities and the housing built for the war heroes are no longer appropriate today.

Space is the problem rather than time or money. And this problem is inextricably tied to an architecture of home and neighborhood that celebrates a mid-nineteenth century ideal of separate spheres for women and men. This was an artificial environment that the most fanatical Victorian moralists only dreamed about, a utopia of male-female segregation they never expected the twentieth century to build. While maxims about true womanhood and manly dominance were the staple of Christian, bourgeois Victorian culture in the United States, England, and many other countries, only in the United States in the twentieth century were so many material resources committed to reinforcing these ideals by spatial design.

The veteran, his young wife, and their prospective children appeared as the model family of 1945. Millions of them confronted a serious housing shortage. In the aftermath of war, employing the veretans and removing women from the paid labor force was a national priority. So was building more housing, but the two ideals were conflated. Developers argued that a particular kind of house would help the veteran change from an aggressive air ace to a commuting salesman who loved to mow the lawn. He would also assist his wife to forget her skills as Rosie the Riveter and begin to enjoy furnishing her dream house in suburbia. . . . The problem is that the spatial rules could have been written by Catharine Beecher in 1870; by 1920 they were anachronistic; by 1950, preposterous.

The outdated ideal of a particular kind of family life, however, had a function. Exaggerated, socially created male and female roles defined not only the labor market and housing design but also the parameters of urban planning. Postwar propaganda told women that their place was in the home, as nurturers; men were told that their place was in the public realm, as earners and decision makers. This ideal, gender-based division of labor described women's and men's economic, social, and political relationships to the private and public realms as distinctly different. Segregation of roles by gender was so pervasive and accept-able that it was used to justify housing schemes characterized by segregation by age, race, and class that couldn't be so easily advertised. In the richest nation in the world, economic deprivation, ethnic differences, age segregation, and racial segregation were hidden by a spatial prescription for married suburban bliss that emphasized gender as the most salient feature of every citizen's experience and aspirations.

CREATING THE CRITIQUE

One could define the essence of any utopian design as the desire to create a society where no one counts costs, and no one even understands the concept of costs or the human inability to make everything perfect for everyone. A cartoon in the New York *Times* in 1977, showing a dream house devouring a family, expressed a growing panic about our national housing strategy as a utopian design on which the long deferred costs had finally come due. Dream houses got out of control economically, environmentally, and socially because they carried unacknowledged costs: they required large amounts of energy con-sumption; they demanded a great deal of unpaid female labor; they were often unavailable to minorities; and eventually, they overwhelmed the institutions that had traditionally financed them. The *Times'* cartoonist forged two and a half decades of partial, tentative criticism from architects, planners, environ-mentalists, women, minorities, and economists into one powerful image of American life in decline.

The earliest critics of the dream house came from the professions of architec-ture and urban planning. They were angry because the basic building activity had bypassed both professions. Contractors received funding from federal housing agencies, bought farm land in a remote part of a metropolitan area—preferably a place without a planning board—and started "raising houses in-stead of potatoes" (as they said in Long Island). Many architects were appalled by the banal designs the builders threw up. William J. Levitt, for example, was considered one of the best developers of solidly constructed houses. He became a popular hero for the speed with which he built homes for veterans, but he simply built one design over and over in his first development. Praised for his skill in reorganizing the logistics of traditional home construction, he responded to aesthetic critiques by developing three or four "models" that could be alter-nated on every street, a practice still followed by many builders today. Levitt's peace offering was to sponsor interior design contests for Levittown residents and invite well-known designers and architects to be the judges of the interior schemes created by the residents, whether modern, Early American, or country French.

The predictable banality of it all was enforced by the federal agency respon-sible for funding: FHA design guidelines actually penalized any builder who hired a sophisticated architect by lowering the mortgagable values of houses that did not conform to their norms of design. Flat roofs were particularly suspect at the FHA. (Curiously, Nazi policy had also decreed that only peaked-roof houses suited the Aryan race.) But flat roofs had characterized many of the best multi-family housing designs in the twentieth century, including those of Irving Gill, Henry Wright, Clarence Stein, Rudolph Schindler, and other American and European architects who had worked on low cost housing but managed to make it harmonious and often elegant.

Architects gnashed their teeth, but their social and aesthetic critiques failed to address the basic gender division of labor. While they proposed the advantages of hiring skilled designers or of providing more community facilities and more shared spaces, they did not attack the Victorian programming at the heart of dream-house culture. Some American architects . . . had led the world in the development of innovative, nonsexist housing prototypes between 1870 and 1940, but the practitioners of the 1950s could only deal with suburbia by asking for a bigger share of the individual commissions. In truth, most architects loved to design large single-family houses, one at a time, and this predilection shaped the profession's acquiescence.

Urban planners, like architects, were early critics of the dreamhouse strategy, but their concerns, while tied to larger issues of private and public space, still lacked a thorough social foundation. Planners perceived that hasty, uncontrolled suburban developments for veterans' families would produce houses without adequate schools, parks, or other community facilities. They saw that suburban residents would then be taxed to pay for these improvements, while the speculative developers used their profits to build yet another subdivision. They predicted that new suburbs would drain the social and economic activities of the center city, and that urban blight and suburban sprawl would work together to wear away the best pedestrian districts of inner-city areas. Some of them recognized the racism of all-white tracts, and worried about the consequences of "white flight" from inner cities.

All of these events came to pass, and yet, while planners decried haste, shoddy building, and greed, while they deplored racial segregation and lack of public transportation, few spoke about the outworn gender stereotypes embodied in the basic definition of the household. Indeed, planners themselves relied on the Victorian template of patriarchal family life when they exhorted Americans to pay more attention to community facilities to strengthen that same idealized family. Even Lewis Mumford, the most trenchant of all urban critics, rhapsodized: ". . . who can doubt that Victorian domesticity, among the upper half of the middle classes, was encouraged by all the comforts and conveniences, the sense of internal space and peace, that brought the Victorian father back nightly to his snug household." He ardently supported providing "a young couple with a dwelling house and a garden" to continue this model, while adding that the city planner must also "invent public ways of performing economically what the old, three-generation bourgeois family once privately encompassed"—care for the elderly.

Planners also used the same outworn family model to study residential choices and to measure needs for new services. The "head of household" and his "journey to work" framed their locational concerns, instead of detailed analysis of the different needs and different experiences of men, women, and children. Even when caucuses of Marxist urban planners responded to the extreme urban fiscal crises of the late 1970s, they too based their statements about housing reform around an unexamined acceptance of the dream house and the gender division of labor underlying it. They proposed a socialist banking policy to keep traditional housing afloat.

In the late 1960s and early 1970s, the activists of two major social movements generated enough anger about the single-family detached houses to spur broader cultural critiques. Ecologists and feminists took up where the designers and planners left off: the former stressing the dire consequences of environmental decline, the latter emphasizing the crippling effects of stereotyped roles for women and men. Both movements stressed that consciousness must be followed by active protest. They organized the disaffected to rally against some of the excesses of the post–World War II American life style. Both stressed democracy and emphasized that personal life represented political choices; neither put architecture in the foreground, but they generated enough debate to illuminate basic conceptual shortcomings of both architecture and urban design.

ENVIRONMENTAL AWARENESS

Environmentalists and energy planners pointed out that American dream houses and their dispersed settlement pattern used more nonrenewable resources than any society had ever consumed before, because builders had assumed that energy would always be cheaper than materials or labor. Thus Americans, as about six percent of the world's population, account for about a third of the world's nonrenewable resource consumption every year. A white child born to a dream-house family in the United States will consume many times more resources than a Third World child over its lifetime.

These activists showed that the imbalance was partly the result of deliberate but uninformed choices in housing design. When builders of the 1950s constructed millions of dream houses lined up on suburban tracts, they broke with traditional regional responses to climate (typical of the adobes of the Southwest or the saltbox houses of New England) in favor of using standardized plans and materials. Huge picture windows created patterns of heat gain and heat loss that had to be compensated for by year round air-conditioning or intensive heating, depending on whether the standardized house was in Arizona or Massachusetts. Traditional siting also broke down. Builders' bulldozers leveled hills and trees that might have provided shade; the same house was built facing north, south, east, and west because the builders didn't care about the position of the sun so much as the profitability of the tract.

The dream houses, because of their isolation from community facilities and from each other, also required numerous private purchases of appliances such as stoves, clothes washers, and refrigerators. These appliances were often designed to increase rather than minimize the use of energy: in some cases the same manufacturers sold both consumer appliances and municipal generating equipment, as a reinforcement of corporate interests. In addition to the wasteful use of energy, some appliances and all plumbing fixtures intensified the use of water. Toilets, garbage disposals, clothes washers, and dishwashers created an enormous volume of water usage in arid regions as well as in more temperate climates, by continuing the American practice of using water as a medium of carrying waste away, rather than reserving water for needed human use and recycling garbage and human waste as compost.

As the suburbs grew, the infrastructure of municipal water, gas, and power lines and roads expanded, and expanded again. Once on the path to lower densities, many cities found it hard to justify public transit expenditures. The journey to work for Americans averaged nine miles one way in 1976, when Americans owned 41 percent of the world's passenger cars to connect home and paid work. Indeed, they had more cars per household than children. To get to distant houses, thousands of miles of roads and freeways were needed. But very few people wanted their dream house next to a busy freeway or shrouded in smog. To provide gas and electricity for these same houses, storage tanks and generating plants were needed, but no one wanted to be near them either.

Ultimately American corporations had to resort to some desperate strategies to assure continued energy consumption. Oil leases in foreign countries brought the accompanying threat of foreign wars. Nuclear power plants and liquid natural gas (LNG) terminals at home were even riskier strategies because of their long-term vulnerability to accidents and because of the lack of safe disposal procedures for nuclear waste materials. In the late 1970s, *The Ladies' Home Journal* carried a pro-nuclear advertisement showing housewives holding up a variety of home appliances and thanking the utility for creating nuclear power to keep their appliances going. The phrase "dream house" began to acquire ironic overtones. Even those families who would have accepted nearby gas or electrical installations refused to be near a nuclear plant or an LNG terminal.

The political movement launched by environmentalists had one great success by 1982. Steady, sustained political pressure on both utilities and government regulatory agencies had made it clear that nuclear power plants were financially unprofitable to design, build, and operate. This citizen resistance to poor energy planning marked a significant achievement for Americans concerned about the safety of their neighborhoods and the social responsibility of major corporations. Victories were won in the face of massive expenditures by utilities for political contributions and extensive lobbying efforts by utility executives speaking to many different audiences. The environmentalists' common sense dominated the debates; revelations about nukes built on earthquake faults and nukes built from upside-down blueprints did the rest.

When it came to renewable energy sources, the environmentalists produced only partial reforms. Conservation education often stressed saving more than sharing. Retrofitting of existing buildings might involve elaborate technical skills, but economic and social reprograming, essential to the better use of space, was often ignored. Thus ecologists Helga and William Olkowski criticized the ecological and economic parasitism of the suburban dwelling: "The typical home now largely wastes the solar income it daily receives and the mineral resources that pass through it. It takes from the forest for its structure, furnishings, reading materials, and fuel as well. The typical home also takes from the often fragile ecosystems of estuary, swamp, desert and prairie for its food and fiber. It also uses the waterways and mineral riches for its power and the products of the marketplace. The house shelters its occupants, but to the larger community it gives 'wastes.' These latter emerge unappreciated and consequently unsorted: the metals with the glass, organic, paper, and plastic all jumbled together; the toxic mixed with the benign. Because the home is such a total parasite, as are its neighboring urban habitats, it is not surprising that the occupants experience themselves as victims or, at best, ineffectual ciphers in a large, impersonal, centralized system." But the Olkowskis' powerful experiment, the Integral Urban House, a collective project established by six adults, did not stress rethinking family life so much as the introduction of urban agriculture and ecosystems analysis. Other designers of solar homes who received wide publicity had far less to offer; some designs were based on new environmental gadgets for the old dream house but retained the model family in 2,500 square feet of space.

In the same way, discussion of new solar technologies, such as photovoltaic cells, often stopped at a certain level of technological innovation. Big corporations (utilities and defense contractors) received most of the government research and development money to study the profitable future production of these technologies. Neighborhood applications and small-town applications were seldom given the same level of support. Here a mix of economic, social, and technical reforms could have resulted in more innovative programing. Using photovoltaic cells to cover the roof of every existing dream house would turn the United States into a nation of fifty-four million private power plants. Scale is still the most misunderstood environmental issue in the so-called appropriate technology movement. Between the giant corporations and the tiny houses, environmental alternatives require new social, economic, and architectural innovations as well as new, energy-saving inventions. While environmentalists are still developing a very effective accounting of the wasteful, destructive patterns of present resource use, they have not yet come to terms with the reconceptualization of the private home as the key to the next set of public issues they must address.

FEMINIST UNREST

The problems of domestic life documented by the women's movement also revolve around the hidden costs of building millions of homes on the Victorian model. The connections between home ownership, family structure, and women's status are complex. During the last three decades, while the majority of white male workers have achieved the dream houses in suburbia where their fantasies of proprietorship, authority, and consumption could be acted out, the majority of their spouses have entered the world of paid employment. Today, handicapped by the least suitable housing imaginable for employed wives and mothers, more than one out of two married women is in the paid labor force. (In 1890, the figure was one out of twenty.) Employed women often find themselves with two jobs: one at home, one at work. Pulled between unpaid work and paid work, women race from office or factory to home and back again. They know they have no time for themselves. They have to spend an inordinate amount of time simply struggling to get husbands or children to do a little more housework instead of leaving it all for Mom.

While this pattern creates logistical problems for the employed housewife, those who stay home also have serious difficulties. Michele Rosaldo, a cultural anthropologist, argued that women's status is lowest in societies where women are most separated from public life. And in the United States the suburban home is the single most important way of separating women, and thus lowering an individual woman's status. But as Bonnie Loyd, a geographer, points out, much of women's work in the household is status-producing work for the family, connected with the maintenance of the house. So by glorifying her home through executing household tasks, a woman can guarantee her family's social status at the expense of her own. As Loyd notes, such activity often creates psychological conflict. This conflict increases when women who try to create interiors as a focus for entertaining come up against levels of consumption which are in fact new to them because of upward mobility. Terrified housewives who know little about designer furniture or antiques, cabinet work or colors, may consult women's magazines, home and life-style magazines, decorators, and department stores. Loyd quotes one psychiatrist who remarked in the 1950s of his female patients: "There is no time at which a woman is more apt to go to pieces than when she is engaged in decorating her home."

Feminists of the 1960s, beginning with Betty Friedan, examined the relationships among women, advertisers, and mass-produced goods. They saw the home as a box to be filled with commodities. Rugs and carpets need vacuuming, curtains need laundering, upholstered goods need shampooing—all fill up the domestic spaces to form colonial, Mediterranean, French Provincial, or some other ersatz decor. Women also criticized kitchens full of single-purpose appliances requiring frequent attention. These machines are lined up in one room, the kitchen, which is often designed to be isolated from the rest of family life. As one appliance manufacturer put it in *Good Housekeeping* in 1965: "This kitchen has almost everything. Tappan built-in electric range and oven, Tappan dish-washer and Tappan disposal, Tappan refrigerator. Only one thing's really missing. *You.*"

One of the most effective explorations of housewives' frustrations was an exhibit created in 1971, "Womanhouse," which incorporated the combined talents of twenty-six artists to transform an abandoned Los Angeles mansion into a series of environments. At the top of the staircase a mannequin in a wedding dress posed, suggesting the young bride's fascination with the dream house. At the bottom of the stairs her muddy train and two disembodied feet vanished into the wall. In the linen closet, another mannequin was trapped among the sheets and towels. In the kitchen, everything was painted pink, that stereotypically feminine color: the sink, the refrigerator, the potato peeler, the pots and pans, the walls. Inside the kitchen drawers newspaper linings revealed stories about women in public life. The bathtub contained colored sand, in the shape of a woman's body. As visitors to the exhibit touched the sand, the figure receded. After two weeks the woman disappeared. There were also rooms dedicated to a woman's enjoyment of her dream house as a place for privacy, fantasy, and playfulness. One room had huge toys, and in another, a crocheted spider web suggested a woman's place to spin out ideas.

The exhibition included some performances, and in one favorite theater piece, the artist simply walked to an ironing board and ironed sheets for thirty minutes. While the women decided it was hilarious, men were perplexed. "Womanhouse" addressed the ways that Americans have mystified the necessary work done in the house by isolating the housewife who cooks, cleans, and irons in a dream house. The artists illuminated some of women's positive feelings and attachments to domestic spaces as nurturing, controllable places, while criticizing the loneliness and isolation which many housewives encounter. Most effectively, they turned domestic space into public space temporarily by the appropriation of a residential structure for the exhibit, and thousands of visitors toured the house.

In the same way that the artists of "Womanhouse" protested the single-family home as an enclosure for women's lives, so the poets Adrienne Rich and Bernice Johnson Reagon cried out for change. Rich's "A Primary Ground," of 1974, told of the suffocation of traditional family life:

> Sensuality dessicates in words—
> risks of the portage, risks of the glacier
> never taken
> Protection is the genius of your house
> the pressure of the steam iron
> flattens the linen cloth again
> chestnuts puréed with care are dutifully eaten
> in every room the furniture reflects you
> larger than life, or dwindling

Most of all, Rich underlined the waste of female talent in this old pattern of domesticity:

> your wife's twin sister, speechless
> is dying in the house
> You and your wife take turns
> carrying up the trays,
> understanding her case, trying to make her understand.

The image of "understanding her case" resonated through Rich's writings, as well as the demand for new forms of habitation.

In "The Fourth Month of the Landscape Architect," Rich fused images of pregnancy and a demand for the creation of a new kind of social space, as a female designer reviews the historical experience of women in her spatial imagination:

> I start to imagine
> plans for a house, a park
> . . .
> A city waits at the back of my skull
> eating its heart out to be born:
> how design the first
> city of the moon? how shall I see it
> for all of us who are done
> with enclosed spaces, purdah, the salon, the sweatshop loft,
> the ingenuity of the cloister?

To read Rich's poems was to be exhorted to transcend the architecture of gender that diminished so many lives, yet it was only an exhortation and not a plan.

Writer, composer, and scholar, Bernice Johnson Reagon, in "My Black Mothers and Sisters," told feminists what the leaders of that struggle would need to be like:

> She could make space where there was none
> And she could organize the space she had
> My mama
> My grandmama
> Ms. Daniels
> dreamers who believed in being materialists—
> . . .
> We must apply energy to the development of our potential
> as parents
> as creative producers
> as the new way-makers.
> There must not be a woman's place for us
> We must be everywhere our people are
> or might be . . .

To seize and hold more space, to redesign space, to deliver the goods of survival was an adequate definition of the task in its material and cultural dimensions, but still an exhortation.

While these women developed a critique of the suburban house and created a new consciousness that inspired some housewives to leave the seclusion of their homes, the critique did not go far enough. Gender was the culprit; material culture was satirized and criticized, but the architecture of gender was not reworked. The material feminists' idea that the gender division of labor was reinforced by spatial design was a lost intellectual tradition for most feminist activists of the 1970s, just as it was for architects and planners.

Indeed, feminists often agitated for something very like the single-family house even as they proposed to put it under women's control. Articles and manifestos on the housing needs of single-parent mothers stressed their desire not to be stigmatized by special housing "projects," their quite natural desire for their children to feel that their homes were "just like everyone else's." Emergency shelters for battered women and their children—which involved integrated housing, child care, and social service arrangements—were usually seen as temporary solutions to women's housing needs, and the stated goal of such groups was to return the woman and her children to "normal" housing as soon as possible. Not surprisingly, this "normal" housing created great stress when women left the community of the shelter to return to the dream-house world. In the 1970s, campaigns on behalf of employed women that stressed gaining economic justice through increased access to home ownership also accepted the dream-house design. At HUD, Donna Shalala's "Women and Mortgage Credit" program promoted female ownership with the slogan, "If a woman's place is in the home, it might as well be her own." While this pragmatic program met with quick success, HUD's sponsorship of in-depth research by architects and urban planners revealed that long-term problems about the nature of housing design would demand far more complex policy initiatives. Neither a single-family house filled with solar gadgets nor home ownership for single mothers addresses the largest political and spatial issues inherent in the dream-house culture. The need to unite architects, planners, environmentalists, and feminists is urgent. As material conditions change, the shock reverberates. The economic problems of this housing form are finally provoking the intensive public policy review that no previous protest movement was ever able to generate.

RACE, GENDER, AND THE ECONOMIC CRISIS

When Americans discuss the good life, they still speak about their hopes or their fears in terms of buying houses. Home ownership has not only symbolized a family's social status, but also guaranteed its economic security. The home-owner has been an owner-speculator, an identity acknowledged by one Florida developer who advertises his homes with the slogan, "To her, it's a nest; to him, a nest egg." The "nest egg" explains why Americans struggle to "climb the ladder of life from renter to owner." After years of mortgage payments to the bank (and substantial income tax deductions), some older homeowners have needed a speculative profit from the sale of the house to provide adequate retirement income. "For years your house has made you happy. Now it's going to make you rich," claims Jon Douglas, a California real estate agent seeking couples to list their homes for sale with him.

Because home ownership has been closely associated with an individual's tax position and retirement income, it has created a sense of progress through life for the two-thirds of American families who have managed to attain it. The process of entering the market has been a rite of passage for thirty-year-olds equipped with the savings, marriage, and children that make this choice seem logical. Ownership and intense participation in the culture of home have characterized the middle years of life. For the retirees who sell their houses, detachment from gender roles has come with age and the speculative bonus of leaving suburbia.

Of course, one-third of American families have never had a chance to participate in these rituals. The roots of this problem lie in the five groups of Americans that were excluded from home ownership in the late 1940s. First, white women of all classes were expected to gain access to housing through their husbands. Second, the white elderly working class and lower middle class, who were no longer wage earners in the prime of life, were left behind in the old inner–city neighborhoods. Third, minority men of all classes were excluded from suburban home ownership when suburban tracts specifically excluded minority families; the FHA actually had agents whose job it was to keep minorities out, and they pressured any builder or lender who didn't agree. Minority men were expected to become tenants in old slums in the central cities or owners in other segregated neighborhoods vacated by the "white flight" to the suburbs. The majority of housing units in these segregated areas were difficult to finance since banks usually refused to give home mortgages in "redlined" ghetto areas. Fourth, minority women of all classes were not to be homeowners. So minority women often became the domestic servants in other women's suburban houses to earn the money to keep their own families together. Fifth, the minority elderly of all classes were left in the central cities. Close to their offspring, they often remained in three-generation households, sometimes caring for their grandchildren while their daughters worked outside the home.

Home ownership did develop among approximately 40 percent of minority male workers and their families in the late 1960s and 1970s, encouraged by the Fair Housing Act of 1968. The Act outlawed segregation and made blockbusting less possible. Redlining of ghetto areas continued, however, and kept many minority families from buying. Eventually the Equal Credit Opportunity Act of 1973 also made home ownership possible for a small number of women by forbidding discrimination by mortgage lenders on the basis of sex. This meant that mortgage bankers could not apply the so-called rule of thumb (perhaps better described as the rule of uterus) to discount the income of any women of child-bearing age by at least 50 percent when determining mortgage eligibility. Still, very few employed women of any age had the income to qualify as sole owners, so this law helped two earner couples more than female heads of households. In this latter group, a home ownership rate of about 40 percent is similar to the minority rate.

As these groups moved into potential home ownership in the 1970s, they encountered increasingly inflated prices. Between 1970 and 1982, average housing prices across the nation jumped from $28,700 to $87,600. The inflation was exacerbated as thirty million baby-boom children of the post–World War II era came of homebuying age in the 1970s; an equivalent or greater number will reach their thirties in the 1980s. As the price of houses turned into a steadily rising line on real estate agents' graphs, millions of these young Americans, most of them the product of the veterans' suburban tracts, found that they couldn't afford to buy homes. They heard economists predict that they would be tenants most of their lives unless they could inherit their parents' houses. They added their frustrations to those of people long excluded from home ownership, including minorities and women for whom the economic obstacles remained although the legal and institutional barriers to home ownership were decreasing. A frantic scramble ensued as all three groups struggled to get into the housing market with "starter" homes.

As a result of the scramble, a rising percentage of household income was spent on housing. Americans' indebtedness for residential mortgages mushroomed from $661 billion in 1976 to $1,172 billion in 1982. Finally the housing market was declared problematic by all but the most optimistic builders. Some introduced tiny "studio houses" and 300-sq.-ft. condominiums at exorbitant prices, and then attempted to distract attention from the size of these units with minimal furniture. Others introduced "mingles" designs or "double master bedroom" plans to help new kinds of households squeeze themselves into outmoded land use and financing patterns, essentially proposing that two households could share one dream house or one condo, since each one could only afford half the asking price. Makers of mobile homes saw their chance. Changing the name of their product to "manufactured housing," they argued that they, and only they, could make houses cheaply enough to "save the American dream."

Bankers tried to patch up the economic crisis in the housing market with new balloon mortgage plans which deferred some interest payments for certain highly educated young professionals (charging them large sums at age thirty-five rather than at age thirty), with variable rate mortgages, and "growing equity" mortgages. These "creative financing" devices didn't do much for the mass market; they helped affluent people become overextended. Bankers also demanded new government subsidies for home buyers, and federal bailouts for failing savings and loan institutions. Real estate agents who were suffering too (from lack of commissions) began to take full-page advertisements in metropolitan papers, criticizing defense appropriations and deficit spending as harmful to the economy. One advertisement showed a little house with a peaked roof sagging under the weight of a sack of dollars for the Pentagon.

By 1983, two things were clear: certain groups were unable to enter the housing market, and many Americans who had already bought houses discovered that they couldn't afford to move. Others found that they couldn't even afford to stay where they were. Unemployment was high, and some people, caught with mortgage payments they couldn't meet, lost their homes to foreclosures. Neither the anxious owners nor the foreclosing banks could sell out because of the sluggish market. Some pessimistic economists began predicting a housing crash similar to the stock market crash of 1929, which started the Great Depression. They predicted that as high rates caused demand to fall, the building construction industry would slump and even fail. At the same time, rising unemployment in all sectors of the economy would contribute to increasing mortgage defaults, weakening the banking system (housing represents half of all its transactions) and further undermining the real estate market and the construction industry. Just as these economic interdependencies had promoted paper profits and growth, so they could contribute to a downward spiral of decline and even collapse.

Although the crisis did not become a crash, now is the moment of opportunity. The inadequacies of dream-house architecture can no longer be ignored. To renew democratic, self-sufficient traditions and survive as an urbanized, modern society, Americans must search for an adequate way to organize and pay for the spaces we live in, a way more compatible with the human life cycle. As a rich nation, we need to examine these issues in world perspective, if we care at all about world peace or about our international influence as a democracy. As a nation that has pioneered self-awareness and personal growth, we must also examine these housing issues from the perspective of our most intimate psychological and sexual desires as women and men. It is not enough to face the loss of the dream house with nostalgia about the end of an era, or with despair that America's resources stretched just so far and no farther. We need to reconstruct the social, economic, and spatial bases of our beliefs about individual happiness, solid family life, and decent neighborhoods.

COMMUNICATION

Window

to the

World

MARTIN ESSLIN

© Ellis Herwig/The Picture Cube

Television camera in Boston's Fenway Park

AMERICANS HAVE ACCESS to worlds beyond their immediate environment through a variety of media, including books, newspapers, and the telephone. The most profound medium of communication today is television. It brings people close to war and human tragedy, as well as bringing them close to sports events and national celebrations.

In the following selection, Martin Esslin describes how everyday life is influenced by the constraints of the television medium. Modern technology permits live transmission of events—TV takes viewers directly to the scene of the action, making them feel like they are really there. By way of contrast, printed accounts of dramatic events create a distance, permitting readers to see beyond the immediate situation and to look at events from a broader perspective. TV can and has exploited the emotional impact of its images, but it can also convey the tedium that is a part of great events. Since it has difficulty conveying complex, abstract information, it tends to rely on the strength of its visual nature. And, just as James Gordon Bennett sensationalized news to create an audience for the penny press in the nineteenth century, so modern television news uses the dramatic dimension of the medium to entertain viewers and win ratings points. Local news programs feature snippets of crime and violence, narrated by anchors who soothe and reassure their audience. The weather is not announced; it is packaged by an entertainer, the weather person. National news is also packaged in short sequences, narrated by known personalities, and illustrated by the most dramatic footage available.

The ability of TV to influence our way of thinking is best exemplified in sports coverage. The use of close-ups, instant replays, slow motion, and interviews helps to bring viewers closer to the event than are those watching the game in the stadium. In addition, sports coverage encourages a blurring of reality by turning athletes into fantasy figures who perform superhuman feats. Once athletes have become famous, they take the place in our television lives of trusted advisors whose commercial endorsements promise us that we too can be great if we buy their products.

Just as the telephone had to find its niche in a modern system of communications, television is now making its place. And, while it offers much that print and radio cannot, its limitations highlight the strengths of other media, indicating that it will be only one of many means of communication.

A FRENCH AVANT-GARDE PLAY of the late sixties depicted a family, fascinated and thrilled by a war going on in the street below their flat, feeling immensely privileged that their windows gave them a far better view of the skirmishes, ambushes, and executions than did those of their neighbors, who had to crane their necks to get a glimpse of the action. When, however, the war finally invaded their own apartment and confronted them with death and disaster on their hitherto inviolate territory, the members of this family were not only shocked and aggrieved but also indignant that events that had been no more than a thrilling entertainment for them should actually turn out to *involve* them as well. The play, *Tomorrow, from Any Window* by Jean-Claude Grumberg, demonstrated an important aspect of the television age and its consciousness, for the television set is just such a window upon "life": wars, revolutions, floods, earthquakes, an endless series of upheavals and calamities.

Long before the advent of television violent and traumatic events provided material for thrilling stories eagerly absorbed as a welcome diversion by people unaffected by the events themselves. In Goethe's *Faust* two fat and complacent burghers taking an Easter promenade discourse on the pleasure of being able to hear that "far down in Turkey whole nations crash into each other" while they themselves remain snug and comfortable, knowing that they are immune from such shocks. Reality in all its harshness and horror has always been turned into narratives in which fact becomes a kind of fiction, tales of faraway events and places, in short, "history."

Nevertheless television has brought about a radical change in the manner and mode of this process: written accounts, illustrated with drawings or still photographs, put events into perspective and give the recipient of the

---

information a chance to see them as a whole and in the light of reflection; the TV picture, by contrast, takes the viewer directly to the scene of the action and shows it to him as it occurs, in all its closeness and immediacy, so that he feels actually present on the battlefield, at the scene of the demonstration, at the launching of the space rocket. The written account usually combines description with reflection and quiet assessment and is meant to be read in detached solitude; the television image is *drama*, an event experienced by an eyewitness who is emotionally involved and much too close to be able to see the event whole or in a larger context that would enable him to evaluate its true significance.

Moreover television, like all drama, concentrates and intensifies its action by highlighting scenes with the greatest visual and emotional impact, including scenes of violence, while neglecting material that develops slowly or lacks visual drama. In a political demonstration that might have lasted several hours, for example, the thirty seconds during which the policemen's batons were raining down on a group of protesters might be the only episode televised of the entire incident. What is more, that brief segment will be edited in a manner that will give the episode a structure of mounting tension to make it even more dramatic.

There can be no doubt that in a society where most people take most of their information about current events from the TV screen, the public perception of what is going on in the world will be substantially different from that in a society where most information is absorbed through the written word and static illustrations. There is, above all, a shift of emphasis from the large perspective to the isolated incident; a loss of abstract insight as against a greater immediacy in the perception of details selected as often as not by criteria independent of their significance within the whole picture.

Statistics, for example, are notoriously undramatic. Large numbers, whether spoken by an announcer or illustrated in the form of diagrams or moving graphics, remain abstract and lacking in emotional impact. A television picture of a single starving child, on the other hand, will inevitably have a great emotional effect, regardless of whether that child is one of a hundred famine victims, or one of a thousand or tens of thousands. The availability or accessibility of such pictures may seriously distort the TV public's—and the world's—awareness of the overall situation. An area that happens to make the news—because a camera team chanced to be in the vicinity or because the location lay en route to another assignment—may leap into the center of world attention, while other famine areas with greater needs and suffering are ignored. In recent years, for example, considerable attention was focused on the famine in Kampuchea (because it was big news in the aftermath of the Vietnam War and within easy access of Thailand) while severe famines in the drought areas of Central Africa received little or no TV coverage for a long while.

The lack of flexibility, moreover, in the duration of news programs, imposed by the rigidities of TV scheduling, necessitates a high degree of selectivity in the editorial decisions of the news producers. This, in turn, results in highly arbitrary choices even among those items that promise the most visual excitement and drama, while those stories that may be more important in terms of their long-term significance but have little visual, dramatic impact may receive cursory attention. And perhaps—from the television professional's point of view—rightly so. Not only is it very difficult to make abstract issues vivid and exciting on television, but it simply may not be possible for the medium to communicate them very well at all. For example, during the period preceding the 1975 referendum on Britain's decision to join the European Economic Community (EEC), British television made a determined effort to explain to its viewers the complex regulations and operating methods of the EEC and their likely impact upon life in Britain and the country's future economic development. Because the forces for and against the Common Market were allotted equal time to put forth their cases, there was a surfeit of material in all possible forms—discussions, lectures with diagrams, documentary films on industrial and agricultural questions, etc. At the end of this voluminous and protracted campaign there was a general consensus among expert observers that the whole undertaking had produced only a minimal increase in the public's understanding of the issues involved and that the result of the referendum (which was won overwhelmingly by the promarket faction) was largely attributable to the voters' inclination to follow the government line. All the hours of patient indoctrination, explanation, and elucidation seemed to have hardly dented the general ignorance. Whether the programs concerned had simply failed to dramatize the issues sufficiently or whether people had switched off broadcasts that promised to be dry and abstract is difficult to tell. What the episode highlights is the difficulty the medium encounters when it attempts to transmit complex, abstract information. While it is no doubt possible that better ways of structuring such TV programs can and will be found, the basic problem derives from the attitude of viewers to the medium they regard basically as a purveyor of entertainment.

And here we have come to the heart of the matter: in essence a dramatic medium, television from the beginning has been compelled by the special requirements of its nature—its own inner logic—to put its emphasis on material with a dramatic, emotional, personalized content. TV therefore is perceived by its audience primarily as a medium of *entertainment*, and all programming— including the news, documentaries, and political broadcasts—is ultimately judged for its *entertainment value*. The effect is that material about events in the real world has to compete, as entertainment, with the openly fictional material radiated incessantly which constitutes the collective daydreams of the masses. Embedded in a never-ending stream of such material, these fragments of reality, glimpsed through the framed stage of the TV set, merge into the world of fantasy with which TV is preoccupied. The distinctions between daydream and reality are again blurred and distorted.

What are the main psychological benefits the viewer of dramatic entertainment craves? First is excitement in the form of suspense that makes him forget the passing of time; the thrills that come from empathy with characters facing danger and imminent disaster; the relief when the good defeat the forces of evil. Equally important and powerful are the cathartic effects of the "beautiful" emotions, such as patriotic pride, religious uplift, tearful joy at the union of a happy, loving couple, and even the gentle sadness of partings and bereavements. And third there is the craving for amusement, laughter, lights, glamour. These, inevitably, are the criteria by which the offerings of an entertainment medium will be judged. And if those elements in the programming that are meant to achieve quite a different end, namely to convey information about the real world, are perceived as just another ingredient in that vast entertainment package they also will, inevitably, tend to be judged by the same criteria: a good news broadcast will be the one that contains the maximum of excitement, high emotion, and amusement.

In the sphere of excitement, however, there operates a law of diminishing returns: the more accustomed viewers become to violence, the more violent the violence has to become to make an impact. This holds true for the news as well as for prime-time dramatic series. Violence produces "good" television. And because the editors of news programs are constantly in pursuit of stories that have a strong visual and dramatic element, violence is assured of a central place in any news show. To me it seems overwhelmingly clear that the increase in terrorism, bombings, assassinations, kidnappings, and the taking of hostages is closely and organically connected with the nature of television and its rise to its present position as the principal information medium in the world. We have grown accustomed to modern-day outlaws demanding TV time.

But that is by no means the most important aspect of the matter. The *drama*, the intensity of the suspense, and the ongoing news potential of the unfolding events that actions such as embassy takeovers and hostage-taking provide give the perpetrators of these actions an almost ideal field for publicizing themselves, especially when the moment for the final assault or hostage exchange arrives and everything is in place and can be fully and minutely shown on the TV screen. Calculate, for instance, the prime air time an action like the taking of the American hostages in Tehran gave the Iranian terrorists and translate it into the sums that commercials of similar duration would have cost: such a terrorist act is worth literally tens of millions of dollars of free publicity. It is no wonder that the incidence of such terrorism has multiplied throughout the world.

In the end the terrorists might be said to be actually working for television by providing the thrills and the violence that enable the news shows to compete with fictional thrillers and an endless stream of often sadomasochistic drama. The men and women who run television news programs are honorable citizens and compassionate human beings (I count some of them among my friends), but when a disaster occurs somewhere in the world a gleam of excitement and exhilaration comes into their eyes as the report flashes over the telex. The nature of the medium makes this inevitable. A day without a disastrous event is a dull day and will produce a dull broadcast, and a dull broadcast will to them equal personal, professional failure.

There can be no doubt that those who are unscrupulous enough to resort to violence as a means of getting publicity exploit this state of affairs. The tactics of street demonstrators and protesters are dominated by such considerations: route a Nazi or Ku Klux Klan procession through a predominantly Jewish or black neighborhood and you are certain to arouse well-founded expectations of violence that bring out television cameras in force. A phone call to a television news editor promising fisticuffs and fireworks may well secure air time worth many thousands of dollars in free publicity.

Here, then, the nature of television as an entertainment medium, a purveyor of daydreams that transmutes reality into a kind of fictional drama, actually dictates the development of events in the real world. To a certain extent analogous considerations have always played a part: kings and knights of old may have set out on spectacular exploits in the hope of becoming immortalized in an epic poem or a ballad. But in our world today the deliberate creation of sensational events has become a *major* factor in the shaping of developments in the real world, a factor not to be ignored, although very difficult to deal with.

It has been argued that television and other news media should simply ignore the actions of terrorists and not report them at all. This is the practice in the totalitarian countries of the Soviet bloc, where anything that might publicize such tactics is severely restricted if not entirely suppressed and where even plane crashes are not reported, though for different reasons (such information would diminish the official picture of state efficiency and technological superiority). But in the West, coverage of events that have actually taken place cannot be suppressed. Somebody will inevitably report them. In a field like TV where there is competition for the best, the most exciting, and the most entertaining, it would clearly be unthinkable to ignore such dramatic events or to relegate them to a low place on the totem pole.

The viewer who from his grandstand seat at the TV window sees wars, acts of terrorism, murders, and executions—reality turned into thrilling entertainment—is kept in a schizophrenic state of mind the reverse of that produced by soap operas and series, which are fictions perceived not only as fictions but also, at the same time, as realities that are more real than events in the real world. For although the viewer is aware of the reality of the news and documentary material, he nevertheless is also instinctively judging it as though it were fiction. The process may not be a conscious one, but it goes on nevertheless and is observable in the degree of attention (or inattention) given a news broadcast and in the tendency to switch channels if the events being reported are perceived as uninteresting.

It might be asked, for example, to what extent the decreasing interest in U.S. domestic politics is attributable to the influence of television. Can it be that the political material on television suffers by comparison with the more interesting and involving fictional fare that occupies so much air time? Or might it be that the politicians, however much they may now be selected (as they undoubtedly are) on grounds of their attractiveness and drawing power on television, rarely match the glamour and erotic appeal of actors whose whole training and outlook is directed toward producing the maximum of personal magnetism, and who, moreover, are seen in interesting and exciting situations? Or, indeed, might the whole political process—perceived as a show to be passively ingested from the television screen—seem utterly remote and, behind that impenetrable windows, beyond the influence of individual participation or involvement? These questions may never be finally and unequivocably answered but they must be asked; they must be considered and weighed.

If politicians, by and large, seem remote and uninteresting on the screen, it is all the more remarkable and significant that the network anchormen and anchorwomen of television *do* succeed in holding the attention of viewers and commanding their loyalties and confidence. This is, as I have noted previously, a function of their ability to act, to project a personality that may well be an invention different from the broadcaster's private self. But here also it is their familiarity, the frequency and regularity with which they appear, that creates their impact. While the pictures of the real world they present take on the qualities of fiction, their own television personalities become more and more real. They are talked about, adored, quoted, and trusted. The immense salaries these individuals command in a hardheaded commercial world attest to the real power of the illusion they have succeeded in creating.

If the national news in the United States is concerned mainly with national and world stories and the drama and violence of international relations, the local news—such a staple of the television scene in the U.S., where television service is far more decentralized than in most other Western nations—deals mainly with crime and violence on the local level, in much the same fashion, with the more dramatic and sensational stories occupying the foreground. The local news programs, because they are concerned with a smaller geographic area and relatively more mundane material, have become increasingly preoccupied with entertaining their audiences with amusing and titillating features. On an uneventful day with little important news, items have to be invented or created. The local anchormen and anchorwomen take the opportunity to groom their well-loved personalities and cultivate their audience allegiance. They will, especially on slow news days, give practical advice, interact with local characters, highlight amusing features of their area. Even the meteorologist is often turned into a personality: a comedian or clown, or, if female, a sex bomb. These attempts are not always successful, which suggests that the number of people with the actor's ability to project an interesting and intriguing personality is limited or that management has misperceived what the viewing audience finds appealing.

News programs by their very nature tend to be "bitty." As they have to cover the widest possible range of the day's events, they can never treat a subject in much depth. There is thus an immense potential in the medium for longer, in–depth documentaries that might provide the public with the background to the complex issues that lie behind the individual news event, say, the Russian invasion of Afghanistan. How many viewers, for example, have any idea of the long and complex background of the struggle throughout the nineteenth century between the Russians and the British to establish control over that vital area between the Russian Empire and India, the British expeditions into the country that were defeated by the Afghans, the endless fighting in the area around the Khyber Pass? Similarly, there are numerous domestic issues that deserve treatment at length and in depth. In a commercial system like that in the U.S. such programs have become relatively rare: they are extremely costly to produce and do not promise high ratings. Most of the documentaries of this kind are seen on the Public Broadcasting Service and tend to be imported from Britain, Canada, and other countries with publicly financed TV services.

Many of these—and some of the rare "specials" that are produced in the U.S.—succeed in providing insights and deepening understanding. But even in this area of programming the temptation to overdramatize and trivialize is clearly present. Take the example of a recent British documentary about the criteria used to establish when a person can be declared legally dead and how this may affect potential donors of transplant organs. The program's contention that there is a danger that accident victims who are still alive might be wrongly pronounced dead—developed in a sensational manner—led to a dangerous drop in the number of potential donors. The British Medical Association claimed that the subject had been seriously misrepresented in a desire to produce an exciting program. When the BBC offered the BMA the right to reply, the medical organization refused on the grounds that the time made available was too short to deal with so extraordinarily complex a matter.

Whatever the rights and wrongs in this specific case, it illustrates the dangers of this kind of investigative TV journalism. Television documentaries, even those of the extended, in-depth variety, face rigid time pressures owing to the nature of the programming process. An investigative book can reach its organic length, as can a documentary film for cinema showing, whereas their television counterpart, with only rare exceptions, cannot: it must be planned to conform to its preordained, fixed time slot. Moreover, there is also the limitation of the medium itself, its resistance to abstraction and its pull toward personalization. Even so serious and public-spirited a series as the BBC's "Civilisation" could be criticized on the grounds that there was a danger that the subject matter would be eclipsed by the star quality of the personality of its presenter, Sir Kenneth Clark.

The recent TV magazine programs that local and network news departments have developed exhibit the same characteristics to an even greater degree. Designed to be dipped into rather than watched with concentration, they often trivialize their material—insofar as it was not trivial from the outset—and present little more than a glimpse of the personalities shown or a faint taste of the issues or activities with which they are involved.

The same happens with discussion and interview programs, although here more time can be devoted to issues. In the more ambitious discussion programs where a politician or public figure is questioned by journalists, the guest can give some account of his or her ideas and policies. Yet what the audience takes away even from this kind of show is more likely to be an impression of the guest's personality, his fluency, his ability to evade embarrassing issues, his deftness of reaction—in other words, a portrait of his character—rather than a coherent understanding of the issues discussed. The lighter, more trivial interview programs, the talk shows, devoted largely to entertainment, publicizing forthcoming stage or TV appearances or movies or books of well-known show-business personalities, exhibit these characteristics in a more blatant form.

These talk shows and the game shows they sometimes resemble can be assigned to the category of improvised popular drama in which, throughout history, stereotyped characters have played for laughs within a more or less predictable structural framework, be it that of the commedia dell'arte, *Hanns Wurst* play, vaudeville, or circus clowns' interludes between acts. In the game shows this is combined with the built-in drama of a competition for sumptuous prizes and the raw emotions among the contestants provoked by winning and losing.

Though game shows are usually laughed off by their sponsors as being "good clean fun," they seem to me a deplorable manifestation of our culture. Not only are many of them clearly sadomasochistic in that they encourage enjoyment derived from the humiliation and embarrassment of the participants (and in some cases from the embarrassing exposure of intimate details of their participants' lives, as in those involving newlywed couples), but the underlying assumptions of many of the game concepts have disquieting implications. They stress the value of relatively unimportant tidbits of information. And the condescending manner of some of the "hosts" underscores the disquieting features of these programs and makes me think of them as a modern equivalent of the gladiatorial contests of ancient Rome.

The area where the real and the dramatic merge most successfully is in the realm of sports. All spectator sports involving competition contain a built-in element of drama—all sports competitions are after all stylized wars, fictionalized struggles—and are structured in a manner calculated to produce the maximum amount of suspense and excitement. As they are invariably concerned with physical activity, sports also emphasize TV's basically erotic orientation, whether in the direction of sadomasochistic eroticism, as in the more violent forms of sports like boxing and wrestling, or simply by displaying beautiful bodies in graceful action. Witness the increase in the popularity of gymnastics after it had been introduced to television audiences within the framework of the 1972 Olympic games: the spectacular gymnasts like Olga Korbut became instant heroes and heroines among people who previously would have regarded gymnastics as an unexciting sport, if they had thought about it at all. Television similarly brought figure skating, ice dancing, and a number of other sports into sudden prominence.

Although the people, the contest, and the prizes in sports are real, the structure of the competition is severely formalized and basically dramatic—both on the playing field and, even more so, on the TV screen. Television, through close–ups and instant replays, and through mini-interviews with the protagonists, brings the participants in the sports drama closer to the spectator than does attendance at the actual event. In the stadium there is drama seen at a distance, but on television the participants can become characters closely akin to those in a play, and, as fantasy figures in the collective daydream, perform superhuman feats of strength and endurance.

Where fantasy and reality are fused more deeply and inextricably than in any other area of programming, however, is in the commercials. Commercials are drama that turns into reality; they are also reality presented as fantasy. The playlets of the commercials are designed to exert the power of fantasy to make people spend real money on real products. They simultaneously convert those products into agents dispensing imaginary satisfactions; they mythologize real products into quasi-magical agents. The soft drink, the wine, the glass of sparkling water become elixirs of implied delights with associated psychological benefits yielding pleasures beyond their positive material effects (if such can be postulated to exist in the first place).

Fantasies, of course, while being unreal, nonetheless have a powerful and concrete influence on reality: for it is fantasy that often determines human beings' actions in the concrete world of reality. Television's ability—or tragic tendency—to turn reality into a kind of fantasy thus in turn, as previously noted, has its influence and impact on events and developments in the real world. The danger lies in the "false consciousness"—the *fausse conscience* in Sartre's sense—that television produces, which results in attitudes toward the real world that are unrealistic, illusionary, and even harmful. The way TV's treatment of the news publicizes and thus seems actually to inspire the increase in political terrorism is but one case in point. There are many others. For example, to what extent did the TV coverage of the Vietnam War, and of the protest movement against it, in highlighting the horrors of the war on the one hand, overstressing the revulsion of public opinion at home on the other, actually lead to what may, in the long run, turn out to have been a wrong course of action—namely the premature abandonment of the struggle? The Vietnam War was the first war in history to be fully reported on television. Was the image of that war as conveyed to the American public a true one, true not only in showing the horrors of warfare but also in putting them into the correct context? And did not the protesters make, also probably for the first time in history, full and highly intelligent use of the medium's predilection for violent, dramatic images, in creating, quite deliberately, what they called *street theater*: dramatic events that would have the optimal effect on television and compel the maximum exposure for their cause?

Every society has—and is shaped by—its self-image. It seems to me beyond doubt that television plays a significant role in shaping that collective self-image. And I would argue that the image of the U.S. that is presented on television is a false one: more violent, shallow, vulgar than reality; and, above all, pervaded by the hysterical tone of a perpetual hard sell quite unlike the far more relaxed atmosphere of real American life.

The presentation of such a distorted self-image to the rising generation must give cause for anxicty. And so must the fact that, owing to the great popularity of American television programs abroad and their relative cheapness and vast quantity, this image of the society is being exported worldwide to populations who have little chance of correcting and modifying it by direct observation. Both inside and outside the United States, the image of the society displayed by television is bound to have far-reaching cultural and political consequences.

The
Mall

WILLIAM SEVERINI KOWINSKI

© *Robert Perron/Photo Researchers*

Town Center Mall, Stamford, Connecticut

THE NINETEENTH-CENTURY DEPARTMENT STORE transformed shopping from an economic necessity into a leisure activity. The twentieth-century mall has emphasized the pleasurable aspects of shopping, becoming one of urban America's favorite places. As William S. Kowinski points out in the following selection, Americans spend more time at malls than anywhere else, aside from their homes and their jobs. The mall took the concept of one-stop shopping and turned it into the reality of a community in which the customers could not only shop and be entertained; they could also define their social identities.

The mall has become the social center for American suburban life. Sprawling housing subdivisions with no community focus and no traditional Main Street have turned to the mall as their common space. Significantly, the mall is an idealized version of life, a place in which no one is bothered. The enclosed space guarantees that the weather is pleasant; the mall management ensures that there are no encounters with undesirable persons; there is no filth and little noise. Visiting the mall has become so enjoyable that, in fact, shopping is often only the *excuse* for going. In reality, people go there to see and be seen, to cruise, and to enjoy.

In its ultimate form, the mall is a totally self-contained environment. The largest malls have movie theatres, office buildings, apartment complexes, and condominiums. In addition to a wealth of stores, offices, and banks, there are doctors, insurance agents, real estate brokers, and travel agents. There can also be aviaries, aquariums, artificial jungles, and amusement parks. One mall calls itself "the world's largest fun and fashion centre." The mall can provide everything necessary for a full and happy life and a person could, at least theoretically, live out his or her life without ever leaving. Shopping centers have become so central to life in the consumer society that one could say American society has truly been "malled."

NEW SCENARIO FOR THE END OF THE WORLD: Four survivors of an unnatural disaster are searching by helicopter for safety and sustenance—my God! What'll we do? Where will we go? Then, just below, they see it, spread out over 100 acres, one million sheltered square feet of food and clothing, not to mention variable-intensity massagers, quick-diet books, Stayfree Maxi-pads, rat poison, hunting rifles and glittering panels of Pong and pinball, all enclosed in a single climate-controlled fortress complete with trees, fountains and neon. Safe at last! Home free! The biggest, best-equipped fallout shelter imaginable, the consumer culture's Eden, the post-urban cradle, the womb, the home, the *mall*.

Such is the premise of director George Romero's new zombie movie, the follow-up to his famous *Night of the Living Dead*. In *Dawn of the Dead*, Romero releases his ghouls in the Monroeville Mall in western Pennsylvania, but it could just as well have been . . . Olde Towne Mall in California with its fully enclosed amusement park rides and carnival midway-style shops; or Sarasota Square mall in Florida with its six-screen cinema; or Olde Mistick Village in Mystic, Connecticut, a whole shopping center representing a New England village circa 1720; or just plain, old Linda Vista Shopping Center in San Diego; or Towne West Square in Wichita, Kansas; or Big Town Mall in Dallas—or anyplace where stores such as Sears, Nieman-Marcus, J.C. Penney and Gimbels glare down long corridors of Slack Shacks, Thom McAns, Magic Pan Creperies, Waldenbooks and Bath Trends. These meticulously planned and brightly enclosed structures, these *ideas* conveniently located just off the great American highway, have taken the concept of one-stop shopping, as old as the ancient public market, and turned it into a virtual one-stop culture, providing a cornucopia of products nestled in an ecology of community, entertainment and societal identity.

Malls try hard to be all things to all people, and they seem to be succeeding. According to a *U.S. News & World Report* survey, Americans spend more time at shopping malls than anywhere outside their homes and jobs. You can buy anything from diamonds to yogurt in them, go to church or college, register to

SHOPPING AND STORES   By William Severini Kowinski. Originally published under the title "The Malling of America." From *The Malling of America* by William Severini Kowinski, as it appeared in *New Times* (1978). Copyright © 1985 by William Severini Kowinski. By permission of William Morrow & Company.

vote, give blood, bet, score, jog and meditate in them, and in some you can get a motel room, apartment or condominium—and live there.

They're big business, too. Something like $60 billion is tied up in American shopping centers, money invested primarily by large insurance companies such as Connecticut General and Prudential, and banks such as Citibank and Continental Illinois. Investors love shopping centers for very direct reasons: They turn enormous profits and hardly ever fail. "Everybody has figured out that a major regional shopping center has got to be one of the best investments known to man," says Lawrence R. Glenn, real estate vice-president of Citibank. Right now centers do about half ($300 billion in 1977) of all retail business and, with 80 percent of new major chain outlets going into them, this share is getting larger every day.

The mall building business has steamrollered over every obstacle in its path so far—recession, the gasoline crisis of 1974, the energy crunch of 1977, the bankruptcy of W.T. Grant Co. which left thousands of stores suddenly vacant (80 percent of them were leased to other tenants within a year), government environmental regulations, the Federal Trade Commission, the Supreme Court—everything. Though construction slowed down considerably during the 1974–75 slump, shopping centers "proved to be a magnificent and resilient asset," according to Mathias DeVito, president of the Rouse Company. Even during the recession, the Rouse centers managed to increase their profits by 11 percent. And now building is again increasing by hefty yearly percentages. Small wonder that Albert Sussman, executive vice-president of the International Council of Shopping Centers—the mall business' own trade and lobbying organization—could crow at their 1976 convention: "The shopping center business is creative, it's exciting, it's challenging. Most of all, it's profitable."

Has all this been passing you by? You're not alone. "Malls are a classic case of something that fills millions of people's needs but is of no interest to sociologists," says Ralph Keyes, writer and social scientist. "People who shop at Bloomingdale's and write our sociology couldn't care less." (Bloomie's itself, in fact, has joined the trend.) Richard Francaviglia, professor of geography at Antioch College, tried to read a paper that took malls seriously at the Popular Culture Association convention in Chicago. "It nearly started a riot," he said. "Quite literally, scholars were yelling back and forth at each other—and me. It was all very stimulating," he added. "But while we were arguing, 20 million people were shopping in malls and generally enjoying themselves."

So if you want to hear the Chicago Symphony, try Woodfield Mall near Schaumburg. The Dallas Symphony was at the edge of extinction before a series of successful concerts at NorthPark Shopping Center rescued it. A Roy Lichtenstein sculpture stands in the Santa Ana Fashion Park in California, which is not to denigrate the 24-foot-high statue of Sir Walter Raleigh commissioned by North Hills Fashion Mall in Raleigh, North Carolina. You can see a laser show (designed by rock impresario Bill Graham's F.M. Productions) three times a day at Old Chicago mall, and listen to the Old Towne Band in Old Towne Mall. Been wondering where Pat Paulsen has been lately? You can catch him at Maplewood Mall near Minneapolis, sharing the bill with Captain Cookie. If you're celebrity hunting in Chicago, try Watertower Place—Muhammad Ali has been seen there.

Of course, it's not all cash and culture. There's kidnapping, car theft, rape, dope—even dognapping. Terrorist bombs have ripped apart an American-style mall in South Africa. In 1972 George Wallace was gunned down in a shopping center parking lot, and five people caught bullets at a political rally for Senator Benjamin Everett Jordan the same year. But there's love too. Researching a story on women and the bar scene in Washington, D.C., writer Jean Callahan discovered that few women actually met prospective lovers in bars. They met them mostly in shopping malls. And so on, for all ages. . . . A Temple University study shows that malls are the most popular gathering places for teenagers in America. So for the noisy rites of pubescence, for old friends sharing a mall bench quietly, for the mainstream middle-class middle-aged middle Americans, Ralph Keyes says it directly in his book *We, The Lonely People*: "Malls aren't part of the community. They are the community."

Tom Walker, business editor of the *Atlanta Journal*, sums it up just a little differently: "If you had to pick one thing that would typify civilization in the United States in the twentieth century, a front-running candidate would be the suburban shopping mall." Hypnotists and jugglers, disco dancing classes, romance, intrigue and disaster—they've got it all, along with quite a bit of money and quite a bit of the landscape. Almost imperceptibly, the culture of the highway has coalesced in these climate-controlled bubbles. . . . The malling of America is happening now.

PART 1   NEIGHBORS IN NEVER-NEVER LAND

Walter Johnson High School in Bethesda, Maryland, was once in the middle of what was, literally, a cow pasture. There were cow pastures all around it; the team mascot was "Mighty Moo." But when Marcia was in ninth grade, that suddenly changed. And so did everything else.

Because up the hill from the school the Montgomery Mall appeared. A big two-level shopping mall, with four major department stores and the full lineup of other shops—the usual suburban bread-and-butter mall built in its time, about 10 years ago. Nothing outrageous or spectacular . . . but suddenly the students at Walter Johnson could not remember what they did on Saturday afternoon besides call each other up around 1:00 p.m. to ask, "Going to the mall?"

The girls would go shopping at Garfinckel's and Hechts and the ladies' specialty and shoe stores for their school outfits and casual clothes, and then the boys would show up at around 3:00 and everybody would walk around. Sometimes they'd meet in Bresler's 33 Flavors for ice cream, giggles, gossip and even to share some of those transcendent adolescent moments when they tried to figure out parents, teachers and God (if any).

Montgomery Mall soon became an intimate and almost institutional part of Walter Johnson High and the focus of Marcia's suburban *American Graffiti* years. Her senior prom and Christmas dance (the Snow Ball) were held in the mall. She spent many of her "open campus" free periods there, having a chef's salad in the afternoon with a friend or just walking around. The mall capitalized on the school as well. When its fountain filled up with the pennies people tossed in for luck, the mall drew crowds to watch Walter Johnson's head cheerleader and drum majorette wade into the water in bikinis and sweep up the coins.

The mall was such a part of Marcia's world that a poem in the 1970 yearbook elegized it along with the rest of the evening landscape:

> It's getting late.
> The sun collapsed behind Montgomery Mall hours ago.
> These halls are empty tunnels interrupted by piles of dust
>   left by previous life.

The difference Montgomery Mall made in Marcia's world isn't unique. There are nearly 18,000 shopping plazas in America. Most are small neighborhood and open strip centers—just lines of stores strung out with nothing more in common than a large parking lot. But about 1,000 are as big or bigger than Montgomery Mall, and a few hundred are huge, some taking up more than 1 million square feet of store space in a vast landscape that includes parking lots, access roads, prefab landscaping and frequently much more.

In the suburbs, malls have been largely unchallenged as social centers—there simply has been no competition. The suburban landscape as it evolved since World War II, with the assistance of FHA housing loans, federal and state highway programs and a boom in subdivisions and housing "plans," became simply houses and space. The suburbs happened so fast that few foresaw they would become anything but bedroom adjuncts to cities.

But children had to go to school, housewives needed places to shop, and everyone needed some common ground. The malls filled these gaps and fulfilled these needs. In 1973, the Camden County Economic Development Committee evaluated the influence of Cherry Hill Mall, which opened in 1961 in New Jersey. The report concluded that Cherry Hill "revolutionized the retail structure of Camden County. . . . Shopping patterns dramatically changed for thousands." Beyond the business aspect, the report found that Cherry Hill and the other malls that have opened there since "are recognized, too, as more than shopping centers. Their generous contribution of space and facilities have added new dimensions to communal life. They're truly the main street of suburbia."

Mall visionaries understood that their space would be the great common area in suburbs otherwise designed for the privacy of single-family dwellings and the convenience of cars, and they welcomed the opportunity to provide that space. In 1960 pioneer mall designer Victor Gruen wrote that malls "can provide the need, place and opportunity for participation in modern community life that the ancient Greek Agora, the medieval market place, and our own town squares provided in the past."

But that is hardly the whole story. To understand how and how well the mall phenomenon touches new American longings, soothes new fears and satisfies new needs, it is necessary to look at the mall more closely: as a structure, a concept, a medium of magic, safety and myth. See the mall after sunset, when it is empty. See it at night.

From the road, malls don't look like much. In the high bare lights, just long stone mausoleums in a wilderness of asphalt. Inside they are movie soundstages on down-time—still possessing potential magic, like sets for an unknown illusion yet to be performed.

This is Greengate Mall in western Pennsylvania, some miles east of the mall where George Romero is filming, at the end of day. Only McSorley's bar is open. Young management types are drinking and discussing business; if they linger they may talk about merchandising strategy or sex. Before the evening's over, some of McSorley's more loaded customers may even honor the tradition of sliding down the railing of the dormant escalator.

Walking around now and looking at the mall without the animation of people, you see and sense . . . possibility. The white liquidity of light that suffuses it, the areas of relative darkness. The central court. The fountain and the stairs. The balcony effect from the railing on a landing. The aisles and escalators, the now-bracketed store facades, the live greenery. Inside, at night, you understand what is here: protected space. Removed, enclosed, intelligible yet not fully formulated. The potential is enormous and striking.

Outdoor strip shopping centers were built as early as the 1920s in California and became common elsewhere by the late fifties. The big department store owners, realizing that people wanted to shop nearer their homes, next added their bulk and muscle to the shopping center idea. Then designers came up with two major innovations: the two-level mall (introduced by the Rouse Company in Baltimore), which seemed to halve the psychological distance shoppers had to walk, and the most important stroke—the fully enclosed, temperature-controlled mall, the first of which was Southdale Center, built near Minneapolis in 1956 by Victor Gruen Associates for the Dayton Hudson Company.

Gruen enclosed Southdale because of the extremes of Minnesota weather, but the effect was so dramatic that it revolutionized shopping centers everywhere. The malls that followed, even in the sunny climes of Florida and California, were also enclosed. Paul E. Leyton, vice-president of operations of May Stores shopping centers, explains why: "We discovered that the enclosed mall changed the concept. The idea of having an enclosed mall doesn't relate to weather alone. People go to spend time there—they're equally as interested in eating and browsing as in shopping. So now we build only enclosed malls."

When the centers stopped stretching out in a line and "circled up" to form a protected enclosure, they took a profoundly different attitude toward the highways and cars that made them possible in the first place. No longer open to the road as a sustaining environment and especially as a style—freewheeling, frequently vulgar and above all uncontrollable—the shopping malls turned in on themselves to shut out the noise, dirt and danger of cars, as well as the intrusions of the highway, creating inner-directed environments divorced as much as possible from the world outside. Designing for that—the closing off of the outside world and the orchestration of what goes into this protected environment—is the art and science of malls.

In his study "Main Street USA" (the one that triggered the wild reaction at the Popular Culture Association convention), Richard Francaviglia develops a design analysis to show two things: first, that the man who initially built the perfect small town, though it never in fact existed outside his amusement parks, was named Walt Disney. And second, that where Disney left off, the mall builders took over.

Francaviglia demonstrates that by manipulating design elements such as scale and sight-lines, and by mixing the most attractive features of both small towns and cities while leaving out all the bad stuff ("pool halls, bars, second-hand stores, and the kind of people who patronize them"), Disney created a pleasant and aesthetically successful image of what a small town should be. Shopping malls simply took this concept out of Disneyland and gave it to millions just a few automobile-minutes from their homes.

Francaviglia also talks about Disney scaling down the size of his Main Street shops so they would look nostalgically small to adults and uncommonly inviting to kids. Malls are designed for Disney's children. Stores are pressed close together; they have small, low facades. In fact, everything about malls is minimized. Designers go berserk trying to make sure people don't have to walk more than a few hundred feet from their cars to the center. The mall is laid out with few corners and no unused space along store row so that there are no decisions to make—you just flow on.

Enclosure gives the illusion of safety. There is no buffeting wind, no traffic to dodge. The rest of the world may be comprised of spaces too large to feel safe in, too dirty or weird to walk in, or else of enclosures too small to stroll in—school, work place, home. But the mall is a comfortably sized space—danger is kept out, decisions are designed out, the scale is manageable. All the fearful things about the marketplace are minimized. Malls seem to be made for future-shocked agoraphobes.

Mall space isn't just created: It is controlled. Unlike cities or towns, malls have nearly absolute control over which stores to have. Their owners are landlords and the stores are tenants. Stores are usually so eager to be in a mall that they not only pay high rents but "overage rents" (a percentage of their profits over a certain figure), "common area" charges to maintain the mall, and sometimes extra charges to have their own store maintained. And they have to abide by the mall's rules.

At Greengate, for instance, the initial design of all stores—including storefronts, colors and the store logo—all have to be approved by the developer and owner, the Rouse Company, seventh largest mall developer in the country. This is standard throughout much of the industry; a developer has been known to change the name of a store, even an established chain outlet, to make it comply with policy.

Harry Overly is Greengate's manager, and part of his job is enforcing the rules. Stores are required to open no later than 10:00 a.m. and close no earlier than 9:30 p.m., because the mall must be absolutely and uniformly dependable. Harry's security people keep a black book on those who violate this rule by even a minute. Stores are required to keep themselves looking new—not to mention clean—even if it means major overhauls, because, as Harry says, "We don't want a store that looks old."

A management trainee who has worked at several other malls says Overly is a good manager because he's tough and he sees everything. When rules aren't enforced and the manager isn't on top of things, the mall becomes chaotic and demoralized. Of course, some people smile at Overly's fanaticism about hand-lettered signs (which are absolutely forbidden for any purpose) and his disapproval of his employees having affairs with each other (even after, the story goes, two of them got married before he realized they'd been dating). But Overly, in fact, is not as strict as some mall managers. Take Al Taubman of the Taubman Company, builder of Woodfield Mall, who has singlehandedly developed more shopping center space than anyone else. There's a famous industry story to the effect that "Big Al" was showing some celebs around one of his mammoth malls when he chanced to slip on some ice cream that had glopped onto the terrazzo tile. He fell on his ass. The fuming Taubman ordered a chemical analysis of the ice cream to discover where the cone had come from, and then threw the offending vendor out of his mall. For good measure he also stopped everybody else from selling food that could be carried around and maybe spilled on his floor.

The total power of the mall owner, even when civil liberties are involved, has been upheld by the courts. There are some antitrust limitations, some restraints of trade litigations that malls have lost, but according to the Supreme Court, malls can keep out those who threaten—particularly pickets and pamphleteers—to disturb the fantasy world inside. The issue has been whether malls are public community areas under law as well as in promotional literature. At first, it seemed that malls were legally what they aspired to be socially. A 1969 California Superior Court decision stated that ". . . in many instances the contemporary shopping center serves as the analogue of the traditional town square." This decision (in favor of antipollution petitioners in a San Bernardino mall) followed the Warren Court's decision to uphold a union's right to picket a store even inside a mall. Both decisions harkened back to a 1940s Supreme Court case on company towns that said in effect: If a place looks and acts like a town, it is a town, whether or not it is privately owned.

But when war protesters entered an Oregon mall in 1972, the Burger Court decided that the mall doesn't lose its private character "merely because the public is generally invited to use it for designated purposes" and ruled against the protesters, 5 to 4. The Court went that way again in a 1976 ruling against another labor union, despite the dissenting argument by Justices Thurgood Marshall and William Brennan that "shopping center owners have assumed . . . the traditional role of the state in [their] control of historical First Amendment forums."

Mall owners aren't shy about exercising their exclusionary power because they simply do not want anything to interfere with the shopper's freedom to "not be bothered" and to "have fun," as some mall officials put it. "Nothing gets in here unless we let it in," says the manager of Westmoreland Mall, a few miles east of Greengate. Tysons Corner and other Lerner Company malls in the Washington area post quite explicit notices on their doors: "Areas in Tysons Corner Center used by the public are not public ways, but are for the use of the tenants and the public transacting business with them. Permission to use said areas may be revoked at any time."

The success of enclosure has to do with things other than keeping out the weather—but it has something to do with that, too. "I like it because no matter what it's doing outside, it's always the same in here—I don't even know whether it's raining or what," says a young employee at Westmoreland Mall. "It's better for looking at girls, too," his friend adds. "They aren't all bundled up in coats and stuff, even in the winter." The absence of weather in malls is a selling point. In a newspaper sent to consumers by Tamarac Square mall in Denver, there is a cute but pointed weather forecast: "Skies over Tamarac Square's enclosed street scene continued irrelevant through the weekend. Temperatures remained consistent, though thunder was heard through the skylights on at least one occasion. No indoor tornadoes were predicted. Forecast: consistently pleasant."

By keeping weather out and keeping itself always in the present—if not in the future—a mall aspires to create timeless space. Removed from everything else and existing in a world of its own, a mall is also placeless space. And the beauty of the form is that this space can be filled with all kinds of fine-tuned fantasies. Malls can host the ideal image of the small-town street or embody nostalgic themes—an anesthetized version of early America is particularly popular in the Northeast. Or they can create new hybrids with elements otherwise found in amusement parks, public markets, sports arenas and symphony halls—encased in structures that partake of the opulence of grand hotels, European city plazas and the great American railroad stations. (Not surprisingly, malls on the West Coast are the most ebulliently rococo, while the Midwest leans toward a kind of mall classicism and the Sunbelt goes for glassy elegance.)

The mall is simply such an elastic form that virtually anything can be packaged and included, as long as it contributes to the basic consumer fantasy: shopping as entertainment. It's fabulous: controlled as a unit in leasing and operation, politically sealed off from the community to the degree the mall owner wishes, protected from the external environment. The mall is a never-never land, a huge plastic bag in which all the proper factors can be arranged to summon up the right consumer myths so that the mall becomes an absolutely vital part of the lives and lifestyle of the Me People, wherever they may be.

The quality of fantasy is sometimes pushed to the edge of surrealism; even at quiet moments the mall may produce scenes seemingly lifted from paintings by de Chirico or Magritte. This feeling can be better appreciated at some hours than others.

For instance, at a mall called Fashion Island in Newport Beach, California, shortly before sunset. . . . The sun is hanging brightly just above the parking lot in the middle of Newport Center, a planned community of which this mall is the epicenter, the temple. A soft yellow light bathes the white sandstone of the high entrance columns as well-dressed ladies in their soft "neutral-look" separates, clinging short-sleeve sweaters and high-heeled sandals jog neatly up the stone steps. Off to one side maintenance men in their sea-green jump suits and black loafers, check the immaculate trees and shrubs. Off to the other, a series of bell-like objects rises several stories up, like some giant wind chimes. But they make no sound; it is very quiet here. The whole place is so perfect that it's eerie. But why, with all this quiescent concrete, does it feel so . . . unreal? And then it dawns on me: Fashion Island is a three-dimensional, life-size Artist's Conception. One of those flawless sketches or scale models that buildings themselves never quite turn out to be . . . except here.

PART 2 BREAD AND CIRCUSES

Alte Faust, promotional director for Tysons Corner Center mall in Virginia, personally dyed baby elephants pink for Tysons' Christmas parade. Her job, she said, is "show business." No kidding. Rock-a-thons for crippled children, a Ben Franklin Birthday Kite-Flying Competition, "Trace your Scandinavian Roots!" displays, bluegrass jamborees—malls use every trick and "community-service" event from Bozos to blood banks to bring the folks in.

These promotions, of course, become part of the major cultural rites, particularly Christmas, the really big one for retailing when almost $75 billion goes into those *bleep-blip-blip-bleep* computerized cash registers in one month. In 1977 major retail chains reported sales earnings 10 to 20 percent higher than those of December 1976. So they deck the halls of Maplewood Mall in Minneapolis with pink angels hanging from the ceiling around spinning ice cream cones; they bring on the Los Angeles Premier Chorale Strolling Christmas Medieval Feast Ceremony in Costume at the Promenade mall in California; and Santa arrives at thousands of shopping centers in motorized sleighs, firetrucks, helicopters . . . In the days of open strip centers he sometimes dropped from an airplane, until the time an elf who preceded him got squished on the asphalt when his little chute didn't open and Santa refused to jump, or so the mall myth goes.

Sometimes the promotions are entirely manufactured—for instance the parades, strutting majorettes, band blaring and the excited kids banging on the edge of the stage, all for the arrival of Mickey Mouse at Greengate Mall. There's a psychology behind all this, a way that these events fit into an overall plan.

But look around now that the customers have been brought in and the mall is filled. It's Saturday afternoon and here they are: parents with clutches of kids; the couples on shopping dates—the girls in corduroy gaucho skirts, harness-style boots and acrylic knit sweater-coats, poised and smiling, and their sleepy-eyed jockish boyfriends, shrugged into jeans and school insignia nylon taffeta warmup jackets; the blimpy middle-aged women munching yogurt cones; the red-faced middle-aged men wearing company logo baseball caps; the roving gangs of teenage girls with identical Farrah Fawcett hairdos in every imaginable shade of blond, brown and red. They're all moving brightly through the big bazaar, fingering and considering and slapping down the plastic that makes the *bleep-blip-blip-bleep* cash registers sing, for all those electric woks, Telstar Arcade micro processors, Watta Pizzaria electric pizza makers, Marie Osmond fashion dolls, tube sox, smoke detectors, leisure slippers, wicker-look bench hampers, sherpa-lined trailblazers, Star Wars digital wristwatches and ceramic jars holding Aramis Muscle Soothing Soak with the inscription, "Life is a joy and all things show it/I thought so once but now I know it!" (Only $22.00, soak included.)

Do not think this is all happening accidentally. Once the enclosure, the mall form, exists, it has to be filled with the right fantasy, the correct combination of stores for the particular mall serving a particular area—the right mix of stuff in the stores and fun and games on the floor, the right over-all atmosphere to lure people, keep them in the mall as long as possible, and keep them coming back. There are a lot of elements in the making of a successful mall, and this is one of them: the right combination of bread and circuses.

The mall business has countless developers, but there are 50 companies that predominate, owning and managing from 3 million to 40 million square feet of leased space each. Many of the largest developers are men who pioneered the field, the Henry Fords and Andrew Carnegies of shopping centers, men like Al Taubman, Edward DeBartolo and James Rouse. But there are also plenty of faceless conglomerates. Some of the financial arrangements among investors, developers and managers of malls can get quite complicated, resulting in corporate monikers such as Cal-American Income Property Fund IV, the company that runs Century City in Los Angeles.

In 25 years, in fact, the mall business has evolved from an aggressive seat-of-the-pants operation to an aggressive and very complex industry. It has its own publications (*Shopping Center World, Chain Store Age Executive, National Mall Monitor* among them), and its own trade association, the International Council of Shopping Centers, with a budget of over $1 million a year, runs a yearly "college" on mall developing and lobbies for the industry.

The first step in a successful mall is site selection. That used to be the easy part—Edward DeBartolo, the Ohio developer who recently opened Randall Park, a virtual city among shopping centers, once searched out his locations from a Learjet. Now it's not so easy, and major developers carefully weigh the demographics, growth potential and political situation of a proposed site as well as its physical attributes and proximity to highways.

Land acquisition means dealing with government, which also means meeting environmental requirements on all levels. Developers complain most loudly about this—all the red tape involved in satisfying as many as 65 separate agencies. They like to point to a California mall that had to go through 140 public hearings before being approved. It used to take one to three years to get a big mall past the planning stage; now it takes at least four to six.

Besides site selection and physical design, there is the crucial matter of finding the right tenants. This is the art of leasing—renting to the right stores that together adjust the balance of bread and circuses to achieve the perfect synergism. As industry spokesman Albert Sussman says, "We have learned that there is no substitute for leasing to the right mix of tenants. . . . The strength of a shopping center derives from the symbiotic relationship of all the stores within the center."

It took some time to discover the precise mix for the regional shopping mall. For a while the major department stores, indispensable to the mall to such an extent that their influence has increased rather than waned over the years, often insisted that they be the only big stores in their given malls, until it became clear that not only was there enough business to go around but that the more big-store power there was to draw people in, the more everybody in the center would profit.

Regional malls also used to have supermarkets—literally bread, as many as two in a center—but now few enclosed malls have any. Part of the reason is that the shopping pattern of supermarkets is different. People move in and out of them quickly, whereas they are supposed to linger in a mall. So take-home groceries continue to be sold in strip centers. Now virtually all the food the regional mall sells is eaten on the premises: Bread has become part of the circus . . . *Let them eat pizza.*

Of course the mall itself—not just the promotional stunts, but the whole mall—is the real circus. To the basic environment, add the products themselves and the atmosphere—right down to the Muzak, the accompanying soundtrack in the consumer movie. In the mall halls, it is gentle and bright, a stroller's smiling companion. In the stores it is more specific and stimulating, from Vivaldi in the bookstores to Linda Ronstadt in the jeans and tops stores to Steve Miller in the fashion shops.

Developers can fine-tune their malls through design, tenant selection and atmosphere to cater to the characteristics of a special area—to provide its particular fantasy. The Rouse Company has done this with Faneuil Hall in

Boston, and in the process changed the whole downtown. Housed in restored and remodeled buildings first constructed in 1826 on the site of Boston's colonial marketplace, the Quincy, North and South Markets as redone by Rouse now encase a prime selection of small shops and eating places in a contemporary suburban mall framework. The Faneuil Hall project includes some living reminders of the old market place in the area around it, where arts and crafts are sold along with fresh fruit and vegetables in uniform carts and stands rented from Rouse.

Faneuil appeals to Boston's preservationist sense, and its success has helped revive long-dormant city pride. It also caters to Boston's tastes—the low-cal cosmopolitanism and casual consumption of its high-income, highly educated classes. Rouse's gamble has been spectacularly successful, earning $300 a square foot in its first year, which is about three times the usual mall standard. In their respective first years of operation, Faneuil drew more visitors than Walt Disney World. Because of the new market, there are crowds on Boston's water-front again. Suburbanites are there shoulder to shoulder on weekends. Nearby Government Center is virtually deserted at workday lunchtimes—employees from the city, state and federal offices are down at Quincy Market, eating croissants from Au Bon Pain, opulent salads, fried bread, souvlaki sandwiches, prosciutto on bulkie rolls, scallops at the raw bar, ice cream sundaes with "real whipped cream"! Its cafe, Cityside, has become the in-spot even when the rest of the market is closed. It's the perfect new Boston fantasy—an enclosed Paris of yesterday, inside the genteel shell of Boston's feisty past. Standing in the courtyard sunshine, a young man in Icelandic coat, jeans and new Frye boots, who was splitting French bread and Perrier with a companion in expensive casual clothes, stared back at the Faneuil Hall marketplace in blank wonder. "I can't believe it," he said, "It's like another world."

Malls are malleable—able and willing to stretch and contour to the character-istic needs and whims, the particular predilections of the areas they inhabit. What worked for Boston—a stylish but understated townishness—might have bombed in the capital. There, the new Neiman-Marcus Mazza Gallerie is taking the measure of Washington, D.C.'s new-money ambitions by applying Texas-brand conspicuous consumption to the city's craving for high-fashion.

Neiman's building, inserted among Washington's most exclusive stores, is a severe structure of white Italian marble, not unlike what a modern presidential monument on the scale of Lincoln or Jefferson might look like. It opened last winter with a typical Washington event—a black tie celebrity gala, with fund raising for the arts as the excuse for dressing up, and for the private pawing of Neiman's pavé diamond-faced watches, cabochon rubies, mulberry silk dinner dresses, brown velvet evening suits and lambskin patchpocket blazers. The rest of the mall wasn't finished as Neiman's opening was being prepared (a copy of the Social List of Washington 1978 lying on the promotion director's desk amidst sandwiches and ad proofs, Texas-accented pep talks to salespeople about how the whole idea is get the very best clientele of Washington). But even then a panel truck was parked outside the embryonic mall. It was from Muzak.

Neiman-Marcus' isn't the only high-fashion mall in Washington—Bloomie's has two stores in suburban malls including the largest, White Flint, and there is even a theme-fashion mall at the end of the brand-new subway line, called

Crystal Underground Shopping Center. These malls are for the people who agree with the laconically polite pants-suited woman I met at the opening of a new store (Bed 'n Bath) at Crystal City. We were talking for a moment about Tysons Corner, the suburban Virginia mall that used to be considered the most impressive in the area. "It's all right, I suppose," she said. "But it smells like hot dogs."

Of course, fine-tuning to that degree is possible and even necessary for places that have such definable characteristics as Boston and Washington, but for most suburban and small town locations, a less glamorous fantasy is sufficient to be profitable. The basic mall's success depends on playing to the new middle-American lifestyle—a phenomenon that suggests every sociological insight and cliché from the affluent society to the Me Decade, which Henri Lefebvre sums up in his book *Everyday Life in the Modern World*: "It is the transition from a culture based on the curbing of desires, thriftiness and the necessity of eking out goods in short supply to a new culture resulting from production and consumption at their highest ebb, but against a background of general crisis."

Customers come to malls from every possible place, walk of life, economic bracket. But if malls have a mind set, a spiritual epicenter, it's not the city, the suburb or rural America, but out *there*, in between, just off the highway, where you find all the new Naugahyde and hanging-plant bars, with fancily named and priced drinks, foreign beers, wines and goods which 10 years ago were the exclusive preserve of big city life. Easy and quick isn't enough any more; the Highway Comfort Culture has gone beyond hamburgers and wash 'n' wear to a veneer of sophistication. It's Lobster and Löwenbräu, even though the lobster is microwaved and the beer is made in Texas. The stores and restaurants have dressed up their interiors with motifs that suggest haute cuisine and high fashion, while trying to keep the same streamlined delivery system as McDonald's. In retrospect, it seems inevitable that these highway stops would draw together and unite under one roof, the one-stop oasis of splendor, the mall.

Along with the rest of the highway culture, malls have responded to the Me Decade and helped bring it to the heartland. A recent industry survey among customers turned up 10 reasons—besides the wish to buy something—why people frequent malls. They ranged from self-gratification to learning about new trends to sensory stimulation and role playing. It is part of the trick of good mall management to understand and manipulate these motivations correctly, and in particular to understand which people want to play what roles. Greengate, for instance, situated in the heart of an oleo-and-white-bread area like Westmoreland County in western Pennsylvania, is a family-oriented mall, with Penney, Montgomery Ward and a five-and-ten dominating the no-frills box like building. Only five miles away as the highway measures, but considerably more in psychic space, is Westmoreland Mall. About the same size as Greengate but opened last year, Westmoreland is trying to appeal to people who identify with disco, *Cosmo* and high fashion by mixing a lot of specialty shops, jeans-and-tops stores and eating places. Sensible people like Grandpa Walton and Florence Henderson would shop at Greengate, but Westmoreland is trying to inspire the Margaux Hemingway and John Travolta in its customers.

Promotion becomes an extension of the styles reflected in tenant mix and mall image. You are more likely to run into Mickey Mouse at Greengate (or Columbia Plaza mall in Maryland and the Dayton Hudson Minneapolis malls) because the sensible family mall wants to attract kids with paying parents. Westmoreland's promotions are more apt to be skin-care lectures; in the extremely high-fashion malls like the Mazza Gallerie in Washington, D.C., you get personal appearances by Diane von Furstenberg and Bill Blass. They are specialized circuses to sell specific brands of bread.

The line between promotion and product is often a very fine one, which is really the whole point of the mall's appeal. By adjusting their emphasis to their clientele (without going overboard, of course: Greengate has fashionable stores and Westmoreland, to be safe, has Sears), malls create a seamless system for their customers to buy whole—physically, conceptually, socially. It's an endless circus because everyone's having fun, and it's all bread because somehow it sustains them.

PART 3 DAWN OF THE DREAD

It hits you, Barbara said, when you're standing there naked, looking in the mirror of the dressing room. Your clothes are in a pile on the floor or draped over a chair. Maybe it's just a little cubicle with a curtain behind you, and you can still hear the other shoppers and the Muzak. You're about to try on something which you'll have to judge, make decisions about. Then you'll have to take it off and put your own stuff back on. This is about the first thing that's taken any real effort on your part since you came to the mall. And then you realize—*you've been here all day.* Time has in fact been passing while you've been gliding through store after store in a hum of soft lights and soft music, the splash of fountains, the people, but almost no intrusive sound, no one calling to you, nothing to dodge or particularly to look for, just a visual parade of clothes, fabric tags and washing instructions. Prices, displays, cosmetics, books, records. Nice colors. An ice cream cone. All the faces, the customers, are walking models of the mall's products, or just walking models of the weird. Whatever you actually came here for is in the distant past. You've been floating . . . for hours.

So what does this remind you of? How about *Invasion of the Body Snatchers?*—people made mindless and happy by certain seed pods from outer space—a great black-and-white film of the fifties, with Kevin McCarthy, soon to be updated with Leonard Nimoy. The malls don't have to be invaded by zombies: They grow their own.

Barbara came down from Minneapolis, where she teaches high school, to guide me through the Chicago area malls and then drive back with me to the Twin Cities, to look at even more malls in the broad Midwestern landscape. It was a journey across terrain as surely and easily invaded by the shopping mall as time and space is obliterated inside one.

We hit the highway on a cold November day. "Chicagoland," as local radio stations call it, is considered a living mall laboratory because many different kinds were first tried out here.

We started with Oakbrook Shopping Center, opened in 1962 and now ancient by mall standards, a model semi-enclosed mall that's a prototype for Southern California's Century City and Fashion Island. Further out we stopped at Fox Valley Center, a new "advanced design" rural-look mall, which the assistant security chief told us was becoming very popular because customers were escaping from the traffic congestion and crime of the older malls.

At this point in my travels I had seen over a dozen malls of various shapes and sizes. Even the anomalies of Fox Valley—diagonal walkways, burnt-orange sofas and a great deal of wood, a combination of horse country and Flash Gordon—could no longer faze me. Like the people at Devil's Tower after the first saucers swooped by in *Close Encounters of the Third Kind*, I thought I'd seen the whole show . . . until we walked into Woodfield: the Mothership.

I stopped just inside the upper level entrance, stunned by the sound. The sound of people—many, many people; a constant background roar like the ocean, like the hum left over from the universe's big bang. Over a quarter of a million people had come here in one day. You could see them everywhere, flowing across the criss-crossing concourses and down the aisles, from this end of the mall to the blue Sears sign at the other, far in the distance. The floor vibrated with their movement.

Downstairs they flooded by: a moving chaos of kids, suburbanites and the most amazing variety of ethnic, racial and social groups I've ever seen in one place outside New York, or maybe San Francisco—Indians, Hispanics, a Japanese family loaded with cameras and smiles, a black dude in elegant fur, dwarfs, low-lifers, a woman sobbing, jeweled matrons, a whole group of incredibly fat people, beautiful Asiatic girls . . . Where did they come from? The nearest town is Schaumburg, not exactly an international melting pot. Not even Chicago . . . And why are they *here*? Barbara pointed out that comparatively few were carrying packages. Woodfield is not just a shopping space. It is an event.

The invasion continues apace—these strange objects dropped on the landscape like H. G. Wells' Martian cylinders in *War of the Worlds*. While not yet back up to the pre-recession building levels of 1971–74, shopping center construction is increasing again—up 14 percent last year and expected to jump another 35 percent by 1979. Industry figures project 140 million more square feet of leasable space by then—and untold acres of surrounding development—with 75 percent of it slated for the suburbs.

For it's not just the malls—other strange structures follow them. We saw them again and again in Illinois, sitting in open fields unconnected to anything else, as if they'd just landed: big anonymous buildings that could be anything from schools to power plants, but usually were offices and motels, accompanied by colorful satellites with golden arches and red and white buckets. They appear near malls.

They are still coming. They are being invited. We saw large signs in cultivated cornfields on the way to Fox Valley: "For Sale for Industrial Development." Mall packagers are aware of them, and their response is to get as much of the secondary development for themselves as they can, to control it and mold it to their mall's image—and to take in the additional profits. The Rouse Company, for example, realized that their planned new mall in New Jersey was going to attract new housing, so they decided to build it themselves. The result is the Echelon Urban Center—a 1-million-square-foot shopping center in a planned community of 2,900 housing units and landscaped parks. In fact, the "multi-use" mall is becoming a definite trend in suburban and city situations. Urban

Investment, developer of Oakbrook and Fox Valley, calls its downtown Chicago Water Tower Place an "omnicenter": a 74-story complex of condominiums, offices, underground parking, and a Ritz-Carlton hotel, with an eight-level mall fronting it all. The multi-use center is midway between Woodfield—the mall as city—and the planned towns such as Columbia, Maryland, and Irvine, California—the city as mall.

These alien forms, with their magnetic power to attract customers and retailers from everywhere, are rearranging the landscape. The suburban malls found they were creating new traffic patterns, drawing customers from cities and towns and other suburbs as far as 40 to 60 miles away. The resulting ex-flux and competition drained cities to such an extent that dying downtowns had to turn to redevelopment schemes.

Now the malls themselves are moving downtown, into the vacuum they helped create. "If used properly, there is something in redevelopment for everyone," Bud Pichetto, a California redevelopment official, told a recent gathering of shopping center executives. Of nine major projects the Taubman Company is planning or looking into, five are in cities. Oakland's downtown regional mall will soon join other major urban projects in Philadelphia, Atlanta, Kansas City, Santa Monica and New York.

Some of the more flamboyant malls are in the new cities of the Sunbelt—for example, Houston's Galleria, an extravagant expanse of glittering glass rimmed by a brand new jogger's track which provides a constant peripheral counterpoint to the more plodding pace of mere shopping. The Sunbelt is the last clear frontier for malls. Since growth there is so rapid, few cities have a chance to evolve normally. In newly urbanized areas of Texas, Florida and Arizona, malls *are* the downtown, right from the start. "The enclosed shopping center is Houston's equivalent of the traditional town plaza—a clear trend across the country," writes architecture critic Ada Louise Huxtable in the *New York Times*.

But even without more great open spaces to conquer, mall developers haven't given up—they're accelerating their movement into small towns and rural spaces. As Albert Sussman notes, "Before we were building shopping centers to fill a vacuum. Now we're plugging up the holes."

So Yazoo City, Mississippi, is getting its own Yazooville City Shopping Center. Hibbing, Minnesota, Bob Dylan's hometown up in northernmost nothingness, will have a 225,000-square-foot mall with three major department stores late next year. Amityville in New York may have its Horror, but it also has a nice new mall that opened a few months ago. Canal Place One is coming to scenic old New Orleans—an urban "multi-use" center featuring not just a mall but three office towers, two hotels, townhouses, a helipad and an entertainment complex. A big piece of the up-front money for Canal Place One is coming from Iran.

Put it all together and what do you get? "The mall is a great machine," says Cesar Pelli, who used to design shopping centers as a partner in Gruen Associates. Now he's dean of the School of Architecture at Yale and the chief architect of the proposed addition to the Museum of Modern Art. "Malls succeeded because for the first time shopping was approached as an idea," he says, "But now they have become too successful—in the same way that the automobile has become too successful. They are so powerful that they overwhelm everything else—there is nothing strong enough to balance them."

Tall, dark-haired, with a European manner and accent, Pelli speaks in a rapid clip about a social landscape over-saturated with shopping centers, and about the consequences of the mall's magnetism on communities, particularly small ones, that can't compete with the furious retail and social activity the malls generate. One conclusion: "Towns disappear," Pelli says.

Towns disappear! Move over, Godzilla and H.G. Wells. Consider the sadly named town of Aurora, Illinois, for example—first crippled when business moved out to a strip center, then done in by Fox Valley mall. The same has happened in California, Minnesota, Pennsylvania . . . everywhere. Who needs a Martian heat ray?

Malls use up more than 2 billion square feet of retail space; they employ over 4.5 million people. They also pay millions of dollars in state and local real estate taxes and generate an estimated $8.3 billion in sales taxes. So it is no wonder they dominate the space that surrounds them. In jobs alone they exert power—at times DeBartolo's Randall Park employs as many as 5,000 people, which is far more than the population of the nearest community. Malls have quietly entered—and quietly transformed—many communities, but they have also blundered and smashed their way into enough places that even Albert Sussman admits that "some centers have abused the landscape, created eyesores, have produced chaotic traffic conditions and even disrupted local community life."

Several years after Marcia had graduated from Walter Johnson School, and moved to Washington, D.C., leaving Montgomery Mall behind with her high school memories, another mall began moving in on her old neighborhood. But this time it appeared virtually in her parents' backyard—in a quiet residential community which had always protected itself against commercial development.

From the mall developers' first overtures, Marcia's parents and their neighbors in Garrett Park Estates were ambivalent. "People started thinking how it wouldn't be so bad," recalls Chester Flather, the community's representative on the local council. "They liked the idea of having a nice Bloomie's and Lord & Taylor out here and maybe a few more shops—25 or 30. The housewives thought they could work there part-time."

But they were also concerned about pollution and traffic patterns. According to Flather, to soothe them, the Lerner Corporation, Washington's dominant mall developer, made certain promises. Don't oppose us, the company said, in effect, and we'll put it all in writing. And so the Garrett Park Association voted to let the mall in by a margin of two-to-one.

Now, White Flint is a massive reality. Beyond the street where Marcia grew up there is a slight rise and a row of trees. Beyond that, there used to be a golf course. Now there is a white colossus—bigger than any of Garrett Park's residents had ever imagined—the largest shopping mall in the Washington area. More trees were cut down than anyone had expected. The traffic became tremendous. "They lied to us," says Chester Flather.

Some of Garrett Park's residents got mad. Formerly sheltered from the highway culture by woods, distance and money, they now had huge lights glaring down on them at night. There were complaints that covenants Lerner had signed promising landscaping and pedestrian walkways weren't honored. The county government briefly withdrew permits for completion of the mall's interior. There was talk of a boycott. "It really bothers me," Marcia's father says, "that a big corporation can come in here and do as they please."

But the anger was—and still is—mixed with ambivalence. White Flint was not only a *fait accompli*—as Flather talked quietly about closing it down before last Christmas, he acknowledged that his daughter was working there—it soon worked its powerful magnetism even on its critics. It is, after all, one of the poshest, most progressive malls in the Washington area—the first in the country to offer a single credit card good in all its shops. "When I used to tell people I lived off White Flint Road," Marcia recalls, "they'd say *where*? Now White Flint is *it*." "Having the mall is not all bad," Marcia's father admits. "If you live in the suburbs and don't relate to downtown, you have nothing to miss and everything to gain. Out here we had no public space before the mall . . . We never thought of Bethesda as 'our town.'"

What then does White Flint represent in Marcia's world? Malls like to think of themselves as contemporary analogues of the old public markets, but there is a crucial difference. Those markets were really *public*: administered by public agencies for one and all. A more striking analogy from history presents itself, another institution that the malls physically resemble: stone fortresses surrounded by great moats of concrete—aloof, inviting, separate and powerful, but fulfilling the needs of their time better than anything else around . . . Malls are the feudal castles of contemporary America.

There are striking similarities. Castles became internally elaborate, eventually including storehouses, lodgings, chapels and the lord's court. So have malls, and the medieval impression is especially strong at a multi-use mall like Del Amo near Torrance, California, with its numerous structures and defensible perimeters. Individual castles became so powerful and well-known that civil rulers often substituted the name of their principal castle for that of the county. A township in New Jersey likewise changed its name to that of its most prominent shopping center. Castles furnished protection against the environment—wolf packs, thieves and other hazards of the medieval landscape—as much as against armies. Malls also are havens from the outer chaos: the fumes, the noise, the craziness and the cars. . . .

Feudal castles ruled a fragmented landscape and dominated public life. The lords were lord of more than their castles, as are the mall developers and managers today. In his "LA.: In Search of a City" series for *West*, journalist Michael Fessier concluded that the manager of Topanga Plaza was more a mayor than the one Los Angeles elected. Certainly Harry Overly, manager of Greengate Mall and an executive of its parent company, Rouse, is more a lord of central Westmoreland than the major of the county seat, whose part-time salary wouldn't pay for Harry's brogues. At Christmas time, people drive out to Harry's estate to see its fabulous decorations—every corner of the house, all the fences surrounding his land, every branch on the trees in front is outlined with white lights. A Santa and three elvettes in green tights dispense candy to the kids in the cars. The Santa charade is a benefit for Children's Hospital (the elves accept donations), but the whole scene suggests the peasants at the lord's gate on the big holiday.

The analogy can be extended, but actually the malls do the castles one better. Castles sometimes had to compete for dominance with monasteries, but malls have done with religion what they do best—absorbed it.

Many malls have chapels where marriages have been performed. One of the most activist and close-knit Catholic parishes in Chicago is headquartered in the Ford City shopping center. Monroeville Mall has a counseling kiosk, the Talk Shop, where spiritual information is provided along with mall directions. Monroeville also features the John XXIII Chapel (next door to Funland and the Luv Pub) where mass is celebrated daily.

The church groups involved typically deny any special relationship with the mall itself—they claim the facilities are simply the most convenient for their flock. That's also what they said at the services Barbara and I attended in a basement community room of the Rosedale Mall in Minneapolis. The setting was ascetic—bare concrete walls and folding chairs—and the services were unpretentious: for the adults, a modest sermon/discussion on developing inner values led by a young divinity student, and for the kids, Bible school. All of it ended at noon, which is when the mall opens for business on Sunday.

We went upstairs; the mall was already well populated. As we walked among the shoppers, browsers and wanderers, we recognized some of our fellow celebrants from the basement. They mixed right in with the main show now, the crowded mall on Sunday afternoon. Some of them still carried their Bibles, and they were still smiling.

PART 4 WHERE NO MALL HAS GONE BEFORE

On low-clouded nights in Greensburg, Pennsylvania, there are two immense glowing spots in the sky: The one to the west, which is always orange, hovers over Greengate Mall; the one to the east, which for some reason is always white, is the aureole of Westmoreland Mall. These are the signatures written across the night deciding Greensburg's future. They are the culmination of the Highway Comfort Culture's sacking of the city, the drawing out of its middle-class traffic, the abandonment of downtown to those who work in the county courthouse and to motorless old people and students. The city has been slow to adapt to the changes, immersed in the lethargy and squabbling that is sometimes known as the political process. Town governments and merchant associations simply can't function or respond as efficiently as the mall's single management. The town isn't a controllable unit; a lot of people in it are too independent to be controlled anyway. So a large part of what has happened to the culture in the last decade has happened out on the highway: The circus is no longer in town.

Greensburg is not one of those towns that has disappeared, but it has changed since I first left it to go away to college, some 14 years ago. A town of less than 20,000, it was settled before the American Revolution and named after General Nathaniel Greene in 1799. Though Greensburg has gone through many changes in its long history, the most portentous of recent years were on display just before Christmas of 1977.

At Westmoreland Mall in early December, flamenco Muzak was playing as people lined up at Orange Julius and at the glass elevator which goes from one floor to the other. The *Star Wars* soundtrack, animating teenagers in Camelot Music, also surrounded their older siblings knotted in makeshift reunions with dimly recalled high school classmates home for the holidays. The serious shoppers—heart-breaking young women with modified Dorothy Hamill hair-cuts, their frankly svelte figures in pullover split-neck tops and black polyester knit flared pants, each dragging three blond kids and a double-knit-sloppo husband who looked like he'd been drinking beer in a laundromat for 20 years—were spinning through aisles of genuine walnut jewelry boxes with sardonyx Incolay stone tops, Infinity Model Qa speakers with optional pedes-tals, TV Action News Team dolls, imitation Christian Dior velours, anti-cling crepeset lounging pajamas, wrap-tie shawl cardigans, electric crock pots, hand-some wall dividers, multi-option video games . . . While old men sat on benches in the nonshade of the non-palm trees.

And at Greengate Mall on the other end of town, it was much the same—high school girls in tight jeans and cheerleader jackets, a scholarly young man in glasses and V-neck sweater, a couple kissing, a salesman in a cheap snug suit. . . . Movement everywhere, except on the escalators, where people were packed motionless in their cowhide leather coats and Dacron polyester fiberfill arctic-Apollo moon-ski jackets, a tableau suggesting a conveyor belt in a wax museum. Traffic was backed up on the highway.

As always, there were Christmas celebrations in Greensburg, but things were not so merry and bright. A small dispirited parade moved past the ghosts of Christmases past—by the La Rose Shop, holding its going-out-of-business sale after 55 years (appropriately, its two mall branches will remain open—its sale banner said, "The Future Decided"); by the remains of the Bon Ton, a once mighty department store whose facade literally crumbled into the street last spring; and by Troutman's, the biggest store left in town, which will keep its old and long since paid for building here, but will open its new larger store at Westmoreland Mall. The streets are a little less lonely than usual, but not by much. After nightfall, when the malls and the highways are still teeming, these streets are dead.

There is little about this that is strange to the kids who have grown up in Greensburg since I left. Greengate has been around for 13 years, after all—long enough to be simply "the mall" to most people; long enough even for the birds, scarce in the Pennsylvania winter, to nest in its warm places outside. Westmore-land Mall, being brand new, is still somewhat controversial (some people think its terrazzo tile is too hard to walk on), but it, too, is rapidly becoming part of everyday life.

Just how completely malls have been woven into the social fabric became suddenly clear to me when I met Carol at the Boardwalk, the electronic arcade of the Greengate Mall where she dispenses change and keeps order among the kids playing air hockey and Death Race. Over the ringing of pinball and the bleeps of Break Out, Carol told me about herself. She was a runaway at 17, hitching to the West Coast where she "got high a lot and learned more about life in three months than I would have in 20 years in Greensburg." After bum-ming around East Coast beaches, trying school and a number of dead-end jobs and finding Jesus, she wound up here: at the Boardwalk. . . . It was a usual enough story, full of the rites of passage quickly standardized since the sixties, and we were able to compare impressions of places we'd both been and what it was like to be back in our hometown. But there was one big difference in Carol's story: malls. Dozens of them that she remembered, all over the country. She had spent alot of time in them—getting out of the heat and the cold, wandering around when she was broke or just felt like hanging out, eating an ice cream cone and watching.

That wasn't at all strange to her, but it was still strange to me. I was back in Greensburg to write a novel in inexpensive isolation, and I found myself wondering what had happened to the town I grew up in. Greensburg was never an idyllic place to be young—in many ways it was a classically crushing small town environment. The malls have brought certain obvious advantages. In some ways they are more stimulating, and certainly more comfortable. Their nature as fantasylands is peculiarly suited to childhood and adolescence. I tried to imagine what it would be like to grow up in one. The new things the mall provided were clear enough—the protected space, the fountains to groove on, the railings to lean on, the record stores, the pizza shops, the electronic game rooms. But what was missing in the malls that was present in my childhood?

For one thing: the weather. That's what I remember most about growing up mall-less in Greensburg. . . . Like many adolescents, I was a helpless devotee of the "pathetic fallacy," which in literature is a universally condemned device for using the weather to mirror states of mind. But I was applying it to life: playing off my moods against the wind and rain and sunshine, the contours of clouds and the colors of the sky. Weather changed, and it was worth watching. The gradations of weather taught me something about the gradations and complexity of emotion.

In fact, in spite of daycare centers and the Mickey Mouse promotional gimmicks, hermetically sealed mall environments aren't meant for children. They are never-never land for consumers; playpens for adults . . . So where do the children play? At Fashion Island, on the DNA-chain red-and-blue slide in the courtyard by the quaint and useless footbridge over nothing? Near one of those inexplicable mall icons, like the circular purple rug about four feet in diameter surrounded by eight globe lights on tall black stands at Del Amo Fashion Center?

Prefabricated, highly defined space with separated functions is not the same as the organic chaos of a city or town, let alone the natural landscape, even if it's made to look like all of that. And in this sense, the mall is characteristic of the environment many of these kids now inhabit. Growing up, moving from home to school to the mall—from enclosure to enclosure, transported in cars— is a curiously continuous process, without much in the way of contrast or contact with unenclosed and unplanned reality. Places must tend to blur into one another. The mall is just an extension, say, of school—only there's Karmelkorn instead of chem lab, the ice rink instead of gym . . . high school without the impertinence of classes.

But they are at play in the fields of this world and they learn it—they adapt to it and make it adapt somehow to them. It's here that these kids get their street sense—only it's mall sense. They're learning the ways of a large-scale artificial environment: its subtleties and flexibilities, its particular pleasures and resonances, and the attitudes it fosters. Whatever differences and dangers there are in this, these skills may turn out to be very useful after all.

For out of necessity and because we're intrigued with the notion, we are moving inexorably into an age of preplanned and regulated environments. Ironically, we're doing it largely because of ecological concerns: We have to manage our resources of energy, space and life-support. Small steps have already been taken with planned communities; significantly, two of the more successful (Columbia, Maryland and the Irvine Plan in California) are the product of major mall developers (the Rouse and Irvine companies respectively), with malls as their physical and social focal points. Even Arcosanti, the city of the future designed by visionary architect Paolo Soleri, is an extension of the mall concept, as Soleri himself admitted in a television interview when Dick Cavett commented that his plan sounded like living in a shopping center.

The ultimate artificial environment would be totally enclosed, planned, controlled and self-contained—so completely independent that it could exist anywhere. And that ultimate enclosure—in effect, the ultimate mall—has already been conceptualized . . . for outer space.

Astrophysicist Gerald O'Neill and a NASA-sponsored team have designed a self-sustaining artificial space environment for 10,000 people called Island One. A mile in circumference, with landscaped grounds, growing plants, climate control and a profit motive—collecting solar power to be sold back to an energy-starved and overcrowded earth—the first one could be launched by the 1990s if the public and investors (like the Saudis, who are interested) can be convinced that it's worthwhile and feasible. *Feasible*—are you kidding? Century City in space, Southdale of the stars? The cosmic Irvine Plan, Del Amo of the heavens? Welcome to the mallenium: Fashion Island as Island One.

The fantasy is clearly out there at the malls already—all you have to do is check out the blinking sanctums of the Boardwalk at Greengate, or Funland at Monroeville, Piccadilly Circus at Southdale, Le Mans Speedway at Del Amo, Sega Center at Fox Hills . . . any of these places with the panels of lights in the dark, the starry fantasy depths where stoned young minds burn on and occasionally nova. Adolescent denizens can remain hour after hour in that world of inescapable electronic panels right out of *Star Trek*. As they zip out now and then for a cheese stick and Orange Crush, cruising the continuous corridors past the TV screens in the store windows and all the merchandise functioning perfectly—it's obvious that it's all here already: food, clothing, entertainment, information, people; even work. . . . A limited spectrum of events that satisfies basic sensory needs combining in cybernetic excitement, in a safe enclosed area with room to walk around. It's so logical. It's like this . . . starship. "These enterprises do not require outdoor settings," as Huxtable points out. They don't really have to be attached to the earth at all. Give them warp drive and a five-year mission. . . .

The afternoon I talked with Carol in the greenish glow of Pong panels, amidst the truncated high-pitched screams of computer dive bombing, I was completely floored by an innocent question. "What's your *favorite* mall?" she asked. I guess to her, the question was as normal as asking my favorite rock star. If I had been able to answer, we might have gone on to discuss the relative merits of Casa Linda Plaza vs. Snug Harbor Square, just as if we were comparing Linda Ronstadt's version of "Down So Low" to Tracy Nelson's. But the question astonished me. What could it mean—a "favorite" mall? What distinctions could be made? Wasn't it like asking which was my favorite Holiday Inn?

Well, some people probably have a favorite Holiday Inn. And after experiencing some 30 shopping malls in various parts of the country in a six-week period, I could go back and answer—yes, Carol, I have some favorite malls. . . .

I liked Fox Hills in Culver City near Los Angeles on a weekday afternoon when the school kids waiting for buses did their homework on the huge orange tinker-toy tower that connects the two-and-a-half bright and clean-lined levels. In Chicago I liked going to Water Tower Place just for croissants in The Courtyard, and in Boston I enjoyed the amazing salads at Faneuil Hall and the walk along the Waterfront Park. But there is much about malls that remains inexplicable and bizarre. Though I became fairly comfortable and even admiring, I still walk through them feeling like the surrealist painter Giorgio de Chirico who devoted his life to the "interrogation of enigmas." They don't provide many easy answers. Just many, many questions.

Have malls lived up to their potential? Cesar Pelli is among those architects who have designed them who don't think so. "There are no interstices in a mall, nothing to separate one store from another, or one mall from another," Pelli says. "The stores are the same in Detroit or Houston . . . Developers learned they could get away with a minimum of relationship to the community and still attract thousands. . . . They are much, much less than we hoped."

Maybe we ought to be glad that malls haven't realized their full power, especially considering their virtuosity in projecting convincing images. As it is they're somewhere between a potential form of living Newspeak and an ultimate P.T. Barnum wet dream. Come hard times in the economy, malls are perfectly capable of telling us we're really having good times. They might turn themselves into Great Depression theme centers and Ghost Town Amusement Malls—see the tumbleweed blowing through the central court! Feel real rain piped in through special-event holes in the roof! And don't forget the *gruel du jour* at the Bread Line, right here at Tent City Esplanade!

Then, of course, there are the inescapable and chilling similarities between malls and the various enclosed and regimented societies in fiction and film, from *Brave New World* to *THX 1138*, in which the computer priest chants an appropriate shopping center benediction: "Buy more, buy more and be happy!"

But maybe it's just nostalgia for places that have more distinguishing and inspiring characteristics than the relative number of shoe stores. Our lives and literature once centered on a sense of place. But can you imagine William Faulkner writing about the Yoknapatawpha Mall? And what would Ernest Hemingway make of a mall? Would he cherish the local cola? Organize friends to yearly attend Disney at the Dales?

It's hard to accept something like the *Montevideo American News*, a rural newspaper now in its 100th year, carrying under its banner the proud proclamation, "Published in West Central Minnesota's Finest Shopping Center." But there it is, anyway: The malling of America is well underway. With malls like Water Tower Place in Chicago where it's possible to work, eat, drink, sleep, see movies and plays, make love and buy just about anything without ever going out into the Windy City, it becomes clear that the mall concept has come of age and the sky isn't even the limit. Now there remains but one step to sufficiently fix the idea of this "great machine" in the American mythos: a mall movie.

There have been several movies shot in and around malls, including the aforementioned ghoul thriller, *Dawn of the Dead*, from George Romero. (Interestingly, the producer of *Dawn*, Richard Rubinstein, says that the bomb survivors do not fare well in their mall: "Since everything is there, they think they are safe, but it isn't true. They make mistakes because they are so overwhelmed by this vast array of consumer goods.") And there have been plenty of sci-fi movie sets that have looked like malls, and vice versa: Woodfield and Fox Valley are right out of Fritz Lang's *Metropolis*; Water Tower Place is a dead ringer for the future city in *Things to Come* . . . And of course more and more movies are being *seen* in malls, fantasies within fantasies: Several of the biggest theater chains, including General Cinema and Cinemette, are dropping most of their pre-fab screening boxes into shopping centers.

But a movie *about* malls? Why hasn't anyone thought of this before? If they'd just look, they could clearly see—*Mall '78!*: Flamboyant self-made entrepreneur Byron Lord, manager of Esplanade Square Bigdale Mall, is under pressure from the ambitious streamlined on-site development rep, a Mall lifer who has never worked outside climate control. Lord's affair with the chic and worldly manager of Casual Corner is getting tempestuous when—crisis! The sprinkler system was shut down following the dousing of a minor fire (and a quarrelsome county supervisor who got in the way), but another fire erupts, threatening the first floor all the way from Broadway department store past Just Jeans to the Piercing Pagoda. Meanwhile the parking lot is heating up as a suburban motorcycle gang, the Mall Marauders, is mixing it up with a band of Hare Krishnas who've been refused permission to jingle their bells inside. Security is diverted from monitoring middle school truants and observing car thieves to these two scenes, except for young rookie Mick O'Bannion who is delivering a baby on the terrazzo tile in front of Karmelkorn. Of course all this distraction pleases glassy-eyed Dan the Dealer as he peddles his dilithium crystals near the fountain across from Tennis Lady. *But*—dope-crazed Jessica is threatening to throw herself from the second level to the central court Recreational Vehicle display because her mother (currently shopping at Big Woman) doesn't understand her, and her stoned friends are too busy riding the glass elevators to care—except Rodger, who's come to the Mall every day on the pretext of playing air hockey just to see Jessie—he's in the elevator, he looks up, horrified—Jessica's perched outside the sheeny railing, outlined against the bright lights of the National Record Mart. . . .

Social Life
in a
Working-Class
Tavern

E. E. LEMASTERS

© Bobbie Kingsley/Photo Researchers

Clarke's Tavern, New York City

IN THE FOLLOWING SELECTION, E. E. LeMasters argues that a particular neighborhood tavern is the center of social life for a group of skilled craftsmen, or blue-collar aristocrats, as he calls them. It is, for them, equivalent to a country club. At the tavern, they play cards, shuffleboard, and eight-ball; they engage in complicated practical jokes, have parties, sing, and dance. They also coordinate activities that take place outside the tavern; they arrange bowling teams and they share ownership of a boat. They plan their next hunting trip or look back nostalgically on the last fishing expedition.

The contemporary tavern seems to be an evolution of the working-class saloon of the nineteenth century. But it actually serves a much narrower function. The tavern does not play political or economic roles, as with the "poor man's club," "multifunctional frontier saloon," or "colonial coffeehouse," but rather, it serves only a social purpose. Although LeMasters does not explain this shift in purpose, it clearly seems related to the argument made earlier by Philippe Aries in "The Family and the City." Public life has declined in modern cities, and Americans have come to rely more on their families. The tavern, therefore, has become almost an extension of the family, in which regular patrons have created their own private world.

THIS PAPER DESCRIBES those aspects of the social life of blue-collar workers which center in and about a tavern. As we shall see, for many of these men, the tavern is the locus, the focal point, for a major share of their leisure activities. As such, it takes on an importance far beyond that implied by its overt function of selling drinks. There is, of course, no claim here either to typicality or representativeness. What is described is merely one particular tavern with one particular clientele. On the other hand, there is no reason to believe that the Oasis is atypical. One suspects that there are many such taverns, serving similar functions for similar groups of patrons, dotting the contemporary landscape. . . .

I shall begin by describing briefly some salient characteristics of the tavern and its customers, go on to outline the various tavern activities, and end with a few comments on the place and importance of establishments such as the Oasis in the modern world.

THE TAVERN AND ITS CUSTOMERS

The Oasis is a working-class tavern located in a former rural village in Wisconsin which is in the process of becoming a suburb. While the tavern is conveniently situated for transient trade, it relies primarily on a regular and, in some cases, long-time clientele for the bulk of its business. Physically, it is rather unprepossessing, occupying the exposed basement of an old two-story building which dates back to the late 1800s. On one side, it is partially hidden by the more elegant Tuxedo, a bar and dining club. On the other side, it adjoins a cemetery.

As one enters the Oasis, one encounters a horseshoe-shaped bar which seats about thirty customers. To the left, in the corner, is a jukebox. A color television set is perched on a platform in the opposite corner, visible from all the seats at the bar. A small kitchen opens off the corner by the television set and is used for making sandwiches and heating soup, the only foods served. Near the bar, opposite the entrance, is the women's room. Also to the right from the entrance is a beer cooler from which customers help themselves to take-home cartons or cases. Farther to the right is a three-quarter-size pool table operated by a coin slot, and across the room from it is a long shuffleboard. Beyond the pool table and the shuffleboard, to the right of the entrance, is the men's room. Its location, so far from the bar, has been the source of many complaints:

> Goddamnit, Harry, why in the hell did you put the lady's room so close to the bar and the men's room so far? You know the women don't have to go as often as we do!

SOCIAL LIFE IN A WORKING-CLASS TAVERN   By E. E. LeMasters. From *Urban Life and Culture*, Vol. 2, no. 1 (April, 1973): 27–52. Copyright © 1973 by Sage Publications, Inc. Reprinted by permission of Sage Publications, Inc.

I did it on purpose. You guys are getting fat and need the exercise.

Scattered about between the bar, the pool table and the shuffleboard are small tables used for eating, drinking, and playing cards. In a far corner, near the men's room, is a coin telephone, placed there to assure privacy. Here and there, space can be found for dancing, although this is not easy when the bar is crowded.

The Oasis is not a neighborhood tavern. Its customers arrive by car, some of them from several miles away. And while middle-class types are not totally absent from the scene, the overwhelming majority of the regular customers are blue-collar workers and their wives. More specifically, the Oasis is dominated by skilled craftsmen—carpenters, plumbers, plasterers, painters, sheet metal-workers, welders, and a few truck drivers. In short, it is dominated by men who are at the top of the working-class world; by men who are, in a sense, "blue-collar aristocrats."

TAVERN SOCIAL LIFE

For most of the blue-collar aristocrats encountered at the Oasis, the center of life is not the job, but the leisure activities made possible by the job. With a forty-hour week, good wages, and the ability to forget about work when the tools are laid down for the evening, these men are in a position to enjoy their leisure time activities—and most of them do. Having little faith in the next world, viewing this one as "one hell of a mess," and being essentially anti-reformist in outlook, Oasis customers seem determined to get as much enjoyment as they can from their lives. As one of them often remarks, "You only get one throw of the dice in the game of life and you better not crap out." In their pursuit of life's joys, they like to be . . . "where the action is." . . . And, by and large, for many of them, the "action" is at the Oasis.

For those who are its regulars, the Oasis functions much as a country club does for middle- or upper-class persons: it is the center of social life, the major locus for leisure activities. The tavern draws into itself not only the male workers who form the core of this clientele, but their wives and families as well. It is a public drinking place which has become, in many regards, a private club.

Several conditions seem to have facilitated the Oasis' centrality in the leisure lives of its customers.

1. Long-term, continuous operation by an owner who is well liked. Harry owned and personally managed the tavern for over two decades (he sold it in 1969). Unless he were ill, customers could expect to see him whenever they stopped in. Except that he drank no alcohol while tending bar, Harry generally entered into the fun, and among the inner circle of steady patrons, he was considered a member of the group. Of the Oasis, Harry frequently remarked, "This tavern is my home. I spend most of my time here. Have a good time, but remember, you are in my house."

2. Occupational or social-class homogeneity among the clientele. As noted above, most of the customers were skilled construction workers. With similar incomes, occupational hazards, educational levels, and economic conditions, the men and their families had much in common. Even granting the individual variation in personal joys and tragedies, the customers of the Oasis, to a considerable degree, faced the same world.

3. Stable residential patterns. While the particular community in which the Oasis was located was, during the period of study, facing a mass invasion of white-collar families, the blue-collar residents who frequented the tavern had, for the most part, lived in the area for twenty to thirty years. Many had been coming to the tavern for ten to fifteen years, some even longer, and Harry knew the parents of some of his younger customers.

In short, stability and homogeneity combined to create of a tavern something that is more than a tavern.

Let us now look more closely at the rich range of activities which center in and about the Oasis.

RECREATION

BOWLING

During the period of this study, the owner of the Oasis sponsored two bowling teams—a men's and a women's—which competed in local leagues. The teams would often meet at the tavern for a drink before going bowling, and they usually returned to the Oasis for a few beers afterwards. If a team had a good score on a particular night, the first round of drinks would be "on the house." At the end of the bowling season, each team had a banquet financed from a "kitty" built up during the season. The women's team usually competed in a state tournament at the end of the regular season, while the men were more likely to enter tournaments in the local area.

For the team members, bowling provided a great deal of amusement. Other tavern regulars would sometimes go to the bowling establishment to root for the team—and bowling scores were often an item of conversation at the tavern.

> You should have seen old Mel knocking over the pins last night. He had just enough beer in him to see a little crooked and that did the trick. He couldn't miss.

SHUFFLEBOARD

Until 1969, when the Oasis was sold and the new owners removed the game, shuffleboard was played in the tavern itself and provided an opportunity for intersex recreation—the men playing as partners against the women or the couples splitting up so that a wife shot against her husband with the other man as partner. (Since they generally do not shoot pool, the women customers, in particular, miss the shuffleboard game, and its removal has been a source of complaint against the new owners.)

The games were usually played for a small wager—the losers had to buy a drink and put money in the machine for the next game. Some of the skilled male players liked to shoot for a dollar a game, and I have seen a few games played for five dollars a game. .

Some of the players were quite skillful and, at one time,. . . the tavern sponsored a shuffleboard team that competed in a local tavern league. A story still circulates about a tavern proprietor who bet $100 that his shuffleboard team could beat the Oasis. A match was arranged, and the Oasis team walloped the other group.

CARD PLAYING

There is usually a card game in progress at the Oasis. In earlier days, one night a week was set aside for a euchre tournament for married couples, but this era was about over when the study began. Some of the men play cribbage, and sheepshead is also very popular. Card games are always played for some wager; no one seems to play just for enjoyment.

BOATING

Several of the men at the Oasis have a partnership in a pontoon boat. During the winter, the boat is stored in the lot at the rear of the tavern, and a great deal of beer is consumed while the men prepare either to put the boat in the water early in the summer or to get it out of the water before the nearby lake freezes over.

"Mel," Bart will say, "this week we *have* to get that damn boat in the water. My wife is raising hell about it—she wants to use the boat for a birthday party for one of the kids."

"Hell," Mel will reply, "we would have got the damn boat in last Saturday if you hadn't started drinking boiler-makers. I can't put the damn thing in myself."

It is claimed that one year the boat did not get into the lake until the Fourth of July—and some stories report that one year it had to be chopped out of the lake ice sometime in December.

Most of the men at the Oasis own power boats and boating (with fishing) is a major activity during the summer months. (There is a large lake five minutes from the tavern and several others only a short drive away.)

HORSESHOES

In the lot at the rear of the Oasis, there is a place for pitching horseshoes. Periodically, some of the men take a six-pack of beer outside and determine who is the champion horseshoe pitcher. As usual, bets are placed on the outcome.

GAMBLING

Among the men at the Oasis, gambling is a constant activity. . . . They will place a wager on almost any event that has an uncertain outcome—football games, baseball games, horse races, games of pool or shuffleboard, even the outcome of a courtship.

When special sporting events occur, such as the Super Bowl, relatively large sums of money are involved. In 1969, for example, when the New York Jets defeated the Baltimore Colts for the world championship, several hundred dollars changed hands. An automobile mechanic won $150 on this event, and several other customers won or lost $50 to $75. For more routine sporting events—weekly football games, for example—"pools" are frequently formed, but these involve more modest sums; $1 in the pot being the usual price to "buy in."

Pocket billiards or pool is very popular at the Oasis and bets—ranging from $.15 glasses of beer to $5—are invariably placed on the outcome. In fact, most of the men appear not to enjoy shooting pool unless there is a bet riding on the outcome, and for some families such gambling activity is surely a financial liability. For example, I once observed an unemployed truck driver lose $45 of his $60 weekly unemployment compensation shooting pool (eight ball) with a hustler who strayed into the tavern and found a "pigeon."

While it is clear from the above descriptions that anti–gambling legislation has not eliminated the activity in the Oasis, given the propensity to gamble that is so obvious among the customers, it is also clear that the state of Wisconsin has been surprisingly effective in limiting the amount and the nature of the gambling that does go on. There are, for example, no slot machines or punch boards at the Oasis. Prior to the period of this study (1963–1969), tickets on "pools" organized by an underground gambling syndicate had been sold in the tavern, but when the "local representative" was arrested, this practice ceased and did not recur. The in-house pools are tolerated by the Wisconsin liquor commission, since there is no "take" for the house (if the proprietor wants into the pool, he has to put his money in, as the customers do), and because professional or organized gambling interests continue to be uninvolved. While some of the customers do place bets on horse races through "bookies," these transactions do not occur on the premises.

Yet, however limited its amount and nature, gambling is a persistent facet of tavern social life. It might be appropriate at this time to consider why this might be so. To ask, that is, what functions gambling might perform in the lives of Oasis patrons.

Perhaps most obviously, gambling increases *the action*. As one crane operator observed: "A little bet on the total score can make even a lousy baseball game interesting." There is also an element of skill involved in many forms of gambling, and most humans find enjoyment in the exercise of skill.

Status in the group is a factor: a man who wins more than his share is viewed either as a "lucky dog" or a "sharp cookie." Both terms are positive in determining social status in the tavern. . . .

Finally, to a considerable extent, it seems to me, gambling for these men is a defense against boredom. . . . As "action lovers," their primary goal in this world is to avoid a dull life—this can be seen in their frequent references to various life activities (such as marriage) as a "helluva drag." Actually, these blue-collar aristocrats are similar to other aristocrats in their fight against boredom: they have gone to the top of their social world and need not expend time or energy in "social climbing." This means that most of them have the time (and the money) to indulge themselves in various activities (such as gambling) which enhance their lives.

The men do not view gambling at the Oasis as a form of social deviation. They believe, rather, that gambling reflects a deep need of the human spirit, and, as such, should be legal, supervised, and taxed by the state.

HUNTING AND FISHING

Most of the men at the Oasis love to hunt and fish. Before the opening of deer season in the fall, for example, the air is full of stories about guns—new guns, old guns, and "gun swaps."

> I've had that old sonofabitch since 1932 and she shoots as true today as she ever did. I wouldn't sell that bastard for a hundred dollars.

> This guy down at the shop sold me this Remington for forty bucks—said he couldn't hit anything with it. I took it out to the Gun Club and bore sighted

it and she shoots perfect. The dumb bastard never had the sight aligned properly.

My father used this gun and never missed a buck and by God so far I haven't missed one with it either. [The speaker knocked on wood at this point so as not to spoil his luck.]

When the season actually opens, there is a mass exodus of customers from the Oasis as the hunters "head north." For the next week or ten days, the tavern is almost deserted. Then the hunters return and begin to spin their yarns as to how "I got my buck" or—in the sadder cases—how "I missed my buck."

To the men of the Oasis, the deer season (and its accompanying "talk") is the climax of the annual hunting and fishing cycle. To portray this year-long cycle, which plays such an important part in Oasis social life, let us follow one typical man. He may hunt and fish more than the average tavern customer, but he is quite representative of the general attitude toward hunting and fishing that prevails at the Oasis.

Bill is a policeman in the nearby metropolitan community. His occupation influences his hunting in two ways: (1) he is expected to be skilled in the use of firearms, and (2) he can accumulate "time off" and get away from the job whenever the various seasons open.

In the spring, Bill waits for the opening of the trout season. He has several favorite spots not more than an hour's drive from the tavern, and he fishes these streams methodically. If he catches too many trout for immediate consumption, they either go into the family freezer or are given to friends and neighbors.

During the summer, Bill fishes several lakes in the area—one of them less than a mile from his house. From these lakes, he usually takes "pan fish"— perch, bluegills, and so forth.

But fall is the time of year that Bill loves best: rabbits and squirrels, the pheasant season, and then the exciting influx of Canadian geese—the hunter's dream. In the fall, Bill lives in a sort of fantasy world.

Took a drive up toward Spring Green yesterday. Saw a beautiful male pheasant strutting near the road. When the season opens next week, I'm gonna go back up there and we'll see what happens.

There is no doubt but that he has carefully marked the spot and will be back there on opening day.

"Did you get your Canadian geese tag?" I asked him one day. "You're darn right. I had my check in the mail the first day they were for sale. I wouldn't miss that for anything."

Later, he brought a goose he had shot into the tavern. I asked him if he felt any reluctance or guilt about killing the bird.

No. The hunting up there is carefully supervised. There are game wardens all over the place. I wouldn't want any part of it if the birds were being massacred or slaughtered—but this is not the case.

As noted above, deer season is for Bill and for most of the men at the Oasis the climax of the year. Bill takes a week off for the deer season and for the last several years has not failed to bag a buck.

He always hunts at the same place with the same group of men, and the annual pilgrimage "up north" never varies. Bill and his hunting companions leave their homes the day before the season opens and arrive at the farm house that night. They have a few beers, eat a good meal, and then hold their annual "reunion," reliving the hunts of previous years. (Some deer hunters live in various parts of the state and see each other only at the annual hunt.) The next day, everyone is up for the opening of the season at daybreak. One year Bill got his buck fifteen minutes after the season opened.

> Well, it was the damndest thing you ever heard of. Two years ago I saw a buck at this same spot but he took off before I could get a shot at him. So this year, I said to myself—do you suppose by any chance that sucker might come back there again? Anyhow, I found that spot again and had just decided to open my thermos bottle and have a cup of coffee when I looked up and there was this big buck staring right at me, not over fifteen yards away.

> I took one quick look through the sight and hit him right between the eyes. He fell over and hardly took one step. It was the damndest thing that's ever happened to me in all the years I've been hunting.

On opening day, 200,000 or more deer hunters will be in the Wisconsin forests, and fatal shooting accidents are not rare. The men at the Oasis appreciate the chance they take but they feel the excitement of the hunt is worth it. As one man noted:

> Christ sake, everything worth doing in this world is dangerous—friend of mine fell off a bar stool and broke his back, but that's not going to stop me from having a drink when I feel like it.

> [At this point another man said:] Why don't they have seat belts on bar stools like they have in cars? Then your friend wouldn't have been hurt.

After deer season, six to eight weeks of wonderful story-telling may be heard at the Oasis—who got his buck, who did not, and all the details of how it happened. Sometimes a hunter ran into a bear, or perhaps even shot one, and stories about them are always exciting.

> I looked up and there was this big black bear looking down at me from the top of this rock. I was debating whether to shoot or get the hell out of there when somebody else shot and the bear took off. We never saw it again.

There are long conversations as to how deer meat should be cooked, whether bear meat is good to eat or not, and who makes the best venison sausage in the area.

When Bill gets home from the hunt he takes his deer to a small butcher shop in a nearby village and has most of the deer meat made into "summer sausage." He carefully preserves the antlers from his bucks and prepares them for mounting. The antlers are sand papered, varnished, and mounted on attractive wooden plaques which are displayed in various rooms of his home. Sometimes he has a metal plate prepared with the year of the hunt engraved on it.

With the coming of winter, Bill's hunting comes to an end for the year, but he does some ice fishing on the nearby lake "when the mood strikes me."

Bill's wife understands his love for the outdoors and would not think of interfering with his hunting and fishing excursions. She regards him as a good husband, believing that men can have hobbies far worse than his.

Persons who disapprove of hunting and fishing sometimes regard men like Bill as "ruthless killers" or "despoilers of nature." He does not have this image of himself but thinks of himself as a conservationist at heart: he believes in strict regulation of hunting and fishing and abides by the rules established. He wants to preserve the natural environment for future generations to enjoy as he has enjoyed it. In defense of deer hunting, Bill points out that, under modern game management practices, the deer herd in Wisconsin was larger in 1965 than it was in 1920. He sees no reason why fish and other wildlife cannot be protected and preserved by the same methods.

It is an error to think of Bill as merely liking to hunt and fish—he *loves* to hunt and fish. He is an outdoorsman who earns his living in a police patrol car but has never learned to like city life. He is the farm boy who still loves the land. There must be millions like him in America.

TAVERN HUMOR

A great deal of "joshing," bantering, or "kidding" goes on at the Oasis more or less continuously between certain individuals. Some of this exchange has an ethnic flavor. For example, Sully, an Irishman, will stick his head in the door and inquire, "Is it alright if an Irishman joins the dumb Swedes in here for a nip?" Then somebody will yell at the owner, "Harry! For God's sake, can't you do something to keep the trash out of here? Even a public tavern should maintain some standards." Sully will laugh, buy a round of drinks, and the joshing will continue.

In this type of exchange, it is important to have a good reply—otherwise you are being "put down" by your adversary. Here is an example:

> Sully walks into the tavern one Saturday morning with an artificial red poppy pinned on the front of his shirt—poppies that are sold annually by one of the veterans' organizations to raise funds. Mel leans over, looks at the poppy intently, and exclaims: "1964! You cheap sonofabitch!" [This was 1967.]

> Sully's expression never changed. "Mel," he said, "I sure as hell am glad to see that you can read—I was never sure before."

Notice that Sully did not take offense at the word "sonofabitch." Such epithets are acceptable when used by friends or as part of a humorous exchange. If a stranger called Sully a "sonofabitch," a fight would be the immediate result.

Certain members of the Oasis are the acknowledged leaders in the planning of "practical jokes" on members of the inner cirlce. Mel is one of these. There is a story that a few years ago a male customer was drinking beer at the Oasis and loudly lamenting the fact that he had to leave the comfort of the tavern and sow some grass seed around his new house. Mel suggested that the man have a few more beers with his old buddies and then they would help him seed his new lawn. According to the story, Mel bought several packs of vegetable seeds and these were put on the new lawn along with the grass seed. In a week or two the home owner was amazed to see turnips and other vegetables sprouting in his new lawn. Gradually he became aware that his old buddies had played a trick on him.

On another occasion, Mel arranged a "practical joke" on German George, a famous fixture at the Oasis, whose thick accent provides one of the pleasures of sitting at the bar. While George was tending bar (or making hamburgers in the kitchen), Mel arranged to have George's car pushed into a vacant garage at the rear of the tavern. When George left to go home, he searched the parking area but could not find his car. A volatile person, German George came back into the tavern, fuming. "Some goddamn sonofabitch stole my car! I kill that bastard if I find out who did it."

Mel suggested that George cool down, that surely none of the gentlemen at the Oasis would stoop so low as to steal George's car. "Gentleman, my ass!" George shouted. "I kill that bastard if I find him."

Mel said that perhaps George had forgotten the exact spot where he had parked the car, so all of the customers at the bar adjourned to the parking lot "to help George find his car." When the search failed to locate the car, Mel suggested that German George call the police and proceeded to look up the telephone number for him. George rushed to the pay phone at the rear of the barroom and dialed the number given him by Mel. By design, this was a "wrong number"; Mel had given George the number of the county morgue. George did not listen to find out who answered his call, but simply began shouting that "some bastard stole my car." At last it dawned on him that he was not talking to the police.

Mel now suggested that the tavern phone must be out of order and urged German George to go across the street to a public telephone and call the police. As soon as George left, Mel and the other men pushed George's car out of the garage and into the tavern parking lot.

In a few minutes the village police car pulled up at the tavern. George began exclaiming that "some bastard stole my car" and then all at once he saw the car in its usual spot in the parking lot. Mel explained to the policeman that a slight mixup had occurred, and the police car pulled out, with George muttering to himself. German George now laughs when the story of this incident is retold, but he did not think it was very funny the night it happened.

One day during the lunch hour some of the men at the Oasis tried to persuade German George that the Germans did not invent sauerkraut (a dish that George loves), but that the Irish had developed it. George became so excited he could hardly talk. "No, by God!" he yelled, "the goddamn Irish did not invent sauer-kraut—the Germans invent that dish!"

The other men then polled the people at the bar and it was agreed that, indeed, the Irish had been preparing sauerkraut for centuries and, presumably, had developed the dish. Nobody had ever heard about the Germans having invented sauerkraut. At this point German George was beside himself, he could not believe his ears. "Jesus Christ!" he said to me, "you are a professor, tell these dumb bastards who invented sauerkraut."

My reply was that this bit of knowledge was outside my field of specialty but that I had read somewhere that the Irish had learned how to make sauerkraut from the Romans when they invaded Ireland a long time ago.

German George was dumbfounded. "The Romans!" he shouted, "those dumb bastards don't know how to make sauerkraut even today! I went to Italy once and no place could you get good sauerkraut! Those wops are spaghetti eaters—that's all they know how to make."

Somebody at the bar suggested that the Romans might have lost the secret of making sauerkraut—just as the secret of making stained glass windows had been lost during the middle ages. "Bullshit!" German George snorted. "Once you know how to make sauerkraut you never forget—never!"

For months after this, the "joshing" about who developed sauerkraut was revived from time to time.

Many of the humorous anecdotes at the Oasis relate to the male-female struggle, especially involving a husband "tricking" his wife in some fashion. Here is an illustration.

A man who lives near the tavern sometimes had difficulty getting away from the house to join his buddies at the bar. He finally developed a system for the summer months that worked rather well: He would tell his wife he was going out to mow the lawn, fill the power mower with gasoline, start the mower and park it out of his wife's line of vision, with the motor running. He would then hustle over to the tavern [only a block away] for a few beers with his old buddies.

The scheme worked for several weeks until one Saturday when the mower ran out of gas. Hearing nothing, the wife went out into the lawn to investigate. Her husband, of course, was nowhere to be found.

Many of the regular customers at the tavern come from rural backgrounds, and some of their humor reflects this. One favorite story tells how an old farmer was driving his tractor up a hill with a manure spreader hitched behind the tractor. A stranger in a big car who could not pass on the hill because of the slow tractor began to blow his horn and shout at the old farmer to pull over. Without looking back or saying a word, the famer pulled the lever on the manure spreader and threw cow manure all over the big car behind him.

Other jokes or stories relate to automobiles, reflecting the prominent part that cars play in American life. For example:

It seems that a worker has bought a new Volkswagen and is bragging at the plant every day about the wonderful gasoline mileage he is getting. His fellow workers decide to sneak a gallon of gasoline into his car every day or so to inflate the gas mileage. The owner becomes more and more elated. "Sixty miles a gallon!" "That's better than they advertise."

One day the owner announces that he is taking the car into the dealer for a regular check-up and at this point his fellow workers cease adding gasoline to the tank. A few days later the owner is furious. "How do you like that! I was getting 60 miles to a gallon until I took the car into the dealer for a tune-up and now I'm only getting 40 miles to the gallon. What do you suppose those dumb bastards at the garage did to it?"

The men pretend to be puzzled and urge the owner to take the car back and complain to the dealer.

This story has no formal ending. The dealer and the owner are presumably still confused as to what happened.

PARTIES

In a very real sense, there is a "party" every weekend at the Oasis. The men begin drifting in after four on Friday to have a few beers. About six, they go home to change clothes and pick up their wives—for Friday night is "couples night" at the tavern. Wives who may not be seen at any other time will usually appear on Friday evening. About seven or eight, small groups leave to have dinner in a restaurant in the area, after which most of the couples return to drink, dance, play shuffleboard, shoot pool, or just talk. Drinking is heavier than during the week. On this night, even the moderate drinkers will often get "high," and the less temperate frequently end up with Saturday morning "hangovers." The heightened tempo continues through Saturday and Sunday, with the tavern returning to normal on Monday.

Many special events are celebrated at the Oasis. For example: a wife held a large "surprise" birthday party for her husband at the tavern; a widower and his new bride had an informal wedding reception there (the proprietor had introduced them); a large party was held for an old customer and his wife when they retired and were about to move to Indiana; a father gave a party at the tavern when his son returned safely from military duty in Vietnam; former neighbors who return to the community for a visit are entertained at the tavern; visiting relatives are brought in for a few drinks and to be introduced to the group.

Holidays, too, may be the occasions for special celebrating. St. Patrick's Day, for example, usually calls for a party. One year, in fact, two customers, neither of them Irish, continued the celebration at the tavern for a week. "It's because we think the Irish are so goddamn wonderful," one of them explained. New Year's Eve provides the occasion for the biggest party of the year at the Oasis. Paper hats and noisemakers are usually furnished, and, at 1 a.m., the proprietor locks the door and permits the "regular" customers (who make certain to be there by then) to continue the celebration as long as they wish. Transients who try to get in after this time are simply turned away.

For the large parties, various women customers supply the food: baked ham, barbecued beef, baked beans, and so forth. Persons who do not bring food are expected to make a contribution to the cost—a dollar being the usual amount. Free beer is provided by the "sponsor" or from a "kitty" accumulated especially for the event, and live music is frequently furnished by several of the male customers.

TRAGEDY

When the family of a regular customer suffers a tragedy, the group immediately responds. Funerals are attended conscientiously, flowers are sent, hospitals are visited, and funds are collected.

One night when I stopped in at the tavern, I found the people at the bar talking about a man in his 40s who had been a regular patron of the Oasis and who was reported to be dying of cancer. One of the men brought a glass jar over and asked me to contribute to a fund for the man's family. "Lee," he said, "put something in this jar. That poor sonofabitch is up there in that hospital tonight dying of cancer and his four little kids are sitting down in that damn house crying."

When a popular member of the inner group suffered a disastrous fire, losing his home and almost all his furniture and personal property, the regular patrons responded with help of various kinds. And when another popular customer was diagnosed as having active tuberculosis and had to be hospitalized for several months, visits were made to the sanatorium and handicraft items made by the person while hospitalized were sold at the Oasis.

In a very real sense, the inner core of the tavern's patrons functions as a mutual aid society: Psychological support is provided in times of crisis; material help is available if needed; children are cared for; cars are loaned; and so forth.

TELEVISION

As a rule, most of the customers at the Oasis prefer that the "idiot box" (as some of them call it) be turned off. It is not unusual to hear a regular customer exclaim, "For Christ sake, Harry, turn that damn thing off. I came up here for peace and quiet and that thing is polluting the air."

If Harry happens to be watching the news or some special event he may reply, with a smile, "I am only trying to improve some of the minds that come in here—and some of them need it." And if the event is something quite special— such as a State of the Union address by the President—he will simply refuse to turn off the set.

Political attitudes can often be observed in responses to certain programs. During one of the space team recovery programs, for example, it became quite apparent that most of the viewers at the Oasis felt that the space program was costing too much money and had been given too high a priority. One man commented, "I'll be a sonofabitch if I can understand why we have to start exploring the moon when we can't straighten things out on this planet. I don't get it."

The big thing on television at the Oasis is, of course, sporting events— football, basketball, baseball, bowling, boxing, horse racing—the televising of almost any sporting event of any consequence will cause the set to be turned on.

Once in a while, almost by accident, a "soap opera" will be playing while the workers are eating lunch. This invariably produces caustic remarks. One noon a plumber watched a soap opera scene in which a woman was planning to have a baby by another man because her husband was sterile. Furthermore, the woman made it clear that she was doing this *for* her husband, so he could be a "father." When the scene on television ended the plumber shook his head in disbelief. "I'll be a sonofabitch. Now I know where my wife gets some of her crazy ideas. She watches that crap all day long."

MUSIC AND DANCING

There is a jukebox at the Oasis, but, as a rule, the men do not play it unless there are women present—preferring the music of their own conversation. Yet while the women are the ones who usually start the music, once it is started, the men appear to enjoy it and, in fact, put in most of the quarters.

Once the jukebox is playing, some people think of dancing, and soon a few couples will be maneuvering around the tables adjacent to the bar. The desire to dance seems rather unequally divided among the married couples who frequent the tavern, and, as such, many married women have to look to men other than their husbands for dancing partners. As a rule, this produces no problems but occasionally a husband will take offense at the manner in which some man is dancing with his wife.

The jukebox is usually not played during the day, except by transient couples who happen to stop in at the tavern. Actually, there is a tacit agreement among the men *not* to play it on Saturday mornings when many of them have hangovers.

Most of the music that is played is sad, involving stories of broken love and unfaithfulness. The only "happy" songs on the jukebox are the old fashioned polkas—"Roll Out the Barrel," and the like. When these are played, the Oasis really "jumps." No jazz, as such, is heard and very little "rock." Johnny Cash is a favorite singer.

Not all the music at the Oasis is "canned." On occasional evenings, even when no special party is in progress, a customer will come in with his guitar or his accordian and play for the group.

THE PERPETUAL EIGHT BALL GAME

One of the features of the Oasis that first attracted the writer was the apparently continuous eight ball game on the pool table. Every time I stopped at the tavern, a game was in progress.

As eight ball is played at the Oasis (various taverns in the area have their own "house rules" for eight ball), it is a fascinating contest. The game may be played by two or four persons. In the latter case, two persons play as partners. Once the balls are "broken," one side shoots the even numbered balls, while the other side shoots the odd numbered ones. The balls do not have to be shot in any particular sequence, except that the eight ball is a neutral ball and may not be shot until the other seven balls (odd or even) have been made.

At the Oasis, eight ball is played as "last pocket," meaning that one has to sink the eight ball in the same pocket into which one's last ball went. If a player sinks the eight ball before his other seven balls are made, he loses the game. He also loses if the eight ball goes into a pocket other than his "last pocket," and he loses if the cue ball goes into a pocket while he is shooting the eight ball. This last rule means that a player could run off his seven balls, make the eight ball in his last pocket (perhaps on a spectacular shot), and still lose if the cue ball finds an open pocket.

These rules produce an exciting game, because a player (or a team of partners) can be several balls behind and still win the game, either because his opposition makes a mistake (such as accidentally making the eight ball in the wrong pocket) or by a clever "defense"—blocking pockets, playing a combination shot on the eight ball to ruin the opposition's position, and so forth. If the players are fairly comparable in skill, the final outcome of the game is highly unpredictable.

The writer never fully appreciated the expression "behind the eight ball" before shooting pool at the Oasis. Since the eight ball is a neutral ball, it may not be shot until the other seven balls have been made. This means, literally, that a player could have several good shots available but he could not take advantage of them because the cue ball is *behind the eight ball.* "Sonofabitch!" a player will exclaim. "Look at all those shots and I'm behind the goddamned eight ball!" Then he will often add, "That's the story of my life."

It is possible for one individual to play the game continuously for many hours, as I discovered one Saturday when I spent six hours at it. This can happen when a player has a long winning streak and defeats one challenger after another. Until defeated, the player who wins is expected to play anyone in the tavern who wishes to challenge.

As noted earlier, the men at the tavern prefer to place bets when playing eight ball (about the only pool game played at the Oasis). A dollar a game is not unusual, although they often play for a $.15 beer. And the loser invariably is expected to put the $.25 in the slot for the next game.

It is an interesting observation that an individual's pool game appears to reflect his personal and social adjustment of the moment. One man, an excellent pool player, lost consistently during a period of unemployment; another player began losing to almost everybody when his wife sued him for divorce; a third man's game deteriorated rapidly when he became ill and the doctors could not diagnose his illness. (He felt well enough to shoot pool but was "worried" about the nature of his illness. He apparently was afraid that the trouble might be cancer—which it was. He was dead within three months.)

Additionally, if one observes the pool players at the tavern closely over a period of time, one discovers that their style of play reflects their stance toward life. "Big Joe," for example, plays a cautious game. Before each shot, he surveys the entire table to examine the various possibilities, and before shooting he calculates the defense possibilities of each potential shot—what opportunities the opposition will have if he misses his shot. This style also represents Big Joe's approach to life. He tries to avoid being vulnerable and, above all, he tries hard never to be "a sucker" (his words). Another player, Handsome Jack, will step up to the pool table, take a fast look at the situation, and shoot quickly. Once in a while he wins, but usually he does not. The reckless players, when they lose, often use the expression. "That's the story of my life." This is said in a half-humorous, half-serious way—in many cases, it is *literally* the story of their lives.

Note should be made also of the fact that, at the Oasis, a person's skill in shooting pool (or in some other game, such as cards) tends to be reflected in his status in the group. A person who drinks so much that he (or she) can no longer shoot a good game of pool or play a good game of shuffleboard is likely to be labeled an "alcoholic." It is not merely their excessive drinking that is involved. It is also their inability to compete with peers. In other words, such a person becomes a "loser" in more ways than one.

There are "hazards" around the pool table at the Oasis of which strangers are not aware, and sometimes the regular players take advantage of their opponents by utilizing these "hazards" as part of their defense.

For example: a post from floor to ceiling is found about two feet from the side pocket on the left side of the table. If you leave the cue ball in certain positions near this post, your opponent will have difficulty shooting properly; the post will interfere with his cue stick. A "sawed off" cue of about half the usual length has been provided for this emergency but most of the shots attempted with this short cue stick are missed (as the regular players know).

Another hazard is the beer cooler located at the right front corner of the pool table. If the cue ball is left in this corner, the opponent may find that he is unable to make certain shots because the beer cooler will interfere with his stick.

These two hazards provide a lot of humor (and frustration) in the eight ball game at the Oasis. A player will see an easy shot that might win the game and walk up to the table with confidence, only to discover that the post or the beer cooler is blocking his shot. Then the comments will begin.

Goddammit, Harry! When are you going to have this damn post taken out?

With all of the damn carpenters around this place, wouldn't you think one of them could cut that damn post down?

Why in the hell don't the damn sheet metal workers or the plumbers put a bend in the post—that would solve the problem.

Actually, hours have been spent at the Oasis discussing what might be done about "the damn post." It was finally decided that a considerable part of the weight of the upper two stories of the building rests on this post and that any tampering with it (without a major remodeling project) would result in a sudden death ending to any eight ball game that might be in progress.

When the Oasis was sold July 1, 1969, there was a great deal of humorous talk about what the new owners would do about the damn post. "Goddamnit, Harry," one player said, "we've been coming in here to drink beer and shoot pool for 20 years and in all that time you didn't do anything about the damn post—the least you could do would be to put a clause in the new deed that says—'Post at left side of pool table must be relocated so as not to interfere with playing of eight ball'—that would be legal, wouldn't it?" The post remains and players are still to be heard yelling, "Goddamnit, when in the hell are they going to do something about this damn post?"

THE TAVERN IN MODERN SOCIETY

The men at the Oasis are, by and large, first-generation urbanites. They are confronting, as their fathers did not, the problem of leisure and the problem of impersonality. The Oasis—and taverns like it elsewhere—appear to be providing at least partial solutions to both.

The need to "fill time" is, of course, a relatively recent phenomenon. As one of the men at the tavern remarked, "Hell, we didn't have any problem of what to do with our time on the farm. We worked all the time. Now a guy works 40 hours a week and has the rest of the time for himself." As should be apparent from the preceding pages, the activities which center in and about the Oasis are, for the men and women who congregate there, a satisfying and interesting way to "spend" their leisure.

But taverns like the Oasis do more than simply provide settings for leisure activities. They provide—at least for those who are their "regulars"—havens of personal relationships in an impersonal world. Here is a place, beyond the protection of the immediate family, where the individual can still feel that he belongs, that people know who he is, that someone cares about him. . . .

In a more religious society, perhaps, the social life of people like the Oasis customers might revolve about the church. But modern America is increasingly secular, and the tavern seems ready-made for such a society.

Constructing Make-Believe Cities

PAUL GOLDBERGER

© *J. R. Holland/Stock, Boston*

The star attractions at Disneyworld, Orlando, Florida

THE EFFORT BY THE WALT DISNEY ORGANIZATION to carve an updated version of the amusement park out of the farms and marshes of central Florida is part of America's long history of shaping the environment for economic and social ends. Eighteenth-century New England farms, nineteenth-century urban parks, and early twentieth-century amusement parks all reflect such transformations. An earlier selection in this volume, "Designing Places for Mechanized Leisure," by Robert E. Snow and David E. Wright, details the growth of a group of amusement parks on Coney Island whose rise and decline were inextricably tied to the growth of New York City. In the following selection, Paul Goldberger describes Disney World, a development which covers an area twice the size of Manhattan and which can be considered one of the most innovative new towns in the United States.

While Coney Island prospered as an appendage to New York City, Disney World has become a city unto itself, a vacation resort accessible to millions who flock to it by automobile and airplane. Just as the mechanical and electrical wonders attracted people to the ferris wheels and merry-go-rounds of Coney Island, the technological wonders of late twentieth-century life draw millions to see the future at Disney World. Disney has raised to a new level the escape from the drudgery of everyday life offered by most amusement parks; the stages of the Magic Kingdom provide idealized settings in which visitors can live out their fantasies. But there is another level that distinguishes Disney World from other amusement parks; it functions as a city, using technological innovations to handle the heavy demands made by thousands of visitors. A vacuum system wisks garbage away through subterranean tunnels, which are also pathways for underground delivery vehicles and accessways for the repair of water, sewer, and electrical lines. The same tunnels add to the fantasy of the park by allowing costumed characters to appear in and disappear from their appropriate theme lands. Thus, while Disney World is a *working* city, it is not a *real* city; it has no politics, no permanent residents, and no economic life beyond tourism. It is a prototype, standing as testimony that a clean, ordered urban environment is technologically possible, if not politically possible.

LAKE BUENA VISTA, Fla.: There is a nondescript, two-story building in Glendale, Calif., that houses 400 men who may have more influence on the shape America's cities will take than any planners, architects or urban designers could ever hope to.They are not part of a think tank, or a university, or a foundation, or anything remotely like these; their operation, which is called WED Enterprises, Inc., is owned and fully controlled by the company that made Mickey Mouse, Walt Disney Productions.

WED began when Walt Disney decided in 1952 to build Disneyland in Southern California. He had no architects or amusement-park designers on his staff, and he had never much liked the idea of hiring outside consultants, so he put together a design team himself, composed mostly of art directors from the Disney studios, and called the group WED, after his initials. Since the WED staff didn't know anything about how to design an amusement park, it never quite got around to giving Disneyland a roller coaster, a Ferris wheel or a standard carnival midway; instead, WED started from scratch and created a park based largely on Disney characters and themes from his films. The result is probably the most successful amusement park ever built anywhere.

Mickey Mouse has come a long way since then: The Disney organization is now engrossed in the development of Walt Disney World, a 27,000-acre site in central Florida, and WED, as its official design and engineering arm, has entered the city planning business, on a bigger scale than almost any other firm in the United States. Disney World covers an area twice the size of Manhattan island, which means that Disney's old film men who staff WED are in the process of creating a new town that will be bigger than the new cities of Columbia, Md., and Reston, Va., put together.

WED hasn't quite decided what it will do with all that land. But it plans to put a new, experimental city on one segment, and on another it has begun a small condominium community called Lake Buena Vista. Here, a few lucky

CONSTRUCTING MAKE-BELIEVE CITIES By Paul Goldberger. Originally published under the title "Mickey Mouse Teaches the Architects," *New York Times Magazine*, October 22, 1972. Copyright © 1972 by *The New York Times*. Reprinted by permission.

folks are already fulfilling that great childhood dream—to *live* at Disneyland. As for the rest of us, WED has filled yet another section of the site with what it calls the "Vacation Kingdom," the Florida version of the original Disneyland, plus hotels, golf courses and campgrounds. And this small part alone is enough to have caused an increasing number of planners and architects to take a serious look at what WED is doing. Concluded critic and architect Peter Blake after a visit this spring: "In a great many respects, the most interesting New Town in the United States is Walt Disney World."

If Blake has gone mad, he has plenty of company; it seems as though trips to Disney World are suddenly becoming the sort of obligatory pilgrimages for young architects that visits to the great monuments of Europe were for earlier generations. Developer Mel Kaufman, who is responsible for many of New York's less orthodox office buildings, such as the open-air lobby tower at 77 Water Street came to Disney World in April and now wants to bring his entire staff here; Kaufman calls it "a truly great learning experience."

What is it that has got architects and planners so excited? To a certain extent it is Disney World's architecture—or lack of it. The admittedly fake, stage-set architecture of the Magic Kingdom (as Disney executives, with utter serious-ness, insist upon calling the amusement park) is extraordinarily successful, and its appeal to the average visitor is cited by younger architects who have been trying to call into question traditional standards of architectural validity. "Disney World is nearer to what people really want than anything architects have ever given them," says architect Robert Venturi, whose praises of the original Disneyland have aroused the ire of his fellow architects for years. "It's a symbolic American utopia."

But what has interested planners even more than Disney World's architec-ture—which is essentially the same as that of Disneyland—is its technical aspects. Disney World is, by any standard, a remarkable technological achieve-ment; it includes an array of technical innovations that would make any city manager drool. But no real city has seen fit to develop and install them; only Disney's WED has, and in doing so, WED has made Walt Disney World perhaps the most important city planning laboratory in the United States.

The most spectacular technological innovations are behind-the-scenes, off limits to the average tourist. Indeed, the most interesting one is below-the-scenes as well: it is a vast service basement that spreads beneath the entire park. There will never be any "Dig we must" signs at Disney World, for one of the functions of the basement is to carry all water, electric and sewage lines, which are exposed in corridors and thus accessible for easy repair. Through the base-ment run special supply-carrying tractors, so that deliveries can be made with-out disturbing the peace and other-worldliness of the Magic Kingdom above. In fact, the basement really functions as a backstage for the great stage that is the Magic Kingdom; costumed employees heading to work at one of the park's self-contained theme areas (there are five: Main Street, Fantasyland, Frontier-land, Adventureland and Tomorrowland) can reach their stations without walking through another area. Thus illusions are preserved, and horrifying sights, such as that of a costumed spaceman rushing through circa-1900 Main Street on his way to Tomorrowland, are avoided.

The idea of a separate level for all services, and another one for people, is not new. But with the exception of a few multibuilding complexes such as

Rockefeller Center and Lincoln Center, it is an idea that has remained largely a gleam in planners' eyes. No new town, or even large development, had tried it until Disney World came along, despite the fact that it is a highly practical scheme that can cut maintenance costs to a fraction of what they are with traditional systems.

(The idea may be beginning to catch on, though: a letter writer to The Times suggested just last month that "to eliminate the incessant, recurrent and uneconomic drilling that plagues the city," New York consider installing walk-in service tunnels à la Disney along the route of the Second Avenue subway. Given WED's track record and the Transit Authority's, Disney may well invent some new kind of system before New York gets around to trying this one.)

Also below decks is one of the few Disney World innovations that is *not* Disney-WED designed: the Swedish AVAC garbage system, which whisks garbage via vacuum tubes from 15 stations within the park to a compacting plant hidden from view outside the gates. Even the service basement needn't be invaded by garbage trucks; there will never have to be any, anywhere on the site. The Disney system, the largest such installation in the world and one of the few outside Sweden, is capable of handling 50 tons of refuse daily. While one could justifiably call such a system merely a pipe dream for New York, it is, like the service tunnels, a practical possibility for new areas not yet built up.

Disney's best-known technological splurge is, of course, the monorail, a carry-over from Disneyland refined for a new Disney World version. Walt Disney himself had great hopes for the monorail as the answer to the mass-transit problems of the nation's cities, and in 1960 he approached Las Vegas with the idea of installing a monorail down the center of that city's fabled Strip. He was turned down, but the experience was a major factor in leading the Disney organization to believe that their amusement park could possibly serve as a kind of testing ground for urban technology.

The new monorail at Disney World was designed by WED, which, with no more experience in the train business than in any of its other ventures, came up with a sleek new system that was manufactured by the Martin Marietta Corporation, Disney's neighbor in nearby Orlando. The Disney organization thinks that its monorail is as advanced a rail system as there is in the country right now. The one at Disney World is more than just a pleasure ride; it is the primary means of transportation between parking areas, the Magic Kingdom's gate and the two on-premises hotels. (All automobiles are banished to the outlying parking areas, thus disposing of another urban ill totally, if a bit simplistically.)

The train ran into some snags at first, mainly because of an inability to handle the crowds that poured onto it, making the whole experience a great deal more like riding the IRT than Disney's designers would have desired. And unfortunately despite the Disney organization's enthusiasm, the monorail appears to have slim chance of becoming the savior of the nation's rapid-transit systems. Its chief advantage is that the thin beam which serves as its track needs very little room and doesn't smother a street, as the El did to Third Avenue, the monorail can run unobtrusively down the center lane. But engineers have found it difficult—and highly expensive—to build beams smooth enough to permit a fast ride (even the Disney World monorail has a top speed of only 45 miles per hour). The switching system is a complex engineering problem, too, and despite the monorail's attractiveness as a kind of abstract symbol of the future, there seem to be few urban takers for this Disney innovation. Bill Stubee, a partner in the New York firm of Hart, Krivatsy and Stubee, which is assisting Disney in the preparation of a master plan for the 27,000-acre site, sums it up this way: "The monorail is a futuristic idea whose time has passed."

If Walt Disney were alive, he might well have argued with Bill Stubee, for Disney had an immense faith in the ultimate rightness of technological progress, and when one of his innovations proved impractical in real urban situations it rarely fazed him. Much of this faith in technology has remained in his successors; for all of its commercial sophistication, Walt Disney Productions (parent company of WED and all the Disney ventures) and the designers at the helm today believe as firmly as did Disney himself that technology will solve all the problems before them.

All of Disney's dreams about technology came together a few years before his death in 1966, in a project he dubbed EPCOT—the Experimental Prototype Community of Tomorrow. The Disney organization intends to build this experimental city on the Florida site, and it is officially part of the master plan for the 27,000-acre duchy. EPCOT is envisioned, say Disney publicists, as a real, functioning city "where people will actually live a life they can't find anywhere else in the world today."

Disney never quite got around to explaining exactly what that life was that he wanted to see lived in EPCOT, and now that he is dead no one else seems to know, either. But the project has taken on the status of the Disney organization's impossible dream, the elusive goal toward which all the company's efforts are directed. Staffers speak reverently of this or that project being "a step toward EPCOT"; designers say they will "mini-EPCOT" a particular scheme when they want to try it out on a small scale to see if it is worthy of Walt's great City in the Sky. Disney did little in the way of social planning; his EPCOT vision was a purely technological one, and the few sketches prepared before his death show fantasylike constructions with crisscrossing monorails. One sketch shows an enormous skyscraper in the center of a vast, Buck Rogers scheme of smaller buildings and radiating railways; it's a pie-in-the-sky conception that, ironically, doesn't really go much beyond the visionary schemes of such pioneer early 20th century planners as Sant'Elia and Le Corbusier.

Planners Hart, Krivatsy and Stubee have the responsibility of helping the Disney organization come up with a practicable scheme for EPCOT. They hope to move somewhat away from the dream-scheme nature of the operation as it now stands; one project they have in mind is a massive recreation complex with year-round stadiums and exhibition centers and homes for sports-oriented vacationers. No final decision has been made about what kind of EPCOT will finally be built, but while the organization is still officially loyal to Walt's nebulous dream city, there is serious talk of trying to attract the 1980 Olympics to Disney World, a sign taken by some company sources as meaning that Disney is leaning toward the Hart, Krivatsy and Stubee scheme for EPCOT.

One senses that the Disney organization is on somewhat firmer ground when it comes to what's already been built than with EPCOT. The EPCOT scheme, if it ever does get under way as Walt envisioned it, would change constantly to allow for new developments; presumably, the times would never catch up with it. Such a utopian dream would have to involve a great deal of social as well as physical planning, of course, and there Disney's expertise seems to falter. "The Disney organization is fascinated by technical experimentation, but scared to death of social concerns," says Stubee. In the Magic Kingdom and its predecessor, Disneyland, there are no social concerns—no drugs, school boards or welfare disputes. Thus the Disney organization's extraordinary imagination is free to roam with no social consequences, and WED's designers can give technology carte blanche. The "imagineers"—as Disney once dubbed the WED staff—can play to their heart's content. And they do.

The Magic Kingdom is, of course, the reason-for-being of the whole complex. In a sense it is really itself a realization of Disney's city-of-tomorrow dreams, a complete urban environment, which has at times handled as many as 40,000 people at once and with a great deal more ease than most cities half that size manage their populations. The streets are cleaner than in towns a tenth of Disney World's daily population, the trains, tramcars and minibuses run when they are supposed to, the power doesn't black out, or brown out—in short, everything works.

Part of what makes it work is an enormous, R.C.A.-designed electronic communications system that keeps tabs on the entire operation. The computer includes a fire monitoring system that is tied into Disney World's own fire department (as large as that of Orlando, a city of 100,000); it also monitors all rides and mechanical devices throughout the park, automatically shutting down any equipment that shows any sign of malfunctioning.

The whole place is powered by a $20-million energy system that, like so much of the rest of the park, was designed by WED (although here WED, less willing to take chances with engines than with monorails and castles, teamed up with a power consultant). The two jet engines of the system at present provide only 8 megawatts of Disney World's required 23; the rest are bought from the municipal power company. But Disney computers control the entire operation, and Disney engineers can switch parts of the park back and forth from one power source to another at will. The system is ecologically sound, too: it uses recycled waste heat to power the cooling system, cutting costs and making maximum use of energy.

What all of this very real stuff serves, of course, is a very make-believe place. The Magic Kingdom is 100 acres of whimsy, a sprawling architectural fantasy that seems far away indeed from the real problems of our cities. But it does have the uncanny ability to make people happy; planner Bob Hart calls it "probably the best example of an urban environment where people are treated in a humane way." And although the designers of real urban areas know that they cannot have a costumed Mickey Mouse strolling about their town squares, they are beginning to look hard for some elements of Disney World's successful environment that they can transplant.

Developer Mel Kaufman opts for taking Main Street itself, the 600-foot long strip of fake Victorian buildings and shop fronts, most of which hide real stores selling real merchandise. "Main Street's purpose is exactly the same as Korvettes in the Bronx," Kaufman says, "but it manages to make shopping wonderful and pleasant at the same time. I'm sure people buy more when they're happy. Why do we care so much about architectural validity in a shopping center, when the real point should simply be to make the place fun? There is no 'architecture' at Disney World—and I think it's great."

Kaufman says that the design of his lobbyless office building at 77 Water Street, which has a stage-set, eighteen-nineties candy store in its plaza instead of the traditional bland newsstand, was "definitely" the result of the impression Disneyland made on him. Indeed, Kaufman even picked up on the WED design process: instead of hiring an architect to design the candy store, he gave the job to a former stage designer.

Main Street is, of course, all a big stage set (mostly of Fiberglas, by the way), sitting on top of the park's "backstage" service basement. (Disney executives even call the process of hiring workers for the attractions "casting.") But it is a stage set designed with a great deal more care than most buildings; details are meticulously executed, and the scale is under complete control. It's always slightly smaller than in real life, to accentuate the feeling of a toylike, unreal place, but the scale grows smaller with each successive floor, to create the illusion of greater height. The colors are mostly pastels, enhancing the sense of fantasy.

As with most Disney World buildings, there was no model. Main Street was not designed as an imitation of any existing small town street, "but it's what a Main Street *should* be," says John Hench, vice president of WED and one of the top design men from its inception. "Ours is a kind of universally true Main Street—it's better than the real Main Streets of the turn of the century ever could be."

Thus, Main Street provides an ideal setting for the visitor's fantasies. He is himself on stage, and he can play-act and relax in a way that he would never dare to in the parks and squares of his hometown. At Disney World, everything is clean, fresh, innocent and just unreal enough to be completely unthreatening. But at the same time, it fulfills the functions of a bona fide urban space, and architect Charles Moore—who Robert Venturi admits turned him on to Disneyland in the first place—has suggested that one reason the original Disneyland was so successful is that it gave Californians a chance to respond to a public environment, something Los Angeles, a city of suburban tracts and freeways, most emphatically does not have.

What Disneyland really is, Moore says, is the town square of Los Angeles, and he adds: "In an unchartable sea of suburbia, Disney has created a place, indeed, a whole public world, full of sequential occurrences, of big and little drama, of hierarchies of importance and excitement, with opportunities to respond at the speed of rocketing bobsleds or of horsedrawn street cars. . . . No raw edges spoil the picture at Disneyland; everything is as immaculate as in the musical-comedy villages that Hollywood has provided for our viewing pleasure for the last three generations."

Perhaps, then, the lesson of Disney's lands is that a sense of fantasy, and the chance to play-act, are what we really crave in our real urban environments. Most of the vast concrete plazas filling our downtowns today are helpful only to those whose fantasies lean toward Kafka; there is pitifully little of the whimsy, and the irony, that make Disneyland and its offspring Disney World such welcome places.

But there are more tangible lessons to be learned from these places, too— another thing that makes them so successful as environments is their total sense of place, or the identity that they give to their spaces. Each of the "theme lands" is entirely self-contained, and designed in a way that enhances the visitor's illusions by shielding everything else from view. Wherever something outside is visible, it is arranged so as to be consistent with the inside theme; for example, the futuristic Contemporary Resort-Hotel outside the Magic Kingdom proper is visible only from Tomorrowland, and can't shatter the turn-of-the-century view from Main Street. Not only is the architecture different in each area, so are the employee uniforms, the graphics and the trash bins.

If the main point of architecture is, as Philip Johnson has written, "not the design of space [but] the organization of procession," then here again Disney World offers cause for serious study. In terms of its plan, the Magic Kingdom is a masterpiece of balance between clarity and diversity. The entrance down Main Street sends the visitor right to the center of the park and the massive Cinderella Castle, which functions as a theme structure and is visible as a landmark from all points. The "lands" radiate from the castle plaza; and while one can get utterly lost within the small theme areas, it is always an easy matter to return to the castle and axial Main Street to set one's bearings straight again. "Main Street is like Scene One, and then the castle is designed to pull you down Main Street toward what is next, just like a motion picture unfolding," says John Hench.

The buildings are designed according to the principles that Hench explains motivated Main Street: they are, in effect, cinematic, visual images of ideal types. They are symbolic architecture, designed to communicate a message or, in the case of the Walt Disney World castle, "to say something about the idea of being a castle," as Hench puts it. Like Main Street, the other buildings are based on historical associations interpreted freely rather than copied literally. A superficial effect is captured for the facade, while modern construction methods and materials may hide underneath.

Disney World publicity manager Charles Ridgway's description of the Cinderella Castle provides a glimpse into just what the Disney designers were after: "Imagine a full-size fairy-tale castle rivaling Europe's finest and all the dream castles of literary history in space-age America," Ridgway wrote in a news release. "A castle without age-crusted floors and drafty hallways. A palace with air-conditioning, automatic elevators and electric kitchens. A royal home grander than anything Cinderella could have imagined. But a true fairy-tale castle in every way. . . . [WED] produced an ancient castle that looks brand-new—as though each guest had been transported back in time." After that, one hardly needs Chambord.

WED's staffers point with pride to the fact that in the Disney scheme of things the architects and designers have the last say, not the engineers. The standard practice is for a WED project designer to prepare a set of renderings showing how the completed building should look.These are passed along to an engineer who is instructed to devise a means for making the design workable without changing its appearance—exactly the opposite of traditional architectural practice.

"We can't think engineering," says Chuck Myall, like so many WED designers a former art director from the Disney studios. "When we did the Country Bear Jamboree [a Walt Disney World attraction that involves audio-animatronic robots, another WED invention], we designed the show itself, then we sketched plans for the inside of the theater, then the outside. Nobody else in the world would do it that way. We never bothered to figure square feet, site coverage, or any of the other things an architect usually thinks about when he designs a theater."

Myall, who was in charge of planning for the Frontierland and Liberty Square areas, had responsibility also for the Haunted Mansion, a popular attraction that offers visitors perhaps the most dazzling array of WED-designed special effects anywhere in the park. The outside of the Mansion is of the same vaguely Gothic, brick design that marks so many college campuses from the twenties; it is sufficiently imposing and bizarre to instill in the visitor the sense that strange beings lurk within, yet at the same time it blends in well with the Georgian architecture of adjacent Liberty Square.

Time, of course, stands still in Disney World; as the visitor moves from one geographically defined theme area, such as Frontierland or Main Street, he also moves across time. Curiously, Disney's designers seem to see the future as yet another geographical place; not only do they offer us Tomorrowland (or, for that matter, EPCOT) but they have chosen for one of the two on-premises hotels a futuristic theme, placing it alongside the completed "Polynesian Village-Resort" and the planned "Persian," "Asian" and "Venetian" hotels. The modern hotel was given the utterly matter-of-fact, yet marvelously ironic, name of the Contemporary Resort-Hotel.

It is a massive, 14-story A-frame structure, and it is probably the best single building through which to observe the blending of technological innovation and far-out fantasy that is uniquely Disney. It was designed in conjunction with architects Welton Becket and Associates, although Disney spokesmen are quick to point out that these consultants were only brought in because the WED staff hadn't time to develop an expertise in hotel design, and they insist that the company will handle the entire hotel project on an in-house basis next time around.

The Contemporary Hotel is a comic-book artist's vision of modern architecture. The rooms are fitted along the outside of the vast A-frame; inside, looms an awesome 10-story open space called the Grand Canyon Concourse, through which the monorail runs—perhaps the technical *pièce de résistance* of the entire park.

But while the building makes no bones about indulging in Buck Rogers fantasies (one senses that surely here, if nowhere else, the renderings of the completed vision came before anything else) its design nonetheless makes a serious attempt to contribute something to construction technology. The hotel rooms were prefabricated—the first prefab steel units in the country—and constructed by U.S. Steel in a special factory on the Disney site. The on-site location meant that units could be constructed with a width of 14½ feet; most prefab units are limited to 12 feet because they must be moved along normal public roads.

Unfortunately, the system never worked out as planned. The prefab rooms function perfectly well, but the expense of developing the system pushed costs from U.S. Steel's original estimate of $17,000 per room to about $100,000 per room, considerably more than traditional, nonprefab construction. While future prefab modules could undoubtedly be built at somewhat lower cost, there is some question as to the practicality of the whole-room prefab system, since the cost of enclosing "bulk" space—*i.e.*, the main part of the room—is not much different with traditional construction methods or prefab construction. The real saving with prefab is in special areas such as bathrooms, and the Disney-U.S. Steel plant is now engaged in producing a small quantity of prefab bathroom units for a nearby Sheraton motel.

For the moment, the high hopes for the whole-room prefab idea have faded, one of the few misses on the almost-perfect track record of Disney innovation. The total cost of the Contemporary Resort-Hotel ran almost $100-million, perhaps why Disney World has seen fit to charge prices that, as one visitor recently remarked, are higher than at Claridge's—up to $44 a room.

At the same time that the Contemporary Resort-Hotel was under construction, the Polynesian Village, Welton Becket's other joint venture with WED, was going up across the man-made lagoon. In typical Disney fashion, the same steel modules were used for the Polynesian rooms, only this time they were set into long, low buildings, covered with false thatched roofs and elegantly landscaped in what was thought to be Polynesian manner. Here, as within the Magic Kingdom's gates, the joke somehow works: One is never quite willing to believe that he is off on a South Seas island somewhere—he isn't expected to; instead, the sensation is of playing along with Disney's designers in an elaborate, intricately conceived hoax. The juxtaposition of fake thatched roofs and cleanly modern, air-conditioned rooms is an obvious put-on, like Main Street with its tricks of scale. But like Main Street it is such a skillful put-on, and such a joyous one, that we willingly play along with Disney's game and share in its irony.

Clearly, it is no usual company that could entice 10,750,000 people—the total number of visitors to Disney World in its first year, which ended this month—to join in such a game. But Walt Disney Productions has never gone about its business in a very ordinary way. Walt Disney's decision to set up WED to design Disneyland, rather than go to an outside organization, was typical of the way he operated. An essential aim of the Disney organization has always been total control over any venture in which it is involved.

In his penetrating study, "The Disney Version," critic Richard Schickel saw the basis of Disneyland in "Walt Disney's lifelong rage to order, control and keep clean any environment that he inhabited." It is a harsh comment, but probably true: Disney's desire to control manifested itself in his films, for which his studio almost never relinquished any rights, in his television shows and, finally, in his obsession with making Disneyland into a total environment.

The Florida operation represents, in a sense, the ultimate lengths to which this principle can be taken. There is not only a Disney power system, a Disney transportation system and a Disney construction company, there is a Disney telephone company, a Disney laundry (with washing formulas controlled by computer) and a Disney navy (much of it runs on tracks as parts of rides, but if these boats are counted along with the real ones; the navy numbers 256 craft—the ninth-largest navy in the world).

But the real thing to make corporate executives' mouths water is the Disney government. Even I.T.T. has never quite been able to own its own government, but Disney, through Florida statutes passed in 1967, does. It is called the Reedy Creek Improvement District (after a swamp on the property) and it is empowered with all the authority of a county except for police power. Reedy Creek is controlled by the Disney organization and can set air- and water-pollution standards, and tax the landowner—which it does, to the tune of $3-million a year.

Reedy Creek's chairman is General W. E. "Joe" Potter, a retired Army general who Walt spotted when, as Robert Moses' executive vice president at the New York World's Fair, he worked with the Disney organization on its exhibits. Among the operations that fall into Joe Potter's bailiwick are Disney World's environmental-protection operations, which are remarkably thorough considering that, until recently, the Disney organization's interest in the environment consisted largely of making sure litter was picked up efficiently at Disneyland. (In fact, the company's proposed Mineral King resort project in Northern California is still held up in litigation brought on by the Sierra Club's charges that the resort would be ecologically harmful.) But in Florida, Disney executives estimate that they have spent $20-million on environmental controls. And 7,500 acres have been set aside as a conservation area that will remain wilderness.

There are elaborate air- and water-pollution controls, and a willingness to undertake some pretty drastic action where prevention measures can't work. For example, when the 450-acre Bay Lake on the property was deemed too polluted, Disney engineers drained it entirely, removed a layer of organic debris, and dredged white sand up from under the lake and spread it along the beaches. Then they pumped in underground water to refill the lake and finally, as if to spur the jealousy of Lake Erie-side residents, they stocked it with 70,000 fingerling bass.

There is also, on the site, a liquid waste-treatment plant that turns out effluent "that is as clear as gin," according to Joe Potter. That liquid—be it gin, water or some unmentionable—eventually finds its way into another Disney experiment, a 100-acre tree farm, where it is sprayed over eucalyptus trees. The controlled water-reclamation system, the largest such experiment in the East, is being run by Morgan Evans, Walt Disney World's chief landscape architect, with the assistance of University of Florida agriculturists.

Lake Buena Vista, the already-started condominium town on the site, bills itself as "host community to Walt Disney World." The project is the Disney organization's first, cautious attempt to try its hand at providing residential facilities before it goes whole-hog with the EPCOT city. Lake Buena Vista's aim is more modest than EPCOT's; it is merely a community of second homes for the wealthy, and a special attempt is being made to interest corporations in leasing houses as places to entertain clients. The hard sell has just begun, but John Tassos, an ex-New York advertising man who is now Lake Buena Vista's director of marketing, says that 80 homes, at prices ranging up to $100,000, will be occupied by November. The attached row-houses are generally arranged in clusters around golf courses, waterways and common green spaces; the plan recalls such greenbelt experiments as Radburn, N.J., of 1928, and, as in Radburn, the automobile is banished to out-of-the-way service roads.

Disney will be "mini-EPCOTing" some transportation experiments here; residents of Lake Buena Vista will be able to travel throughout the town via a system of electric cars and boats, and no automobiles will be necessary. Once again, the architecture is by WED, and while the concrete houses are a bit bland, they are surely better than the average Florida condominium.

It is a curious irony that today, when large-scale, total planning is looked on with disfavor by many architects and planners, Disney's planning ventures could appear to be providing so many answers. They seem at once too big and too far away, too unreal to have enough bearing on the problems of real cities.

Ultimately, though, this distance from reality is their greatest asset. WED's designers were free to plan Disney World's underground-tunnel system not only because they had a great deal of money at their disposal but because they did not have to bother with maintaining an old, unworkable system. They could develop the monorail because they did not have to bother with fixing the IRT. Too, they were removed from the problems of schools, drugs, welfare and politics, leaving them free to invent new kinds of ecological controls, power systems and pleasing urban spaces—all things that "real" cities could never afford to develop and test themselves.

In part, then, Disney World works because its task is narrower, and its available resources can all be concentrated on finite problems. But the fact of its working is no less valid because of this. An old Tammany politician once said that the way to keep in office is to be sure to keep the potholes in the streets repaired; at Disney World, they always are, because there aren't the concerns that exist elsewhere that would prevent them from being fixed.

But Disney World is not yet, by any stretch of the imagination, a real city— not only are there no politics, there are virtually no permanent residents. It does, of course, have an economic base, tourism, but this base operates under such unusual circumstances that Disney World cannot be called a real city economically, either. The lessons for real cities center around its technological innovations and its approach to design and planning, and to be of value these things must be seen outside of Disney World's context. The whole of Disney World is not, in any sense, itself a prototype for new towns.

The real test for the Disney organization—and WED especially—will come in the next few years, as Lake Buena Vista nears completion and the EPCOT scheme gets under way in some form. At the moment, since Lake Buena Vista is mainly a second-home community, social planning means putting the golf course in the right place. But EPCOT, presumably, will be different; if Disney is serious, people will have to live daily lives here, not merely leisure-time existences, and whether super-appliances, pollution-free vehicles and clean open spaces can truly affect the quality of life remains to be seen. Up to now a combination of pleasing spaces and wizard technology is all Disney has needed to produce successful environments, but when it builds a full-scale city there will be much more than potholes to worry about.

Heroes
on the
Playing Field

BENJAMIN G. RADER

Babe Ruth with a group of young fans

BY THE 1920S, most Americans recognized that their country had become a different kind of place. Many found the changes unpleasant, frightening, and disorienting. In the following selection, Benjamin G. Rader argues that the sports heroes of the 1920's— men such as Babe Ruth, Red Grange, and Jack Dempsey—epitomized traditional American values and seemed to reaffirm the fundamental beliefs in the culture, thereby helping ordinary Americans overcome the feeling of powerlessness and alienation that accompanied social change.

Ruth, Grange, and Dempsey all represented fantasies of power and instant success; they were men who rose to fame and fortune because of natural ability and sheer determination. The talents they used to transcend humble backgrounds—the exceptional power of Ruth's swing, the speed of Grange's legs, and the power of Dempsey's punches—suggested to the average American that anyone with real ability could still make it to the top, even in a highly bureaucratic and scientific world. In this way, sports heroes reassured Americans that success was still possible, made it easier for them to accept the passing of the world they had always known.

THE DECADE OF THE 1920s, often hailed as the Golden Age of American Sport, teemed with sport heroes. "Never before, nor since, have so many transcendent performers arisen contemporaneously in almost every field of competitive athletics as graced the 1920s," concluded veteran sports reporters Allison Danzig and Peter Brandwein in 1948.[1] Each sport had its magic name: George Herman "Babe" Ruth in baseball, William Harrison "Jack" Dempsey in boxing, Harold "Red" Grange in football, Robert T. "Bobby" Jones in golf and William T. "Big Bill" Tilden in tennis. Many others stood close to the magic circle.

Why sport idols in the 1920s? The public acclaim accorded star athletes sprang from something more than performance, though indeed their athletic feats were often phenomenal. The same skill and shrewd promotion which successfully hawked automobiles, breakfast foods and lipstick also sold athletes to the public. Behind the sport heroes stood professional pitch men: George "Tex" Rickard, Jack "Doc" Kearns, Charles C. "Cash and Carry" Pyle and Christy Walsh, to name a few. And journalists and radio broadcasters, such as Grantland Rice, Arch Wood, Paul Gallico and Graham McNamee—were also prone to hyperbole. They created images of athletes which often overwhelmed the athlete's actual achievements. Yet the public idolization of athletes went even deeper than the skillful ballyhooing of the promoters and journalistic flights of fancy. Ultimately, the emergence of a dazzling galaxy of sport idols was a creation of the American public itself. The athletes as public heroes served a compensatory cultural function. They assisted the public in compensating for the passing of the traditional dream of success, the erosion of Victorian values and feelings of individual powerlessness. As the society became more complicated and systematized and as success had to be won increasingly in bureaucracies, the need for heroes who leaped to fame and fortune outside the rules of the system seemed to grow. No longer were the heroes the lone business tycoon or the statesmen, but the "stars"—from the movies and sports.[2]

Beginning in the decade of the 1920s a popular culture of compensation flourished. The media helped create defense mechanisms for the helpless individual that rested upon a complex set of images, fantasies and myths. Some were comic: Charlie Chaplin in the movies was the carefree little tramp who eluded cops, bullies and pompous officials. Even the machine could not bring him to heel. Some were dashing and romantic: Douglas Fairbanks slashed his way through hordes of swift-sworded villains. Some were tough: the classic western hero was brave and handsome. He killed bad men and Indians, thus dramatically serving the forces of "good" while saving white America from the "savages." The popular culture of compensation also projected images of heroes vaulting to the top. In the 19th century drama and fiction the hero won the

HEROES ON THE PLAYING FIELD   By Benjamin G. Rader. Originally published under the title "Compensatory Sports Heroes: Ruth, Grange, and Dempsey." From the *Journal of Popular Culture, 16* (1983): 11–22.

hand of the rich man's daughter through his virtuous character; Rudolph Valentino won her through his irresistible physical charm. Even the kings of organized crime, who themselves enjoyed something of a celebrity status in the 1920s, furnished forceful images of power and success.

Above all, fantasies and images of power and instant success flourished in the world of sport. In sport—or so it seemed—one could still catapult to fame and fortune without the benefit of years of arduous training or acquiesence to the demanding requirements of bureaucracies. Unlike most vocations, sheer natural ability coupled with a firm commitment to sport for its own sake could propel the athlete to the top. Determining the level of success of a doctor, lawyer or business manager might be difficult to ascertain, but achievement in the world of sport was unambiguous. It could be precisely measured in home runs, knock-outs, touchdowns scored, victories and even in salaries. Those standing on the assembly lines and those sitting at their desks in the bureaucracies found the most satisfaction in the athletic hero who presented an image of all-conquering power. Thus they preferred the towering home runs of Babe Ruth to the "scientific" style of base hits, base stealing, sacrifices and hit-and-run plays personified by Ty Cobb; they preferred the smashing knockout blows of Jack Dempsey to the "scientific" boxing skills displayed by Gene Tunney. Perhaps it was little wonder that boys now dreamed of becoming athletic heroes rather than captains of industry and girls dreamed of Hollywood stardom rather than the hearth.

No modern athletic hero exceeded Babe Ruth's capacity to project multiple images of brute power, the natural, uninhibited man and the fulfillment of the American success dream. Ruth was living proof that the lone individual could still rise from mean, vulgar beginnings to fame and fortune, to a position of public recognition equalled by few men in American history. With nothing but his bat, Ruth revolutionized the National Game of baseball. Ruth's towering home runs represented a dramatic finality, a total clearing of the bases with one mighty swat. Everything about Ruth was extraordinary—his size, strength, coordination, his appetite for the things of the flesh, and even his salary. He transcended the world of ordinary mortals, and yet he was the most mortal of men. He loved to play baseball, to swear and play practical jokes, to eat, drink and take girls to bed. Despite his gross crudities, wrote Billy Evans, a big league umpire, "Ruth is a big, likeable kid. He has been well named, Babe. Ruth has never grown up and probably never will. Success on the ball field has in no way changed him. Everybody likes him. You just can't help it."[3]

Ruth saw himself as a prime example of the classic American success story. "The greatest thing about this country," he wrote in his autobiography, "is the wonderful fact that it doesn't matter which side of the tracks you were born on, or whether you're homeless or homely or friendless. The chance is still there, I know."[4] Ruth encouraged the legend that he had been an orphaned child. While the story had no basis in fact, his early years were indeed grim. He grew up in a tough waterfront neighborhood in Baltimore. His saloon-keeping father and sickly mother had no time for the boy; he received little or no paternal affection. By his own admission, he became a "bad kid," who smoked, chewed tobacco and engaged in petty thievery. At the age of seven his parents sent him to the St. Mary's Industrial Home for Boys, an institution in Baltimore run by the Xaverian Order for orphans, young indigents and delinquents. Except for brief interludes at home, Ruth spent the next twelve years at St. Mary's. There as a teenager he won a reputation for his baseball prowess and in 1914 signed a professional contract with the Baltimore Orioles of the International League. In the same year the Boston Red Sox purchased him as a left-handed pitcher.

Ruth never had to struggle for success in baseball. For him both pitching and hitting were natural talents rather than acquired skills. Converted from a top pitching star to an outfielder, Ruth surprised the world of baseball in 1919 by hitting twenty-nine home runs, two more than the existing major league record which had been set in a crackerbox ball park in 1884. He followed in 1920 as a member of the New York Yankees with a stunning total of fifty-four four baggers, which was a larger number than any entire team (except the Yankees) in the major leagues compiled. For Ruth, this was only the beginning. From 1918 through 1934 he led the American League in homers twelve times with an average of more than forty a season; from 1926 through 1931 he averaged slightly more than fifty home runs per season. In every 11.7 times at bat he hit a round tripper. In addition, Ruth hit an exceptionally high average. His lifetime mark of .342 has been equalled by few players in baseball history.

The public responded to Ruth's feats with overwhelming enthusiasm. Before Ruth, the Yankee's best annual attendance had been 600,000, but with him the fans poured out to the ball parks to see the Yankees play, apparently caring little whether the home team won or lost, only hoping to witness the Babe hammer a pitch out of the park. Even Ruth's mighty swings that failed to connect brought forth a chorus of awed "Oooooooohs," as the audience realized the enormous power that had gone to waste and the narrow escape that the pitcher had temporarily enjoyed. Each day millions of Americans turned to the sports page of their newspaper to see if Ruth had hit another homer. Indeed the response may have been unique in the annals of American sport. "In times past," Paul Gallico, a perceptive sportswriter reflected, "We had been interested in and excited by prize fighters and baseball players, but we had never been so individually involved or joined in such a mass outpouring of affection as we did for Ruth." To players and fans alike, Ruth was a pioneer exploring "the uncharted wilderness of sport. There was something almost of the supernatural and the miraculous connected with him too," continued Gallico.[5] "I am not so certain now that Ruth is human," added Cleveland catcher Chet Thomas. "At least he does things you couldn't expect a mere batter with two arms and legs to do. I can't explain him. Nobody can explain him. He just exists."[6]

The Ruthian image of home run blasts ran counter to the increasingly dominant world of bureaucracies, scientific management and "organization men." Ruth was the antithesis of science and rationality. Whereas Cobb relied upon "brains rather than brawn," upon, as he put it, the "hit-and-run, the steal and double-steal, the bunt in all its varieties, the squeeze, the ball hit to the opposite field and the ball punched through openings in the defense for a single," Ruth, on the other hand, swung for the fences.[7] Ruth, according to sportswriter F.C. Lane in 1921, "throws science itself to the wind and hews out a rough path for himself by the sheer weight of his unequalled talents."[9] Ruth seemed to embody the public preference for a compensatory hero with mere brute strength rather than one who exercised intelligence. Ruth played baseball instinctively; he seemed to need no practice or special training. He loved the game for its own sake. "With him the game *is* the thing. He loves baseball; loves just to play it," asserted a sportswriter.[9] No ulterior motives seemed to tarnish his pure love of the game.

The Ruthian image also ran counter to Victorian values. Ruth's appetite for things of the flesh was legendary. He drank heroic quantities of bootleg liquor; his hotel suite was always well stocked with beer and whiskey. People watched him eat with awe; he sometimes ate as many as eighteen eggs for breakfast and washed them down with seven or eight bottles of soda pop. In each town on the spring training tours and each big league city, Ruth always found a bevy of willing female followers. His escapades were well known enough that a sports-writer wrote a parody of them. "I wonder where Baby Ruth is tonight? He grabbed his hat and coat and ducked from sight. I wonder where he will be at half past three? . . . I know he's with a dame. I wonder what's her name?"[10] Ruth probably did not know her name, for he had a notorious reputation for being unable to remember the names of even his closest friends. In the 1920s, to those many Americans who were rejecting what they called "Puritanism," Ruth could be identified as a fellow rebel. Marshall Smelser has written that Ruth "met an elemental need of the crowd. Every hero must have his human flaw which he shares with his followers. In Ruth it was hedonism, as exagger-ated in folklore and fable."[11]

Of America's legendary heroes, Ruth is the country's preeminent athletic hero. Even in an age which takes a special delight in smashing false idols, Ruth remains the demigod of sports. His astonishing success reassured those who feared that America had become a society in which the traditional conditions conducive to the success of the ordinary person no longer existed. He tran-scended the world of sport to establish an undefinable benchmark for outstand-ing performances in all fields of human endeavor. The media have hailed Willie Sutton as "the Babe Ruth of bank robbers," Chuck Stearns as "the Babe Ruth of water skiing," Jimmy Conners as "the Babe Ruth of tennis," and Franco Corelli as "the Babe Ruth of operatic tenors." The list could be continued indefinitely. Americans resented anyone who threatened to tarnish Ruth's he-roic stature. When Henry Aaron approached Ruth's career record of 714 home runs, he said, "I can't recall a day this year or last when I did not hear the name of Babe Ruth."[12] Roger Maris, when he broke Ruth's mark of sixty home runs in one season in 1961, found himself the victim of a steady stream of abuse from fans, sportswriters and people in the streets. They repeatedly noted that Ruth had compiled sixty home runs in a 154-game season while Maris had only fifty nine after 154 games. After the 1961 season, Maris quickly sank into obscurity but the legend of Babe Ruth lived on. Long after the 1920s Ruth continued to be a peerless compensatory hero.

Pitch-men and journalists also found in Red Grange an almost perfect subject for elevation to the status of compensatory hero. Like Ruth, Grange projected an image of swift, decisive, all-conquering power. Rather than methodically grinding down the opposition with power plays, Grange's forte was the sudden and total breakthrough, the punt return, the kickoff return, or the long run from scrimmage that climaxed in a touchdown. By exhibiting his phenomenal talent for open field running in a game against Michigan in 1924, Grange stunned the football world. Before the game, Fielding H. Yost, the veteran mentor of many powerful Michigan elevens, assured everyone that the Illinois redhead could be stopped. With 67,000 fans present at the opening of Illinois' new stadium, Grange responded by scoring four touchdowns in the first twelve minutes of the game. He took the opening kick-off for a ninety-five yard touchdown run; he then had touchdown runs of sixty-seven, fifty-six and forty-five yards from the line of scrimmage.[13] Modern technology accentuated the dramatic quality of Grange's feats. While few Americans were able to see Grange perform in the flesh, millions saw him in the newsreel of thousands of theaters. The image of Grange, speeded up by the flickering screen, was almost eerie, as it darted, slashed, cut away from would-be tacklers and crossed the goal line one, two, three or even five times within a few brief seconds. Little wonder that Grantland Rice hailed Grange as the "Galloping Ghost of the Gridiron."

Grange's career seemed to confirm traditional virtues and the survival of the dream of the self-made man. Like Ruth, he began life under adverse circumstance. One of five children, he was born in the small rustic town of Forksville, Pennsylvania, where his father supported the family by working in local lumber camps. When Grange was but five years old, the family began to break up. His mother died and his father moved to Wheaton, Illinois, a town on the outskirts of Chicago. Shortly, the elder Grange decided he could not raise his three daughters without a mother and sent them back to Pennsylvania to live with his wife's relatives. As a youth Red Grange, unlike Ruth, practiced all the Victorian virtues that seemed to be fast disappearing in the United States of the 20th century. He neither drank nor smoked. He was modest, soft-spoken, and hardworking; in both his high school and college days he toted ice to Wheaton residents. These character traits, according to Grange in his autobiography, paid dividends. Athletics "was my whole life and I put everything I had into it," he wrote. "The future took care of itself. When the breaks came I was ready for them." Confirming the legendary dream of American success, he wrote: "Any boy can realize his dreams if he's willing to work and make sacrifices along the way."[14]

Grange, of course, exaggerated. He owed his success to more than hard work and impeccable personal habits. He enjoyed marvelous natural talents for quickness afoot and the ability to change directions while carrying a football. In high school he was the Illinois sprints and hurdles champion. As a high school football player at Wheaton he created something of a sensation by scoring seventy-two touchdowns in three seasons of play. Contacted by the alumni of several mid-western colleges who wanted to bring his talents to their campuses, Grange finally resolved to attend the University of Illinois. In the fall scrimmages of 1922 he led the freshmen team to several victories over the varsity. Robert "Zup" Zuppke, the Illinois head coach, recognized in Grange a potential immortal. In the spring practice of 1923 he designed a powerful single wing formation with Grange running at tailback. "I got a great break at Illinois," Grange later confessed ". . . I ended up making most of the team's touchdowns and getting all the publicity, because Coach Bob Zuppke let me carry the ball 90 percent of the time. In most of the games I carried the ball thirty or forty times."[15]

Bare statistics give only a partial indication of Grange's outstanding collegiate performance. In three seasons he scored thirty-one touchdowns, gained 3,637 yards on the ground (including kick-off and punt returns) and passed for an additional 653 yards. He accounted for an average of 214 yards for each of the college games in which he appeared. By the close of the 1925 season Grange was, according to the New York *Times*, "the most famous, the most talked of, and written about, the most photographed and most picturesque player the game has ever produced."[16]

After the final game of the 1925 season Grange immediately left the University of Illinois to become a professional player. Instrumental in his decision was Charles C. "Cash and Carry" Pyle, a sports impresario who was almost the equal of Tex Rickard.[17] Without any prior experience in managing athletes or staging sporting spectacles, Pyle approached Red Grange in the fall season of 1925. According to Grange's recollection, Pyle simply said: "How would you like to make one hundred thousand dollars, or maybe even a million?"[18] Without waiting to hear the details Grange replied in the affirmative. Pyle left Champaign, Illinois, the next day for Chicago to confer with George Halas and Ed Sternamen, co-owners of the Chicago Bears, a professional football team in the fledgling National Football League. Secretly the two parties reached a tentative agreement. Grange would join the Bears immediately after the college season to play the remaining league games of the Bears and then he and the team would go on an exhibition tour to be staged by Pyle. Gate receipts for the games would be shared fifty-fifty. Of the Pyle-Grange 50 percent, Grange was to receive 60 percent.[19]

Today we take it for granted that outstanding college athletes will attempt to benefit personally from their exploits, but in 1925 Grange's decision initiated a national debate. By abandoning his studies for a blatantly commercial career, he openly flaunted the myth of the college athlete as a gentleman-amateur who played merely for the fun of the game and the glory of his school. Grange's Illinois coach joined a host of academics in condemning Grange. Not only was professional football held in low moral esteem, but to them it was unethical for Grange to capitalize upon a reputation he had acquired in college for direct, personal gain. An idol of the nation's youth and an exemplar of amateur sports simply should not accept "tainted" money.[20] Initially, sympathetic newsmen depicted Grange as an "innocent, decent, trusting chap," who was the "victim of a kind of conspiracy of get-rich-quick promoters who did not care how far they went in prostituting him to their ends."[21] But Grange was hardly an innocent victim. He publicly acknowledged that "I'm out to get the money, and I don't care who knows it." Furthermore, "my advice to everybody is to get the money while the getting's good."[22] He did promise his admirers that he would at some future date finish his senior year in college, a promise he never kept.

While the Galloping Ghost was still attracting headlines, Pyle and Grange went all out to maximize their profits. Five days after Grange's final game with Illinois, he played with the Bears at Wrigley Field in Chicago on Thanksgiving Day, 1925. The publicity barrage accompanying Grange's departure from Illinois helped to attract 35,000 fans, to that date the largest crowd ever to attend a professional game. (At the time the National Football league consisted of eighteen make-shift teams located mostly in smaller cities. The Bears considered 5,000 to be a good draw in Chicago.) The Bears, with Red Grange obliged to play at least half of each game, then played a grueling schedule of ten games in seventeen days.

Everywhere they went—St. Louis, Philadelphia, New York twice, Boston, Providence, Washington and Pittsburgh—they broke professional football attendance records. In New York 65,000 fans packed the Polo Grounds and an estimated 20,000 had to be turned away. Until the "Grange Tour" arrived, the New York Giants had been losing money. After taking an eight-day rest in Chicago, Grange and the Bears embarked upon Pyle's 7,000 mile, thirty-five day, fourteen game, barnstorming tour of the South and West. In matches against "pick up" teams of mostly former collegians, Pyle insisted upon a $25,000 guarantee from local promoters. Newspapers and press syndicates assigned their most distinguished sports writers to accompany Grange. Westbrook Pegler, Damon Runyan and Ford Frick, among others, reported daily every facet of Grange's behavior both on and off the field of play. Never had such a tour by an athletic team attracted so much publicity nor been so financially rewarding. Ironically the Galloping Ghost's performance—perhaps because of a nagging injury—was far less spectacular than it had been as a collegian.

Emboldened by his spectacular financial success with Grange in the winter of 1925–26, Pyle expanded his promotional horizons. He first demanded that he and Grange be granted one-third ownership of the Bears. When Halas and Sternamen refused, he attempted to place a second NFL team in New York, only to be blocked by the owner of the New York Giants. He then formed a new professional loop, the American Football League, with Grange and himself as co-owners of the New York Yankees. Because of Grange, the Yankees drew large crowds, but the other teams lost money. After the 1926 season the new league collapsed. Pyle, with Grange and the financial losses suffered by NFL teams during the 1926 season as leverage, forced the NFL to admit the Yankees as a "road team" for the 1927 season. A permanent knee injury suffered by Grange in the third game of the 1927 season brought financial ruin to the Yankees. Grange and Pyle amicably severed their partnership. Pyle went on to other forms of sport promotion—professional tennis tours and two long-distance walking contests ("Bunion Derbies"). Grange returned to the Bears as a superb defensive back and above average straight-ahead running back. He played his last game in 1935. In the 1940s and 1950s he became a successful radio and television sportscaster.

On the face of it, Jack Dempsey was an unlikely prospect for a compensatory hero.[23] True, his social origins were modest; he was born into a poor, peripatetic Irish-American family at Manassa, Colorado. But until Jack Kearns became his manager in 1917, Dempsey had been little more than a saloon brawler, fighting in western tank towns for a hundred dollars or less per bout. Dempsey's reputation as a peerless slugger rested as much on myth as fact. He himself had been the victim of a knockout in 1917 and he had lost a decision in 1918. His career knockout percentage of .613 was unexceptional, well below that of Floyd Patterson and Primo Carnera, for instance, and only slightly above that of Tommy Burns who is considered the worst of all heavyweight champions by ring historians. As champion, Dempsey defended his title only six times in seven years and met only two genuinely formidable foes. As a potential hero, Dempsey suffered from an even more serious liability. Having not served in the armed forces in World War I, the federal government in 1920 charged him with being a "slacker." Although acquitted on the grounds that he had provided financial support to his wife and mother, the issue clouded Dempsey's heroic image.[24]

Dempsey acquired the reputation of being "Jack the Giant-Killer" largely through the hokum of his manager, Jack Kearns, and Tex Rickard, the "King" of boxing promoters in the 1920s. Dempsey had the good fortune of meeting Jess Willard, the "Pottowatomie Giant," in a championship bout staged by Rickard at Toledo, Ohio, in 1919. Willard towered over Dempsey. He stood six feet and six inches tall and weighted 245 pounds. Dempsey floored the massive Willard five times in the first round; at the end of the third round, Willard, his face swollen twice its normal size, bloody and bewildered, conceded defeat. The image of Dempsey as a giant-killer caught on at once. Publicity stunts, such as having Dempsey's sparring partners wear inflated chest protectors and catcher's masks, reinforced the image. The public accepted the mistaken notion that Dempsey was a little man. As Dempsey told it: "Jack Kearns' ballyhoo that made me 'Jack the Giant-Killer' was partially responsible. Various pictures that were published of my different fights, too, added to the misconception. Repeatedly they showed me fighting against men who were inches taller than I and many pounds heavier."[25]

Tex Rickard exhibited the full aresenal of his promotional skills in the Dempsey-Georges Carpentier fight of 1921. Because of political hostility at the State Capitol in Albany, Rickard transferred the fight to Jersey City where he had a huge wooden statue built. As Dempsey later confessed, Rickard "dug up" Carpentier, the light heavyweight champion of Europe, and set out to convince the public that the fragile Frenchman was a serious contender for the crown. Rickard explained to Dempsey and Kearns how he planned to ballyhoo the bout. It would be a "foreign foe" versus an American; a war hero—Carpentier had twice been decorated for valor in World War I—versus a "slacker," the "rapier" of the skilled fencer versus the "broadsword" of the peasant; the civilized man versus the "abysmal brute." "That's you, Jack," the elated Rickard reputedly exclaimed.[26] The contrast in images was almost perfect. Ike Dorgan, Rickard's assistant, nicknamed Carpentier the "Orchid Man," set up his training camp on Long Island amidst the "social crowd," refused to allow reporters to watch Carpentier spar, and declaimed long upon the Frenchman's attractions to women. According to Dorgan and the press, Carpentier was handsome, debonair, a "boulevardier" who danced beautifully and sang French Chansonnettes.[27]

As Rickard had hoped, the nation took sides. The American Legion passed a resolution condemning Dempsey for his lack of military service in World War I; the Veterans of Foreign Wars retaliated by siding with the champ. In general the "low brows"—workingmen, ethnics and perhaps many from the white collar class as well—favored Dempsey. The "highbrows," especially the nation's literati, supported Carpentier. Even George Bernard Shaw, the distinguished British playwright, enlisted his vast literary talents in Carpentier's behalf. The fans at Boyle's Thirty Acres near Jersey City gave Carpentier a larger welcoming applause than Dempsey. As a financial event, the fight was an unprecedented success. Over 80,000 fans paid $1,789,238 to see the fight. Present were the "Who's Who of the social, financial and entertainment world."[28] As an athletic contest, the bout was a farce. Dempsey had little difficulty in knocking Carpentier out in the fourth round. Nonetheless, everyone seemed satisfied. Even the dignified New York *Times* announced the results of the fight in three streamer, front page headlines. Few Americans were left untouched by the spectacle at Boyle's Thirty Acres.

Rickard used similar tactics in promoting his next bonanza: Dempsey's fight with Luis Angel Firpo at the Polo Grounds in New York in 1923. Firpo, formerly a bottle washer from a Buenos Aires pharmacy, had come to the United States looking for easy money. Rickard corralled for Firpo a "proper assortment of weak-chinned or canary hearted boxers ... to pole-ax into unconsciousness."[29] Firpo, a big, awkward man, soon won appellations by the press as the "Argentine Giant" and the "Wild Bull of the Pampas." Rickard hoped to convince the public that the bout would be "two cave men fightin' with tooth and claw."[30] The actual fight conformed to the ballyhoo much better than anyone expected. In less than four minutes of action Firpo went down to the canvas ten times, Dempsey twice. After the seventh knockdown of Firpo in the first round, Firpo arose and shot a right to Dempsey's jaw that sent the champion toppling through the ropes. (George Bellows memorialized the event in his renowned painting *Dempsey–Firpo*.) Reporters boosted Dempsey back into the ring and the champ finished the round on unsteady legs. But in the next round Dempsey, swinging both fists wildly, crushed Firpo for a knockout. The exciting battle produced boxing's second million dollar gate, Bruce Bliven wrote in the *New Republic*, but within the confines of the boxing ring both Firpo and Dempsey had decided "their own fates."[31] No sport exceeded boxing's capacity to furnish compensatory heroes.

The famous Dempsey-Tunney fights revealed the complex dynamics of compensatory heroism. For the first fight scheduled for September 23, 1926, Rickard chose Philadelphia's Sesquecentennial Stadium as the site. The build-up followed Rickard's familiar formula. In the "Battle of the Century" it was the dark, savage-visaged, mauling Dempsey versus the smooth, "scientific" boxer Tunney. To the surprise of nearly all the 120,757 fans present and several million listeners to Graham MacNamee's radio broadcast, Tunney defeated Dempsey in the ten-round match on points. While scoring repeatedly on solid but non-lethal blows, Tunney simply avoided Dempsey's famed rushes. The fight was reminiscent of James J. Corbett's upset of John L. Sullivan in 1892. The gate exceeded one and three quarter million dollars and Dempsey collected $711,268 for one night's work.

Shortly the demand grew for a return bout. Rickard achieved the pinnacle of his promotional career with the second "Fight of the Century" between Tunney and Dempsey in 1927. Over 104,000 customers paid $2,658,660 to witness the event at Soldier Field in Chicago, both marks that still stand today. Spectators on the outer perimeter of the stadium sat as far as 200 yards from the ring, making the boxers almost undiscernible. An estimated fifty million Americans heard Graham MacNamee's broadcast from one of seventy-three stations connected to the NBC radio network. For the first six rounds the fight seemed to be a replay of the Philadelphia bout. Then in the seventh round Dempsey landed a series of blows which crumpled Tunney to the mat. As the referee began the count, he waved Dempsey to a neutral corner of the ring. Dempsey ignored the motion, an action that may have cost him the heavyweight crown. By the time the referee convinced Dempsey to retire to a neutral corner, several seconds had expired. The referee then began the count anew, reaching nine before Tunney came to his feet. Although the referee's action conformed to the Illinois boxing codes, the legendary "long count" furnished a source of endless debate among fight fans. Tunney survived the seventh round and outboxed Dempsey in the final three rounds to win a unanimous decision. In defeat Dempsey's popularity soared even higher than when he had held the championship.

The contrast in the popularity of Dempsey and Tunney reflects the type of compensatory hero sought by the American public. The image of Dempsey as the mauler who relied upon quick, physical solutions was far more satisfying to the public than Tunney's exhibition of complex defensive finesse. Doubtless, millions of Americans who worked in large corporations, bureaucracies and on assembly lines dreamed of equally direct and decisive answers to their countless frustrations. In addition, Dempsey seemed more human than Tunney. Tunney projected an image of snobbery and intellectuality. He married a socialite, had lectured to a class at Yale on Shakespeare, and was a personal friend of the novelist Thornton Wilder. He remained aloof from the everyday world of ordinary people. He was disdainful of reporters and the comraderie of the "hangers-on" in the fight game. Americans wanted their heroes to be "average" in all respects except their specialty. Leo Lowenthal has written: "It is some comfort for the little man who has become expelled from the Horatio Alger dream, who despairs of penetrating the thicket of grand strategy in politics and business, to see his heroes as a lot of guys who like or dislike highballs, cigarettes, tomato juice, golf, and social gatherings—just like himself."[32] The "little man" could find confirmation of his own pleasures and discomforts by participating in those of Dempsey.

Dempsey's defeat by Tunney signalled the end of the Golden Age of American boxing. The public did not respond to the new heavyweight king; in 1928 Rickard lost some $400,000 in promoting the Tunney-Tom Henney bout. After the fight Tunney retired from the ring, leaving the heavyweight scene in chaos. Then, in 1929, Rickard, while launching an elimination series to determine a new champion, suddenly died from an attack of appendicitis. Rickard's funeral revealed that the peerless promoter was in his own right a public celebrity. Over 15,000 persons filed past his ornate $15,000 bronze casket in the main arena of Madison Square Garden. The next day 9,000 attended his funeral. No new impressario replaced Rickard and in the Great Depression of the 1930s gangsters seized control of boxing. The age of athletic heroes seemed to be over. "After 1930 our stream of super-champions ran dry, replaced by a turgid brook," wrote John R. Tunis in 1934. "The champions were now just ordinary mortals, good players but nothing more."[33]

NOTES

[1]Danzig and Brandewein, eds. *Sports Golden Age: A Close-Up of the Fabulous Twenties* (New York: Harper & Bros., 1948), p. xi.

[2]Most efforts to explain the American need for heroes in the 1920s see the heroes as fulfilling cherished American ideals or myths. For instance Leo Lowenthal in *Literature, Popular Culture and Society* (Englewood Cliffs, N.J.: Prentice-Hall, 1961), pp. 109–140 has interpreted the heroes of the pre-1920 era as "idols of production"—from industry, business and science—and those of the post 1920 era as "idols of consumption"—from the world of entertainment. The heroes of the post 1920 era thus furnished guides to the public on how to consume rather than produce. For a provocative study that in part confirms Lowenthal but came to my attention too late to be incorporated in this essay, see Lary May, *Screening Out the Past: The Birth of Mass Culture and the Motion Picture Industry* (New York: Oxford University Press, 1980). In "The Meaning of

Lindbergh's Flight," in Joseph J. Kwiat and May C. Turpie, eds. *Studies in American Culture: Dominant Ideas and Images* (Minneapolis: University of Minnesota Press, 1960), John W. Ward finds that in Lindbergh the American people paradoxically celebrated both the self-sufficient individual and the machine. Roderick Nash, in *The Nervous Generation: American Thought, 1917–1930* (Chicago: Rand McNally, 1970), pp. 126–137, finds the sport heroes of the 1920s to be surrogate frontiersmen.

[3] As quoted in Leverett T. Smith, Jr., *The American Dream and the National Game* (Bowling Green, Oh.: Popular Press, 1975), p. 207. Smith offers an interesting interpretation of Ruth and Cobb in different terms than mine. To Smith, Cobb was the representative of a community "identified with a democratic capitalistic world," Ruth with an "authoritarian," "paternalistic" and "hierarchical society." See also Tristram Potter Coffin, *The Old Ball Game: Baseball in Folklore and Fiction* (New York: Herder and Herder, 1971), Chap. 4.

[4] Babe Ruth and Bob Considine, *The Babe Ruth Story* (New York: Scholastic Books, 1969), p. 9. There are many biographies of Ruth. Tom Meany, Martin Weldon, Claire Ruth and Bill Slocum, Lee Allen, Daniel M. Daniel and Waite Hoyte wrote early biographies. Four recent books are superior in most respects to the earlier works: Ken Sobel, *Babe Ruth and the American Dream* (New York: Ballantine, 1974); Kal Wagenheim, *Babe Ruth: His Life and Legend* (New York: Praeger, 1974); Robert W. Creamer *Ruth* (New York: Simon and Schuster, 1974); Marshall Smelser, *The Life that Ruth Built* New York: Quadrangle/Doubleday, 1965).

[6] As quoted in Smith, *The American Dream*, p. 190.

[7] Ty Cobb with Al Stump, *My Life in Baseball—The True Record* (Garden City, N.Y.: Doubleday, 1961), p. 280.

[8] As quoted in Smith, *The American Dream*, p. 190.

[9] Ibid., p. 205.

[10] Quoted in Harold Seymour, *Baseball: The Golden Age* (New York: Oxford, 1971), p. 431.

[11] Marshall M. Smelser, "The Babe on Balance," *American Scholar*, 44 (Spring 1975), 299.

[12] Creamer, *Babe*, p. 16.

[13] Allison Danzig and Peter Brandewein, eds., *The Greatest Sports Stories from the New York Times* (New York: Barnes, 1951), pp. 218–229, offers a convenient source for this game.

[14] Red Grange as told to Ira Morton, *The Red Grange Story* (New York: Putnam's Sons, 1953), p. 178.

[15] Ibid., pp. 174–75. See also "Debunking the 'All-American' Football Team Fiction," *Literary Digest*, 91 (Nov. 27, 1926), 60.

[16] New York *Times*, Nov. 22, 1925.

[17] On Pyle, see New York *Times*, Feb. 4, 1939; Hugh Leamy, "Net Profits," *Colliers*, 78 (Oct. 2, 1926), 9, 32; Myron Cope, "The Game That Was," *Sports Illustrated*, 31 (Oct. 13, 1969), 93–96, 102–103.

[18] Grange, *The Red Grange Story*, p. 91.

[19] Ibid., p. 92; George Halas with Gwen Morgan and Arthur Veysey, *Halas by Halas* (New York: McGraw-Hill, 1979), p. 104. According to George Vass, *George Halas and the Chicago Bears* (Chicago: Henry Regney, 1971), p. 76, Grange and Pyle were to receive a guarantee of $2,000 per game, 10 percent of the first $5,000 of the gate, 20 percent of the five, and forty cents of every dollar above that. It is unclear whether the agreements described by Grange, Halas and Vass applied to both tours or only the first one.

[20] See responses in "Football History as Made by the Illinois Ice Man," *Literary Digest*, 87 (Dec. 26, 1925), 29–34 and Grange, *The Red Grange Story*, pp. 89–90, 92–96.

[21] "Football History as Made by the Illinois Ice Man," 30.

[22] As quoted in John B. Kennedy, "The Saddest Young Man in America," *Colliers*, 77 (Jan. 16, 1926), 15.

[23] On the legalization and financial aspects of prize fighting in the twenties see Jesse Frederick Steiner, *Americans at Play: Recent Trends in Recreation and Leisure Time Activities* (New York: McGraw-Hill, 1933), pp. 94–97. Among the best quasi-analytical accounts of boxing in the

twenties are James P. Dawson, "Boxing," in Danzig and Brandewein, eds. *Sports Golden Age*, pp. 38–85; Paul Gallico, *Farewell to Sport* (New York: Knopf, 1938), Chaps. II, VII, VIII, XIII; Randy Roberts, "Jack Dempsey: An American Hero in the 1920s," *Journal of Popular Culture*, 8 (Fall, 1974), 411–426; and Roberts, *Jack Dempsey: The Manassa Mauler* (Baton Rouge: Louisiana State University Press, 1979). Roberts interprets Dempsey as a major symbol of the 1920s.

[24] Roberts, "Jack Dempsey," 413; "War Record of Dempsey," *Literary Digest* 64 (Feb. 14, 1920), 122–124.

[25] Jack Dempsey, *Round by Round: An Autobiography* (New York: McGraw-Hill, 1940), p. 176.

[26] Jack Dempsey with Charles J. McGuirk, "The Golden Gates," *Saturday Evening Post*, 107 (Oct. 20, 1934), 11.

[27] See especially Paul Gallico, *A Farewell to Sport*, p. 95.

[28] Jack "Doc" Kearns with Oscar Fraley, *The Million Dollar Gate* (New York: Macmillan, 1966), pp. 147–148; Roberts, "Jack Dempsey," 415–419.

[29] Jack Koefoed, "The Master of Ballyhoo," *North American Review*, 227 (Mar. 1929), p. 285.

[30] Dempsey, "The Golden Gates," p. 75.

[31] As quoted in Roberts, *Jack Dempsey*, p. 181.

[32] Lowenthal, *Literature, Popular Culture and Society*, p. 135.

[33] John R. Tunis, "Changing Trends in Sport," *Harper's Monthly Magazine*, 170 (Dec. 1934), 78.